BUILDING DREXEL

EDITED BY RICHARDSON DILWORTH

AND SCOTT GABRIEL KNOWLES

BUILDING DREXEL

THE UNIVERSITY AND ITS CITY,

1891–2016

TEMPLE UNIVERSITY PRESS

Philadelphia • Rome • Tokyo

TEMPLE UNIVERSITY PRESS
Philadelphia, Pennsylvania 19122
www.temple.edu/tempress

Library of Congress Cataloging-in-Publication Data

Names: Dilworth, Richardson, 1971- editor. | Knowles, Scott Gabriel, editor.
Title: Building Drexel : the university and its city, 1891–2016 / edited by
   Richardson Dilworth and Scott Gabriel Knowles.
Description: Philadelphia : Temple University Press, 2016. | Includes
   bibliographical references and index.
Identifiers: LCCN 2016022122 (print) | LCCN 2016033362 (ebook) | ISBN
   9781439914205 (hardback : alk. paper) | ISBN 9781439914229 (E-book)
Subjects: LCSH: Drexel University—History. | BISAC: HISTORY / United
   States / State & Local / Middle Atlantic (DC, DE, MD, NJ, NY, PA). |
   EDUCATION / Higher.
Classification: LCC LD1725.D62 B85 2016 (print) | LCC LD1725.D62
   (ebook) | DDC 378.748/11—dc23
LC record available at https://lccn.loc.gov/2016022122

♾ The paper used in this publication meets the requirements of the
American National Standard for Information Sciences—Permanence of
Paper for Printed Library Materials, ANSI Z39.48-1992

Printed in the United States of America

9 8 7 6 5 4 3 2 1

A COMMEMORATIVE EDITION

Sponsored by the

DREXEL UNIVERSITY ALUMNI ASSOCIATION

Contents

Foreword

ANTHONY J. DREXEL was a man who, among his many accomplishments, conceived and created an institution unlike any other of its day, one whose mission and values continue to be aspirational to many institutes of higher learning today. Author Cordelia Biddle (in this volume) describes Drexel as one who "embodied the American immigrant ideal that hard work, perspicacity, and enterprise can engender a better and more prosperous life" and who succeeded in "creating a co-educational institution whose purpose was to provide young men and women with both academic and applied knowledge, enabling them to improve their earning potential and enhance their lives."

One hundred twenty-five years after its founding, Drexel University's over 200,000 alumni have benefitted from Anthony Drexel's vision and have built careers, businesses, and families as a result. Many of us may never have had the opportunity to seek higher education had our founder chosen a less altruistic purpose to deploy his vast wealth. Drexel University's unique focus on experiential learning, through the co-op program, provided a way to finance one's education, and virtually assured its graduates of a career. This model has been emulated by other universities, as a testament to its success.

As the representative of Drexel's Alumni Association participating in this effort, it is both exciting and humbling to be able to help tell the story that describes the legacy of our founder. *Building Drexel*: *The University and Its City* celebrates the accomplishments of the institution, but more importantly, celebrates the impact that Drexel made on its alumni and, in turn, the impact its alumni have made on the city of Philadelphia, our country, and the world.

I was fortunate to have attended Drexel in the mid-1970s and to have witnessed, firsthand, the evolution of Drexel from what was a commuter school for engineers into the multifaceted, internationally recognized university it has become today.

Yet with all of that success and growth, chronicled in the chapters to follow, I am sure that I am not alone in knowing that Drexel, as an integral part of the fabric of our lives, left an indelible mark on each of us; the magnificent Great Court, the orange brick buildings, the Dragons and our long-lost football team, the food trucks, the fraternities and sororities, the Pi Kapp Show, the May 10 Block Party, the DAC, the Regatta, the Jail House, the green beach, Cavanaugh's, Drexel Pizza, and Colonel Conway.

These people, places, and events inspire memories in all of us . . . of the times when our lives were ahead of us; we experienced life at its fullest; we grew into adults; we met our friends and our future families and our futures were bright. On behalf of the Alumni Association Board of Governors, who have sponsored the research, writing, and production of this historical volume, it is my hope that everyone who reads *Building Drexel* finds something within the book that will bring them back to those memories.

Anthony M. Noce, chair,
Alumni Association Board of Governors, 2016

ACKNOWLEDGMENTS

L IKE DREXEL ITSELF, this book is very much the product of a collective effort. Thanks go first to President John Fry, who had the idea for a book-length history of Drexel in honor of its 125th anniversary—the first book that would cover the full history of the institution. In his enlightened vision of the role universities play as agents of social change, President Fry also understands the importance of learning from their histories.

The financial commitment of the Drexel University Alumni Association to the creation of this book is a testament to the strong spirit of Drexel's alumni all over the world. We sincerely appreciate the leadership of Ira Taffer and Anthony Noce, each of whom offered insight and support throughout the process. Cynthia Leesman also served as a wonderful resource to us as we coordinated with Drexel's extraordinary alumni community.

David Unruh and the staff of the Office of Institutional Advancement served similarly as a constant source of support from the proposal stage all the way through to production of the volume.

We are very grateful to the 125th Anniversary Committee, especially Jan Biros, Lori Doyle, Rosalind Remer, and Eric Zillmer who helped champion and shape the proposal for the volume at an early stage.

When this book was just an idea it was supported by the former university archivist, Robert Sieczkiewicz. The dean of libraries, Danuta A.

Nitecki, and libraries/archives staff have consistently risen to the occasion—answering our *many* requests for materials and providing a space to work. The university archives staff to John Wiggins, Anita Lai, and Alexis Morris. The university archives is an extraordinary repository, and we hope that this book marks a launching point for increased attention to the creation and curation of Drexel's history.

Our student research staff worked tirelessly conducting interviews, transcribing, assembling the documentary record, assisting with writing, and answering e-mails and calls from anxious editors day and night. These are historians in the making. Special thanks to our talented history co-op students, Daniel Johnson and Christina Schweingruber. Also, thanks to Madison Boerner, Elizabeth Burdett, Sebnem Dugmeqglu, Jason Ludwig, Maegan Madrigal, Carley Roche, Nathaniel Stanton, and Virginia Theerman.

In University Communications, Alissa Falcone was a crucial resource for materials. Ms. Falcone is a Drexel graduate herself who has written widely on the university's history (including in this volume). Thanks also to Mark Eggerts for his assistance with the Introduction and with the speeches of Constantine Papadakis. The publications of this office—especially *DrexelNow* and the *Drexel Magazine* were highly useful to this project.

This book would not exist were it not for the studious work of the chapter authors, nearly all of whom are Drexel faculty and administrators (who did this on top of their normal Drexel-like packed schedules). For outside perspectives, we also enlisted James Wolfinger from DePaul University in Chicago, and Jeannine Keefer from the University of Richmond. We are grateful to both for lending their expertise to this project.

Melissa Mansfield, department administrator for the departments of history and politics, managed everything beautifully behind the scenes so that the researchers, authors, and editors could get their work done on time and with the resources they needed.

We thank the numerous members of the Drexel community—faculty, administrators, staff, alumni, and students—who shared their documents, their photos, and their memories with us.

Finally, thanks go to the team at Temple University Press, including Kate Nichols, Gary Kramer, and David Wilson—and to Micah Kleit, for his excitement about Drexel's history, and his eagerness to help us bring it to life in one comprehensive book.

Richardson Dilworth
Scott Gabriel Knowles
Philadelphia, 2016

Timeline of Drexel History, 1889–Present

1889   Work begins on the Main Building at Thirty-Second and Chestnut Streets, and plans for the Drexel Institute are made public

1891   First school president, James MacAlister, appointed

       Drexel Institute of Art, Science, and Industry is dedicated

       Departments are organized under the following academic divisions: Art Department, Scientific Department, Department of Mechanic Arts, Department of Domestic Economy, Technical Department, Business Department, Department of Physical Training, Normal Department for the training of teachers, Department of Lectures and Evening Classes, Library and Reading Room, and Museum

1892   Classes begin

       Third school in the country to train librarians opens at Drexel

1893   Houses on Thirty-Second Street purchased for lab and classroom space

       School founder Anthony J. Drexel dies in Carlsbad, Germany

1894   Department of Domestic Science and Arts offers three specialized programs: domestic science, cookery, and dressmaking and millinery

Technical Department and Scientific Department merge to form Department of Science and Technology

Howard Pyle begins School of Illustration

School incorporated under the laws of the Commonwealth of Pennsylvania

First school-wide commencement; commencement previously held at the department level

1895   Athletic association is formed

Thomas Eakins teaches briefly

First alumni association is formed

1896   First two class books, *The Hanseatic* and *The Eccentric*, are published

Department of Free Public Lectures and Entertainment established, previously affiliated with the Evening School

Evening architecture extends requirements for certificate

1897   Free evening classes in choral music are offered

Violet Oakley attends classes in School of Illustration

Lucina A. Ball, first secretary and registrar, resigns

1899   Virginia Castleman writes lyrics to "Drexel Ode," which is performed at commencement for the first time

Houses leased on Chestnut Street above Thirty-Second for the School of Architecture

Formal committee appointed to oversee social activities for students

1900   Department of Electrical Engineering opens

Pauline Conway becomes first woman to complete the architecture program

William Pittman, African-American scholarship recipient from Tuskegee Institute, completes architecture program

Courses are offered in mathematics, physics, and chemistry

Domestic Science and Arts are separated into junior and advanced programs with technical-level courses in Domestic Science and Domestic Arts as separate departments

Howard Pyle resigns from Drexel

1902   Randell Hall (originally called East Hall) opens

Picture gallery opens in Randell Hall

1903   Engineering course becomes School of Electrical Engineering grouped under the Department of Science and Technology

Training for nurses is briefly offered

Library school requires entrance examination

Choral music department is reconstituted as Department of Evening Classes in Choral Music

1905   Architecture becomes independent department

Fine and applied arts is officially terminated

Board of trustees decides not to offer a degree

Evening School offers course to prepare students to pass State Board of Examiners of Public Accountants

Marble bust of A. J. Drexel, done by Moses Ezekiel, is presented to school by Sarah Drexel Van Rensselaer, daughter of the founder

1906   Science courses become School of Science

School of Electrical Engineering becomes School of Engineering under the Department of Science and Technology, offering electrical, mechanical, and civil engineering

New alumni constitution is prepared

1907   First alumni day is held

1908   Training for nurses is discontinued

Choral music course is discontinued

Industry subsidizes employees' attendance at Drexel Evening School

Board of trustees president James W. Paul, son-in-law of the founder, dies; Alexander Van Rensselaer becomes board president

1909 Architecture offers three-year course

Frances MacIntyre replaces Frances J. Dill as school's secretary

1910 Evening School alumni form separate group

Associated alumni of evening classes form constitution

1911 First yearbook is offered

Charles E. Etting Fund established as the first general scholarship fund

1912 Men's student government is formed

1913 *Lexerd* published under present name

President James MacAlister resigns, then dies shortly after

President James Horace Churchman serves pro tem

1914 Hollis Godfrey becomes president, implements a major restructuring of academic divisions

Academic departments reorganized under four schools: School of Engineering, Secretarial School, Evening School, and School of Domestic Science and Arts

Technical training becomes a division under the School of Domestic Science and Arts

Architecture drops from day curriculum, becomes a division of Evening School

Secretarial School created through the dissolution of the Department of Commerce and Finance

Department of Domestic Science and Department of Domestic Arts consolidated under School of Domestic Science and Arts

Courses in pure and physical science, technical courses, and electrical engineering consolidate to form School of Engineering

State grants rights to offer bachelor of science degree in engineering

Free lectures and public concerts discontinued

Library school is discontinued

Henry V. Gummere heads newly reorganized Evening School, lengthens course offerings with policy of non-duplication with area schools

1915   Controlled summer program begins, predecessor to co-op program

1916   First home management practice house opens for the School of Domestic Science and Arts

Lower school is discontinued

1917   Bachelor of science in secretarial studies is offered

Bachelor of science in domestic science and arts is offered

State grants rights to offer master of science in domestic science and arts

Twenty-fifth anniversary convocation held

1918   Students' Army Training Corps begins

War course for women initiated in dietetics, occupational therapy, and preparatory work for the civil service

First student houses for women under direct Drexel control are set up

1919   First regular summer school begins

Reserve Officers' Training Corps (ROTC) begins

Terms become quarters

Four-year engineering co-op is established

Harold C. Bales is appointed first director of co-op

Elizabeth L. Cowan and Ruth E. Green are the first women to receive bachelor's degrees in domestic science and arts

Evening diploma school is organized

1920   Evening School offers preparatory curriculum

M. J. McAvoy, first full-time coach, is hired

1921   Hollis Godfrey resigns

Administrative board runs the institute in the interim between presidents

1922   Kenneth Gordon Matheson becomes president

Evening School faculty consists of regular college faculty, secondary school teachers, and persons from industry

John Arnett comes to Drexel as physician

New Home Management House opens

Cecil A. Kapp is appointed new director of cooperative work

Two-year dietetics course is offered

Helen Goodspeed is director of home economics and advisor to women

First alumnus, Horace P. Liversidge, is elected to board of trustees

Seven scholarships are granted to students from local schools

Secretarial School is renamed the School of Business Administration

Women's student government is formed

Office of dean of men is created and dean of women's functions are expanded

Faculty council of president is formed, composed of deans and directors, department heads, and chairmen of committees

Functions of registrar and comptroller are divided

Preparatory nurses course is started

Library school is reestablished under directorship of Anne Wallace Howland

1923   Drexel alumni write new constitution

Grace Godfrey succeeds Helen Goodspeed as director of home economics and advisor to women

Dietetics becomes four-year major

Four-year cooperative degree in chemical engineering is offered, as are business administration, four-year commercial teaching, four-year secretarial studies, and two-year secretarial course for diploma

1924   First evening diploma to women in accounting is offered

Five-year commerce and engineering course is offered

Robert C. Disque becomes academic dean

Endowment drive begins

Evening College alumni amend constitution

John Arnett begins systematic program of student health

Faculty athletic council is formed

1925   Chemical engineering becomes five-year co-op

1926   Department of Education and Psychology is established

        The Triangle begins publication

1927   Nursery playschool is developed

        Walter H. Halas hired as full-time coach, responsible for baseball, basketball, and football

        State grants charter amendment for bachelor of science and master of science degrees in secretarial studies, commerce, home economics, library science, and civil, electrical, mechanical, and chemical engineering

1928   Cyrus H. K. Curtis gives pipe organ to institute

        Edith M. Rood becomes first woman editor of *The Triangle*

1929   Annuity plan for faculty is approved by board of trustees

        Home economics offers textile merchandising

        Curtis Hall is completed

1930   Home Management House and nursery school building open

        Nurses course is established

1931   Drexel Lodge, gift of A. J. Drexel Paul, is dedicated

        Cornerstone is laid for Sarah Drexel Van Rensselaer Dormitory for Women

        Charter is amended to give honorary degrees

        Graduate work begins in home economics

President Matheson dies

Executive committee runs Drexel: academic dean (R. C. Disque), comptroller (W. R. Wagenseller), dean of men (L. D. Stratton), and director of Evening School (W. T. Spivey)

Sarah Drexel Van Rensselaer Dormitory opens

1932   Parke R. Kolbe becomes president

Open house for high school students, parents, and faculty is held

Alexander Van Rensselaer starts first loan fund for Evening School students

1933   Home economics holds first vocational conference

Faculties with broad self-governing powers are formed in each school: business administration, engineering, home economics, and library science; administrative head of school is to be called dean

Business administration offers retail management

1934   Men's faculty club room is established, with corresponding Ryder Club for the women of the faculty and administrative staff

Provision of indefinite tenure for the faculty with rank of assistant professor and higher is passed by the board of trustees

1935   Home economics offers general home economics course

1936   Drexel Institute is renamed Drexel Institute of Technology

Carl Altmaier undertakes history of Drexel

Marie Hamilton Law succeeds Anne Wallace Howland as director of library school

Engineering Council for Professional Development accredits School of Engineering

1937   Alumni help in selecting promising students

1938   George C. Galphin starts guidance clinic

Library school discontinues noncredit summer work

Technical Journal begins publication

1939   Student Building opens

New alumni association constitution subordinates class and school interests to those of the institute as a whole

1940 Engineering defense training program offered

1941 Training begins in the engineering defense program and the engineering, science, and management of war program

1942 George Peters Rea becomes president

Edward D. McDonald and Edward M. Hinton's history of Drexel, covering the first fifty years of the institute, is published

1943 First women enroll in the School of Engineering

1944 Financial crisis caused by falling enrollment during World War II forces the sale of Drexel's collection of art and original manuscripts; the auction for the material brings in $75,000

President Rea resigns; Dean Disque serves as acting president

1945 James Creese becomes president

Athletics recognized as a department under the dean of faculty

1946 Drexel Society of Women Engineers founded

1947 Day college and evening school unite, making credits from both of equal value

Don Yonker appointed men's soccer coach, beginning a thirty-year career

1948 Evening students receive their diplomas with students from the day colleges in a combined ceremony

1950 Evening School becomes Evening College

1955 Stratton Hall (originally called the Basic Sciences Building) is completed

Men's football team goes undefeated for the first time

1956 Tidewater Grain elevator explosion causes considerable damage to Drexel buildings

The United States Army Corps of Engineers report on the educational qualifications of engineering graduates ranks Drexel alumni second in the nation

1958   Men's soccer team wins national championship after a 12-0 season

1959   M.S. in biomedical engineering and science is offered

New library (current Korman Center), which includes space for the library school and an audiovisual center, opens

1960   Red Lion Warehouse, adjacent to the Main Building, is purchased

1961   Rush Hospital on Thirty-Third Street is purchased

1962   Drexel graduate Paul Baran (class of 1949) invents "packet switching," a key component in the development of the Internet

John Semanik (class of 1956) becomes athletic director, the first alumnus to hold the position

1963   William Walsh Hagerty becomes president

Creese Student Center opens

Commonwealth of Pennsylvania grants institute the right to confer Ph.D. in physics, chemistry, materials engineering, applied mechanics, and mathematics

1964   Red Lion Warehouse is converted into classrooms and reopened as Commonwealth Hall. A bridge over Ludlow Street connects Commonwealth with the Main Building

1965   Mary Semanik becomes Drexel's women's director of athletics

1966   Rush Hospital is converted into classrooms and opens as the Graduate School of Library Science (Rush Building)

A. J. Drexel statue moved from Fairmount Park to the Drexel campus

1967   Women's basketball team completes its second consecutive undefeated season

Disque Hall opens

Richard J. Mortimer earns the first Ph.D. awarded by Drexel

1968   College of Engineering and College of Science are founded out of the previously established College of Engineering and Science

1970   Drexel Institute of Technology is renamed Drexel University

Nesbitt Hall is completed

1972   Drexel's four-oar crew wins the school's first gold medal at the Dad Vail Regatta

1973   Mandell Theater opens

1974   Lancaster Avenue (between Thirty-Second and Thirty-Third) is converted to a sidewalk

The Educational Activities Center (later renamed MacAlister Hall) opens

1975   The Physical Education Athletic Center (later renamed Daskalakis Athletic Center) opens; *Running Free* sculpture of three horses is installed

1981   Men's soccer team wins its first East Coast Conference championship

1983   Drexel announces plan to require all students to have access to a personal computer

1984   W. W. Hagerty Library opens

First Macintosh computers distributed to Drexel students

President Hagerty retires

William S. Gaither becomes president

1987   Harold Myers begins his service as interim president

Wrestling team has its winningest season ever (17-5-1)

1988   Richard Breslin becomes president

Academic Building is purchased to be used for administration

1988   Neuropsycholgy Ph.D. program approved

1989   LeBow Engineering Center opens

Michael Anderson (class of 1989) becomes first Drexel alumnus to play in the National Basketball Association

1990   The Center for Automation Technology opens

College of Science becomes the College of Arts and Sciences

1993   One Drexel Plaza is purchased at a December auction; it later becomes the home of the College of Evening and Professional Studies

1994   Chuck Pennoni serves as interim president upon the resignation of Richard Breslin

1995   Constantine Papadakis becomes president

1996   Men's basketball team sets a record by winning twenty-seven games

1997   School of Biomedical Engineering, Science and Health Systems begins

School of Education begins

1999   North Residence Hall opens

2000   Caneris Residence Hall (formerly East Hall) Dormitory opens

2002   Drexel University College of Medicine established, successor to MCP Hahnemann University School of Medicine

Pearlstein Business Learning Center building opens

University Crossings opens as a dormitory

2005   Bossone Research Enterprise Center for Scientific Research opens for biomedical engineering courses

Classes begin in the College of Law

2007   College of Law Building opens

Race Street Residences opens

2009   Constantine Papadakis dies; Chuck Pennoni resumes service as interim president

Millennium Hall opens

2010   John Anderson Fry becomes president

Recreation Center opens

2011   Papadakis Integrated Sciences Building opens

The Center for Interdisciplinary Inquiry, part of Pennoni Honors College, offers the custom-designed major

Drexel affiliates with the Academy of Natural Sciences

2012   Men's basketball team sets a record by winning twenty-nine games

The URBN Center, new home of Westphal College, opens in the former Institute of Scientific Information (ISI) building

2013   Gerri C. LeBow Hall opens

The College of Computing and Informatics (CCI) is created, combining the College of Information Science and Technology (the iSchool), the Department of Computer Science in the College of Engineering, and the Department of Computing and Security Technology in Goodwin College

The Center for Hospitality and Sport Management is established

Women's basketball team wins the Women's National Invitation Tournament; Hollie Mershon is named tournament MVP

Men's and women's crew teams combine to win the overall points trophy at the Dad Vail Regatta; Drexel repeats this victory in 2014

Charles D. Close School of Entrepreneurship is launched

2014   The College of Computing and Informatics (CCI) enrolls its first class of students

The School of Public Health moves from the Center City campus to Nesbitt Hall in the University City campus

Dornsife Center for Neighborhood Partnerships opens

President Obama announces the first of five Promise zones, one of which is in Philadelphia, with Drexel as a partner

2015   School of Public Health is renamed the Dana and David Dornsife School of Public Health after the Dornsifes promise $45 million to the school

M. Brian Blake is named provost and executive vice president for academic affairs.

2016   Drexel and Brandywine Realty Trust unveil plans for Schuylkill Yards, a $3.5 billion investment to create a new fourteen-acre neighborhood immediately west of Thirtieth Street Station

BUILDING DREXEL

Introduction

Drexel at 125 and 150

Celebrating History with an Eye to the Future

John A. Fry

THE APPROACH of a significant anniversary invites us to look backward in time. But I think such milestones are more valuable for the chance to take stock of today, and especially to think about what tomorrow can and should hold. As Drexel University celebrates 125 years, I'm tempted to try a thought experiment about the future: What might this university and its environs look like at its next big anniversary in 2041?

Our founder, the financier and philanthropist Anthony J. Drexel, was a keen thinker and a prescient futurist. If he had engaged in such an experiment to imagine his Drexel Institute today, he might have hoped that his highest ideals would still animate it—and indeed they do. We who have custody of Mr. Drexel's legacy remain committed to showing our students where the world is headed, and preparing them accordingly, to leading society's efforts to meet its biggest challenges, and to weaving a strong, resilient urban fabric in our home city of Philadelphia. As Mr. Drexel once wished, a Drexel education is still "not only good, but good for something."

As he built his father's currency-trading bank into the first modern financial institution, Anthony J. Drexel helped lay the foundation for a century in which new technologies would forge a new type of industrial city. He saw a future with plenty of modern jobs that demanded educated workers. What he didn't see was an institution prepared to educate those workers—so he created one. The Drexel Institute of Art, Science, and

President John A. Fry, appointed in 2010, is the fourteenth president to serve Drexel. (Office of University Communications. Photo by Jeff Fusco.)

Industry was unique in 1891 for opening its doors to all, without regard to barriers such as wealth or gender, and for devoting itself to outstanding practical education.

Today, we again see a future in which prosperity relies on fostering a culture of innovation in urban environments. The difference this time is that comprehensive research universities like Drexel can't simply work to fill tomorrow's jobs—we must help create them. We are expected to educate the next generation of leaders, discoverers, and creators, while being engines of sustainable, equitable economic growth in our own right. And that growth must favor enterprises in which innovators work with entrepreneurs to address the critical problems facing us today, from energy to human health to the environment. These are the responsibilities that will shape the next quarter century at Drexel.

I believe that some aspects of this university will look very much the same to those of us lucky enough to compare 2041 with 2016. First and foremost, experiential learning will continue to be the core of a Drexel education, most clearly embodied by the Drexel Co-op. I hope that the norm for our students will eventually be a sequence of three co-op assignments placing them in greater Philadelphia, another region of the United States, and an international location. More students will be able to undertake co-ops in the nonprofit service sector thanks to increased funding, and some students will use the entrepreneurial co-op as a springboard to developing their own businesses. Beyond co-op, students will be deeply involved in research, clinical work and academically driven service. Drexel will serve as a global model for how to build a constant dialogue between classroom learning and the real-world demands that graduates face in their fields.

In a quarter century, an observer from today will recognize Drexel's world-class research enterprise, and in particular its excellence in translational research that turns new knowledge into important technologies. Drexel has the potential to move up through the ranks of the top one hundred American research universities as measured by sponsored research funding. And the university's expanding capacity for technology commercialization means that future generations of Drexel researchers will be among the highest-impact innovators in the world. They will save lives, help us live better, and grow the economy.

Drexel in 2041 will also be familiar for its trusted partnerships with business, government, and civic leaders in Philadelphia. Co-op, research, consulting, and technology commercialization will continue to connect the university to a thriving regional business community. Drexel will be a sought-after source of policy expertise in greater Philadelphia and beyond. Deep, generational relationships with community and neighborhood service organizations will be the hallmark of the university's core commitment to civic engagement, and will have clearly established Drexel as the most civically engaged university in the United States.

It is fairly straightforward to imagine these continuities between today's Drexel University and tomorrow's. Other aspects of the university's future require a larger leap of faith to envision. But they also grow from the seeds sowed by Anthony J. Drexel, and cultivated by every generation up to the present.

By 2041, I believe that Drexel will be the focal point of an urban innovation district that rivals any in the nation. A once-in-a-generation opportunity exists right now to leverage University City's academic ecosystem, entrepreneurial energy, and unsurpassed locational advantage into a new center of technology and job creation.

Planners, researchers, and public policy experts recognize the unique potential for cities to catalyze twenty-first-century prosperity. Urban innovation districts are arising because of the way city neighborhoods can foster human networks, which are the key to knowledge exchange and collaboration. Such districts integrate universities and hospitals, research-oriented firms, entrepreneurs, and investors. They also meet the growing demand for places where professionals, academics, and artists can work and live in proximity to retail and open-space amenities, cultural venues, and mass transit.

"Anchor institutions" like Drexel have both the ability to create innovation districts and the responsibility to make sure that their impact goes far beyond real estate development. The world desperately needs solutions to problems that affect the quality of life for everyone. Climate change, the need for sustainable energy, new health crises such as the rising prevalence of autism—our best hope to meet these threats is at the intersection of academic excellence, groundbreaking research, and entrepreneurship. Drexel of 2041, and the innovation district it leads, will be where that intersection happens.

A time frame of twenty-five years is just about right to imagine Drexel and its neighbors as driving not just economic and social growth in greater Philadelphia, but also American competitiveness and global progress. We are committed to this vision. The traveler of 2041 will arrive at Amtrak's Thirtieth Street Station via a high-speed rail trip of less than an hour from New York or Washington to find Drexel and the innovation district waiting outside the door, with Center City's business center just across the Schuylkill River. In a Philadelphia famous for William Penn's original five public squares, the gateway to our university at Thirtieth Street will be the sixth: Drexel Square.

Drexel is developing ten acres of land alongside Thirtieth Street Station— land that was underutilized for decades before Drexel's acquisition—as a mixed-use academic and commercial neighborhood featuring all the building blocks of innovation. There, corporate and academic partners will work with Drexel faculty and students on entrepreneurial solutions to the problems I've described, and to other challenges we can only begin to imagine. The indicators of success for this undertaking will include businesses that move from the university lab to find funding and incubation help and eventually provide good jobs in their own thriving space in the neighborhood, opportunities for Drexel students to prove once again that they outpace their peers in real-world readiness, and technologies and ideas that change the world.

Drexel's project dovetails with transformational new facilities by the University of Pennsylvania and Children's Hospital of Philadelphia. And by 2041, this groundswell of growth will hopefully be capped by another mixed-use, waterfront development above some eighty-five acres of rail yards north of Thirtieth Street Station. Drexel, Amtrak, the Southeastern

Pennsylvania Transportation Authority, and the Brandywine Realty Trust are among the principals involved in crafting a comprehensive Philadelphia Thirtieth Street Station District Plan.

Drexel can drive Philadelphia's innovation future because of the university's experiential approach to education, its translational research expertise, and its focus on new-venture skills through the Charles D. Close School of Entrepreneurship. The groundwork for this role is being laid already: Drexel Ventures helps faculty commercialize their research through a variety of support and funding opportunities, and initiatives like the Baiada Institute for Entrepreneurship and the Innovation Center at 3401 Market Street are incubating and accelerating the growth of new businesses. The neighborhood that travelers see as they disembark twenty-five years from now will be the physical manifestation of an innovation culture that has taken root today. And Drexel is the connector that makes all of this possible.

The future Drexel that I've imagined here represents a bold and complex undertaking. Though it will require the commitment and talents of a generation of faculty, administrators, and students to come to fruition, I am confident that we will rise to the challenge. But perhaps the most important measure of Drexel's quest for educational excellence and economic leadership is whether this progress will be shared by all of our Philadelphia neighbors and colleagues.

The neighborhoods around Drexel's campus are beset today by generational poverty exacerbated by economic inequality. If we want to honor our founder's vision, Drexel cannot be an island of privilege surrounded by privation. We must build a better city alongside community partners with whom we share a love for Philadelphia and a commitment to vital streets where families thrive and opportunity abounds. Both education and economic development are roads to prosperity—we must travel those roads together with our neighbors, if we want to make University City a new center of gravity for innovation. That is how an anchor institution fulfills its purpose.

As the nation's experiential education leader, Drexel must ensure that each new student's experience includes joining a peer group that represents Philadelphia and America. We have provided more than three hundred full-tuition scholarships over the past seven years to Philadelphia residents with economic need through our Liberty Scholars program. This has been a great means of improving diversity and access at Drexel, but it's a stopgap measure. In the long run, we must bring the cost of an undergraduate education within the means of families from all economic strata, while keeping the value of that education high for those families. This is a challenge for all of higher education, but it is especially acute for an urban university founded to facilitate educational and economic improvement for its city's residents.

As an economic engine, Drexel must wield its growing influence so that the developing innovation district leads to broad-based gains. The district cannot be self-contained, but rather must connect to neighborhoods like Mantua and Powelton Village both physically and psychologically. Its amenities should improve quality of life for workers and for residents, both new and long established. Drexel must be an active partner in providing a first-rate primary and secondary education to every child living in the area. And Drexel must also open jobs and entrepreneurial opportunities to West Philadelphians, and help them gain the skills and connections to benefit. That work has begun at our Dornsife Center for Neighborhood Partnerships and Lindy Center for Civic Engagement, where Drexel experts collaborate with neighbors on a wide range of solutions.

Drexel has been integral to Philadelphia's progress throughout our history. This university has always embraced its role as an anchor institution, and today more than ever, our vision for Drexel's future must serve Philadelphia's future as well. I am excited to help Drexel spark a new innovation district, tied to long-term solutions for both urban and global problems, because that is the highest purpose I can imagine for a university in America.

The celebration of Drexel's 125th anniversary reminds me how fortunate I am to be at an institution where my colleagues and I can envision an exciting future and begin to make it happen. It also reminds me that I am but a small part of a long legacy of educators and innovators, connected by the desire to shape future generations and build a stronger community. That knowledge is deeply humbling, and I am honored to accept the responsibility that comes with it.

Drexel, Philadelphia, and the Urban Ecology of Higher Education

Richardson Dilworth

I N 1891 the Drexel Institute of Art, Science, and Industry first opened its doors, at what is today known as the Main Building of what is now Drexel University. And thus in 2016, the year of this book's publication, Drexel celebrates its 125th anniversary. Yet the Drexel of today includes a medical school that traces its origins back to 1848 and the Academy of Natural Sciences (ANS), which was founded in 1812. And while Drexel Institute was established in response to the educational needs of a booming industrial city, the medical school and the ANS are part of an older tradition, when Philadelphia was the "Athens of America"—a center of free thought, learning, and scientific experimentation.

The units that compose Drexel today reflect a broad swath of the educational and cultural traditions, and the economic and social forces, that shaped the city of which the university is an intimate part. We can attribute much of the university's success to the pioneering vision of its founder, Anthony Drexel. Yet the path by which Drexel became one of the prime institutional stewards of Philadelphia has not been a straight one—the university has survived through numerous external crises, internal convulsions, and disruptive transformations. As I describe briefly in this chapter, many similar institutions have fallen by the wayside over the past 125 years. What has marked Drexel's development since its founding has been a commitment to the core values of community, innovation, experimentation, and the pursuit of practical knowledge; countless cadres of faculty, researchers, administrators, students, and alumni who have found a shared sense of purpose in those core values (to which this book is a testament); and an institutional flexibility that has allowed the school to adapt to new conditions and seize on opportunities—and which has made it, in my personal experience, a wonderful place to work.

In this chapter I provide an overview of Drexel's history, placing it in the larger story of Philadelphia, introducing and contextualizing the chapters to follow in this book, and providing brief sketches of several moments when the university faced relatively clear choices regarding its developmental path. Drexel has been around long enough, and is big enough (it is currently the fourteenth largest private university in the United States, in terms of student enrollment) that it is impossible in the space of a single book to document all of its many different parts. Those covered here and subsequently are meant as a sampling that we believe provides a good sense of the larger whole, and of the overall spirit of the institution.

————

IN 1766 a twenty-three-year-old Thomas Jefferson visited Philadelphia for the primary purpose of receiving a smallpox inoculation, a somewhat risky treatment revolutionary enough that it had inspired mob violence in Boston and was officially banned in New York.[1] That the inoculation was only available in Philadelphia suggests the unique role of the city as a center of science and useful knowledge—a place where Benjamin Franklin found a receptive audience for his Library Company (founded in 1731), American Philosophical Society (cofounded in 1743 with the botanist John Bartram, whose forty-five-acre "garden" along the Schuylkill still attracts close to 40,000 visitors a year), Pennsylvania Hospital (1751), and Academy and Charitable School in the Province of Pennsylvania (1751), which would become the University of Pennsylvania (or "Penn" as it is typically known).

The institutions founded by Franklin were just a small sampling of the rich fabric of medical, scientific, and educational organizations in the city that were established in the eighteenth and early nineteenth centuries, which included as well the Philadelphia Society for Promoting Agriculture (1785), College of Physicians (1787), Pennsylvania Society for the Encouragement of Manufactures and the Useful Arts (1787), Pennsylvania Academy for the Fine Arts (1805), Academy of Natural Sciences (1812), Philadelphia College of Pharmacy (1821, now the University of the Sciences), and the Franklin Institute (1824). Given the adventurous, liberal, and experimental nature of Philadelphia's intellectual communities, it comes as no surprise that the city was also a leader in municipal infrastructure technology, with the first steam-powered public water system (designed by a young architect and engineer, Benjamin Latrobe, who President Jefferson later hired as the Surveyor of the Public Buildings of the United States) that used what were then the largest steam engines in the country, construction of which began in 1799.[2]

Among Philadelphia's early cultural and educational institutions, the Academy of Natural Sciences would, nearly two centuries after its founding, become part of Drexel, and many of its scientists are now professors in Drexel's Department of Biodiversity, Earth, and Environmental Sciences. As Lloyd Ackert discusses in Chapter 4, the merger between Drexel and ANS built upon the university's long-standing commitment to the sciences, while also expanding its resources in environmental studies, a topic discussed by Charles Haas in Chapter 16.

ANS is the most significant of what was a group of institutions devoted to natural history and sciences, preceded by Charles Willson Peale's namesake museum. Founded in 1786, its collection provided "primary sources for every significant natural history monograph on ornithology, entomology, zoology and paleontology written in the United States during the first three decades of the nineteenth century." Peale's museum had itself been preceded by Pierre Eugene Du Simitiere's American Museum, devoted to "natural curiosities."[3] And in the 1840s, William Wagner, a Penn graduate and later a successful merchant who learned his trade under Stephen Girard, built an extension on his house to hold his sizable collection of natural artifacts, in which he began to hold free lectures in 1847. In 1855 Wagner's collection moved to the Wagner Institute at Thirteenth and Spring Garden Streets, and in 1865 moved to North Philadelphia, where it has remained largely unchanged from the nineteenth century.[4]

Francis Drexel, an aspiring artist from the small Austrian town of Dornbirn who had been wandering Europe for eight years (staying away from his hometown to avoid being drafted into Napoleon's army), and who possibly on a whim decided to travel to the United States, landed in Philadelphia in 1817, in the midst of the city's tremendous intellectual, economic, and population growth. Setting up shop as a portrait painter, Drexel "achieved almost instant social and professional acceptance" if not necessarily fame and fortune. Four years after arriving, Drexel married Catherine Hookey, and five years after that he was off to South America, in what turned out to be a misguided business venture, to paint portraits of Simon Bolivar. Yet the trip was apparently worthwhile as it inspired Drexel to turn from painting to trading currencies, and in 1838 he opened up a currency exchange business in Philadelphia's financial district on Third Street.[5]

When Francis Drexel left for South America in 1826, he left behind his wife and two small children (Mary Johanna and Francis Anthony), with a third child—Anthony Joseph, the founder of Drexel Institute—on the way. In Chapter 2 of this book, Cordelia Biddle (herself a direct descendant of Francis Drexel and Second Bank president Nicholas Biddle, and thus a physical embodiment of journalist Charles Morley's description of Philadelphia in 1920 as "a surprisingly large town at the confluence of the Biddle and Drexel families"),[6] discusses the rise of Anthony Drexel in the world of banking, first as the heir apparent to his father's business, then as a partner with his father and brother in Drexel and Company, and later as a mentor and partner to John Pierpont Morgan.

Early on Anthony Drexel established partnerships with bankers in New York City—most notably with Pierpont Morgan in the establishment of Drexel, Morgan and Company in 1871, which by 1873 was housed in the largest building on Wall Street.[7] Drexel's move reflected a larger shift, as Philadelphia lost its status as the financial capital of the country to New York by the middle of the nineteenth century and evolved into a center for industry, manufacturing, education, and medicine.[8] Yet Anthony Drexel himself remained in Philadelphia, attending to business at the Drexel and Company building on Third Street, to which he commuted from his Italianate villa in West Philadelphia, far from the fashionable residences around Rittenhouse Square—part of his desire to stay out of the limelight, so much so that he failed to attend the grand opening of his institute.

As Anthony Drexel was building an international financial empire, Philadelphia was truly becoming the medical center of the country. The first American medical college was founded in Philadelphia in 1765, under the auspices of the University of Pennsylvania, and the city's second medical school, Jefferson Medical College, was established in 1825 (first under the auspices of Jefferson College in Canonsburg, and made independent in 1838), but it was the period from 1840 to 1850 that saw a veritable explosion in medical education, with the establishment of Pennsylvania Medical College (1840), Franklin Medical College (1846), the Philadelphia College of Medicine (1847), Homeopathic Medical College of Philadelphia (1848), and the Female Medical College of Pennsylvania (1850). Dental schools were quick to follow, with the establishment of the Philadelphia College of Dental Surgery in 1852, Philadelphia Dental College in 1863, and the dental department of the University of Pennsylvania in 1878. Later medical schools established around the same time as the Drexel Institute were the Medico-Chirurgical College (1881), Philadelphia College of Osteopathy (1899), and Temple University's School of Medicine (1901).[9]

As medical professor John Kastor noted of Philadelphia at the beginning of the twenty-first century, "About one-fourth of the country's doctors have worked in the city at some time during their careers, as medical students, trainees, practitioners, or faculty members."[10]

Franklin Medical College quickly disappeared. Pennsylvania Medical College and the Philadelphia College of Medicine merged in 1859 but then went out of business during the Civil War. More successful was the Homeopathic Medical College of Philadelphia, which later expanded to become Hahnemann Medical College.[11] Hahnemann and the Female Medical College (later the Medical College of Pennsylvania, or MCP) formed the two original institutions that would in 2002 become three new units of Drexel—the College of Medicine, College of Nursing and Health Professions, and what is now the Dornsife School of Public Health, all of which are discussed in detail in Chapters 19, 20, and 21.

In the mid-1840s, the medical student had already become an established Philadelphia character. As novelist George Lippard described it, "long hair and [a] characteristic look of frankness and recklessness combined, betrayed the Medical Student of the Quaker City."[12] Lippard's description suggests a general suspicion of the medical professions. Indeed, at the time of the founding of Philadelphia's first medical school, doctors and their students were often the subjects of violence, based on moral apprehension regarding the dissection of human bodies, and a suspicion, often well-founded, that medical students were robbing graves in order to get bodies. By the time of the medical school boom of the 1840s, public fear and suspicion in Philadelphia had shifted away from doctors and students to abolitionists, Irish immigrants, and Catholics, including a pitched battle over several days in 1844 between Catholics and Nativists leaving many dead and injured—a riot that still stands as the largest and most significant physical attack on the Catholic Church in the United States. Rampant and violent Nativism was perhaps one reason the Drexels converted from Catholicism to Episcopalianism—with the later exception, of course, of Saint Katharine Drexel, Anthony Drexel's niece.

Less than a decade after the 1844 Nativist riots, Philadelphia's Catholics began organizing colleges, beginning with courses offered at Old Saint Joseph's Church in 1851, which Saint Joseph's University identifies as its founding; and then with the establishment of La Salle College in lower Kensington in 1863, which La Salle contends establishes it as the first Catholic college in the city.

Nativism and anti-Catholicism were in part a function of industrialization, as at least some in the city's working class feared for their job security against an increasing tide of new European immigrants. And as Philadelphia's financial preeminence was eclipsed by New York, it became instead one of the country's most important industrial and manufacturing centers, drawing increasingly large numbers to work in its numerous factories and offices. The prominence of industry and manufacturing in the city presaged a school devoted to the "mechanical arts"—a medieval term that gained new significance in the industrial age.

As its name implied, the Drexel Institute of Art, Science, and Industry was a response to the new educational needs of the city's burgeoning industrial population. This was frankly not a new idea, as the Drexel Institute was itself modeled after such schools as New York's Cooper Union for the Advancement of Science and Art (established in 1859), the Pratt Institute (established 1887), and Philadelphia's own Pennsylvania Museum and School of Industrial Art (founded in 1876, the museum later became the Philadelphia Museum of Art and the school became the University of the Arts). All of these institutions, including Drexel, were designed to be highly accessible and focused on upward mobility rather than maintaining elite status; offered low cost tuition; were open to all genders, races, and creeds; and focused on practical subjects such as, in the case of Drexel, "business, chemistry, cooking, dressmaking, art, and library science."[13]

Prior to the Drexel Institute there were also several schools in Philadelphia devoted specifically to technical and business education, including the Spring Garden Institute (founded in 1851, it later became Spring Garden College), Union Business College (founded in 1865, which later became Pierce College), and the Philadelphia Textile School (founded in 1884, for, as its name suggests, somewhat more specific purposes, tied to the city's large textiles industry). Temple University's founding, in 1884 in North Philadelphia (just a few blocks from the Wagner Institute) to a certain extent fits this mold as well. Though Temple's origins lie in Latin classes begun by the Baptist minister Russell Conwell, the goal from its very beginning was egalitarian in nature. As Conwell's biographer Robert Shackleton described Temple's early students, they "have come largely from among railroad clerks, bank clerks, bookkeepers, teachers, preachers, mechanics, salesman, drug clerks, city and United States government employees, widows, nurses, housekeepers, brakeman, firemen, engineers, motormen, conductors, and shop hands."[14] Certainly the other schools were targeting this same market of potential students.

What distinguished Drexel from most of the new educational institutions in Philadelphia was, first and foremost, the wealth and influence of its founder, which provided for an impressive building, a substantial initial endowment of $3 million (adjusted for inflation, still the largest single gift to the university), and which meant that the opening ceremonies were attended by the likes of Andrew Carnegie, Thomas Edison, and, of course, Pierpont Morgan. Second, from its beginning Drexel Institute clearly intended to offer more than simply the vocational educations offered by the likes of the Spring Garden Institute and Union Business College. As Amy Slaton notes of the early institute in Chapter 5, "The appearance of Drexel's first building, declared at top volume that industrial learning and labor and the transmission of Western high culture were inseparable undertakings."

Third, Drexel's focus on library science also distinguished it from Philadelphia's other technical and industrial schools. As Danuta Nitecki and David Fenske both note (in Chapters 9 and 10, respectively), Drexel's library training program was the third established in the country (Columbia University's was the first, established by Melvil Dewey in 1887, followed by Pratt's library school in 1890), and thus part of an incipient national trend, reflected as well in the establishment of the Free Library of Philadelphia in 1891 by medical doctor William Pepper, in the same spirit of egalitarianism and uplift as the Drexel Institute—and in some respects in reaction against the more elite subscription libraries such as the Philadelphia Athenaeum.

One of the most distinctive elements of Drexel's educational program was added nearly thirty years after the school's founding—cooperative education, where students alternate between their studies and short-term employment in industry, arranged by the school. As discussed in more detail in Chapter 3, cooperative education at Drexel began after World War I with a pilot program for engineering students in 1919, which by 1920 had been incorporated into the institute more broadly, and the school moved from the semester to the quarter system to accommodate the change.

The founding of Drexel and similar schools reflected an optimism about the urban, industrial future of the country that was at odds with the attitudes of many contemporary thinkers who saw in urbanization a grave threat to the national spirit. Just two years after Drexel's founding, the historian Frederick Jackson Turner famously announced the end of the Western frontier that, he argued, had been the wellspring for the American spirit of democracy and individualism.[15] And James Bryce commented in his classic *American Commonwealth*, first published in 1888, that "the growth of great cities has been among the most significant and least fortunate changes in the character of the population of the United States during the century that has passed since 1787."[16]

A baseball game is played on the grounds next to the Main Building, now the site
of Stratton Hall, 1916. (Drexel University Archives. PC 3 Early photographs
of the Drexel Institute of Art, Science, and Industry.)

In the first few years, Drexel's administrators faced what appears (at least in hindsight) to have been a choice as to what the institute was to become. Drexel had a magnificent building with a library and museum, and it offered courses but no degrees, and in that respect was similar to Philadelphia institutions such as the Franklin and Wagner Institutes. And while the Franklin Institute has evolved into what is largely a contemporary museum (and IMAX movie theater), and the Wagner Institute has in some respects become a time capsule of a nineteenth-century natural history museum, Drexel became a university—a path that was quite clearly established early in its history, though it ostensibly might have gone in a different direction.

Certainly Drexel's industrial focus suggests that becoming a museum, with its core function as a repository of objects, was a less likely outcome than it was for other institutions. Yet in 1893, just such a museum, devoted to industry—the Philadelphia Commercial Museum—was founded, in part as a permanent world's fair (such as Philadelphia's Centennial celebration in 1876 or Chicago's Columbian Exposition in 1893) but also as something of a hybrid between a contemporary think tank and chamber of commerce.[17] As the commercial museum became increasingly irrelevant starting in the 1920s, was absorbed into the Philadelphia Civic Center in 1952, and ultimately closed in 1994, the decision to focus on education and training seems to have been a good one for Drexel.

As explained in Chapter 3, under its second president, Hollis Godfrey, Drexel Institute changed tracks, from offering basic instruction through thirteen largely autonomous departments, to a degree-granting institution organized into four schools (Engineering, Domestic Science and Art, Secretarial, and the Evening School), and added two new buildings beyond the original one financed by Drexel himself. By the onset of the Great Depression, Drexel had clearly chosen a different route than either Spring Garden or Pierce College, which remained largely vocational schools, and joined Temple, Penn, La Salle, and Saint Joseph's as a general purpose institution of higher education, though one more focused in practical subjects, and, with the co-op central to its program, job readiness. As Miriam Kotzin notes in her history of Drexel, the more vocational orientation of the original institute was preserved in what began as the Department of Lectures and Evening Classes in 1892, which became the Evening School in 1918, and the Evening College and Diploma School in 1950, when it began granting degrees.[18] (In 2001 the Evening College became the Goodwin College of Professional Studies, as discussed in more detail in Chapter 21.)

Drexel's early growth was cut short by the Great Depression, and though the institute was energized with federal grants during the war, it was by 1943 nearly insolvent, and saved only by a large gift from the estate of one of Anthony Drexel's children, George Childs Drexel.[19] In 1936, the school changed its name to the Drexel Institute of Technology—a reflection of the trajectory established by President Godfrey and reinforced by nearly every successive president until Richard Breslin (1988–1994), who was charged with developing the university's liberal arts focus. As discussed in more detail in Chapter 3, Godfrey, inspired by the scientific management philosophy of Frederick Taylor, had a vision of Drexel engineering graduates as future industrial managers who would oversee the entire productive process, rather than technical-area specialists. It was through Godfrey's vision that both engineering and business became two of the university's central foci.

Anthony Drexel's significant founding gift (combined with later contributions from Cyrus Curtis, Alexander Van Rensselaer, the Rockefeller Foundation, and several Drexel family members, among others) had allowed

*Aerial view of Drexel campus, looking north from Thirty-Second
and Walnut Streets, c. 1956. (Drexel University Archives.)*

the institute to charge minimal tuition, though as a result of financial pressures during the Depression tuition increased under President Kenneth Matheson. Yet during the 1950s and 1960s, under the eighteen-year presidency of James Creese (from 1945 to 1963), tuition as a proportion of university revenue fell from approximately 90 to 60 percent, and the university doubled its physical plant. This momentum was maintained under William Hagerty (president from 1963 to 1984), who oversaw the institute's transition to Drexel University, the establishment of several new schools and colleges, a further expansion in the size of the campus, and a virtual explosion in the number of students.

The thirty-nine years' combined presidencies of Creese and Hagerty mark a period of stability in leadership during which Drexel, despite facing financial insolvency and massive dislocations resulting from wartime mobilization, also gradually took on the shape of a comprehensive research university. To a great extent, the two presidents, and Hagerty especially, were responding to, and taking advantage of, a major period of growth for nearly all American colleges and universities, as the college participation rate for

Aerial view of Drexel campus, looking south from Market Street—Matheson Hall in the foreground, 1967. (Drexel University Archives. PC 5 Buildings and campus photographs.)

high school graduates increased, thus boosting enrollments, and institutions of higher education, with the help of federal funding, took on a larger national role in research.

Different universities responded in different ways to postwar growth. To accommodate growth while keeping tuition low, for instance, Temple University in 1965 became a state-affiliated institution. Drexel, by contrast, provided financial support through the co-op, by which students could earn money as part of their undergraduate educations and thus ease the financial burden of going to college. In essence, while Temple affiliated itself with state government, Drexel reinforced its affiliation with private industry—as Nitecki points out in Chapter 9, the new library built in the 1950s was financed by subscriptions from private business—and in doing so maintained its focus on engineering, business, and experiential learning.

As Eric Zillmer notes in Chapter 6, another important decision made by Drexel administrators during the Hagerty years was to compete successfully in NCAA Division I athletics by focusing on basketball and dropping the football program. In a 2016 *Wall Street Journal* editorial, President John Fry emphasized the wisdom of that choice, noting the great expense of most college football programs, that in most cases require large annual subsidies.[20] Certainly Temple's problems with its plan to build a football stadium, which have embroiled it in conflicts with the city government and its North Philadelphia neighborhood, speak to the benefits of the choice made by Drexel.[21]

Drexel's focus on industry made it a conservative institution. As James Wolfinger points out in Chapter 13, the civil rights and Black Power movements had a minimal impact on the largely white institution, especially relative to other schools. And as Jonson Miller points out in Chapter 15, the antiwar movement at Drexel was a muted one. Similarly, Charles Haas notes in Chapter 16 that, though there have been educational and degree programs at Drexel focused on the environment in one way or another since the 1890s, these have virtually all been until very recently technically focused and thus not reflective of the environmental activism that emerged in the 1960s and 1970s. There is no evidence, for instance, that anyone at Drexel celebrated the first Earth Day in 1970.

Yet as Paula Cohen points out in Chapter 17, by the 1980s, largely as a result of Hagerty's efforts to make Drexel a comprehensive university, humanities and social science faculty and degree programs were an increasing presence on campus, which provided at least a light counterweight to the predominance of engineering and business. By the 1990s there was even an African American studies program on campus (which is now Africana studies).

As Drexel grew after World War II, Philadelphia shrank, from a peak population of nearly 2.1 million in 1950, to a postwar low of 1.5 million in 2000, with especially dramatic declines in the 1970s (the effects of which Wolfinger discusses in more detail in Chapter 13). At the same time, the city's African-American population was increasing—in 1950 Philadelphia was approximately 82 percent white and 18 percent black (with a negligible amount of other races), and by 1980, when Hagerty was preparing to retire, the city was 58 percent white and 38 percent black. Meanwhile, the surrounding suburbs were booming with primarily white residents who were moving out of the city. Between 1950 and 1960, for instance, the population of neighboring Montgomery County increased by more than 45 percent, from 353,068 to 516,682 people. When Temple acquired a campus in Montgomery County in 1958 (by absorbing the Pennsylvania School of Horticulture for Women), there was some speculation that it portended the move of the entire university to the suburbs.[22]

From the 1964 North Philadelphia race riot (one of the first of a wave that would sweep across American cities every summer for the next decade),

Aerial view of Drexel campus, looking south from Thirty-Third Street
and Powelton Avenue, 1979. (Drexel University Archives. PC 5 Buildings
and campus photographs.)

demonstrations to integrate Girard College (achieved in 1968), and the election of a "white backlash" mayor, Frank Rizzo, in 1971, racial conflict was
a leitmotif in postwar Philadelphia. Around Penn and Drexel, racial conflict focused in part on urban "renewal" under the auspices of the West
Philadelphia Corporation (WPC), a joint project by Penn, Drexel, the
Philadelphia College of Pharmacy and Science, Presbyterian Hospital, and
the Philadelphia College of Osteopathy to create a new joint "science center"
that was also part of a larger plan to brand the neighborhood around Penn
and Drexel as "University City."[23]

    With construction begun in 1964, the University City Science Center
ultimately displaced approximately a thousand mostly black residents (though
the figures vary, with those provided by university and city government being
notably lower than those estimated through U.S. Census figures), generating
neighborhood and student resistance as it gradually built new buildings westward along Market Street, starting with its original building at Thirty-Fourth
Street.[24] As Jeannine Keefer discusses in Chapter 14, Drexel's primary role in
the University City renewal focused on a portion of land known as Area V

or Unit 5, in which the university planned primarily to place dormitories. As the university moved forward with its plans, it faced resistance from both students and community members, and created conflicts with the residents that lasted until at least the 1980s.

As discussed in more detail in Chapter 24, north of Drexel are two neighborhoods, Powelton Village and Mantua, relatively starkly divided by race and class. Powelton Village was (and still is) a racially mixed but predominantly white and upper-middle-class, professional neighborhood, the postwar origins of which lay in a liberal progressive belief in counterculture and racial integration, but which more recently had become home to many young urban professionals more concerned with their property values. Mantua, by contrast, was a black working-class neighborhood that had fallen on hard times as deindustrialization decimated the blue-collar jobs in the city, and the crack cocaine epidemic increased street crime.[25]

For administrators and faculty, the neighborhoods surrounding the university were of little significance. As David Paul, a former Drexel administrator, has commented, "The president of the university traditionally lived in one of the Main Line towns that were homes to the Philadelphia aristocracy. . . . The faculty also commuted into the university to teach."[26] The only residence hall was one for women, Sarah Van Rensselaer Dormitory, which opened in the 1930s, and even after the second dormitory, Kelly Hall, was built, in 1967, the majority of students were commuters. The major exceptions were the fraternities and sororities, which, as Michael Kelley and Anthony Noce relate in Chapter 7, were establishing houses in Powelton Village, starting with Alpha Pi Lambda's "castle on the corner" in 1939. By the 1980s there were racial tensions between the neighborhood and at least one of the fraternities, at one point leading Mayor Wilson Goode to order one fraternity house closed for being a "threat to the public safety of the city."[27]

Conflicts with its neighbors were one of the smaller problems faced by Drexel at the end of the 1980s and the beginnings of the 1990s. After President Hagerty retired in 1984, William Gaither was appointed the new president, and while he was successful in increasing donations and research money, he also became embroiled in a pitched battle with faculty and deans that ultimately ended his tenure after just three years.[28] His successor, Richard Breslin, was ultimately dismissed himself in 1994 after an era that saw declines in nearly all indicators—such as, for instance, an entering freshmen class half the size as that in the year that Hagerty retired.

Drexel's decline in the late 1980s and early 1990s was a combination of several factors: a university that was awkwardly attempting to transition from a technical institute to a comprehensive university, fewer students and more competition from public schools such as Temple and Penn State, and increasing frictions between faculty, administration, and the board of trustees. It is worth noting that many schools faced pressures during this period, and some fared worse than Drexel. Spring Garden College, which had also expanded after World War II and had moved to a thirty-three-acre campus in the Mount Airy neighborhood, suffered declining enrollments and closed for good in 1992.

The financial pressures faced by many universities in the 1980s and 1990s forced them to shutter some of their weaker programs, and library programs were especially vulnerable. In 1990 Columbia announced that it would close its library school, as did the University of Southern California, University of Chicago, and Vanderbilt University around the same time.[29] By contrast, Drexel and Pratt's library schools have evolved into schools of information and computer science, and Drexel's library now views itself more as an "information hub" than a repository of printed materials. And as David Raizman discusses in Chapter 12, Drexel's College of Home Economics also successfully avoided extinction by transitioning away from what had become an anachronistic discipline into a college of design arts, which is today the Westphal College of Media Arts and Design.

As David Paul argues, Breslin's strategy of cost-cutting put Drexel into a downward spiral, where decreased resources attracted fewer students, leading to further cuts combined with tuition increases, and so on.[30] This strategy changed under the new president appointed to replace Breslin, Constantine Papadakis, a former chief of engineering at Bechtel who the *Wall Street Journal* described in 2005 as "part showman—a promotional CD-ROM is tucked inside a pocket on his business card—and part numbers jockey" who "exhorts his marketing staff to find more paying 'customers,' better known as students."[31]

Under Papadakis, Drexel resumed the growth trajectory that had defined the university under Creese and Hagerty—the result, in part, of a dynamic new leader focused on enrollments, combined with demographics, as the "baby boom echo" increased the number of high school graduates, and thus college applicants, by 1995. Yet Papadakis also fundamentally reshaped Drexel by building upon Hagerty's efforts to transform it from an institute of technology to a comprehensive research university. Two of the most important elements in this transformation were the acquisition of MCP Hahnemann University (MCPHU) in 2002 and the creation of a law school in 2006.

Similar to Drexel, though for different reasons, Hahnemann University and the Medical College of Pennsylvania (MCP) were both struggling in the 1980s—in large part because Philadelphia's rich medical heritage had by the end of the twentieth century created a fragmented and highly competitive market for medical schools and health systems. At the other end of the state, in Pittsburgh, Allegheny Health Services, Inc. (AHSI), under an ambitious president, was looking to expand through the acquisition of a medical school. As described in Chapters 19 and 20, what ensued was more than a decade of rapid—and chaotic—organizational change. In 1988, AHSI absorbed MCP; in 1991, it acquired four hospitals in the Philadelphia region and was reorganized and renamed the Allegheny Health, Education and Research Foundation (AHERF); in 1993, AHERF absorbed Hahnemann University (HU) and its hospital; and in 1996, MCP and HU were merged to form the Allegheny University of the Health Sciences (AUHS), and AHERF also acquired the Graduate Health System, which consisted of five hospitals and 110 primary care practices. As part of the expansion and reorganization, a new nursing school and school of public health were established, in 1994 and 1995, respectively.

Then came the unraveling. In 1997 AHERF laid off 6 percent of its workforce, and in 1998 it entered agreements to sell eight of its hospitals in the Philadelphia area, and to file for bankruptcy. The hospitals were ultimately sold to Tenet Healthcare, in an agreement where Drexel would manage AUHS, the name of which had been converted back to MCPHU.[32]

As Roger Dennis describes in Chapter 22, the ink was hardly dry on the Drexel-MCPHU merger before Papadakis began planning for the establishment of a new law school, which opened for business in 2006. As it turned out, the law school faced extremely hard circumstances. Its first class graduated in 2009, into one of the worst markets for new lawyers in American history, and as a result new law school applications plummeted nationally—while at the same time the costs of running law schools had increased. Yet Drexel's law school has persevered, succeeding in developing a unique niche through its cooperative program, and securing a major gift from one of the country's top trial lawyers, Thomas Kline.

Just as Drexel in the 1990s under Papadakis was experiencing a resurgence, so was Philadelphia. The city's mayor elected in 1991, Ed Rendell, was as much a booster of his city as Papadakis was a promoter of his university. And the population loss that had defined the city in the 1970s and 1980s at least began to slow down (and by the 2000s the city's net population would stabilize and then begin to grow for the first time in half a century). Yet in the 1990s Philadelphia was also the home of a crime wave, felt traumatically at Penn, with the well-publicized murders of a researcher,

Vladimir Sled, in 1996, and the shooting of graduate student Al-Moez Ali-mohamed, in 1994.

In the same year as Alimohamed was killed and a year before Papadakis was appointed Drexel's president, Judith Rodin was appointed president of the University of Pennsylvania, where she was immediately confronted with a crime-ridden campus. In 1995 Rodin hired education consultant John Fry as the university's chief operating officer, responsible for developing and implementing the 1996–2001 comprehensive strategic plan. Fry focused in part on improving the neighborhood to the west of the university in response to crime, known collectively as the "West Philadelphia Initiatives," including commercial development along the Fortieth Street corridor, subsidies for Penn faculty and staff who agreed to buy homes near the university, and a partnership between Penn and the School District of Philadelphia to fund and run a new elementary and junior high school in West Philadelphia.[33]

In 2002 John Fry left Penn to become president of Franklin and Marshall College in Lancaster, and in 2010 he returned to Philadelphia to become Drexel's fourteenth president. Picking up from his work at Penn, Fry declared his goal for Drexel to be "the most civically engaged university in the United States." Toward that end, the university has established the Dornsife Center for Neighborhood Partnerships, located right along the border of Powelton Village and Mantua, which is currently in the process of preparing to become home to a new public middle school, in partnership with Science Leadership Academy. Under Fry the university has also committed to densifying University City by leasing land for new private student housing and retail, and planning for an entirely new "innovation neighborhood" next to Thirtieth Street Station, described in more detail in the president's introduction to this volume.

As the contents of this book attest, Drexel has changed significantly over time, especially as it has absorbed other institutions and taken on their missions. Had it not changed, it most likely would no longer exist—and as is true of many institutions that have been around for more than a century, its continued existence has on more than one occasion been open to doubt. To a great extent, Drexel's fortunes have ebbed and flowed with those of its home city, even as it has now emerged as one of the city's primary employers and economic drivers—an outcome that would most likely have surprised its founder, who lived at a time when Philadelphia was an industrial powerhouse, the Pennsylvania Railroad dominated everything, and only approximately 2 percent of Americans aged eighteen to twenty-four were enrolled in a college or university.[34] And yet Anthony Drexel's imprint on the school he founded is still readily apparent in its focus on innovation, technology, and experiential education. Even the university's newer units, most notably the schools of law, and nursing and health professions, have become integral parts of the larger institution by embracing experiential education. Similarly, the university's leadership has committed the university to its city and neighborhood in ways that it never had in the past, yet which at the same time builds on Drexel's tradition as an urban university. No one knows what the future will bring, but there is certainly a clear trajectory.

NOTES

1. Dumas Malone, *Jefferson the Virginian* (Boston: Little, Brown, 1948), 98–100.

2. See the *Water Works of the City of Philadelphia: The Story of their Development and Engineering Specifications*, compiled by Walter Graf, available at www.phillyh2o.org /backpages/GrafHistory_HSP.htm#Preface. See also Nelson Blake, *Water for the Cities: A History of the Urban Water Supply Problem in the United States* (Syracuse, NY: Syracuse University Press, 1956), chs. 2 and 5.

3. Robert Schofield, "The Science Education of an Enlightened Engineer: Charles Willson Peale and His Philadelphia Museum, 1784–1827," *American Studies* 30 (Fall 1989): 22, 25; quote from 22.

4. See the "finding aid" for the Robert Chambers collection on William Wagner and the history of the Wagner Free Institute of Science, 90-015, Library and Archives of the Wagner Free Institute of Science, available at http://hdl.library.upenn.edu/1017/d/pacscl /WFIS_WFIS90015.

5. Dan Rottenberg, *The Man Who Made Wall Street: Anthony J. Drexel and the Rise of Modern Finance* (Philadelphia: University of Pennsylvania Press, 2001), ch. 2; quote on 21.

6. Kan Kalfus, ed., *Charles Morley's Philadelphia* (New York: Fordham University Press, 1990), 4.

7. Rottenberg, *The Man Who Made Wall Street*, 103–4.

8. See Jerome Hodos, *Second Cities: Globalization and Local Politics in Manchester and Philadelphia* (Philadelphia: Temple University Press, 2011).

9. "Introduction," in *Founders Week Memorial Volume, Containing an Account of the Two Hundred and Twenty-fifth Anniversary of the City of Philadelphia, and Histories of its Principal Scientific Institutions, Medical Colleges, Hospitals, etc.*, ed. Frederick Henry (Philadelphia, 1909).

10. John Kastor, *Governance of Teaching Hospitals: Turmoil at Penn and Hopkins* (Baltimore: Johns Hopkins University Press, 2004), ch. 3.

11. "Introduction," in *Founders Week Memorial Volume*.

12. George Lippard, *The Quaker City, or, The Monks of Monk Hall: A Romance of Philadelphia Life, Mystery, and Crime*, ed. David Reynolds (1845; repr. Amherst: University of Massachusetts Press, 1995), 437.

13. Rottenberg, *The Man Who Made Wall Street*, 157–58.

14. Robert Shackleton's biography of Conwell ("His Life and Achievements") is included in Russell Conwell, *Acres of Diamonds* (New York: Harper and Brothers, 1915), 63–170; quote is from 137–38.

15. See Frederick Jackson Turner, "The Significance of the Frontier in American History," *Annual Report of the American Historical Association for the Year 1893* (Washington, DC: Government Printing Office, 1894), 197–227.

16. James Bryce, *American Commonwealth*, vol. 1 (Chicago: Charles H. Sergel, 1891), 593.

17. Steven Conn, "An Epistemology for Empire: The Philadelphia Commercial Museum, 1893–1926," *Diplomatic History* 22 (fall 1998): 533–63.

18. Miriam Kotzin, *A History of Drexel University, 1941–1963* (Philadelphia: Drexel University, 1983), 12.

19. Constantine Papadakis, "A University with a Difference: The Unique Vision of Anthony J. Drexel," paper delivered at the Greater Delaware Valley meeting of the Newcomen Society of the United States, Drexel University, Philadelphia, December 6, 2001, available at www.drexel.edu/papadakis/newcomen/.

20. John Fry, "We're Glad We Say No to College Football," *Wall Street Journal*, January 3, 2016.

21. See, for instance, Chris Brennan, "Protest May Stall Timeline, but Temple Will Get Its Way with Stadium," *Philadelphia Inquirer*, February 15, 2016.

22. These speculations were apparently not grounded in fact according to James Hilty, *Temple University: 125 Years of Service to Philadelphia, the Nation, and the World* (Philadelphia: Temple University Press, 2010), 266.

23. MacKenzie Carlson, "A History of the University City Science Center," University Archives and Records Center, University of Pennsylvania, 1999, available at www .archives.upenn.edu/histy/features/upwphil/ucsc.html.

24. Ibid.

25. On Powelton Village and Mantua, see Elijah Anderson, *Steetwise: Race, Class and Change in an Urban Community* (Chicago: University of Chicago Press, 1990).

26. David Paul, *When the Pot Boils: The Decline and Turnaround of Drexel University* (Albany: State University of New York, 2008), 23.

27. Quoted in ibid.

28. See Huntly Collins and Martha Woodall, "Gaither's Future Hinges on Board Vote This Week," *Philadelphia Inquirer*, October 18, 1987. Gaither faced sexual harassment charges, which Paul suggests were not the determining factor in his dismissal (see *When the Pot Boils*, ch. 4).

29. Wolfgang Saxon, "Columbia to Close Library School," *New York Times*, June 6, 1990.

30. Paul, *When the Pot Boils*, chs. 6–7.

31. Bernard Wysocki, "How Dr. Papadakis Runs a University Like a Company," *Wall Street Journal*, February 23, 2005.

32. This history is described in more detail in Judith Swazey, *Merger Games: The Medical College of Pennsylvania, Hahnemann University, and the Rise and Fall of the Allegheny Health Care System* (Philadelphia: Temple University Press, 2012).

33. John Kromer and Lucy Kerman, *West Philadelphia Initiatives: A Case Study in Urban Revitalization* (Philadelphia: Fels Institute of Government, University of Pennsylvania, 2004).

34. Thomas D. Snyder, ed., *120 Years of American Education; A Statistical Portrait* (Washington, DC: National Center for Education Statistics, U.S. Department of Education, 1993), 64.

Anthony Joseph Drexel's memory loomed large over my childhood. His daughter, Emilie (born 1851), was the mother of my grandfather Livingston Biddle (b. 1877). Her full-length portrait—dressed for her wedding to Edward Biddle—graced my grandparents' dining room. She died young; my grandfather went to live with Anthony and his wife, Ellen. Emilie's youngest brother, George (b. 1868), became Livingston's lifelong friend as well as uncle.

For Livingston Biddle, it was a given that Anthony Drexel had been a great man and a visionary. This might appear to be the normal adulation of a grandson for his grandfather, but Biddle believed that the founding of the university and its bold mission of inclusion were not only remarkable but meriting financial support. He became a Drexel trustee in 1916, joining relatives John R. Fell, A. J. Drexel Paul, and Anthony's sons, A. J. Drexel, and George C., and others.

Convinced of the university's value, Biddle altered the trust fund his grandfather had established for himself and his heirs, so that the university—rather than his descendants—would benefit. In 2002, at the death of Biddle's surviving child (my father), that wish was fulfilled. Drexel's gift to his grandson became a gift to the institution.

—CORDELIA FRANCES BIDDLE

2

Anthony Joseph Drexel

The Evolution of a Philanthropist

CORDELIA FRANCES BIDDLE

His father had old-fashioned notions of what was to be expected
of a boy. While there were regular hours for others, there were
none for him. He was expected to come early and stay late.
From his boyhood on he never knew what it was to be idle.[1]

ANTHONY JOSEPH DREXEL embodied the American immigrant
ideal that hard work, perspicacity, and enterprise can engender a
better and more prosperous life. The son of a poor Austrian émi-
gré who arrived in Philadelphia in 1817 intending to make his name and
fortune as a portrait painter, Drexel's great wealth set him apart from most
first-generation Americans, inspiring and then enabling an expansive philanthropy. Having had no formal education past the age of thirteen, and of
a naturally introspective disposition, he felt ill at ease with colleagues who
held university degrees and could readily quote from the classics. "I make
no pretensions to oratory," he replied after being called upon for an
after-dinner speech. "On the contrary, I much prefer to be quiet. All that I
wish to say is that whenever any thing is wanted, call on me."[2] When President Ulysses S. Grant asked Drexel to become Secretary of the Treasury,
the same humility induced him to decline the honor. After Drexel's death,
the Right Reverend Henry C. Potter, Bishop of New York, described him
as "lenient, patient, a liberal creditor, a generous employer, considerate of
and sympathetic with everyone who worked for him."[3] Potter knew whereof
he spoke. As a boy laboring in a Philadelphia accounting firm, he had encountered the then august financier. According to Potter, Drexel's "unceas-
ing stream of private and personal munificence"[4] originated in his rise
"from modest beginnings."[5]

————————

ON JULY 27, 1817, the "John of Baltimore" docked at the foot of Callow-
hill Street following a grueling seventy-two-day journey from Amsterdam.
Aboard was nineteen-year-old Francis Martin Drexel, who had been born
April 7, 1792, in Dornbirn, the largest town in Tyrolese Vorarlberg. The
region's proximity to Switzerland, Germany, and Liechtenstein made trade
a crucial element to the economy. Drexel's father (the variations of whose
name's spellings are "Drachsl" and "Dråxl," a *drechsen* being a wheelwright),
a successful merchant, had the financial resources to send his eleven-year-
old son to the prestigious Convent della Madonna in Saronno, north of
Milan. Thirteen months later, Francis was forced to abandon his studies.
Napoleon's Austrian campaign and the nation's subsequent economic woes
had bankrupted the family. On December 2, 1805, Napoleon vanquished
the Austrians at Austerlitz. The impoverished Drexels now lived under foreign rule. Having shown artistic talent, Francis was apprenticed to a painter
five miles from Dornbirn. In a memoir prepared for his children, "The Life
and Travels of F. M. Drexel, 1792–1826," he commented upon this reversal: "I was able to follow my natural inclination for painting which I had
from infancy. I never had any inclination for mercantile affairs."[6] A behavioral pattern had emerged; obstacles became opportunities.

In 1809, every able-bodied man and boy became liable for conscrip-
tion into Bonaparte's forces. To avoid service in the enemy army, seventeen-
year-old Francis fled to Switzerland, then roamed Switzerland, France, and
Italy, finding sporadic employment, or bartering work for food and lodgings. By the time of Napoleon's defeat, Francis had honed his craft, but
financial success eluded him. America, with its seemingly limitless opportunities, beckoned. "I reasoned to myself since my native place having but five thousand inhabitants would never employ me professionally,
and being obliged to be from home it would be no wether [*sic*] I was One
Hundred or Ten Thousand miles off. . . . If I did not do well [I] would
return after six months, but if on the contrary six years, but by no means
stay."[7]

Stay, he did, marrying Catherine Huki (anglicized to Hookey) the
daughter of a grocer, and subsequently opening a studio in 1821 at 40 South
Sixth Street that advertised "Francis M. Drexel, Portraits and Miniatures
at very Reasonable Prices."[8] He and Catherine had two children, Mary
Johanna and Francis "Frank" born in 1822 and 1824, respectively. However,
Drexel's peripatetic nature resurfaced, prompting him to leave Philadelphia
for Latin America in May 1826 in order to paint portraits of the nations'
emerging leaders. Catherine gave birth to Anthony Joseph Drexel four

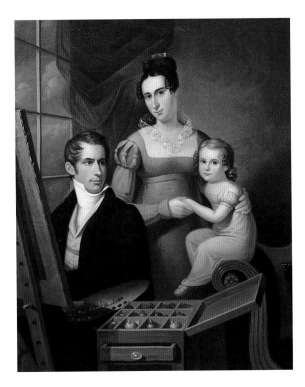

Self-Portrait with
Family, *by Francis
Martin Drexel, c. 1824.
(The Drexel Collection.)*

months after her husband's departure. (The Drexels eventually had six
children.) Anthony didn't meet his father until April 1830. Fundamental
differences in personality between father and son are traceable from this
period: Francis, impulsive, autocratic, and determined to outwit all adver-
saries. And Anthony, reserved, analytical, and deliberate.

President Andrew Jackson's war on the Second Bank of the United States
gave the elder Drexel the opportunity he'd craved when he wrote, "I left
my native place again for the wide world to make a fortune."[9] Prior to cam-
paigning for a second term, Jackson, who harbored a deep mistrust of centralized banking, had warned Nicholas Biddle, president of the Second
Bank, against making the bank's recharter an issue (the charter was due to
expire in 1836). Biddle refused to acquiesce, declaring: "This worthy President thinks that because he has scalped Indians and imprisoned Judges, he
is to have his way with the Bank. He is mistaken—and he may as well send
at once and engage lodgings in Arabia."[10] Biddle lost the fight. In 1836,
Jackson issued a Specie Circular, requiring that purchasers of government
lands pay in hard currency instead of paper. One consequence of the mandate was a run on the banks, instigating the Panic of 1837.

With the U.S. currency in flux, Drexel utilized his Latin American connections, starting a new business trading in the stable species of Spain and Germany, as well as in gold and silver. He opened a currency exchange office in Louisville, Kentucky—a city that served as gateway to the west while also providing access to the south via the Ohio River. In January 1838, he returned to Philadelphia, no longer as an artist, but as head of F. M. Drexel, Exchange Broker.

The city's economic landscape had altered during the previous two decades. Matthias Baldwin's Locomotive Works at Broad and Hamilton Streets met the needs for a burgeoning railway industry. Henry Deringer's firearms manufactory in the Northern Liberties produced the eponymous derringer. In Fishtown, William Cramp built iron ships in the largest shipyard in the United States. Francis Drexel, shrewd and canny, joined the city's rising men. Like many immigrants, he believed business should be a family affair. His eldest sons, Frank and Anthony, began working for their father when in their early teens. Their days at the brokerage house were long; Anthony took his meals while still standing in his designated space: cold food prepared by his mother and concealed beneath the counter.

By 1847, the artist turned banker had become so prosperous that he was able to float the U.S. Treasury a loan of upward of $49 million to finance the Mexican War. The same year, he made Frank, twenty-three, and Anthony, twenty-one, partners in the family concern, although it was Anthony rather than his elder brother who was chosen as heir apparent. F. M. Drexel, Exchange Broker, was now Drexel & Co. The gold rush of 1849 saw Francis on the move again. He traveled to California in 1850, opening the banking house of Drexel, Sather and Church in San Francisco in 1851, and didn't return to Philadelphia permanently until 1857.

———

ANTHONY J. DREXEL'S career as a financier has been well chronicled, from his Civil War alliance with Jay Cooke to the death of Francis Martin Drexel in 1863, from his leadership of the House of Drexel and savvy partnerships in London and New York with Junius Spencer Morgan and his son, John Pierpont Morgan, to the efficacy of Drexel's Paris office during the Franco-Prussian War, and Drexel & Co.'s involvement in the Panama Canal syndicate, as well as the funding of the nation's railroads. Internationally respected because of its "sound and sure transactions,"[11] the firm's growth necessitated an expansion of its offices at 428 Chestnut Street in 1888: 398 rooms spread over ten stories in what was then a prototype of a modern office structure. The building also housed the Philadelphia Stock Exchange, adding luster to Drexel & Co.'s reputation.

Drexel's success as a man of affairs led to civic engagement, philanthropy, and ultimately to the founding of the Drexel Institute of Art, Science, and Industry. As *Harper's Weekly* stated in its January 2, 1892, issue, "He has always acted as though his great wealth conferred certain obligations on him."[12] The front cover of *Harper's* carried a photographic portrait of Drexel. Page four was devoted to images of the newly dedicated institute: "Entrance Hall, Central Court and Organ and Screens in Auditorium."[13] The attention of a popular weekly magazine must have made Drexel uncomfortable. After all, here was a man who once stated, "You know, I consider that wealth comes to men by accident. I do not see why a man who has become wealthy should be different from the poor man who hoes corn or drives a street car."[14]

The psychological shift from financier to philanthropist had its roots in Drexel's moral imperative. Whether he had achieved wealth by "accident," or through sagacity and foresight, what good was affluence if it couldn't be used in service to others? His wife, Ellen Rozét Drexel, shared his views. As helpmeet and partner, she encouraged her husband's philanthropy; when she died in November 1891, he was overcome with grief. The couple had married in August 1850, when Anthony was twenty-three; Ellen Rozét, eighteen. She was vivacious and as young as her years. His life experiences and early responsibilities made him seem older than a man in his early twenties. Then too, his father's work ethic had left little room for pleasure. Ellen's father, John, a merchant of French descent, was a Protestant, meaning that Anthony had left his birth faith for that of his wife—a not insignificant choice given his religious beliefs and later service to the Episcopal Church as a vestryman of the Church of the Savior.

With Ellen and his growing family (the couple had nine children born between 1851 and 1868), Anthony experienced a sense of belonging he'd never before known. He indulged Ellen and his children, sparing no expense for their comfort and happiness. If she desired a gold terrapin set with which to entertain guests or wished only white flowers[15] to grace her reception rooms, white flowers were procured despite the cost. The house, an Italianate villa at William and Walnut Streets (between Thirty-Eighth and Thirty-Ninth), boasted a morning room, a conservatory, music room with two pianos (one of which was covered in gold leaf), a billiard room, and numerous guest and servants' rooms.[16] This haven served a dual purpose; it provided time and space for Drexel to escape from work, and also created a buffer between the financier and the social elite of Philadelphia. Because the house was located in "WP," as the unfashionable area west of the

Schuylkill was called, Anthony and Ellen could avoid the tightly knit clan of old money Philadelphia, and with it any perceived censure of the Drexels as *arrivistes*.

During lively house parties for extended family members at the couple's summer residence in Long Branch, New Jersey, and country estate, Runnymede, near Lansdowne, Ellen tossed convention to the winds, while Anthony indulged his passion for music, performing duets and quartets with his daughters.[17] Because he believed in keeping physically fit, he rode horseback as often as possible, and daily strode eastward through the city from Thirty-Eighth Street to his office on lower Chestnut Street. During Drexel Institute's construction and later its management, he stopped daily to discuss its needs. Although preferring intimate gatherings to large dinners and receptions, he and Ellen entertained Ulysses S. Grant and his wife at a reception for seven hundred at their home on December 19, 1879, and invited the Grant family to the 1872 marriage of Emilie (the Drexels' eldest child) to Edward Biddle. For a sitting president to attend what was then a strictly family celebration proves how far up the ladder the Drexels had come.

Drexel's closest friend—almost his alter ego—was the publisher George William Childs (1829–1894), with whom he had purchased the *Philadelphia Ledger* in 1864. Childs, also a self-made man, relished the limelight that Drexel shunned, speaking publicly when Anthony demurred, and aiding his plans for civic engagement. A poor boy from Baltimore who had arrived alone in Philadelphia at the age of fourteen, Childs understood the power of the press, utilizing it to champion the downtrodden. He and his wife, Emma (née Peterson), entertained lavishly in America and abroad, where their dinners for Charles Dickens, Henry Wadsworth Longfellow, and other literary luminaries and statesmen made news. *Harper's Weekly* wrote of the decades-long bond between the two men: "His most intimate friend is Mr. George W. Childs, with whom he is interested in many other charities. Their intimacy, indeed, is so close that it seems almost sentimental in its nature."[18]

"Sentimental" may seem a curious word to describe a man whose reserve could make him appear forbidding, but sentimental is how his family perceived him. Despite his insistence on punctuality, and a childhood in which he admitted that his father's discipline had been "exacting,"[19] he encouraged a tradition of boisterous amateur theatrics that carried on into subsequent Drexel generations. Most of his correspondence was destroyed after his death, but the few letters that remain reveal a tenderhearted, nurturing nature. The welfare of his "dear Children"[20] was a constant. He was no less magnanimous with those outside his family. As Childs recalled, "His

George W. Childs with Anthony J. Drexel, seated. (Drexel University Archives. MC 1 Drexel family collection.)

purse was always open, and his heart was as large as suffering and needs were great."[21]

IN MARCH 1862, at Childs's suggestion, Matthew Vassar wrote to Drexel, providing information regarding the "first meeting of the trustees of Vassar Female College. I trust you will find these proceedings not devoid of interest to an intelligent and generous mind, fully appreciating the importance of educating the mothers of coming generations. . . . If God please to spare my life, I hope to witness great and blessed results flowing from these investments."[22] With Vassar as an example, Drexel began considering creating an educational institution for women.

It wasn't until 1876 and an introduction to the social activist Eliza Sproat Turner (1826–1903), author of the suffragist tract *Four Quite New Reasons Why You Should Want Your Wife to Vote*, that he found the beginnings of a pragmatic solution to his plan. The nation's centennial celebration, "The

International Exhibition of Arts, Manufacturers, and Products of the Soil and Mine," which Drexel helped shepherd into being, promoted America as a pioneer in technology and industry. The Main Building—then the largest in the world—covered twenty-one and a half acres; however, women were denied permission to exhibit within it. The Women's Pavilion became the focal point for suffragist issues, distributing *The New Century for Women*, a newspaper Turner edited. A popular exhibit featured a woman tending a steam engine while dressed in formal clothing (the message being that laboring over a hot stove was more arduous). Recognizing that large numbers of women entering the workforce had no support services, Turner subsequently founded the New Century Guild of Working Women in 1882, to which Drexel contributed financially. Their collaboration continued beyond that of activist and patron. Turner served on Drexel Institute's first Women's Advisory Board; the guild's classes became part of the institute's curriculum in 1892.

Doubtless, Drexel's niece Katharine (St. Katharine Drexel, 1858–1955) also participated in discussions regarding a school for women. Passionate about providing education to African-Americans and Native Americans, "Kate," as her uncle called her, possessed a similar sense of purpose and duty. Although devoted to his children, it was Katharine with whom Anthony shared a special bond of moral obligation and dedication.

Resolved upon establishing an industrial college for women, Drexel purchased "Louella," an eighty-room estate in Wayne in 1880. In the Drexel University Archives, an embossed seal stamp of "The Drexel Industrial College for Girls 1889" serves as a reminder of that goal. Bucolic Wayne, however, was far from the city and working-class youth whose needs Drexel had known intimately as a boy. He decided to expand his approach, creating a coeducational institution whose purpose was to provide young men and women with both academic and applied knowledge, enabling them to improve their earning potential and enhance their lives. Dr. James MacAlister, former head of schools in Philadelphia, became the institute's first president. Recalling Drexel's decision, MacAlister said, "After a good deal of that careful consideration which he was accustomed to give to all his undertakings, he came to the conclusion that in no way could his money be so well spent as in promoting the education of the people."[23]

To construct the Main Building of the institute, Drexel hired the Philadelphia firm of Wilson Brothers & Co, which had designed and constructed his banking house. The finest materials were to be used throughout. No detail in the construction of the Renaissance-inspired building was too small for his attention: from an innovative ventilation system in the attic, to a

*Anthony J. Drexel, c. 1890.
(Drexel University Archives.
MC 1 Drexel family collection.)*

*Anthony J. Drexel, c. 1890.
(Drexel University Archives.
MC 1 Drexel family collection.)*

heating network that allowed for each room to be warmed independent of the others, or a "gymnasium fitted out with the latest athletic appliances."[24] *Harper's Weekly* was lavish in its praise: "Its curriculum is such that when a young man or young woman goes forth from its doors with its diploma in hand, he or she may find a situation open and waiting. It will afford training—and that is practical education—to the masses, who have undoubted ability, but no possibility of attaining development under present scholastic conditions. The Drexel Institute starts upon a course of broad philanthropy, of which no man can consider the possible bounds."[25] Drexel absented himself from the dedication ceremony on December 17, 1891. His excuse was Ellen's death, but in reality, he would have felt supremely uncomfortable listening to laudatory speeches while surrounded by a panoply of dignitaries. His priority, as always, was on the success of his endeavors, rather than himself.

Ill health sent him to a spa in Carlsbad, Germany, in May of 1893. As he did with all his travels, he brought business with him, corresponding daily and informing the Drexel offices of any change in his itinerary. He planned to sail for home July 29, meeting with Walter Hayes Burns, head of the house's London office en route. On June 29, he drafted a letter to Burns, writing in pencil and in a shaky hand, "In consequence of the pleurisy causing short breathing & a feeling of suffocation I could not go to bed but have to pass the night in a chair . . . I am hors du combat." That small jest aside, he delved into the problematic restructuring of the Reading Railroad, underlining the words *"I would advise going very slowly about RR reorganization*. In my judgment you cannot improve on the plan just withdrawn."[26]

The next day, he took up his pencil again, telling Burns about "a most careful nurse & lots of sympathy & friends who are very kind."[27] Astute even when ailing, he returned to business affairs, taking comfort in the cogent and concrete. With words of caution against "silver interests"[28] in the United States Senate, he closed what would become his final letter. That afternoon at two o'clock, a cablegram arrived at the New York office bringing news that Anthony Joseph Drexel had died.

———

DURING HIS LIFE, Drexel contributed liberally to local charitable causes, and was recognized as "among the first on the list of large subscribers"[29] who reached beyond Philadelphia to address suffering wherever it was found, whether the victims of the 1889 Johnstown Flood or the 1892–93 Russian Famine, or a Home for Invalid Printers in Colorado that he and Childs established in 1886. However, his will named bequests to only two institutions: $100,000 for the German Hospital of Philadelphia (now Lankenau Medical Center) in honor of his brother-in-law, John Diederich Lankenau (who, in turn, willed his art collection to the Drexel Institute), and $1 million for the "erection and maintenance of an Art Gallery, Museum or other Public Institution"[30] to serve the student body and general public. Having spent $500,000 on the institute's building and grounds and another $1.23 million to ensure an annual $50,000 to maintain and grow the school, this was a princely sum to devote to art. It was Anthony Drexel's final desire that those studying at his institute experience beauty amid the practical.

NOTES

1. Series 1: Scrapbooks, box 1, no. 11, 12, Drexel Family Collection, Drexel University Archives. Certain primary sources are found in the Drexel Family Collection, Drexel University Archives. Among them are newspaper death notices, the most extensive of which is the *Philadelphia Press*. Additional primary sources include *Harper's Weekly: A Journal of Civilization* 36, no. 1828 (January 2, 1892); *Poulson's American Daily Advertiser*, October 23, 1821. Secondary sources include Reginald C. McGrane, ed., *The Correspondence of Nicholas Biddle Dealing with National Affairs, 1807–1844* (Boston: Houghton Mifflin, 1919); Boies Penrose, "The Early Life of F. M. Drexel, 1792–1837: The Peregrinations of a Philadelphia Painter-Banker," *The Pennsylvania Magazine of History and Biography* 60 (October 1936); Dan Rottenberg, *The Man Who Made Wall Street* (Philadelphia: University of Pennsylvania Press, 2006); Robert E. Wright, *The First Wall Street: Chestnut Street,*

Philadelphia, and the Birth of American Finance (Chicago: The University of Chicago Press, 2005).

2. Series 1: Scrapbooks, box 1, no. 13, 14, Drexel Family Collection, Drexel University Archives.

3. "Service in Memory of Anthony Joseph Drexel 1894," 46, Drexel Family Collection, Drexel University Archives.

4. Ibid., 57.

5. Ibid., 56.

6. Francis Martin Drexel, "The Life and Travels of F. M. Drexel, 1792–1826," MC 1, box 7, no. 1A, Drexel Family Collection, Drexel University Archives.

7. Ibid.

8. *Poulson's American Daily Advertiser* (Philadelphia), October 23, 1821.

9. Francis Martin Drexel, "The Life and Travels of F. M. Drexel, 1792–1826."

10. Reginald C. McGrane, ed., *The Correspondence of Nicholas Biddle Dealing with National Affairs 1807–1844* (Boston: Houghton Mifflin, 1919), 222.

11. Series 1: Scrapbooks, box 1, no. 15, 16, Drexel Family Collection, Drexel University Archives.

12. "Anthony Joseph Drexel," *Harper's Weekly: A Journal of Civilization* 36, no. 1828 (January 2, 1892): 6.

13. Ibid., 4.

14. Series 1: Scrapbooks, box 1, no. 13, 14, Drexel Family Collection, Drexel University Archives.

15. Biographical Essays, F. M. Drexel and His Sons, MC 1, box 7, no. 13, Drexel Family Collection, Drexel University Archives.

16. Ibid.

17. Ibid.

18. "Anthony Joseph Drexel."

19. Biographical Essays, F. M. Drexel and His Sons, MC 1, box 7, no. 13, Drexel Family Collection, Drexel University Archives.

20. Marie Elizabeth Letterhouse, *The Francis A. Drexel Family* (Cornwells Heights, PA: The Sisters of the Blessed Sacrament, 1939), 244.

21. Biographical Essays, F. M. Drexel and His Sons, MC 1, box 1, no. 9, 10, Drexel Family Collection, Drexel University Archives.

22. Matthew Vassar to Anthony J. Driscoll, March 25, 1862, MC1, box 7, no. 8, Drexel Family Collection, Drexel University Archives.

23. James MacAlister, introductory address, "Service in Memory of Anthony Joseph Drexel 1894," 25, Drexel Family Collection, Drexel University Archives.

24. "The Drexel Institute," *Harper's Weekly: A Journal of Civilization* 36, no. 1828 (January 2, 1892): 9.

25. Ibid.

26. Anthony J. Drexel to Burns, June 29, 1893, MC 1, box 1, no. 3, Drexel Family Papers, Drexel University Archives.

27. Anthony J. Drexel to Burns, June 30, 1893, MC 1, box 7, no. 4, Drexel Family Papers, Drexel University Archives.

28. Ibid.

29. Series 1: Scrapbooks, box 1, no. 13, 14, Drexel Family Collection, Drexel University Archives.

30. Anthony Joseph Drexel, "Last Will and Testament," July 20, 1893, MC 1, box 14, no. 30, Drexel Family Papers, Drexel University Archives.

I was accepted into the electrical engineering program of the Drexel Institute of Technology after graduating from high school in Philadelphia in 1953. In those days the Philadelphia school system had two graduations a year, one in May and another in January. Drexel accommodated the winter graduates with a winter freshman term, called February Freshmen. It lasted only six weeks but it covered ten weeks' worth of material. We were told to look either side of you, only one of you will complete the first term; they were right!

Engineering students at this time used slide rulers to perform calculations. Several years later, about 1958, HP came out with a hand calculator that most of our engineering students used; it cost about thirty-five dollars. To give you a feel for the time, tuition was only three hundred a quarter, and the first textbook I bought was only $3.50, used! And, I still have it; it was a calculus textbook.

The Drexel Co-op program helped me make my career choice. I knew I did not want to punch a clock every morning and evening. Instead of looking for a job in industry when I graduated in 1957, I accepted a teaching position in the Electrical Engineering Department as an instructor . . . my salary was four thousand dollars a year (not a term). I was assigned a twelve-hour teaching load and assigned to develop a new electronics lab. I stared in 1957 by changing our electronics lab from a vacuum tube into a solid-state electronics (transistors) lab. In 1980 I received an NSF grant of $10,000 to develop an undergraduate lab course utilizing computers to perform computerized lab experiments; later I learned that it was the first one in world. It did in less than a minute what it took us hours to do before!

I have been here for sixty years, more than half of Drexel's existence.

—E. L. GERBER, PH.D.

Continuous Reinvention

A History of Engineering Education at Drexel University

ALISSA FALCONE, SCOTT GABRIEL KNOWLES,
JONSON MILLER, TIAGO SARAIVA, AND AMY E. SLATON

O N DECEMBER 17, 1891, over two thousand people gathered in the auditorium of Main Building for the dedication of the Drexel Institute.[1] This was not the dedication of an engineering school, but rather of an institute for the children of the working class, who would largely remain in the working class. It was only later that formal engineering education arrived at Drexel.

Since at least the 1820s, there had been calls for new forms of education for the laboring classes that taught "useful knowledge," including mathematics and the sciences. Some of the schools that were established, especially public and private military schools in the South, and later the land-grant colleges, would lift meritorious boys out of the laboring classes by training them as civil engineers, yet the great majority of engineers at the time learned on the job rather than through formal education. "Manual labor schools," on the other hand, would elevate the status of labor itself by cultivating the virtues of working-class boys.[2]

Railroad lawyer and occasional New York politician Chauncey Mitchell Depew made clear the purpose of the new Drexel Institute in his oration at its dedication ceremony. He criticized traditional forms of higher education as tradition-bound and unable to keep up with social and industrial changes that continually made obsolete the knowledge and skills of the working class. "The old education," he said, "simply trained the mind. The new trains the mind, the muscles, and the senses. The old education gave the intellect a vast mass of information useful in the library and useless in the shop." Even night classes for workmen were insufficient for the new needs of laborers. "For the vast army which must live by labor, and upon the results of whose labor depends the welfare of the country, no adequate provision has yet been made." New schools like Drexel would provide a proper education that included a thorough and formal training with machines, in drawing and scientific principles, as well as in the arts.[3]

Drexel's graduates were not going to rise up out of the working class to become engineers or inventors. Instead, Depew said, "They will hail the inventor as their friend and follow with keen delight his discoveries and improvements." Those inventions might make the workers' old methods obsolete, but "their thorough grounding in principles will enable them instantly to understand [the inventor's] device and adapt themselves to the fresh roads they must tread." Thus they will be able to "keep pace with progress and earn living wages in the fierce strife and heat of modern competition." Moreover, through education the students would acquire the "disciplined mind" and "habits of work" that traditional higher education imparted to its graduates. Drexel graduates would go to work in industry with that discipline, skipping "the apprentice period" yet knowing "more than the apprentice could ever know." The Drexel Institute would produce a superior mechanic and laborer able to better serve industry and to maintain a career by keeping pace with constant technological change.[4]

Founding an Engineering College

In January 1913 the City of Philadelphia hired the consultant engineer Hollis Godfrey to inspect streetlights. Finding it impractical to have the lights brought to a testing facility, Godfrey put together a moving photometric laboratory mounted on a fifteen-hundred-pound motortruck. Six hundred tests undertaken by "nine leading illuminating engineers" offered the city reliable data to dispute its bills from the Welsbach Street Lighting Company of America, whereby it ultimately saved some $55,000.[5] Impressed with the gains in efficiency produced by his survey of the city's lights, Drexel's board of trustees invited Godfrey to employ the same methodology to their own institution, and then hired him as the institute's president.[6]

When Godfrey arrived at Drexel, the institute had thirteen departments, each operating more or less independently, and responsible for developing their own curricula.[7] Drexel positioned itself as a vocational institute, occupying the space between college and high school, not accredited to grant either the degrees of the first or the diplomas of the second. As

James MacAlister, president of Drexel University,
1891–1913. (Drexel University Archives. PC 4
People photographs.)

president James MacAlister had candidly
recognized in 1900, "Drexel has not yet
found its right place in the educational
economy of the country, and it is not easy
to define what that position should be."[8]
After becoming president, at the end of 1913
Godfrey consolidated the departments by
grouping them into four schools: Engineering, Domestic Science and Arts (later Home
Economics), the Secretarial School (later
Business Administration), and the Evening School. Every school offered a
two-year curriculum leading to certification, and the engineering school
also offered a four-year curriculum leading to the bachelor of science degree. The other three schools were granted the right to award B.S. degrees
in 1917.

The engineering school's move away from vocational training should
be understood together with the efforts of increasing efficiency in Philadelphia street lighting, as part of the emerging trend in "scientific management," or "Taylorism" (named after Frederick Taylor, one of the inventors
of management consulting, and a Philadelphia native).[9] In more emphatic
words, the engineering school came into being through the Taylorization
of Drexel. Taylor had first developed his proposals for the rationalization
of labor and production while working as chief engineer for Midvale Steel in
Philadelphia, and Godfrey—a disciple and associate of Taylor—planned
to make Drexel a "demonstration plant" of the value of scientific management in engineering education.[10] Every element of the system that formed
the institute was Taylorized: facilities reformed; curricula remade; student
admissions regulated; "inefficient" faculty dispensed and new professors
hired. The main instrument Godfrey developed was the institutional budget, the elements of which were "like raw materials . . . worked over until
they assume the form of parts—the index, the summary, the detail, and
the explanatory sheets, which when assembled produce . . . an effective
mechanism by which proper educational stresses can be brought about and
coherent policies of educational advance obtained."[11]

One of Godfrey's first acts as Drexel president was to commission a survey that was to identify "the place of Drexel in the scheme of education."

Hollis Godfrey, president of Drexel University, 1913–1921, photo 1915. (Drexel University Archives. UR 12.8 Yearbooks.)

This was the first of many surveys under Godfrey, which collectively were "undoubtedly the largest continued examination of educational facts and policies ever carried on by a single institution."[12] From these surveys, he developed a vision that Drexel's engineering graduates would be generalists "who can bring together the work designed by the electrical, civil, or mechanical engineer and make it available to industry."[13] Those seeking specialized training should look for other schools, namely the neighboring University of Pennsylvania, as suggested in Godfrey's 1914 commencement speech.

While Drexel was originally designed for machinists and foremen who wanted to improve their condition and prospects by learning the principles guiding their industries, the institute under Godfrey moved to produce engineers that were to take control over the industrial production process. Foremen, who determined the components needed for jobs, ordered the raw materials, and wrote out job cards for the machinists, would be replaced by planning departments staffed with engineers who produced detailed instructions about which machines to use, the allocation of materials and manpower, and, crucially, how much time should be spent in each different task, always guaranteeing that no bottlenecks halted production.[14] As historian of technology Thomas Hughes has described the introduction of scientific management in American industries, "[U]pwardly mobile young graduates from the rising engineering schools were soon displacing their fathers, the foremen."[15] What Hughes didn't notice was that Drexel was the engineering school at the forefront of this move.

For the promoters of the scientific approach to engineering education, increased productivity in industry was supposed to lead to both rising wages

Engineering School faculty and students building motor in machine shop, c. 1916. (Drexel University Archives. PC 3 Early photographs of the Drexel Institute of Art, Science, and Industry.)

Mechanic Arts Department, electrical laboratory. (Drexel University Archives. PC 3 Early photographs of the Drexel Institute of Art, Science, and Industry.)

and higher profits, thus resolving conflict between laborers and capitalists and reestablishing the social harmony lost during the Gilded Age. Never mind that workers' unions fiercely fought against the Taylorization of the workplace, forcing Taylor's early retirement to his house in Philadelphia's affluent Chestnut Hill neighborhood, where he applied his scientific methods to his gardening and to designing golf clubs.[16]

World War I provided the opportunity for Taylor's apostles to prove at a large scale the value of scientific management for American democracy. Long before the United States declared war on the German empire in April 1917, American industries were already supporting the British and French. In 1916 President Woodrow Wilson formed the Council of National Defense (CND), in response to the chaos caused by ten different procurement agencies in the army alone, and by government contractors competing among themselves for fuels and raw materials. In order to fight all the waste of time and resources, the CND was to apply scientific management principles at the national scale.[17]

Godfrey was the chief architect of the CND and determined its composition, which included the secretaries of war, navy, interior, commerce, labor, and agriculture, and an advisory council that included Godfrey himself and representatives from companies such as Sears, the Baltimore & Ohio Railroad, AT&T, the Hudson Motor Company, and the American Federation of Labor. Godfrey also chaired the CND's "Committee on Science and Research, Including Engineering and Education," the purpose of which was to guarantee the technical preparation of American military personnel while also preventing excessive recruiting from engineering colleges before students finished their training.[18] Drexel participated in the effort, offering courses for men and women to support the war effort, and training students as officers. Drexel, it was noted in 1918, "with the single purpose of serving most effectively in the present crisis, has put its engineering school absolutely on a war basis."[19]

World War I fundamentally redefined Drexel, as it led to the creation of the cooperative program, instituted in 1919, in which work experiences with private firms were incorporated into undergraduate education. Godfrey explained the co-op program as being "based on the new principles of engineering education developed by the experience of the war . . . this newly designed system of engineering education shows you how to make your services of more value to . . . your country, enabling you to fight more intelligently for the industrial democracy of our nation and to make complete the military victory we have won."[20] For Godfrey, work experience was

Kenneth Gordon Matheson, president of Drexel University, 1921–1931, photo 1922. (Drexel University Archives. UR 12.8 Yearbooks.)

Parke R. Kolbe, president of Drexel University, 1932–1942, photo 1933. (Drexel University Archives. UR 12.8 Yearbooks.)

obligatory for the generalist engineers produced by Drexel, as it provided them the opportunity to understand the challenges faced by a business organization.

After the war Drexel established co-op positions for students at Honeywell in 1922, Bell and RCA in 1923, Bethlehem Steel and Link Belt in 1924, General Electric in 1925, Westinghouse in 1926, and IBM in 1939. While big companies were responsible for the largest chunk of co-op placements, there were also opportunities at Philadelphia's smaller firms, such as Alan Wood Steel Company, Electric Battery Storage Company, Proctor & Schwartz, and Lee Rubber and Tire.[21] By 1925 all of the institute's engineering programs were placed on a five-year cooperative basis. In 1926 the co-op was extended to the business administration program, and in 1929 to retail management, drawing mostly on the commercial and financial companies of the Philadelphia area.

During the Great Depression, Drexel found co-ops in government agencies such as the Tennessee Valley Authority and the U.S. Bureau of Reclamation. The era also exposed tensions with organized labor; unions didn't easily accept the prospect of co-op students occupying positions during this period of high unemployment. Cecil Kapp, who directed the co-op program for forty years, considered union conflicts an advantage for students, who learned how to handle labor issues. He saw strikes in particular as a major educational opportunity.[22]

World War II and the Cold War Era

During World War II Drexel participated in the Engineering, Science and Management War Training Program organized by the U.S. Office of Education to "meet the shortages of trained personal [*sic*] in fields essential to the national defense." These were mostly twelve- to sixteen-week courses (in, among other things, chemical, electrical, mechanical, aeronautical, and general engineering; and welding, engineering drawing, inspection, circuits, and engineering mathematics) paid for by the federal government, for both men and women, separate from Drexel's regular classes and programs.[23] Drexel encouraged women to participate in the war-training program because they were "filling many jobs formerly held by men who had been called to military service." War industries needed women for "drafting, chemical laboratory work, design, inspection, and junior engineering."[24]

After the war, anxiety was prevalent among Americans, including Drexel's president James Creese, of being unable to compete technologically with the Soviets. As part of Soviet premier Nikita Khrushchev's cultural exchange programs, Creese traveled with his family to the Soviet

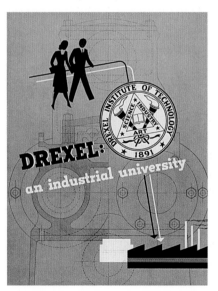

Union to tour the country's institutions of "higher technological education" and industrial facilities. What he found worried him. Of secondary education, he said, they "are *strong in mathematics and science*, just where our secondary schools are criticized for weakness." He reported that after finishing their ten years of primary and secondary schooling, Soviet students had taken ten years of mathematics,

"Drexel: An Industrial University," pamphlet front cover, 1947. (Drexel University Archives.)

George P. Rea, president of Drexel University,
1942–1944, photo 1943. (Drexel University
Archives. PC 4 People photographs.)

six years of biology, five years of physics, and
four years of chemistry. While the laboratories
in the USSR's higher technical schools were
either below American standards or absent,
students made up for it by spending two and a
half months in industrial plants under technicians and engineers. Not surprisingly, then, all
of the educators, engineers, and managers Creese
spoke with took an interest in Drexel's co-op program.

Creese's concerns went beyond just the intensity of scientific and technological training at all levels of education in the Soviet Union; he was also
impressed by the fact that one-third of the graduates of the higher technical schools were women, "a source of human power which we in America
have only begun to use." Despite feeling that the United States was falling
behind the Soviets, he urged Americans not to become alarmed, and to have
faith in the power of education to lift people up and presumably to change
the government of the Soviet Union. Nonetheless, Drexel as well as even
the most traditional colleges in America had to step up their scientific and
engineering training.[25]

The launch of Sputnik in 1957 intensified Americans' anxiety about
their standing in the arms and space races. One response was the National
Defense Education Act (NDEA), which spurred exactly the sort of increased
emphasis on technical education for which President Creese had called. The
NDEA program provided Drexel with funds to provide loans to students
studying fields that would contribute to America's Cold War fight, namely
education, engineering, and science.[26]

To receive loans under the NDEA, students had to sign an oath of loyalty, indicating that they would "support and defend the Constitution and
laws of the United States against all its enemies, foreign and domestic" and
an affidavit disavowing membership in any organization advocating the
overthrow of the government "by force or violence or any illegal or uncon-
stitutional methods." President Creese and the faculty in general opposed
the affidavit on several grounds, including its vagueness, that it targeted students as a class, and that it was "not helpful." A faculty motion, with the
support of Creese, advocated the repeal of both the oath and affidavit, but
especially the affidavit. To get around these requirements, Drexel offered

*President James Creese placing cement on the cornerstone of the Creese Student
Center, dedication ceremony, May 10, 1962. Creese served as president
of Drexel University from 1945 to 1963. (Drexel University Archives.
PC Chronological photographs.)*

alternative loans to students, and the institute joined 104 other schools and
the American Civil Liberties Union to protest the requirements. Drexel did
receive some push-back for its actions, as some companies and individuals
who supported the oath and affidavit threatened to withhold future donations, but Creese did not back down.[27]

From Technical Institute to Research University: The Hagerty Years

William Hagerty succeeded James Creese as president of Drexel in 1963, during a time of massive expansion for American universities. During Hagerty's
presidency, "Drexel's campus grew from ten to nearly forty acres. Student
enrollment doubled to 14,000 and the budget grew from 8 to 80 million . . .
20 buildings were either built or acquired for campus."[28] Hagerty envisioned
a fully realized university, with graduate-level instruction in technical fields
and the introduction of a liberal arts faculty.

Drexel president William Walsh Hagerty with President Lyndon B. Johnson. Hagerty served as president of Drexel from 1963 to 1984. (Drexel University Archives. PC 4 People photographs.)

What Hagerty was expanding upon was a finely tuned machine of local technical education, though, as engineering professor Bruce Eisenstein put it, "not a research institution." As Eisenstein elaborated,

> It was well I guess what you would call a plane pipe rack kind of institution. The philosophy had always been, keep the tuition as low as possible so the bare
bones tuition provided bare bones service, a lot of part time faculty, and a lot of people with industrial experience teaching. Tuition was about 700 or 800 dollars a year, it was easy enough to earn enough [through co-op placement] to cover your five years of tuition in Drexel for engineering. The College of Engineering had one or two researchers.[29]

"Great institutions," Hagerty argued, "always educate for the future and hence play a role in what the future is to be. It immediately follows that only through graduate study and research can a school ensure that its people are not being slighted." A graduate program would "attract and retain a brilliant faculty . . . who can add to our knowledge through research and who can stimulate not only their students but their fellow teachers."[30]

Drexel awarded its first Ph.D. to Richard Mortimer in mechanical engineering in 1967, and the College of Engineering added an electrical engineering program by the 1970s. The proportion of faculty with Ph.D.s increased from 24 to 94 percent between 1963 and 1984. Engineering and the sciences had been combined into a single college in 1964, but in 1969 they were split into a separate College of Engineering and College of Science. And by 1968 Hagerty was ready to initiate the transition of the Drexel Institute into a university. "Hagerty sent alumni a letter addressing the idea of changing the institution's name from Drexel Institute of Technology to Drexel University. The proposal was met with approval by alumni and staff, and once permitted by the Commonwealth of Pennsylvania, the new name was celebrated on University Day, February 27, 1970."[31]

The Society of Women Engineers at Drexel

In 1947, Joan Rubin became the first woman to graduate from Drexel with a bachelor's in electrical engineering, and Alice Forbes became the first woman to graduate with a bachelor's in chemical engineering. Two years earlier, women made up half of one percent of the country's graduating engineering class, even though women first joined the American engineering field in the late nineteenth century. By the time the Nineteenth Amendment guaranteeing women the right to vote was ratified in 1920, women had earned all levels of degrees in a variety of engineering fields, though they were a select few. Opportunities for female engineers became more pronounced after the draft for World War II, though employers and the general public still doubted their abilities and suitability to the engineering field.

During World War II, in 1943, Drexel enrolled its first class of women engineers, seventeen students, some of whom created or joined a student organization to support each other through challenges on campus, paving the way for the Society of Women Engineers (SWE), a nonprofit professional organization that currently has about 30,000 members and chapters on three hundred college campuses,

Alma Forman, the first woman to graduate Drexel with a bachelor's in civil engineering, was told by one of her male professors that she was the biggest mistake in the class (though she did pass his course). Joan Rubin's calculus professor told the class they didn't have to worry about her being at school to catch a man, since she was already married. Not only was prejudice to be expected, but it was expected to be dealt with individually. Though they were easy to single out, Drexel's women engineers didn't know one another because they didn't take the same classes. And some didn't stick around long: of the four women who started as female chemical engineering majors alongside Forbes, she was the only one left at the end of her freshman year, and every year until graduation.

In an effort to bring the women engineers closer, the dean of women, Dorothy Young, hosted a tea party in 1945 to introduce the students to each other. It was so successful that the women started eating lunch together every day to discuss their similar experiences. By the following fall, about twenty women had formalized their lunchtime support group as an academic and social club called the Society of Women Engineers. The first year's program consisted of technical speakers, social events, and dinners for graduating seniors like Forbes, who is thought to have been the club's first president. As the club grew and gained recognition at Drexel, so did

Members of the Society of Women Engineers, 1950.
(Drexel University Archives. UR 12.8 Yearbooks.)

the number of women engineers on other college campuses, especially on the East Coast. But they were just as isolated and independent as the Drexel students had been. Some spark, some catalyst, was needed to bring them together.

As it turns out, the idea of a greater "Society of Women Engineers" came from a freshman English term paper that was written by Drexel mechanical engineering student Phyllis Diamond Rose in the summer of 1948. As Forman recalls, "She decided to write about women in engineering and when she brought this up, we started thinking about what other colleges had women engineers."[32]

In the spring, the Drexel students sent questionnaires to major engineering colleges asking if those institutions accepted women in engineering courses, if they had an organization similar to the society at Drexel, and what those students did after graduation. The answers revealed that although some of the colleges did accept women, they weren't organized in any groups, and they either hadn't graduated yet or revealed what kind of jobs they might be holding.

It was up to the Drexel women to unify their colleagues, and they succeeded beyond their wildest expectations. The group, chaired by Forman, held a regional conference for women engineers in April 1949 that was attended by eighty-three engineering students from nineteen colleges. Held at the Sarah Van Rensselaer Dormitory (which was then women-only), the event was completely financed by Drexel, thanks to Forman's collaboration with President Creese and the dean of the engineering school, Robert Disque, who spoke at the event.

Several of the founding and charter members of the Society of Women Engineers were Drexel students, including Forman, Rose, Phyllis "Sandy" Evans Miller, Eleanor Gabriel, and Doris McNulty. As A. W. Grosvenor, an assistant professor in the mechanical engineering department and the Drexel group's faculty advisor, would later say, "The initial members of the Drexel group, the nucleus from which grew the National Society of Women Engineers, were enthusiastic and hard working. They were determined to prove themselves in a profession dominated by men."[33]

Rubin and Forbes's legacies as Drexel's first women engineers remain an important part of the College of Engineering, which in 2014 celebrated one hundred years since conferring its first degree. Rubin worked at Bell Laboratories and RCA before teaching high school math and working with her engineering husband. Forbes worked as a chemist in the Franklin Institute's rubber lab before raising ten kids; she passed away in 2013.

After paving the way for future women engineers, Drexel's first class of SWE members continued to work with those who followed in their footsteps. Forman, Miller, and McNulty all remained involved with SWE through various leadership roles, with Miller starting a SWE section in Pittsburgh and Forman doing the same at Temple University. After working in the industry, Forman later became a professor of mechanical engineering and later the director of computer services for Temple's School of Engineering and Architecture.

Though Miller passed away in 1982, the "first ladies" continued to occasionally meet, even after McNulty died in 2009. The bond that birthed the Drexel and national SWE groups holds up even seventy years later. "The Society of Women Engineers is a great developing tool for women," Forman says. "It develops leadership. It's great for networking. You find support in unusual ways. And that's why it was formed in the first place: as a support group."[34]

Generations of these support groups have passed through college campuses across the country, but it's a special tradition at Drexel, which since World War II has graduated large numbers of women engineers. Today's SWE Drexel chapter has approximately 130 members, including twenty officers. Much like the national organization, the Drexel chapter holds workshops, guest speakers, community outreach events and other opportunities to help women engineers grow academically, professionally and socially. "While Drexel is where I learned to be an engineer, Drexel SWE is where

I found my passion for being one," says Meaghan Paulosky, a 2015 graduate and recent former president of the group. "I've learned so many lessons that will carry me throughout my engineering career and eventually bring me back to Drexel SWE to share with the next generation of students."

As a member of the first generation, Forman reflected on what SWE accomplished when speaking at the Philadelphia SWE conference held on campus in the winter of 2015. "It's kind of awesome looking back at this group that is now so large. It gives you a feeling of growth and satisfaction that there was a need, especially when there's still a need today."

Going National: The Macintosh at Drexel

According to Bernie Sagik, former vice president for academic affairs and a close advisor to President Hagerty,

> When I came here, I guess 1980, my preaching to the faculty was largely about demographic decline and what you do to counter it. You either hunker down, shrink the faculty, in keeping with the shrinking eighteen-year-old pool, or you go national. If you go national you compete against every other first rate national institution. . . . I felt we had to trade on what Drexel had already, that was unique to us, that was co-op, very applied programs built on a solid theoretical base, those are things that we can sell.[35]

Drexel "went national" in a big way in the 1980s when it became the first university in the world to require students to use microcomputers. In a first-of-its-kind partnership with Apple Computer, Drexel rolled out the program in 1984, and results were immediate. Student enrollments spiked the next year and a wave of positive press followed. According to David Paul's history of Drexel, in the 1980s and 1990s, Sagik's idea to bring the computer to campus was initially rejected by Hagerty, "as he believed computers to be a passing fad." Yet Hagerty was "convinced by business colleagues outside of Drexel that it would be a source of great publicity," and the idea was ratified by the Board of Trustees in 1982.[36] Models from IBM and Apple Computer were under consideration, and electrical engineering professor Bruce Eisenstein was sent by Sagik to a secretive "unveiling" of the new Apple Macintosh in a hotel room in Boston. Impressed by its functionality and the thousand-dollar all-inclusive price, Eisenstein recommended the Macintosh to the selection committee.

Drexel was one of the twenty-four universities participating in the Apple University Consortium, a strategy crafted to introduce a new consumer base to Apple products and destabilize the control IBM exerted over the national computer market.[37] The *Philadelphia Inquirer* described the program and the scene on campus in January of 1984 when the computers were first shown to faculty and students:

> At precisely 3 p.m., a folding wall in a Drexel University auditorium rolled aside to reveal two uniformed security guards standing at attention, flanking a computer. But it was no ordinary computer. It was the new-generation, super-secret Macintosh personal computer, made by Apple Computer Inc., that all Drexel University freshmen must purchase for $1,000—a hefty discount from Apple's suggested retail price of $2,495. . . . Last October, Drexel became the first university in the United States to require all freshmen . . . to purchase their own personal computer. Until yesterday, Drexel officials had not revealed which computer they had selected . . . the contract represents a major sale for Apple, a computer company begun in 1977 in a garage in Cupertino, Calif. . . . Students will buy a basic Macintosh machine with a keyboard, a 9-inch black-and-white screen, and a "mouse," which is a small box used, instead of keys, to control the cursor. Printers will be installed throughout the university for student use.[38]

"The Macintosh caught on almost instantly," remembers former provost Mark L. Greenberg, who was then an assistant professor of English. "And, in typical fashion, the students were probably ahead of the faculty. The melding of technology and higher education occurred at Drexel within the first year. And we never looked back."[39] Bruce Eisenstein witnessed the impact of the Macintosh gambit in his classrooms and among his faculty. "So that's how we got the Macintosh," Eisenstein explains. "The secondary effect of that was in 1984 enrollment in the electrical engineering

Students waiting in line to pick up their Macintosh microcomputers, 1984. (Drexel University Archives, PC 8 Events photographs. Drexel University Archives. PC 11 Academic photographs.)

President Hagerty and his wife, Mary E. Hagerty, in the Hagerty Library atrium, second floor. (Drexel University Archives. PC 4 People photographs.)

department swelled to over 400 students, entering students, where we previously had 120–130. All of them were interested in computers. . . . I had to add faculty like mad . . . I had to transform people who had been teaching circuits and electronics into computer people."[40]

Apple CEO Steve Jobs visited the campus in the spring of 1985 to watch the premiere of a documentary titled *Going National*, produced by two faculty—Dave Jones and Paula Cohen—about the Drexel microcomputer program. "After the viewing, dressed in a . . . tuxedo and noticeably pleased by what he'd seen, what he'd started, Jobs spoke, calling Drexel 'a pioneer for being the first university to fully incorporate the Macintosh' into its curricula."[41]

E4 at Drexel

In the late 1980s, pressure to enroll and retain undergraduate students who would then achieve success working for industry, was a priority for Drexel's College of Engineering. High-level research and graduate education still represented relatively small parts of the university's identity (compared to what they would become a decade later), and increased undergraduate enrollments, preparation for work through coursework and co-op, and the attainment of successful careers upon graduation, were central to the College of Engineering's, and very possibly the university's, survival.

The emphasis on undergraduate education created a setting in which members of Drexel's engineering college revamped their approach to pedagogy through the Enhanced Educational Experience for Engineers (E4). E4 was an effort to "drastically reformulate" the first two years of the undergraduate engineering curricula and, as described by its planners, to challenge national norms of engineering education. Its main features remained in place through the 1990s, as part of what became the four-year "Drexel

Curriculum," in 1994. There is little doubt among E4's founders, even today, that it was the decision, under a new engineering dean in 2000, to make research and graduate education the central focus of the college, that brought an end to the integrated and applied pedagogy inherent in E4. A look at the rise and fall of E4 at Drexel can help us understand not just Drexel's own history, but how support for, and obstacles to, pedagogical reform in the science, technology, engineering, and math fields come to be.[42]

The E4 curriculum, initiated under the leadership of engineering deans and faculty including Richard Woodring, Robert Quinn, and Eli Fromm, garnered praise from the engineering education sector from its initial development in 1988, receiving significant early support from the National Science Foundation and the General Electric Foundation. The program represented to some educators nothing less than a "Revolution in Engineering Education."[43]

The E4 program admitted its first ninety-eight students in 1989, and by 1993 some five hundred students and fifty faculty had participated.[44] E4's most conspicuous innovation was to put in place an "engineering up front" approach that provided students an immediate, practical experience of technical understanding from their first days in college. At many American engineering schools, students did not handle physical materials until they had taken foundational classes; engineering students would customarily watch instructors or technicians do things that they themselves were not yet allowed to do, much as they had for the past hundred years. In the E4 program, experiments and other lab experiences began for students in the introductory course, Fundamentals of Engineering. Full-blown engineering projects and formal presentations, normally found only in senior design courses, were now challenges that freshmen undertook. Students in E4 used and learned on software that they owned and used across different courses, and which was put to the production of "definite oral and written deliverables."[45]

The E4 curriculum was also multidisciplinary in a way that replicated the conditions of technical employment much more closely than traditional training. The rejection of traditional disciplinary structures was certainly not a new idea among U.S. engineering schools, shaping public and private institutions particularly through the 1960s and 1970s, but these were never many in number and where it had been tried it represented a strong departure from convention.[46] E4's model of integrated and team teaching was time-intensive and relied on a range of faculty, including those in math, physics, humanities, and other departments outside of the College of Engineering. Moreover, given the interdisciplinary nature of the program, a

E4: The Drexel Curriculum lab, 1994. (Drexel University Archives.
PC 11 Academic photographs.)

calculus instructor might be asked to sit in on his student's mechanics class, for example, to make sure all instruction was well coordinated. Without support for such participation from the university's upper administration, it would have been difficult for any program to enlist other disciplines.

The E4 freshman course, Mathematical and Scientific Foundations of Engineering, covered mathematics, mechanics, electromagnetic theory, thermodynamics, and less traditional subjects such as "nature, structure, and interactions of matter," and "living systems." There were traditional lectures and recitations, but through hands-on exercises, students in the E4 program learned basic principles and methodologies. For instance, the act of "making measurements of length, mass, force, time, frequency and current, voltage, resistance, power and sound" became in essence a unified body of practice in this format, rather than discrete skills pertaining only to discrete physical phenomena.[47] This introduction to the "unifying rather than the parochial aspects of engineering" allowed students to experience the heterogeneous and unpredictable intellectual requirements found, according to E4's planners, in the world of engineering work.[48]

E4 directors recorded improved student retention, computer and laboratory skills, and, more generally, enjoyment and excitement. The end product, the Drexel-trained engineer of the 1990s, also departed in important ways from those more traditionally educated. Co-op employers, for example, identified a set of unusual facilities among E4 students, who brought their conjoined mathematical, physical, and technical skills to bear on the day-to-day work of engineering.[49]

Preparation for a lifetime of industrial employment motivated the design of the E4 curriculum. Thus an engineering seminar taken by all E4 students required a "series of presentations in the form of a briefing that a professional engineer would make to a CEO, a corporate director . . . a House or Senate Subcommittee . . . or perhaps a Stockholders' Meeting."[50] At the same time, self-reflection was also an important part of the curriculum. Students kept journals in which their ideas about their own education were recorded, and these were seen by E4's directors to be helpful with program evaluation. Feedback from students to instructors was systematic. Within a month of the first E4 classes starting, students began participating in weekly faculty team meetings and were asked for ideas on programming, mentoring, and other aspects of the program.[51] This reflection too was seen by E4's designers as a skill of use to industry, as students were being taught to think critically about activities and processes going on around them and in which they were participating, and even more important, to speak out.[52]

For Robert Quinn, Eli Fromm, Donald Thomas, Alan Lawley, Richard Woodring, and other strong E4 proponents among the engineering faculty, changes to engineering education quite simply made for a changed profession.[53] It was not merely that the "engineering up front" experience could match Drexel graduates to industry job descriptions; it could alter and improve the way in which such jobs were undertaken. For college administrators in the late 1990s, and especially after 2000, by contrast, undergraduate education seemed to have little connection to the nature of engineering as a body of knowledge, as the shaping of that knowledge was seen to be the purview of research alone. That demarcated (and tiered) understanding of education and discovery in the sciences is of course not unique to Drexel; it characterizes much of the complex history of engineering education globally.[54] It certainly offers a metric whereby research today constitutes a more prestigious activity for an engineering school (and its faculty) than does teaching. But by detaching the acquisition of technical knowledge from its application, we raise an artificial and convenient firewall between engineers and the world in which they labor; not only does education reproduce the professions for which it prepares entrants, it determines what will and will not become part of professional practice. Only by a very selective logic does undergraduate engineering instruction have no role in the worldly life of engineering. If we are genuinely interested in deep questions about the customary aims of American engineering (questions that can be informed by social justice, sustainability, or global security concerns) or about the inefficiencies of conventional engineering planning and management (questions that may prompt radical restructuring of the engineering workplace and labor market), we must introduce critique as a central aspiration for the learner.[55]

The basic premises of E4 are necessary to any authentically critical engagement with engineering as a social enterprise. In obvious ways the integration of multiple bodies of knowledge and ongoing habits of self-reflection such as those encouraged by E4 both support responsible, societally focused technical work. In perhaps less obvious but even deeper ways, E4's curriculum enforced attention to linkages between learning and practice, and in so doing it kept students, instructors, and administrators tuned to the worldly realities of engineering. That is an awareness that is foundational to socially responsible and impactful practice. In this sense E4 may not itself have been revolutionary, but it identified tools and techniques required for transformative changes in technical pedagogy. In other words, if the E4 program did not permanently change Drexel's College of Engineering, we can nonetheless understand that its founding ideas might yet help change engineering.

New Directions in Drexel Engineering

Drexel's College of Engineering—under the leadership of Dean Joseph Hughes since his arrival in 2012—has expanded in both the scope and size of programs and degrees offered in fields that would have been inconceivable when the institute first offered its engineering course in 1893 and offered its first four-year degree program in 1914.[56]

The School of Biomedical Engineering, Science and Health Systems was established in 1997, growing out of the Biomedical Engineering and Science Institute (the nation's first) founded by Professor Hun H. Sun in 1961 (see Chapter 21).

The A. J. Drexel Nanomaterials Institute was established in 2003 to coordinate research, education, and partnerships in nanotechnology,[57] the study of matter on a nanoscale ("nano" means one-billionth, so one nanometer is one-billionth of a meter). Led by founder Yury Gogotsi, Distinguished University and Trustee Chair Professor in the Materials Science and Engineering, the institute is considered an international authority on carbon-based nanomaterials as well as new materials Drexel professors have discovered such as MXenes, a nanosheet only five atoms thick but with huge potential for possible uses in energy storage.[58]

The Nanomaterials Institute has explored developing smart fabrics and wearable technology with the Shima Seiki Haute Tech Lab at Drexel's Expressive and Creative Interaction Technologies (ExCITe) Center. The Shima Seiki Haute Tech Lab focuses on exploring the capacity of knit structures and new materials to push development in the field of wearable technology.[59] The nanomaterials studied by Drexel professors and students are perfect candidates to be incorporated in advanced textile technologies such as wearable fabric batteries and turning textiles into energy storage devices.[60]

That multidisciplinary research collaboration is a perfect example of why the ExCITe Center was started in 2013, and directed by Dr. Youngmoo Kim, as a university-wide strategic initiative for research innovation. The ExCITe Center pursues activities at the intersection of technology, design, and entrepreneurship—a modern update to the Drexel Institute's original founding pillars of art, science, and industry. Students and professors involved with multidisciplinary collaboration at the ExCITe Center have worked on everything from digital media, health care, performing arts, computer and information science, product design, and more.[61] In addition to the Shima Seiki Haute Tech Lab, ExCITe also houses the Entrepreneurial Game Studio (an incubator for student game design startups),[62] the Music and Entertainment Technology Lab (for research in digital media technologies),[63] as well as various seed projects.[64] Outside of the university, the ExCITe Center has forged partnerships with civic, arts, and cultural groups as well as industry and various institutions and organizations in Philadelphia.

Within the College of Engineering, the number of graduate and undergraduate students has continually increased over the years. Drexel's is the largest private engineering college in the nation according to undergraduate class size, with seven departments focusing on education, research, and engineering leadership. About 98 percent of undergraduate engineering students have successfully found and completed co-ops, and the average salary of a co-op for an engineering student ranks at the top of co-op salaries across the university.[65]

After graduation, engineering alumni have gone on to make great innovations in their field. Most visibly, three engineering alums have explored outer space as NASA astronauts. The first, Dr. James P. Bagian (B.S., mechanical engineering, 1973), flew on two space shuttle missions in 1989 and 1991 and became the first physician to develop now-standard treatments for space motion sickness.[66] Paul Richards (B.S., mechanical engineering,

1987), flew in the STS-102, the eighth shuttle mission to visit the International Space Station, in 2001.[67] Chris Ferguson (B.S., mechanical engineering, 1984, Hon. 2009), captained the final space shuttle flight, that of the shuttle *Atlantis,* in 2011.[68]

Using the foundation forged by Drexel engineers in the past one hundred years, those involved with the ExCITe Center, the College of Engineering, and the School of Biomedical Engineering, Science and Health Systems are carrying forward what has been a process of continuous reinvention in Drexel engineering.

NOTES

1. Drexel Institute, *Art, Science, and Industry: Dedication Ceremonies* (Philadelphia, 1893), 9.

2. Terry S. Reynolds, "The Engineer in 19th-Century America," in *The Engineer in America: A Historical Anthology from "Technology and Culture,"* ed. Terry S. Reynolds (Chicago: University of Chicago Press, 1991), 7–26; Terry S. Reynolds, "The Education of Engineers in America Before the Morrill Act of 1862," *History of Education Quarterly* 32 (1992): 459–82; Roger L. Geiger, "The Rise and Fall of Useful Knowledge: Higher Education for Science, Agriculture, and the Mechanic Arts, 1850–1875," in *The American College in the Nineteenth Century,* ed. Roger Geiger (Nashville, TN: Vanderbilt University Press, 2000), 47–65; Robert H. Kargon and Scott G. Knowles, "Knowledge for Use: Science, Higher Learning, and America's New Industrial Heartland, 1880–1915," *Annals of Science* 59 (2002): 1–20; Jeffrey A. Mullins, "'In the Sweat of Thy Brow': Education, Manual Labor, and the Market Revolution," in *Cultural Changes and the Market Revolution in America, 1789–1860,* ed. Scott C. Martin (New York: Rowman & Littlefield, 2005), 143–80; Jonson Miller, "Pathways and Purposes of the 'French Tradition' of Engineering in Antebellum America: The Case of the Virginia Military Institute," *Engineering Studies* 5 (2013): 117–36.

3. Drexel Institute, *Art, Science, and Industry: Dedication Ceremonies,* 15–17, 20–21.

4. Ibid., 16–17, 21–22.

5. "New Standards for the Buying of Street Lights," *Municipal Review* 2 (1913): 695.

6. Edward D. McDonald and Edward M. Hinton, *Drexel Institute of Technology 1891–1941: A Memorial History* (Philadelphia: Drexel Institute of Technology, 1942), 54–69; Hollis Godfrey, *The Drexel Idea: Policies Based on Facts* (Philadelphia: Drexel Institute, 1919).

7. The Department of Engineering, offering a three-year curriculum, was formed in 1906, having as its direct predecessor the Department of Electrical Engineering. It should be emphasized that electrical engineering was the field leading to the formation of the school of engineering moving Drexel away from its original focus on vocational training.

8. Quoted in McDonald and Hinton, *Drexel Institute of Technology,* 51.

9. David F. Noble, *America by Design: Science, Technology, and the Rise of American Capitalism* (New York: Alfred Knopf, 1977), 268–77; Thomas P. Hughes, *American Genesis: A Century of Invention and Technological Enthusiasm 1870–1970* (New York: Viking, 1989), 188–203; Edwin T. Layton Jr., *The Revolt of the Engineers: Social Responsibility and the American Engineering Profession* (Baltimore: Johns Hopkins University Press, 1986).

10. Noble, *America by Design,* 209.

11. Hollis Godfrey, *The Institutional Budget* (Washington, DC: Department of the Interior, Bureau of Education, 1914).

12. Godfrey, *The Drexel Idea,* 7–8.

13. Hollis Godfrey, "Summary of Speech Delivered at the Commencement Exercises of the Drexel Institute of Art, Science and Industry, June 11, 1914," 5, Hollis Godfrey Papers, Drexel University Archives.

14. Hollis Godfrey, "The Foreman," *Annals of the American Academy of Political and Social Science* 85 (1919): 146–51; Hollis Godfrey, "The Training of Industrial Engineers." *The Journal of Political Economy* (1913): 494–99.

15. Hughes, *American Genesis,* 193.

16. Donald Stabile, *Prophets of Order: The Rise of the New Class, Technocracy and Socialism in America* (Boston: South End Press, 1984); Hughes, *American Genesis,* 193–200.

17. Kyle Bruce, "Scientific Management and the American Planning Experience of WWI: the Case of the Industries War Board," *History of Economics Review* 23 (1995): 37–60; Carroll Pursell, "Engineering Organization and the Scientist in World War I: The Search for National Service and Recognition," *Prometheus* 24 (2006): 257–68; Adam Tooze, *The Deluge: The Great War, America and the Remaking of the Global Order, 1916–1931* (New York: Penguin, 2014); Noble, *America by Design,* 150–57; Hughes, *American Genesis,* 115–37.

18. Noble, *America by Design,* 213.

19. "Students' Army Training Corps" (c. 1918), UR 10.7 ROTC 1918–1969, 3, Drexel University Archives.

20. *Cooperative Industrial Engineering Education Afforded by Drexel Institute, Philadelphia,* 1919, Hollis Godfrey Papers, Drexel University Archives.

21. *Drexel Institute of Technology Three-Quarter Century Fund,* Drexel University Archives.

22. Joseph Barbeau, *Cooperative Education in America: Its Historical Development, 1906–1971* (Boston: Northeastern University, 1973).

23. *Engineering, Science and Management War Training Program, 1943–1944,* UR6.16, World War II Collection, 1943–1951 2006-143-01, 2–4, Drexel University Archives.

24. Ibid., 4.

25. James Creese, "Technical Education in the U.S.S.R," *Alumni News* 8 (1956): 2–4. Miriam N. Kotzin, *A History of Drexel University, 1941–1963* (Philadelphia: Drexel University, 1983), 114.

26. Dean Toombs letter to Dr. Hagerty, November 16, 1963, UR 1.8/56/9: National Defense Education Act of 1958, 1958–1964, Drexel University Archives.

27. Patrick Murphy Malin and Louis M. Hacker letter to Dr. James Creese, September 9, 1960, UR 1.8/56/9, National Defense Education Act of 1958, 1958–1964, Drexel University Archives; National Defense Education Act Faculty Motion, UR 1.8/56/9, National Defense Education Act of 1958, 1958–1964, Drexel University Archives; James Creese to Arthur Adams, UR 1.8/56/9, National Defense Education Act of 1958, 1958–1964, Drexel University Archives; Office of Development Memorandum, January 5, 1960, UR 1.8/56/9, National Defense Education Act of 1958, 1958–1964, Drexel University Archives; James Creese letter to Philip L. Corson, January 6, 1960, UR 1.8/56/9, National Defense Education Act of 1958, 1958–1964, Drexel University Archives.

28. Kotzin, *A History of Drexel University.*

29. Ibid.

30. Ibid.

31. Ibid.

32. Alma Forman personal communication with Alissa Falcone, February 27, 2015.

33. "Remarks By A.W. Grosvenor—April 19, 1963," Philadelphia Society of Women Engineers, available at http://philadelphia.swe.org/uploads/2/3/6/6/23664278/aw_grosvenor_remarks.jpg.

34. Alma Forman personal communication with Alissa Falcone, February 27, 2015.

35. D.B. Jones, *Going National: Introduction of the Micocomputer at Drexel University* (Philadelphia: Drexel University, 1985).

36. David A. Paul, *When the Pot Boils*, 26.

37. Joseph Master, "When the Mac Came to Market Street," LeBow College of Business, Drexel University, available at www.lebow.drexel.edu/news/when-mac-came-market-street.

38. Dick Pothier, "With a Little Fanfare Students Meet Their New Computer," *Philadelphia Inquirer*, January 25, 1984, B7.

39. Master, "When the Mac Came to Market Street."

40. Eisenstein interview, November 23, 2015.

41. Master, "When the Mac Came to Market Street."

42. James Mitchell, "Evaluation of the E4 Program; Notes on the Process," memo, 1994, Drexel University Archives.

43. Brochure, "Energy Symposium, 1992," Drexel University Archives.

44. Robert G. Quinn, "Drexel's E4 Program: A Different Professional Experience for Drexel Faculty and Students," *Journal of Engineering Education* 82 (1993): 196–202.

45. Robert G. Quinn, "An Enhanced Educational Experience for Engineering Students: Project Chronology and History 1988–1994," September 12, 1994, 3–5, Drexel University Archives, 3–5.

46. Amy E. Slaton, *Race, Rigor and Selectivity in U.S. Engineering: The History of an Occupational Color Line* (Cambridge, MA: Harvard University Press, 2010).

47. Quinn, "An Enhanced Educational Experience," 4.

48. Quinn, "Drexel's E4 Program," 197.

49. Amy Slaton interview with Eli Fromm, January 29, 2016.

50. Quinn, "An Enhanced Educational Experience," 4–5.

51. Quinn, "Drexel's E4 Program," 196; Duncan Widman, "Revolutionary E4 Program a Continuing Success," *The Triangle*, November 15, 1991, 6.

52. Quinn, "An Enhanced Educational Experience," 196.

53. Ibid.

54. Gary Lee Downey and Juan C. Lucena, "Knowledge and Professional Identity in Engineering: Code-Switching and Metrics of Progress," *History and Technology* 12 (2004): 393–420.

55. Donna M. Riley and Yann Lambrinidou, "Canons against Cannons? Social Justice and the Engineering Ethics Imaginary," *Proceedings of the ASEE Annual Meeting*, Seattle, WA, June 14–16, 2015.

56. Joseph Hughes, "State of the College," College of Engineering, Drexel University, available at drexel.edu/engineering/about/state-of-the-college/.

57. "History," A. J. Drexel Nanomaterials Institute, Drexel University, available at nano.drexel.edu/about-dni/history/.

58. "Shaping the Future of Energy Storage with Conductive Clay," *DrexelNow*, November 26, 2014, available at drexel.edu/now/archive/2014/November/MXene-clay/.

59. "Shima Seiki Haute Technology Laboratory," ExCITe Center, Drexel University, available at drexel.edu/excite/research/shimaSeiki/.

60. "Holding Energy by the Threads: Drexel Researchers Spin Cotton into Capacitive Yarn," *DrexelNow*, March 5, 2015, available at drexel.edu/now/archive/2015/March /capacitive-yarn/.

61. Personal correspondence, Youngmoo Kim to Scott Gabriel Knowles, February 2, 2016.

62. "Entrepreneurial Game Studio," ExCITe Center, Drexel University, available at drexel.edu/excite/research/egs/.

63. "Met-Lab," ExCITe Center, Drexel University, available at drexel.edu/excite /research/met-lab/.

64. "Seed Projects," ExCITe Center, Drexel University, available at http://drexel.edu /excite/research/seedProjects/.

65. Alissa Falcone, "Drexel Co-ops by College," *DrexelNow*, October 26, 2015, available at drexel.edu/now/archive/2015/October/Co-op-Report/.

66. ASAP Member: Dr. James Bagian, MD, PE, National Aeronautics and Space Administration. http://oiir.hq.nasa.gov/asap/bios/bagian.html.

67. "Biographical Data: Paul William Richards, NASA Astronaut," National Aeronautics and Space Administration, available at www.jsc.nasa.gov/Bios/htmlbios/richardsp .html.

68. "Drexel Astronauts Talk about Future of Space Program at Alma Mater," *Newsworks*, October 26, 2011, available at www.newsworks.org/index.php/local/healthscience /28931-drexel-astronauts-talk-about-future-of-space-program-at-alma-mater.

Other than having fewer buildings than we have today, Drexel's campus still has somewhat the same feel as when I graduated in 1983. As a chemistry major I, spent a lot of time in Disque Hall and Stratton Hall, so that quad area near what's now the Korman Center (which was the library) was where you spent most of your time. So, that core part is still pretty much the same. Of course nearly everyone was a commuter, so I took the Chestnut Hill local here with about eight or nine other people who either went to my high school or who were from the same suburban area, and we would all be together, taking the train, especially in our freshmen year when all our courses were pretty much the same no matter what your major. We would do homework on the train ride home, we'd be doing our calculus homework or physics homework on the train ride home.

The campus being in the city, things that happened in the city you knew about. Probably the biggest thing that happened at that time was the MOVE movement. MOVE was right up the street from here, and I had friends who lived right around their house, and in the last year before Frank Rizzo took it over there was a large police presence; they used the Armory as their headquarters and there were always dozens of police walking around there, so everyone was very aware. I can say of the years that I was here, several friends' houses and apartments backed right up against the MOVE house and there were never any issues. In fact, you used to be able to pull your car up in front of their house and they'd wash your car for a dollar. So, it never caused any issues, but it was something that you were well aware of and knew about and, of course when there was the big shootout and they tore down the house in the same day it was newsworthy, but nothing stopped on campus. Kids came in looking a little scared when they said they woke up to gunfire, but other than that it was business as usual.

I have been connected to Drexel since starting as a freshman in 1974. The university, as you would imagine, played an important role in my life. Not only did it mold me as a person having spent my formative years here. I started as a young adult at eighteen years old and left as a much more mature young man at age twenty-seven. Drexel also played a big part in my professional life. As I started a chemical company upon graduation it was a source of employees and advice from the same mentors that guided my education. Over the years the bond grew stronger and I increased my involvement in a number of ways. I see this as a way of giving something back to ensure other students can have the opportunity and experience that I had.

—IRA TAFFER

4

The Sciences at Drexel

Instruction, Service, and Research

LLOYD ACKERT

T HE RELATIONSHIP BETWEEN the sciences, engineering education, and technology research is complex and has shifted across time.[1] Since the late nineteenth century, engineering curricula have been oriented toward either "science" or "practice." Drexel struck a balance between these two approaches; the curriculum combined both a desire to apply the scientific theories, methods, and instruments defined by the basic sciences with a sincere belief that these must be employed to solve realistic engineering problems in an economically viable way.[2]

Science as Instruction, 1893–1918

Drexel's early physics faculty trained students "to use the fundamental laws and principles in new cases . . . in a common sense way . . . in deducing new conclusions."[3] Drawing on his experiences at Johns Hopkins University, Professor A. J. Rowland conducted limited basic and applied research. A Franklin Institute member in 1899, he advanced optics research by assessing a new portable photometer, provided by the Electric Motor and Equipment Company of Newark, New Jersey.[4] Research sensibilities also drove the main productions in physics. Both Rowland and Homer J. Hotchkiss (Professor of Physics after 1906) published textbooks for conducting experiments. Between 1905 and 1924, Rowland's *Applied Electricity for Practical Men* stressed the practical application of theory and experiment to industry.[5] Hotchkiss had the same goals with his 1913 *Principles of Experimental Physics for Students of Science and Technology*.[6] The 1897 program taught courses in electricity ranging from electrostatics to electromotive force in dynamo machines. Seniors studied the theory and practice of alternating currents, which included the design of apparatuses and solving practical engineering problems.[7] By 1909 the curriculum included "Advanced Experimental Physics" and laboratory work.[8]

The faculty in mathematics, Henry Gummere and Katherine D. Brown, both served on the Philadelphia section of the Association of Teachers of Mathematics.[9] Their curriculum supported technical studies by applying mathematics to solve original problems.[10] Courses included algebra, geometry, analytical geometry, differential and integral calculus, and several practical courses in surveying and mechanics.[11]

In chemistry, Professors Ernest Congdon and Abraham Henwood conducted research and highlighted it in their textbooks. Congdon's *Laboratory Instruction in General Chemistry* and Henwood's *Laboratory Work in Applied Chemistry* taught basic principles aimed at industrial work. In 1918, Henwood worked as a chemist at the Hercules Powder Company, an explosives manufactory (previously part of DuPont but separated in 1912 as a result of an antitrust suit), which by 1917 had become a major military supplier.[12] In *The Industrial Chemist* Henwood recommended teaching chemists a proper balance between basic principles and how to apply them to industry. The best educational organizations taught "business organization, corporate finance, economic and social conditions (including housing problems, sanitation, attractiveness and comfort in living conditions)." That is, "the all important human element."[13]

Biology was taught only in the "normal course" of the domestic science program. Albert P. Brubaker (Professor of Anatomy, Physiology, and Hygiene) taught human anatomy and physiology. His research paralleled the work of leading European scientists such as Hermann von Helmholtz. Between 1888 and 1893 he also collaborated locally with Henry Chapman at the Jefferson Medical College and Academy of Natural Sciences on respiration, cornea size, and physiology.[14] Chapman's collaboration was novel for Drexel at the time, but would become common practice. The biology curriculum added other courses reflecting new research trends—in 1899, for example, Catherine J. Coolidge, an instructor in bacteriology, lectured on fermentation and the relationship of microorganisms to disease.[15]

In 1908, recognizing the close connections between the sciences, Drexel founded its School of Science to teach students in mathematics, physics, and chemistry.[16] The school was restructured in 1912, becoming three separate courses in the Department of Science and Technology, which also included the School of Engineering. The faculty and students were formed into disciplinary cohorts. Physics and mathematics students, for example, could concentrate on the applied sciences, in which they would work and teach.[17]

The Early Research Era, 1918–1950

Faculty retirements during World War I—including Rowland (dean of the School of Engineering), Henwood (chemistry), and Gummere (mathematics)—and the beginning of the cooperative system made the 1918–1919 academic year a crucial one in Drexel's history. President Kenneth Matheson's administration hired several new faculty and established the four-year co-op curriculum, which was expanded to a five-year program in 1925.[18]

Chemistry offered the most extensive curriculum, with more than forty courses, compared to ten courses in physics and six in mathematics. As with the previous School of Science, the "chemistry seminar" required students to conduct research projects with faculty mentors.[19] In the late 1920s Leon D. Stratton, head of the Department of Chemistry, created a degree program in chemical engineering that reflected a transition from providing "service courses" to specialized courses and research. This included organizing a new laboratory in Curtis Hall, and new courses in thermodynamics, electrochemistry, and physical chemistry.[20] Stratton's 1949 textbook, *Food Chemistry*, reflects his research interests in chemistry, nutrition, and human physiology and his commitment to domestic science.[21] Of the three assistant professors in chemistry, D. C. Lichtenwalner conducted important research in agricultural chemistry, and Robert S. Hanson published textbooks and laboratory manuals in the late 1940s.

James E. Shrader, the faculty member in charge of physics, following the directive for science faculty to publish textbooks, wrote six between 1932 and 1939, all specifically for Drexel students.[22] He is better known for his award-winning invention of the tridimensional vibrograph, and, after 1939, his membership in the National Defense Research Committee's instrument division.[23] The physics assistant professors, James J. Barrett, Floyd L. Nutting, and W. W. Steffey, were mainly instructors, but also participated in local and national physics and science societies.

Henry C. Wolff, the head of mathematics, blended research and pedagogy by applying mathematical analysis in geology (e.g., regarding the rotation of the Earth) and writing basic algebra and calculus textbooks for agricultural students. His administrative and instructional efforts were mirrored by the assistant professors in mathematics and statistics: Clarence G. Dill, James E. Davis, Frank H. M. Williams, and Leda F. White.

The biological sciences continued to be taught in the School of Domestic Science and Arts. By 1922, for example, students studied dietetics and nutrition through courses on physiological and pathological chemistry.[24] The faculty (Grace Godfrey, Professor of Domestic Science; and Edna B. Dayton and Gwendolyn H. Mason, instructors in Physiological Chemistry, Bacteriology, and Physiology) did not conduct research. After 1927, however, nutrition and biology courses included both laboratory and field research.[25]

The Post–World War II and Cold War Years

By the 1950s, chemistry could boast of five laboratories, with the three largest dedicated to general study and basic organic and analytical chemistry, the fourth dedicated to experimental research in physical and electrochemistry, and the fifth dedicated to textile chemistry. Physics offered three laboratories for instruction in thermodynamics, electricity, and spectrochemistry, and one devoted to the new science of atomic physics. Biology, no longer restricted to the School of Domestic Science and Arts, organized laboratories for research and instruction in general biology, bacteriology, biochemistry, and public health. To facilitate research and teaching in the sciences, Drexel began plans for a new Basic Science Building (built in 1955 and dedicated to Dean Leon D. Stratton in 1967).[26] Beginning in 1951 these institutional investments reflected an expansion of the science curriculum to include graduate studies.[27] Among the new graduate faculty in mechanical, civil, chemical, aeronautical, and electrical engineering were junior and senior professors in physics, mathematics, and chemistry.

With Robert S. Hanson as its head, the Department of Chemistry expanded its curriculum to over sixty courses divided into series of inorganic and organic chemistry, with both qualitative and quantitative analysis, and a number of specialized topics such as advanced textile chemistry, petroleum chemistry, and history of science. Select seniors had the opportunity to conduct original research, which was also required in the "research problems" seminar.[28]

Among the chemistry faculty, Elwyn F. Chase's articles in the *Journal of the American Chemical Society* demonstrated that, like the other faculty in the department, his work was not only at the leading edge of research, but stood at the nexus of basic chemistry, physics, and medicine.[29]

Likewise, in the 1960s George Sasin investigated ester reactions in organic chemistry.[30]

Physics grew faster than the other sciences during the decades after World War II. Directed by department head George M. Carlton, physics offered over forty courses at the undergraduate and advanced level. Junior and senior majors were required to take atomic physics with a three-hour lab each week. Advanced optics, thermodynamics, theoretical electricity and magnetism, x-rays, mechanics, and spectroscopy rounded out the program.

Mathematics was guided by James E. Davis and then Alexander Tartler, with Miltiades S. Demos and Samuel S. McNeary as additional faculty. McNeary, who taught from 1936 to 1978, offered the first courses in statistics and numerical analysis, and conducted research in hydraulics. With collaborators, he applied his statistical skills in an eleven-year analysis of smoking by Drexel students.[31] Reflecting the high level of service provided by the Department of Mathematics, more than twenty adjunct professors and instructors taught in the college division.

In the 1960s, biology for the first time matched the other basic sciences in the number of faculty, range of course offerings, and research laboratories. The departments of biology, biochemistry, and physiology offered new curricula, including instruction in a thermodynamics approach to the human body, biophysics, evolutionary anatomy, and a radioisotope laboratory course.[32] The biology department by 1966 ran fourteen laboratories devoted to endocrinology, animal physiology, developmental, and radiation biology, and a greenhouse for plant physiology.[33]

After World War II, Drexel, like other universities, benefited from dramatically increased government funding for scientific research, often through collaborations with the military and private corporations. It is difficult to overstate the dramatic rise in sophistication of Drexel's science curriculum during this period. In each department, new courses taught by new faculty addressed the pressing research questions of the day. Mathematics offered "data handling" related to analog and digital computers; the Department of Physics added instruction in nuclear physics; and the Department of Chemistry taught a radiochemistry laboratory and quantum mechanics.[34] After 1963, Drexel created a master's degree program in biomedical engineering, admitting students along two tracks: those with advanced degrees in the life sciences, and those with engineering and physical science backgrounds.

In 1968 Drexel established a new College of Science, which offered a comprehensive basic science curriculum at both the undergraduate and graduate levels. Each science department began to blend the liberal arts with its established programing.[35] Biology, for example, now taught twenty-three courses, including a seminar series and special independent studies; and physics created a five-quarter directed research sequence.[36]

Reflecting new sensibilities about the role of science in society, programs in the history and philosophy of science, and the history of technology, were organized in 1967 to address the "Social Implications of Twentieth Century Technology."[37] Drexel graduate and history professor Richard Rosen recalls taking a history of science course in the social science department, which, combined with his participation in a televised General Electric "College Bowl," led him to pursue a doctorate in this new field. His subsequent long career at Drexel as a professor and dean often bridged the humanities and engineering departments.[38]

Drexel's expanded commitment to research necessitated the costly re-cruitment of outstanding faculty and construction of the facilities required to attract them. This was accompanied by the administration's increased emphasis on faculty publications and research grants, which were adver-tised in university reports.[39] In the 1982 *Bulletin*, for example, each Col-lege of Science department listed core faculty research interests, and annual reports detailed their grants, publications, and society affiliations.[40]

The College of Arts and Sciences

In 1990 the College of Science and the College of Humanities and Social Sciences were combined to form the new College of Arts and Sciences. In the 1990s, the Department of Chemistry offered graduate degrees in analytical, inorganic, organic, physical, and polymer chemistry. The de-partment's laboratories and curriculum educated students in both funda-mental research (gaining proficiency in digital electronic methods) and applied problem solving. Faculty offered expertise in molecular analysis of air and water; applications of solar, fossil, and nuclear energy; and carcino-gen toxicity. Supported by the Polymer Laboratory with its gel-permeation chromatograph and differential scanning calorimeter, and the GC-Mass Spectrometer Laboratory with a Finnegan 4000 GC-MS, faculty investi-gated new areas of research such as the synthesis of conducting polymeric materials, environmental chemistry (water treatment), and atmospheric photochemistry and the chemistry of hemoglobin.[41]

Physics faculty during the 1980s and 1990s conducted research in a variety of interdisciplinary fields, split evenly across atmospheric science, experimental physics and biophysics, and theoretical physics. In the 1980s, department faculty used LIDAR (Laser Radar) to investigate atmospheric composition at the molecular level, and also large-scale atmospheric dynamics. They also used lasers to study biophysical kinetics, quantum optics (for laser development), and solar collector design.[42] After 1989, investigations in the new Biophysics Laser Laboratory demonstrated interdisciplinary possibilities such as in the biophysics of sickle-cell hemoglobin polymers. Faculty also collaborated outside the university—some worked at Brookhaven's National Synchrotron Light Source to investigate the cross-bridge cycle in muscle contractions.[43]

Mathematics became one of the fastest-growing departments during the 1980s and 1990s, as it integrated computer science into its faculty, curriculum, and research programs. The Center for Scientific Computation, directed by William G. Gordon, was a multidisciplinary graduate research facility that applied computer graphics to large-scale computational problems in science and engineering. The central piece of equipment was the Prime 550 Minicomputer, which along with the department's IBM mainframe and microcomputers allowed the twenty-six faculty to conduct research in fields from applied mathematics to artificial intelligence. The latter opened several avenues for interdisciplinary research, such as in modeling and control theory in biological systems, combinatorics, family planning evaluation, and solar collection systems.[44]

Biology undergraduates learn about evolution by studying the variety of vertebrate life-forms alive today. (College of Arts and Sciences.)

In 1995, the department operated a university-wide local area network (LAN) that united the campus and connected it to the World Wide Web. Their Sun System Unix and Macintosh servers offered students and faculty a creative lab space not only in the department classrooms, but also in the dormitories.[45]

In order to emphasize and provide focus for expanded programs in biotechnology and the biological sciences, the university established a new Division of Life Sciences, consisting of the renamed Department of Bioscience and Biotechnology, and the Department of Nutrition and Food Sciences. Directed by Wayne E. Magee, a professor of biochemistry and head of the bioscience and biotechnology department, the Division of Life Sciences applied studies of theoretical and basic science to practical areas such as human and animal health, food processing and food safety, environmental protection, and genetic engineering.[46] Researchers in both departments collaborated internally at Drexel—and conducted research at several Philadelphia medical institutions including Thomas Jefferson University Hospital.

Recent Developments

Under Donna Murasko, a biology professor, former chair of MCP Hahnemann's Department of Microbiology and Immunology, and now dean of the College of Arts and Sciences, Drexel built the Papadakis Integrated Sciences Building (PISB), which was completed in 2011. Speaking at the PISB dedication ceremony, Dean Murasko described the relationship between the PISB's unique physicality and its intellectual pursuits:

> The essence of this structure—a place for faculty and students to interact, to discover and to discuss ideas—is felt from the open atrium up to the collaboratories on the second, third, and fourth floors and into the brightly lit classrooms and laboratories, which reveal and reinforce the energy of our students and faculty. The stimulating environment is further reflected in the ceiling and skylights, with the light streaming in as a symbol of inspiration and our constant upward gaze towards the next great discovery. The beautiful spiral staircase, although not quite a double helix, evokes the image of DNA and also reminds us of the powerful integration of art and science, the essence of our College.[47]

Murasko also highlighted the importance of the PISB for another ongoing project, Drexel's official affiliation with the Academy of Natural Sciences

In 2011, Drexel celebrated its merger with the Academy of Natural Sciences, a storied Center City Philadelphia institution with roots in the earliest origins of conservation and ecology. At the podium is Academy of Natural Sciences president and CEO George W. Gephart Jr. (Office of University Communications.)

(ANS): "Little did we know then that at the time of this opening the university would have made another significant commitment to sustainability by partnering with the Academy of Natural Sciences. We are delighted by what this means for both the University and for the College of Arts and Sciences."[48]

Founded in 1812, the ANS mission is to encourage and cultivate the sciences. The Drexel ANS affiliation in 2011 offered both institutions new resources, such as shared faculty, facilities, and endowments.[49] In many ways the affiliation represents the continuation of a long-standing tradition of collaboration. Since Drexel's founding, its faculty have attended and presented at ANS's colloquia and seminars. Academy scientists worked with Drexel researchers in the Environmental Studies Institute from 1963 to 1997, and from 1997 to 2002 with the School of Environmental Science, Engineering and Policy. According to Gary Rosenberg, when he served as vice president of the ANS's Center for Systematic Biology and Evolution, he and Donna Murasko discussed possible collaborations between ANS and Drexel's biologists.[50] Rosenberg, who is now both a professor in Drexel's Department of Biodiversity, Earth and Environmental Science (BEES) and Pilsbry Chair of Malacology at ANS, agrees that the affiliation has worked because it is a meeting of research interests from below and administrative interests from above.

The most extensive collaborative connection between Drexel and ANS has been the establishment of BEES. Dean Murasko created this new department in 2012, to create an interdisciplinary institutional framework for thirteen ANS senior scientists (most of whom became tenured or tenure-track Drexel faculty) and six faculty from Drexel's biology department. The combined expertise in BEES, in environmental science, earth science, ecology and conservation, biodiversity and evolution, geoscience, and paleontology, has offered new curricular possibilities for both undergraduate and graduate science students.[51]

ANS scientists have found new opportunities for joint grant proposals and professional development.[52] The affiliation has also allowed over one hundred Drexel students to complete one of their co-ops at ANS.[53] Rosenberg noted that integrating co-op students into ANS research requires an adjustment ("you need to find a new way to work") and that this will result in joint publications with students.[54]

The history of the sciences at Drexel, especially the later developments in physics, chemistry, mathematics, and biology, tells in microcosm the story of the history of modern science. This history is at the core of the university's commitment to science education and creative research that reflects local, national, and international movements.

NOTES

1. For an excellent survey of the relevant literature on this topic, see Jonathan Harwood, "Engineering Education between Science and Practice: Rethinking the Historiography," *History and Technology* 22 (2006): 53–79.

2. Ibid., 54–55.

3. Drexel Institute of Art, Science, and Industry, Circulars (1906–1907), 11.

4. Arthur J. Rowland, "The Photometry of Incandescent Lamps," *Journal of the Franklin Institute* 148 (1899): 376–83.

5. For example, see Arthur J. Rowland, *Applied Electricity for Practical Men* (New York: McGraw Hill, 1916).

6. Homer J. Hotchikss and Floyd C. Fairbanks, *Principle for Experimental Physics for Students of Science and Technology* (Philadelphia, 1913).

7. Drexel Institute Course in Electrical Engineering, 1896–1897, 10–11.

8. Drexel Institute Circulars of the Departments and Courses of Instruction, 1906–1907, 12.

9. W. H. Metzer, ed., *The Mathematics Teacher*, vol. 4 (Syracuse, NY: New Era Printing, 1912), 175, and vol. 9 (1917), 58.

10. Drexel University, *Year-book*, 1908–1909, 121–22.

11. Ibid., 115–17.

12. William A. Lacock, "Hercules Powder Company," *The Analysts Journal* 9 (1953): 143–47.

13. Abraham Henwood, "Importance of Fundamentals," in *The Industrial Chemist: His Place in the Chemical Industry, His Opportunities and Responsibilities, His Training and Rewards: A Symposium* (D. O. Haynes, 1918), 10.

14. Edward J. Nolan, "A Biographical Notice of Henry Cadwalader Chapman," *Proceedings of the Academy of Natural Sciences* (Philadelphia, 1910), 263.

15. Drexel University, *Year-book*, 1899–1900, 127.

16. Drexel University, *Year-book*, 1908–1909, "School of Science," 108–9.

17. Drexel University, *Year-book*, 1912–1913, 76–77.

18. Edward D. McDonald and Edward M. Hinton, "Drexel Institute of Technology 1891–1941, a Memorial History," *Year Book* (Camden, NJ: The Haddon Craftsmen, 1942), 173–75, 178–79.

19. The Drexel Institute Register, 1930–1931, 89.

20. McDonald and Hinton, "Drexel Institute of Technology 1891–1941, a Memorial History," 182.

21. Leon Stratton, "A Factor in the Etiology of a Sub-Breathing Stammerer: Metabolism as Indicated by Urinary Creatine and Creatinine," *Journal of Comparative Psychology* 4 (1924): 325–45; and Leon Stratton et al., *Food Chemistry: A Laboratory Manual for Students in Home Economics* (Philadelphia: Stephenson Brothers, 1949).

22. For example, see James Edmond Shrader, *Physics for Students of Applied Science* (New York: McGraw-Hill, 1937).

23. He had won the Franklin Institute's John Price Wetherill Medal; see the *Journal of the Franklin Institute*, 1934, 116; McDonald and Hinton, "Drexel Institute of Technology 1891–1941, a Memorial History," 183.

24. McDonald and Hinton, "Drexel Institute of Technology 1891–1941, a Memorial History," 198.

25. The Drexel Institute Register, 1926–1927, 81.

26. "Science Buildings Dedicated to Deans Disque and Stratton," *The Triangle*, June 2, 1967, 1.

27. "College Courses with Majors in Biological Sciences, Chemistry, Physics," *Drexel Bulletin* 28, no. 7 (August 1951).

28. *Drexel Bulletin*, 1951–1952, 164–71.

29. See for example, Elwyn F. Chase and Martin Kilpatrick Jr., "The Classical Dissociation of Bromcresol Green, Chlorphenol Red and Methyl Red in Potassium Chloride Solutions," *Journal of the American Chemical Society* 54 (1932): 2284–92. For background on biochemistry during this period, see Joseph Stewart Fruton, *Contrasts in Scientific Style: Research Groups in the Chemical and Biochemical Sciences*, vol. 191 (American Philosophical Society, 1990), 252–65.

30. For the later work, see D. A. Lutz et al., "X-ray Diffraction Powder Studies of Some Dithiol Diesters of Long Chain Acids," *Lipids* 1 (1966): 6.

31. Bill Price, "An Obituary of S. McNeary, Professor Emeritus," *Philadelphia Inquirer*, July 4, 1996; J. H. Arnett, M. W. Black, and S. S. McNeary, "An Eleven-Year Study of Cigarette Smoking Habits of Students Entering Drexel University, Philadelphia," *American Journal of Public Health* 64 (1974): 120–23.

32. *Drexel Bulletin*, College of Engineering, 1960–1961, 21.

33. *Drexel Bulletin*, College of Engineering and Science, Graduate Curriculum, 1966–1967, 21.

34. *Drexel Bulletin*, College of Engineering, 1960–1961, 22–29.

35. *Drexel Bulletin*, College of Engineering and Science, Graduate Curriculum, 1966–1967, 73–83.

36. Ibid., 130–140.

37. Ibid., 148.

38. Dick Rosen, interviewed by Scott Knowles, December 10, 2015, Drexel University Archives.

39. Martin Whitehead, " 'Proposal or Perish' Policy Becomes Major Issue: Some Faculty Leaving for Failure to Garner Research," *The Triangle*, June 2, 1967, 1.

40. *Drexel Graduate Bulletin*, 1983, 2–16.

41. *Drexel Graduate Bulletin*, 1988–1989, 148–49.

42. *Drexel Graduate Bulletin*, 1986–1987, 167.

43. *Drexel Graduate Bulletin*, 1989–1990, 147–48.

44. *Drexel Graduate Bulletin*, 1985–1986, 162–63.

45. *Drexel Graduate Bulletin*, 1996–1997, 56–57.

46. *Drexel Graduate Bulletin*, 1986–1987, 151–56.

47. Dean Murasko speech, opening of the Papadakis Integrated Sciences Building, September 20, 2011.

48. Ibid.

49. "Drexel University and The Academy of Natural Sciences and Drexel University Announce an Historic Affiliation," *Economics & Business Week*, June 4, 2011, 1293.

50. Ibid.

51. Carolyn Belardo, "Drexel-Academy Partnership Ushers in Future of Environmental Science Education," press release, Academy of Natural Sciences, June 8, 2012, available at www.ansp.org/about/press-room/releases/2012/bees/.

52. See the announcement "Drexel Areas of Research Excellence," available at drexel.edu/research/news-and-events/news/DARE/.

53. Gary Rosenberg, interviewed by Lloyd Ackert, January 29, 2016.

54. Ibid.

William Sidney Pittman, Department of Fine and Applied Art, class of 1900 (back row, second from right). (Drexel University Archives. PC 3 Early photographs of the Drexel Institute of Art, Science, and Industry.)

African-American architect William Sidney Pittman graduated from the Drexel Institute of Art, Science, and Industry in 1900. Ten years later, a profile written on the young architect stated simply: "Mr. Pittman is considered the leading architect of his race." Over the course of a relatively short career, Pittman is credited with forty designs or additions, mainly in the vicinity of Washington, DC, and the state of Texas.

William Sidney Pittman, Tuskegee Institute graduate and protégé of Booker T. Washington, arrived at the Drexel Institute in early November 1897. According to a letter written soon after his arrival . . . President James Macalister and Professor of Architecture Arthur Truscott greeted him "warmly and pleasantly." MacAlister wrote a letter of introduction to a "Reverend Phillips" who secured Pittman a room in a boarding house for the "reasonable rate of fourteen dollars per month."

Pittman told Washington in his first letter from Philadelphia that "a very different but more extraordinary and a more elaborate course than usual was made in particular for me—something unusual indeed I assure." This course would allow Pittman to finish his course work at Drexel in three years and receive specialized training in Mechanical Arts and Architectural Drawing. In a letter in 1898, Pittman wrote that he had a hard time convincing the administration that he could take on such a course load and that "it was not easy to have them understand the idea but they don't know what some Negroes can do."

At the beginning of his final academic year at Drexel, Pittman commented: "My treatment has been extraordinarily good and the work down here, and what is to be done this year will cover all and more too than is required to help with the work at Tuskegee." Pittman continued to maintain a hectic schedule but also seemed content with his life in the city, writing that his schoolwork was "progressing and interesting." His enjoyment was evident in a letter in which he wrote, "My class on top of city hall today sketching—extraordinary!" At the end of 1899, he was paid three dollars by the head of the architecture department to complete a "large scale drawing of the Institute's library." He also sold a watercolor to the Institute for "permanent exhibit." Pittman attended the graduation ceremony on June 8, 1900 and returned to Tuskegee soon after to begin his work as an instructor there.

Pittman graduated from Drexel and returned to Tuskegee, where he taught and paid back the loan for living expenses he received from Washington and the Tuskegee Institute. In the fall of 1906, he entered and won the competition to design the Negro Building at the Jamestown Tri-Centennial Exposition. Pittman relocated to Texas in 1912 after being awarded a series of contracts in the South.

—Kevin Martin; revised by Robert Sieczkiewicz, Rebecca Goldman, and Zachary Mohn

5

Drexel's Architecture

Encountering the Urban Campus

Amy E. Slaton

THE GERMAN POET Goethe's larger-than-life-size terra-cotta bust, placed alongside similar portrayals of Humboldt, Bach, and eight other famous Western thinkers of past eras, has looked down from the portal of Drexel University's Main Building at Thirty-Second and Chestnut Streets since the school first opened its doors in 1891. Goethe's gaze faces westward, toward a distant horizon, and for decades, with the river and rail yards behind him, he would have seen block after block of three- and four-story houses and small Philadelphia businesses stretching before him to the north and west. The University of Pennsylvania's campus lies a few blocks to the southwest, but through the 1940s, both schools were surrounded by residential streets with just a few factories and warehouses scattered among them.

In the 1950s, Goethe's view began to change dramatically as the Drexel Institute expanded its facilities and a series of clean-lined, purpose-built low-rise structures emerged. A tidy, unified campus was taking shape, and the new buildings, virtually all featuring unadorned concrete and, most conspicuously, the school's trademark orange brick, continued to appear into the 1970s. Finally, after a period of little change when Goethe could have been forgiven for doubting the institution's future, in the late 1990s a steady stream of new and architecturally varied research, teaching, and dormitory structures began to rise; and in our own time, new ten-, fifteen-,

Detail of a column in the main entrance archway with "Goethe, Poetry" in the background. (Drexel University Archives. PC 5 Buildings and campus photographs.)

and even twenty-story buildings are appearing each year on Drexel's campus, taking the place of the school's older structures. Some orange bricks remain, but many of these now hide behind a new coat of white paint, and the few still of original color seem almost a nostalgic token, surrounded by gleaming expanses of glass and stone.

Following the changing character of Drexel University's buildings through the institution's 125-year history reveals the powerful ways in which, in the words of the innovative college campus planner M. Perry Chapman, a university functions "as narrative." A college's campus layout and the structures built or chosen for teaching, research, housing, and administration are the physical expressions of a school's "mission, its history, its traditions, its aspirations."[1] Crucially, the character of a university's built environment also helps determine the experiences of all who come in contact with it: students, faculty, staff, administrators, civic patrons of the university, and community members. No less important are those indirectly affected by a university's building choices: those who do not receive public resources (whether money or land) because a federal or state government has given them to an individual school in order that it may build or expand a physical plant; those who cannot afford to attend a particular college because its decisions regarding facilities have resulted in, or justified, higher tuition costs. In short, the visual and material building choices made by Drexel's leaders and supporters since its opening can tell us about the school's intended meanings in the world and its actual impacts.

This short essay cannot offer a comprehensive overview of all the campus buildings erected, purchased, renovated, or destroyed, which now number in the many dozens, over the course of Drexel's history.[2] The apartments and houses in which generations of students, faculty, and staff have lived; nearby stores and restaurants; and nearby infrastructural features such as roads, railroad trestles, trolley lines, and even the Philadelphia skyline visible from campus might also be considered important parts of Drexel's architectural history. Not least influential in the history of Drexel's design choices were the appearances of other cultural institutions in and beyond

Philadelphia to which the school might have been compared well or poorly, including that of Drexel's Ivy League neighbor, the University of Pennsylvania.[3] Each of these has its own aesthetic and material history that might be part of our overview given a longer essay. But with a few well-chosen examples we might begin to see what sorts of economic, cultural, and social priorities have occupied those in charge of shaping and maintaining the school's physical plant between 1891 and 2016, and formulate some guidelines for asking historical questions about other structures and cityscapes that have been part of Drexel's history.

Looking at the school's architecture helps us detect what, in the 1890s, 1930s, 1970s, or 2000s, Drexel's leaders might have believed about what the school was or could be in the higher education marketplace. Certainly at no point would anyone have mistaken Drexel's campus for that of its Ivy League neighbor, or for the idyllic academic clichés of literature or cinema; no sweeping greenswards, tree-lined allées, or classical facades here. Nor at midcentury did Drexel choose to hire the celebrated modernists then responsible for other urban campuses in America, such as Mies van der Rohe or the firm of Skidmore, Owings and Merrill.[4] When many U.S. universities began seriously competing with one another for students in the 1980s, Drexel's campus came to be labeled by a great many people as bland and utilitarian; famously, the Princeton Review ranked it the nation's ugliest at one point.[5] But rather than counter or accede to such judgments we will try to understand how Drexel's buildings came to be, in different historical periods; after all, the exteriors of all buildings express prevailing cultural ideologies, and even seemingly functionalist choices to minimize decoration or use mass-produced materials are value-laden. And of course, no building or campus is ugly (at least in any simple way) to those who design and pay for it.[6]

We will try as well to get some sense of how those without influence over Drexel's architecture have lived or worked in or around the school's buildings. A central element of this piece is the very question of where the line between these two interest groups might be drawn in different eras; in other words, where the "inside" and "outside" of Drexel's operations might be located. This is not a simple question, and although Drexel is a private institution the question is not one readily answered with ideas of private/public distinctions, or even delineations between Drexel-affiliated and unaffiliated stakeholders. Drexel students, their parents, university faculty, and staff are surely "insiders" when compared to nearby community members, but all of these groups have at different times found themselves well outside processes of decision-making about the school's physical plant. Patterns of defense sector and corporate patronage experienced by Drexel, enhanced as the government-industry-academy "triple helix" solidified over the later twentieth century, have complicated the inside/outside demarcation still further. While the university's buildings themselves are interesting and in some instances innovative or visually striking, what really motivates our close look at Drexel's architecture is understanding the plays of power and influence across many different stakeholder groups in the university's history.

With that in mind, I will focus on three buildings that reflect both ambition and conflict in Drexel's history as a technically focused, urban institution. All modern universities blend the aims of knowledge transfer and production (or teaching and research), vocational preparation, and institutional self-preservation, and Drexel has always added to that recipe some sense of civic mission; I have tried to choose buildings that make that combination clear. Each of the three has housed technical programming and thus also reveals Drexel leaders' cultural understandings of technology, knowledge, and higher education in general as well as the more specific (if aspirational) meanings of a Drexel credential, or, in the case of faculty researchers or clinical practitioners, affiliation.

The first building I discuss expresses the founder's view of these complicated and vital elements of institutional operation: the lavishly decorated Main Building, commissioned directly by Anthony Drexel from his favorite Philadelphia architects, and upon which he expended a huge amount of money and attention. His conception of conjoined economic opportunity and cultural uplift for Philadelphia's working-class residents shaped every feature of this building, which still stands as a fully functioning part of the campus and a seat of administrative power, housing the president's and provost's offices.

The second building I discuss is, at first glance, but only at first glance, at the other extreme of architectural ambition: the utilitarian Stratton Hall. Completed as the Basic Sciences Building in 1955, it represents the first of the so-called orange brick buildings and would appear to express few deliberate aesthetic aims.[7] Yet Drexel's simple, blunt buildings of this period actually reflect President Creese's and other leaders' understanding of the American university as a vital responder to Cold War–era geopolitics and local, racialized urban unrest, arguably two of the most complex social and cultural challenges of the latter half of the twentieth century.

The third building, the Bossone Research Center, built in 2005 to hold engineering labs, classrooms, and offices, can help us follow Drexel's ideas regarding its context and constituencies into a very different historical moment. The university had by this time passed through its most uncertain stage, recovering dramatically under President Constantine Papadakis. The turn to a famous architectural firm and an eye-catching design for Bossone expressed a university more confident of its own sustainability in a modernizing world and city, with everyone involved dedicated to facilitating integrated corporate and government patronage of the sciences.

Fascinatingly, we may detect in the design of Bossone and other new campus buildings of the 2000s an echo of the technically ambitious Main Building, a return to the high architectural drama and panache of the school's earliest moments, perhaps expressing a sort of renewed institutional self-assurance to mark the end of more modest eras. We can also trace strategies across the generations for meshing the institution with the socially complex neighborhood in which it is located. With their materials, styles, and explicit and implicit messages, all three buildings help us see how Drexel has approached the ever-present and sometimes incompatible demands of students, employees, research patrons, and private and civic sponsors, and the needs and expectations of a changing nation and community.

Main Building

Guests attending the 1891 dedication of Drexel Institute could not have been more prominent: Andrew Carnegie, J. P. Morgan, and Thomas Edison were all on hand while politicians and philanthropists, wealthy merchants, and tastemakers of the eastern seaboard filled out the crowd.[8] Surely their willingness to attend was in part due to Anthony Drexel's well-established social networks, but there was also an indication that the opening of a new educational institution for urban, working-class students signaled to these men and women a significant cultural endeavor. Drexel's educational mission was by no means a social project readily associated with the more elite functions of the American academy, but it was widely seen among the influential as a creditable contribution nonetheless.

Functioning during the day and evening to serve working people, the school would disseminate practical occupational skills to many parts of the industrial economy. A set of aesthetic and humanistic lessons would pervade this technical curricula; students would attend concerts and visit the Free Library for exposure to fine arts and literature.[9] Industry, science, and art were all seen as essential to a healthy polity, and the new Main Building, in both its exterior and interior, made this balance of priorities almost inescapable for all who encountered it. The appearance of Drexel's first

Main Building, exterior, looking northeast, 1891. (Drexel University Archives. PC 3 Early photographs of the Drexel Institute of Art, Science, and Industry.)

building declared at top volume that industrial learning and labor and the transmission of Western high culture were inseparable undertakings.

As historians Jeffrey Cohen and Leslie Beller have described the imposing 500,000-square-foot, four-story structure, an exterior featuring light buff brick and a huge variety of terra-cotta decorative elements produced a memorable effect for Main Building. Distinguished immediately from the tall Gothic and Victorian structures of the University of Pennsylvania's campus a few blocks away, and from the eclectic profiles of Philadelphia's nearby banking and railroad buildings, Main Building had more in common with the imposing Beaux Arts styling of Memorial Hall, built by Herman Schwarzmann for the 1876 Centennial Exposition in Philadelphia.[10] Main Building was the result of Anthony Drexel's large budget and focused vision, and undeniably of his own notions of what counted as humankind's more valuable cultural contributions. The eleven portrait medallions, of which Goethe was one, arrayed in an archway surmounted by a winged nude female figure representing "the Genius of Knowledge," were the building's most fully rendered exterior sculptures, but reliefs made up of floral and geometric motifs decorated much of the outside surface.[11] Passing into the recessed main entry, reached by stairs from Chestnut Street, forced students to consider that Faraday, Columbus, Shakespeare, and William of Sens (master builder of Canterbury Cathedral) had endowed modern civilization with their lasting brilliance, but anywhere the eye rested on the building's exterior would have revealed some reference to classical architecture or the design preferences of antiquity. The orderly but nearly numberless patterns covering the walls seem almost like a catalog of previous architectural styles. By including arched windows, elaborate friezes, and dozens of distinct motifs from curb to roofline, the institution's planners were drawing on the most durable cultural past they could imagine and in so doing projecting the school itself, and its graduates, into the future.

To our twenty-first-century eyes this astonishingly detailed surface likely appears excessive. To some it may even signal a retrograde naïveté: Surely many Drexel students and visitors today understand that Columbus is not an unalloyed hero, and that the white, male "geniuses" and their naked female muse are not necessarily representative of all human intellectual attainment, if they notice these decorations at all. But when erected on the former site of a large private home owned by a friend of Anthony Drexel, Main Building stood out as an example of cultural abundance. One did not need to know the exact cost of the building to understand the scale of Drexel's investment in the institution. Main Building would have likely signaled a concentration of wealth and enviable taste compared to the small wood or plain brick buildings around it, but it also conveyed the cultural educability of those inside. Drexel famously saw his school as a means of economic inclusion for those without access to existing post-secondary options, whether due to ethnic, gender, or class proscriptions. Main Building's outward aesthetic placed the teaching and learning going on within (including that of Catholic, female, and working-class students) in an unbroken chain of Anglo-European efforts at cultural reproduction.

To achieve this expression of his cultural and educational vision, Drexel turned, interestingly, to architects with a commercial and industrial portfolio. Joseph Wilson and his brother John had already provided the Drexel family with homes and with buildings for their banking concern, but notably they had also designed massive railway terminal sheds for the Pennsylvania Railroad, some of the most ambitiously engineered structures in Philadelphia at that point. The interior of Main Building features a soaring atrium, and its uninterrupted span surely involved some of the same technical acumen that Wilson Brothers architects had deployed for those functional commissions. Joseph Wilson served as president of both the Franklin Institute and the American Institute of Civil Engineers, and published on the benefits of American emulation of European trades and

Main Building, Great Court, with view of painted ceiling, completed in 1892.
(Drexel University Archives. PC 3 Early photographs of the Drexel
Institute of Art, Science, and Industry.)

technical education, a kind of cosmopolitan concern that was not inciden-
tal to Wilson's ideas about appropriate architectural styling, as Paul Hirshorn, Drexel professor of architecture, has made clear.[12] Joseph Wilson
would likely have been seen by Anthony Drexel as combining exactly those
forms of expertise needed for the new school's combination of practical and
arts education.[13]

Main Building's atrium featured arched and balustraded galleries, a
wide double stairway, and richly tiled floors that filled the space with conventional aesthetic details, but the overall impression is again one of unusual abundance and informed accomplishment, of wealth intelligently
spent for the common good. Drexel could be assured that anyone entering
the space would either be intimidated, inspired, or, perhaps in keeping with
his goals of expanding his students' educational ambitions, both.

Within a decade of its opening, Drexel Institute had expanded considerably, and the Wilson Brothers returned to extend Main Building eastward
with a somewhat simpler addition (now Randell Hall). In the 1920s a further addition (Curtis Hall) appeared, each new exterior bearing less detail

The Drexel Institute of Technology, west side entrance to Main Building.
(Drexel University Archives.)

than the last. All of the additions are of the same height and all of their facades line up neatly along Chestnut Street. But to walk eastward along this length of streetscape is to realize that Drexel's 1891 blend of industrial practicality and high-culture inculcation did not drive the institution in perpetuity, as he might have wished.

In the half-century following the financier's death in 1893, two world wars and a major depression brought the nation a steadily heightening sense of science and technology as guarantors of national security and wealth. For

many Americans of cultural influence and means, it was increasingly a pragmatic modernity that seemed to assure cultural continuity, rather than the
rearguard lessons of classical antiquity or of the traditional European academy. By the 1950s, as the nation moved from hot war to cold, and Philadelphia like many cities faced unprecedented social upheaval along lines of
race and class, Drexel's architecture came to express a clear-eyed presentism
rather than celebrate the lofty and esoteric intellectual achievements of past
epochs. The intended local, national, and global functions of the school were
changing as well, bringing new articulations of individual and collective
good to which the institution might contribute. These were ideological shifts
that the Basic Sciences Building makes clear.

Basic Sciences Building (Stratton Hall)

During his lengthy Drexel presidency (1945–1963), James Creese consistently made a priority of national security, seeking to understand how the
institution might play a greater role on the contemporary economic and political landscape. This was a focus that reflected federal trends in science
and technology funding: a massive postwar jump in public support for
cutting-edge instruction and research across engineering, the life and hard
sciences, and a host of other disciplines, seen by many as central to meeting the country's daunting geopolitical and domestic challenges. Drexel had
gradually built its enrollment through the 1920s and 1930s and played a
significant role in training technical personnel during World War II. However, the strains of wartime mobilization and the Soviet's test of an atomic
bomb in 1949, even before the launch of Sputnik in 1957, made the prospect
of American scientific shortfalls seem both real and profoundly threatening
for the nation's leaders.[14] Government funding for college students, along
with a perceived shortage of engineering personnel nationwide, poised Drexel
Institute to become a major player in the response to looming defense and
economic crises. In the early 1950s a plan for dramatically expanding the
school, to be supported by private and public funding, was formulated.[15]

Yet despite President Creese's clear articulation of geopolitical anxiety
(he visited the USSR in 1956 and, as Drexel historian Miriam Kotzin writes,
"was astounded at the high level of technical education" he saw there),[16] we
must be careful to avoid ascribing this growth in American higher education and at Drexel itself only to international tensions. The abstracted understanding of science in the United States as an answer to societal ills also
arose from a national confrontation with the country's history of racial
discrimination and social injustice. White flight deeply eroded property

values and tax bases in northern cities through the 1950s and 1960s. The strengthening of large, white-dominated urban institutions, including colleges, hospitals, and businesses seen to be at the vanguard of American science and technology, was seen by many policy makers and civic leaders as the answer, and enacting this plan invariably and not coincidentally involved the eradication of "blighted" inner-city black communities.

Through the 1960s urban renewal would help expand research universities in many nervous city neighborhoods across the United States. Ostensibly this sometimes occurred in the service of expanded urban higher education opportunities, but historians have questioned the depth of that commitment and certainly the mocking alternative term for urban renewal, "negro removal," was often apt.[17] Drexel's physical growth in this era captures this dovetailed commitment to science as a source of both national and domestic security and hints as well at emergent questions of how the school, founded on the premise of economic inclusion, would approach the minority community in which it was now sited. Its architectural choices can help us link the institution to wider cultural subjectivities then circulating around both matters.

The design of the Basic Sciences Building, eventually named Stratton Hall and completed in 1955, powerfully expresses Drexel's civic, educational, and industrial priorities of this period. Massed in two- and four-story wings along Thirty-Second and Chestnut Streets, respectively, the building's erection followed the construction of the Alumni Engineering Laboratories in 1952, one of a tiny handful of new facilities that had been established by that point beyond the Main Building complex. The creation of this additional building, intended to house a range of science and engineering departments, represented a moment of "such weight and peril" for Creese, Kotzin explains, that he saw the board's deliberation on the matter as calling "for prayerful consideration."[18] Stratton Hall's seemingly pared down, utilitarian appearance, positively Spartan compared to that of the Main Building standing just across Thirty-Second Street, might at first seem to reflect simply an economizing move, saving the costs of materials and labor clearly needed for a more decorative exterior. But this negative explanation would miss the building's intentional aesthetic function, and the civic, pedagogical, and even bureaucratic meanings it held for its makers.

In addition to the use of orange brick, a mass-produced alternative to the carved-stone masonry still favored in the 1950s by many more traditional universities for their architecture, the design of Stratton Hall highlighted construction materials as an explicit sign of efficiency, technical knowledge, and institutional purpose. Although they have recently been replaced by more varied elements, Stratton's original metal windows and door frames, and the exterior panels placed between some windows, all bluntly expressed their mass-produced and uniform character; their use also signaled a departure from the artisanal products (and employment) of skilled carpenters or masons. The overall look of the building stressed repetition: windows on all floors are of identical shape and size and evenly spaced (compared to the taller, elaborated windows seen on the first story of the Main Building, for example). In short, not only were repeated, standardized forms the essence of Stratton Hall's aesthetic; it was difficult for anyone encountering the building to detect any reference to previous academic architectural styles.

Many buildings in America, as long as they were not functioning as residences, museums, or places of worship, were tending by the 1930s toward a more functionalist look, and universities were edging away from buildings that looked as if they could have been built in Europe in an earlier century; major accretions of classical, Gothic, Victorian, and other sorts of retrograde detailing were losing favor.[19] Complex rooflines and elaborate surface treatments were giving way to cleaner, squared-off profiles. Yet many universities through the middle decades of the century still incorporated hints of traditional architectural styling such as towering tall clock or bell towers or carved stone entry ways, sills, and lintels. New engineering schools built by private universities (consider Northwestern's massive "Tech" building) and public institutions (the University of Wyoming is one example) still commonly brought a note of cultural tradition to their exteriors. Drexel's science and engineering buildings of this period, by contrast, placed a premium on the present.

A fund-raising campaign designed to attract donors for the new science and engineering building reveals a remarkably detailed set of cultural associations between Drexel and the polity in which it functioned. Drexel was to be seen as a modern, supremely efficient factory for the mass production of technical workers in the American economy, and the new building represented the necessary physical plant for such production. A chart in the fund-raising brochure lays out the "Factors in Quality Production" in two parallel lines that equate the manufacturing of what appears to be a complex machining device ("Plenty of Good Raw Material + Plenty of Skilled Operators + A Modern Precision Tool = A Top Quality Product") to the education of Drexel graduates ("An Abundance of Able Students . . . [Which Drexel Has!] + An Able Faculty . . . [Which Drexel Has!] + A Modern and Adequate Building . . . [Which Drexel *Does Not* Have!] = A Continuing Supply of Well-Trained Scientists, Engineers and Technicians [Which You

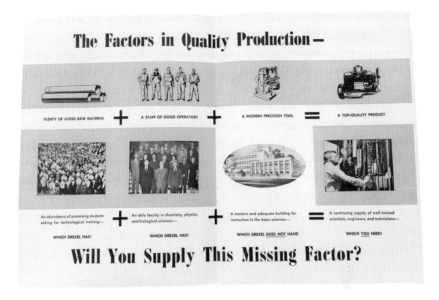

The Factors in Quality Production —

PLENTY OF GOOD RAW MATERIAL + A STAFF OF GOOD OPERATORS + A MODERN PRECISION TOOL = A TOP-QUALITY PRODUCT

An abundance of promising students asking for technological training— + An able faculty in chemistry, physics, and biological sciences— + A modern and adequate building for instruction in the basic sciences— = A continuing supply of well-trained scientists, engineers, and technicians—

WHICH DREXEL HAS! WHICH DREXEL HAS! WHICH DREXEL DOES NOT HAVE! WHICH YOU NEED!

Will You Supply This Missing Factor?

Drexel University Pamphlet, "Will You Supply This Missing Factor?"
(Drexel University Archives.)

Need!]"). At the bottom of the page potential donors are asked, "Will You Supply the Missing Factor?"[20]

Two powerful messages are delivered here. First, the chart clearly conveys that Drexel shared the values and literal techniques of its industrial audiences, upon which it relied for donations and the employment of its graduates. But perhaps less obviously, the education of technical workers is itself cast here as a predictable production process with a known and reliably functioning output. Drexel Institute, in short, is not a place for the cultivation of individual economic or political sensibilities among young people, not a site of undirected energies or unpredictable critical thought. It is a place for the reproduction of knowledge and practices of proven value to American industry; in short, a source of order in an uncertain world. The visual elements and technological style of Stratton Hall, resonant with a great many commercial and industrial buildings of the time, expressed this sensibility beautifully.

In retrospect, promotional choices of this kind might be seen as ultimately having limited the school's status. Treating graduates as mass-produced objects hardly positions them for stellar careers—and indeed, careers in scientific research or upper management were not the norm for most Drexel graduates through much of the twentieth century. But the association of Drexel with the needs of the American industrial economy,

conservatively imagined, did sustain the school. Donations for the construction of Stratton Hall were forthcoming. What's more, by the end of the
1950s, a set of public/private initiatives provided Drexel with more reliable
means for growth and a distinct rationale for making an enlarged, mod-
ernized college campus.

Local redevelopment initiatives channeled money to Drexel and the
University of Pennsylvania for the direct funding of new construction, but
also, tellingly, to help relocate families and businesses seen to be standing
in the way of that institutional expansion.[21] The close of the decade saw a
revision of the Federal Housing Act that allowed cities to use federal urban
renewal monies for university-related construction. The University of Pennsylvania and Drexel, with the nearby Philadelphia College of Pharmacy
and Science, the Philadelphia College of Osteopathy, and Presbyterian
Hospital, formed a nonprofit entity that helped to organize and legitimize institutional growth in West Philadelphia.[22] In 1963, an explicitly
science-focused urban-planning initiative created the University Science Center, but as historian Margaret Pugh O'Mara has recognized, the nickname
"University City" on its own had begun to mark the disappearing poorer or
black residential communities nearby as undeserving of preservation. It was
universities that would control and prosper on this swath of city land.[23]

My final example, Bossone Hall, traces the race- and class-driven ideology of urban planning, and the role of technical knowledge in this formulation of American society, through the coming decades.

Enterprise Research Center (Bossone Hall)

As other chapters in this book detail, Drexel achieved a new status in the
1970s and 1980s (becoming a university in 1970, creating a larger campus
with many more students in residence, and attracting new kinds of research
funding) while it also began to feel the effects of deeply troubling economic
and planning problems. In his account of this period, David Paul traces
the often well-intentioned strategies that brought Drexel to near dissolution, and the 180-degree turn in fortunes that accompanied the arrival of
President Constantine Papadakis in 1995.[24]

Bossone Research Center—one of many new buildings constructed
through Papadakis's efforts between his arrival in 1995 and death in 2009,
sometimes at a rate of one per year[25]—represents many ideas regarding
Drexel's identity among institutions of higher education and within the city
of Philadelphia that have continued under the current administration of
John Fry. Bossone offers a lens on a period of tremendous expansion of

Drexel as a private institution of higher education and nonprofit business, and concomitantly on its civic and global influence. An explosion in applications and student body size, the acquisition of a medical school, the creation of a law school, and the annexation of one of the nation's foremost natural science museums and research centers over the Papadakis and Fry years unquestionably signaled a different notion of Drexel's cultural identity than those developed in earlier decades. Studying Bossone may help us investigate these aspirations and attainments as those within and outside of the Drexel community have understood them.

Papadakis, accomplished as an engineer and manager of huge civil engineering projects, famously brought the skills and priorities of business to his oversight of Drexel, and he was especially masterful in the gathering of private and public funding for the university. The plan to create a "Research Enterprise Center" at Market and Thirty-Second Streets indicated his concerted integration of teaching, research, and industrial priorities, and the appeal of that integration to potential sponsors.[26] This combination of interests had of course always been present at Drexel, but for Papadakis unlike for earlier leaders, participation at the very highest levels of academic, government, and corporate sectors was paramount. The identity of the university was to change through marketing, funding, and standards for admissions and hiring. In what may be a telling indication of his sense of cultural mission, many of the construction projects Papadakis led at Drexel built on dramatic design and big-name architects. They were in this sense closer to Anthony Drexel's striking aesthetic choices for the Main Building than to the deliberate but visually restrained architectural expressions of the Creese era.

Beginning around 2000, Drexel planned for the creation of a new 150,000-square-foot "Research Enterprise Center" along Market Street, revamping portions of the existing Commonwealth Hall and expanding its footprint to hold laboratories, offices, classrooms, an auditorium, and other common spaces for engineering and related fields. With Papadakis's trademark ability to garner public monies, and a $10 million contribution from the Bossone family, planning went ahead on the projected $30 million project (its total cost eventually approached $40 million).[27] Papadakis and Drexel's board of trustees chose the firm of Pei Cobb to design the building. Although the project also brought in Burt Hill Kosar Rittelmann, a Philadelphia firm engaged with other Drexel buildings, the choice of Pei Cobb involved celebrated architect I. M. Pei, whom Drexel promotional materials soon referred to as "the architect renowned for the Louvre's glass pyramid."[28] A previous Papadakis project at Drexel, the North Residence

The Edmund D. Bossone Research Enterprise Center, home to the College of Engineering, was completed in 2005 as part of Drexel's mission to support innovative multidisciplinary research. (Office of University Communications. Photo by Halkin/Mason Photography.)

Hall, had employed architect Robert Graves; a slightly later project, Pearlstein Business Learning Center, turned to the firm of Philip Johnson. Papadakis, a consummate corporate observer attuned to the ways in which an enterprise gained status and thereby security, was actively associating Drexel with signature architects.

The design of Bossone clearly echoed that of Pei's best-known structure. Its towering seven-story glass atrium, rising over Market Street and the 1876 bank building of Frank Furness just to its west (a historic landmark renovated and reopened as Drexel's Paul Peck Alumni Center in 1999), comes to a sharp point and reveals its internal structural elements much as does the Louvre's pyramid. In some foundational ways the building continues the midcentury modernist styling seen on Stratton and Drexel's other orange-brick buildings, displaying a rejection of nineteenth-century motifs and elaborate decoration and a reliance on repeated, standardized elements and clean lines. But unlike earlier Drexel buildings, institutional efficiency and routine are emphatically not conveyed by the 2005 structure. In addition to its almost intimidatingly pointed glass corner, Bossone's large open lobby offers a space for meetings and receptions and includes a glass-walled robotics lab; it is clearly meant to be a showplace for the engineering research taking place elsewhere in the building and also for the technical expertise involved in creating the atrium's soaring span. Here Bossone may remind us of the Wilson Brothers' Main Building atrium. But it is the creativity and inventive drive of enterprise-focused technical research—the core of that twenty-first-century buzzword "innovation"—that is most clearly being advertised in Bossone and other one-of-a-kind structures of the Papadakis era at Drexel. The campus is no longer attempting to remind viewers of a mass-production operation. The aesthetic boldness associated with the Graves, Johnson, or Pei name—each architect has been at different moments celebrated as the leading edge of postmodern design—is taken on as a signal of Drexel's own innovative energy. Their cultural prestige becomes something that Drexel University, as a patron of the world-renowned designers, may share.

But like all attempts at shaping cultural meaning, this is one that does not necessarily extend to all audiences. For one thing, seen in a certain way, Bossone's lobby is not an example of cutting-edge design but instead echoes well-established trends in American academic and corporate architecture, looking much like a 1972 glass atrium at Cleveland State University, designed by Don M. Hisaka, for example; or even reminding us of the multistory glass walls fronting undistinguished suburban industrial headquarters.[29] This comparison is not meant to point out any weakness of the Pei Cobb building, ignore its nuanced design, or deny its visual impact, but only to indicate that Bossone is not in any obvious way one of Pei's convention-smashing buildings, any more than Drexel's Pearlstein Center could be mistaken for Johnson's seminal, postmodernist AT&T Building, designed with his partner John Burgee to transform the Manhattan skyline in 1984.

Without doubt, in the eyes of many observers, Drexel's newer buildings are more handsome and memorable than those of the preceding generations. Part of their job, aesthetically, is to show that Drexel is a cultural
arbiter for its community. For example, the Millenium Hall dorm of 2009,
designed by the distinguished Philadelphia firm of Erdy-McHenry, offers,
in *Philadelphia Inquirer* architecture critic Ingrid Saffron's view, an "abrupt
change" from the Victorian homes lining the nearby streets of Powelton and
Mantua.[30] Historian Taleb Rifai has described this demarcation of school
from neighborhood as a prime function of urban university architecture.[31]
In addition to such a demarcation, many of the buildings of the Papadakis
and Fry years also represent a clear move away from the architecture generated by the lesser ambitions shaping Drexel's previous incarnations. Above
all, many structures built at Drexel since 1995 are "buildings that brand,"
in Saffron's words.[32] But in each case, the "brand" being developed is unquestionably one of established tastes, not one of cultural transgression.

Conclusion

Even the boldest of modernist or postmodernist architects' designs have
not always furthered the cause of societal change. The conservative features of buildings commissioned by leaders of government, industry, and
the academy are well documented by architectural scholars, and really not
particularly surprising if we follow the ways in which the wealth required
to commission, produce, and maintain such structures is obtained.[33]
Drexel at the end of the twentieth century strove for and attained a more
selective and elite (and expensive) status among universities, leaving behind
the mass-production model of technical education featured in the Stratton
fund-raising brochure. It was embracing conventional ideas of corporate
and industrial success, moving beyond a perceived ceiling that had limited
early growth and status by projecting a compatibility of that success and
academic learning and research. With the University of Pennsylvania (for
which John Fry served as executive vice president between 1995 and 2002,
shaping much of its community and land use policy), Drexel has focused
on developing West Philadelphia as a center for technology related to the
needs of business and industry; in O'Mara's term, this is a "city of knowledge," the inventive and entrepreneurial priorities of which Bossone could
easily express.

But what kind of metropolis is this city of knowledge, this "technopolis"?[34] Consider for a moment an encounter with Drexel's campus not on
the part of the school's administrators or board members, the architects and

designers they have selected, or the city's influential economic policy makers. Instead, picture a West Philadelphia resident walking eastward along Market Street, perhaps approaching the entrance to the subway at Thirty-First Street. She is not a student, parent, faculty, staff member, or donor to Drexel University; she is a neighbor. Passing by Bossone at street level, she can look through the transparent facade and see a robotics demonstration or reception underway in the lobby. She can follow the building's exposed beams and columns upward along the wall of glass rising high overhead. But she cannot enter; this is not a place built for her use, or possibly, for her appreciation.

She may not wish to come in, of course, and she may not care about how this structure looks. There is not necessarily an intention or feeling of exclusion operating here; we should perhaps not seek or even expect the kind of conflict that has erupted at various moments in Drexel's history between the community and those in charge of the university's campus.[35] But how can we know what this neighbor might desire or expect when the university and its community are increasingly defined, a priori, as socially and culturally distinct, as naturally possessing different interests from one another? What we can recognize in Drexel's campus and architectural choices is a use of space and public resources, a shaping of the urban landscape in ways that primarily serve the university, not any collective understanding of city life, and we should attend to that choice. In so doing we can reflect on where a private university, bent on participating at the highest level of corporate and scientific activity, and doing so globally, chooses to and might fit within its community.

This is of course the situation facing all urban institutions. Without a complete rejection of its urban roots and current identity, Drexel cannot exchange its city setting for the isolated quiet and greater perceived safety of the suburban or rural campus. It is not a public university, and does not "owe" a particular use of public funding to a particular sector of the public. But as the university in 2016 embraces a plan to increase the height and density of its buildings, and does so with an eye toward profit-making retail and residential opportunities, it may be instructive to think about the physical presence of Drexel-owned and sponsored architecture. As I write this, President Fry is initiating new means of making more permeable the university/community boundary. Some of these programs have raised the prospect of drawing community members into Drexel's core instructional and research activities, and thinking critically about how the school and city have meshed, or not, over time may guide us to the most radical such interventions possible. Whatever Goethe may be seeing today or over the coming decades, we can try to imagine it not merely as a university campus, but as a neighborhood as well.

NOTES

1. M. Perry Chapman, introduction to *American Places: In Search of the Twenty-First Century Campus* (Westport, CT: Praeger Publishers, 2006), xxiii.

2. Miriam Kotzin's invaluable history of Drexel operations between 1941 and 1963 details patterns of growth and curricular priorities behind many of these architectural and campus planning choices; Miriam Kotzin, *A History of Drexel University 1941–1963* (Philadelphia: Drexel University, 1983). A timeline of Drexel buildings, including those on the Center City and Queen Lane campuses, is available at https://www.library.drexel.edu/drexel-buildings-1891-present.

3. On the idea that in any given point in its history, Drexel's architecture functioned to distinguish the school's character and leadership from that of previous eras, see Paul Hirshorn, interviewed by Scott Knowles, October 26, 2015, Drexel University Archives.

4. Taleb Dia Ed-Deed Ar-Rifai, "The New University Environment: A 20th Century Urban Ideal," Ph.D. diss., University of Pennsylvania, 1983; Amy E. Slaton, *Race, Rigor, and Selectivity in U.S. Engineering: The History of an Occupational Color Line* (Cambridge, MA: Harvard University Press, 2010).

5. "Drexel Tops 'Unsightly' Campus List," *Temple News*, September 12, 2006, http://temple-news.com/news/drexel-tops-unsightly-campus-list/.

6. Amy E. Slaton, *Reinforced Concrete and the Modernization of American Building* (Baltimore: Johns Hopkins University Press, 2001).

7. Kotzin, *A History of Drexel University*, 85.

8. George Thomas, *Drexel University: An Architectural History of the Main Building* (Philadelphia: Drexel University, 2008).

9. "Drexel Industrial Institute, Philadelphia," *Public Ledger*, ca. 1890.

10. Jeffrey Cohen and Leslie Beller, "Philadelphia 1870–1895," in George Thomas and Carl Doebley, *Philadelphia* (n.p., 1976); on the architectural distinctiveness and aesthetic ambition of the Main Building, see also Paul Hirshorn, interviewed by Scott Knowles, October 26, 2015.

11. Thomas, *Drexel University*, 5–7.

12. Paul Hirshorn, interviewed by Scott Knowles, October 26, 2015.

13. Thomas, *Drexel University*, 7.

14. Audra Wolfe, *Competing with the Soviets* (Baltimore: Johns Hopkins University Press, 2012).

15. Kotzin, *A History of Drexel University*, 110–15.

16. Ibid., 114.

17. Slaton, *Race, Rigor, and Selectivity*, 79–113.

18. Kotzin, *A History of Drexel University*, 85.

19. Slaton, *Race, Rigor, and Selectivity*; Richard P. Dober, *Campus Architecture* (New York: McGraw Hill, 1996); Chapman, *American Places*, 27–46.

20. The brochure is available in the Drexel University Archives.

21. "Drexel to Add Two New Buildings," *Evening Bulletin,* April 5, 1960.

22. Margaret Pugh O'Mara, *Cities of Knowledge: Cold War Science and the Search for the Next Silicon Valley* (Princeton, NJ: Princeton University Press, 2004), 159.

23. Ibid., 162.

24. David Paul, *When the Pot Boils: The Decline and Turnaround of Drexel University* (Albany: SUNY Press, 2008).

25. "Drexel University President's Report, 2002," 11, Drexel University Archives.

26. "Report of the Board of Trustees, February 26, 2003," Drexel University Archives.

27. Katrina Beach, "Research Center Slated to Open in 2004," *The Triangle*, August 22, 2003.

28. "Engineering New Frontiers: Drexel University College of Engineering" (brochure), n.d., Drexel University Archives.

29. Dober, *Campus Architecture*, 208; Louise A. Mozingo, *Pastoral Capitalism: A History of Suburban Corporate Landscapes* (Cambridge, MA: MIT Press, 2011).

30. Ingrid Saffron, "Changing Skyline," *Philadelphia Inquirer*, September 25, 2009.

31. Rifai, "The New University Environment," 95.

32. Saffron, "Changing Skyline."

33. Slaton, *Reinforced Concrete*.

34. Joseph Straubhaar, Zeynep Tufekci, Jeremiah Spence, and Viviana Rojas, "Digital Inequity in the Austin Technopolis: An Introduction," in *Inequity in the Technopolis: Race, Class, Gender, and the Digital Divide in Austin*, ed. Joseph Straubhaar, Zeynep Tufekci, Jeremiah Spence, and Viviana Rojas (Austin: University of Texas Press, 2012), 1–2.

35. See, for example, Samuel J. Lin, "Neighbors Slam Drexel University Project," *Philadelphia Inquirer,* July 14, 2005, available at http://articles.philly.com/2005-07-14/news /25433065_1_drexel-university-apartment-building-student-housing.

Drexel's mascot, the Dragon, has a mysterious history. For the longest time nobody knew exactly how this mythical nickname originated. Rumors included Drexel meant "dragon" in German, a nod to Anthony J. Drexel's Austrian heritage (it is drechseln, *or woodturning). Some believed the Dragon must have been Chinese. Not true, the Drexel Dragon is more Japanese; it is fire-breathing and has wings.*

The actual origin of the Dragon is related to a 1928 edition of The Triangle *in which the football team was characterized as fighting like Dragons! This must have stuck, because a Dragon logo appears on the jerseys of the men's basketball team the next year. Before then, the school's sports teams were known as the Blue and Gold, the Engineers, and the Drexelites. But by the 1950s the sports teams were absolutely thought of as the Dragons, and Drexel's identity only grew over the next decades.*

Today, there are more than 350 NCAA Division I teams, but Drexel is the only school to have the Dragon as its mascot. The Drexel Dragon has several advantages. It is not an actual animal so it does not have to be fed, it is not politically offensive, it is gender neutral, and it has many positive attributes.

The Dragon is now known as "Mario the Magnificent" in honor of the late Mario Mascioli '45, who never missed a Drexel basketball game. Shortly before his passing, Mario shared that what he would miss most were those afternoons cheering on his Dragons.

Let's go, Dragons!

—Eric A. Zillmer

6

The History of Athletics and Student
Life at Drexel University

Eric A. Zillmer

ATHLETICS HAS HAD several important phases in the history of
Drexel. From the institute's early days after its founding in 1891, to
the 1950s, an era of emerging student life, and the parallel development of fraternities/sororities and competitive athletic teams fueling
school spirit. The 1970s saw the discontinuation of football, the initiation of
Title IX legislation, the opening of the Physical Education and Athletic
Center, and the move to NCAA Division I. The 1980s and 1990s witnessed
the emergence of men's basketball as a powerhouse. Finally, the most recent
chapter of athletics is the one being written in the twenty-first century. This
period is marked by the evolution of a comprehensive athletics department,
the emergence of competitive women's sports, a focus on infrastructure expansion and development, and the aspiration to compete nationally and
even internationally. As a result, the history of Drexel athletics is more
meaningfully communicated through the lens of these important milestones, rather than with a strict linear or chronological approach.

The Drexel Main Building Gymnasium

From the very beginning, Anthony Drexel's institute included an athletic
curriculum as well as dedicated space in which the foremost concern was
athletic competition and physical education. Architect Joseph Wilson replicated the ancient idea of physical education by including a gymnasium in

*The women's gymnasium, 1904. (Drexel University Archives. PC 3 Early
photographs of the Drexel Institute of Art, Science, and Industry.)*

the top floor of the Main Building. The gymnasium still exists today, but
serves as a teaching studio. By including physical space for athletics, Drexel's
Institute broke new ground by reinforcing that physical education was an
important ingredient of A. J. Drexel's educational philosophy of learning by doing.

Early History of Sports Teams
at Drexel University

The beginning of Drexel athletics can be traced to 1895, when an athletic
association was formed that governed all sports utilizing the gym Anthony J.
Drexel had built. Historic pictures survive from as early as 1896 of a women's
basketball team and of a men's basketball team from 1897. This discovery
is fascinating for two reasons. First, Canadian physical education instructor James Naismith invented the game of basketball in 1891 in Springfield,
Massachusetts. Therefore, Drexel was one of the first educational institutions to have formed an organized basketball team. Secondly, the idea that
women not only enrolled in an institution of higher education but also played
organized sports was revolutionary.

Members of the men's basketball team, 1897–1898. (Drexel University Archives. PC 3 Early photographs of the Drexel Institute of Art, Science, and Industry.)

Members of the women's basketball team, 1905. (Drexel University Archives. PC 3 Early photographs of the Drexel Institute of Art, Science, and Industry.)

The 1950s—New Pride and Unity: The
Beginning of Student Life at Drexel

For the next fifty years there was a movement of increasingly organized sports. Sports in those decades were thought of as more recreational and all students participating on the various teams exclusively came from the student body already attending Drexel. This changed in the postwar 1950s, which were a time of renewed energy and optimism, not only for our nation, but also for Drexel. *The Triangle*, the independent weekly student-run newspaper first published in 1926, reported, "In the future, [the year 1955] may be looked upon as a starting point of a new student feeling, a feeling that has either been dormant or suppressed."[1] The physical footprint of Drexel had remained much the same since the institute's beginning, but there was a different culture among the student body that attended the institute during the 1950s. Most students commuted to Drexel, others lived in the dozen fraternities and sororities, and many female students lived in Van Rensselaer Hall, Drexel's first-built dormitory, constructed in 1931. Regardless of where students lived, everyone wanted to be part of this evolving spirit of athletic pride and student unity that was embracing Drexel.

Helen Callas Reiner, a Drexel Hall of Famer and a member of the 1957 U.S. national field hockey team, recalled, "I was a commuter student, but it did not matter, we all came together as friends to meet up at the fraternities, the sororities, or the athletic events."[2] Different factors contributed to this sociological phenomenon, including an increased focus on staging social events and a collective need by the student body to be part of a group, to form an identity as a Drexel student. The co-op structure ensured that entire classes of students would go through their Drexel curriculum together as a group. For the first time there was a commitment at Drexel to celebrate large social events, as well as competitive sports by attending games and organizing pep rallies in support of the teams. Taken together, the 1950s represented an extraordinary period in the history of Drexel University and marked the beginning of student life on campus.

All athletic competition was executed under the watchful eyes of the athletic director, retired Major General Douglass Greene, a graduate of the class of 1913 from the U.S. Military Academy, who often appeared at sporting events in full uniform. The women's rifle team shot its way to the national championship, and the men's basketball team, under legendary coach Sam Cozen, fielded championship-caliber teams. Homecomings grew bigger and bigger each year, and there was even a demand to add fraternities. There were pep rallies in the Great Court with speeches and music on Fridays. "We would decorate all morning. Then in the afternoon, everyone came, the coaches, the cheerleaders, even the engineers. It was wall-to-wall students," recalled Callas Reiner. "One of the biggest pep rallies was held after the 1955 football team won its last game to complete the undefeated season. That rally began in the early morning as students arrived for classes and just gained momentum all day." At one point that day a progression of students marched into President James Creese's office and demanded that all classes be canceled that afternoon. And for that one time, the students' wish was granted!

Drexel's Undefeated Football Season

Football attracted considerable attention from the student body. There were cheerleaders at every game as well as a small military band composed of ROTC students. Often the school organized buses for fans and friends to travel to away contests. Everyone was on the bandwagon in 1955 as the team went on to complete a perfect 8-0 season. "The year 1955 saw the rebirth of Drexel spirit among the student body, which started with the West Chester game and gathered momentum with each succeeding week's victory and exploded in the spontaneous combustion and dance following the great Philadelphia Military College game," head coach Eddie Allen summarized this milestone in *The Triangle*. "The atmosphere was terrific."[3]

Vince Vidas was Drexel's best football player. Playing both offense and defense, Vidas was a menace to his opponents. His size and strength were remarkable, bolstered by his experience assisting his father's piano storage business in South Philadelphia. Vince reported how he often helped his dad move pianos, with his bare hands, up and down the stairs, "It is all about leverage."[4] A game film in the Drexel University Archives shows how Vince would cover the field with great speed and plow over anyone that came in his way. Off the field, Vince was the nicest guy you could meet. His wife, Judy, met Vince while attending Drexel, and the two of them have become longtime supporters of Drexel athletics. "We love this place," she said. Today, the athletics fields at Forty-Third and Powelton are named after Vidas. The season-ending 20–6 win by the football team over Philadelphia Military College was "the big one" and sealed an undefeated season, one for the record books. "It was a cold, snowy day, which made the game at Philadelphia Military College somehow even better," Judy Vidas remembers. "We all warmed up at halftime at the Frog Pond, a Chester bar, and then we were ready for the second half. This game was a big deal!"[5]

The 1958 Men's Soccer National Championship

The 1958 men's soccer team posted an undefeated season, and also a national championship. The 1958 Dragons steamrolled through their twelve-game schedule undefeated and untied (12-0-0). They opened their season with a 7–1 win over Western Maryland and ended it with a 5–2 victory against Lehigh in the Mid-Atlantic Conference championship game. Overall, the Dragons outscored their opponents by a combined score of 76 to 15 and beat every one of their opponents by at least two goals. "No opponent even approached victory over this vaunted team," proclaimed *The Triangle*.[6]

The team had an exceptional coach in Don Yonker. Over his twenty-nine years as coach, from 1947 to 1976, he compiled a 184-119-34 record. Of all the first generation U.S. coaches, Yonker is credited to be the first to study the international game. Al Laverson, Drexel's assistant soccer coach, stated, "Don should be credited with being the most influential coach of his time. He was the first American coach to stress work with the ball. He was a consummate gentleman, creative, innovative and articulate. He made a significant impression on soccer nationwide, but his crowning achievement was a national championship with Drexel."[7]

Scrapbook pages detail Drexel's 1958 national championship soccer team.
(Drexel University Archives. UR 12.8 Yearbooks.)

Drexel was a team with three All-Americans, plus another player who set the Drexel goal-scoring record of twenty-two that still stands today. That player was Igor Lissy.[8] Igor remembers the 1958 championship game as if it were yesterday. "We had a great team, even the referee commented on that," Lissy said. Going into the game with a perfect 11-0 record, "we just wanted to win the game to win the Mid-Atlantic Conference championship. A national championship was the furthest thing from our minds," he said. Drexel dispatched Lehigh 5–2 on home soil. The Dragons' record-breaking season yielded that all important title. In January, the Intercollegiate Soccer Football Association of America, then the governing body of men's college soccer, voted unanimously to name Drexel's twenty-two-man squad the national champion of 1958.

Basketball under Sam Cozen

Samuel Cozen guided Drexel's men's basketball team for sixteen years (1952–68), leading the Dragons to eleven MAC championships. Cozen goes down in history as one of the best coaches to have ever stepped onto Drexel's campus. He recruited talent, and was also able to put it together on the court. His coaching techniques were legendary, and some have survived to this day, including a 1954 document entitled, "The 50 Morale Builders for Basketball," which includes as its first point, "Develop a good shot. Baskets win games." Other Cozen nuggets of wisdom include, "refrain from slumping mentally and you will not slump physically," and "when the team is losing they need your help, not when they are winning."

Cozen also coached at Overbrook High School during the 1940s and the 1950s. For one season, he coached NBA Hall of Famer Wilt Chamberlain. Once Chamberlain came to Drexel to scrimmage on their tiny court in the Main Building and help sharpen the Dragons defense. Cozen coached five players to Hall of Fame careers, including Bob Buckley, Bobby Morgan, Mike McCurdy, Ronald Kleppinger, and Dan Promislo. Besides being a great basketball player, Promislo was also in the middle of Drexel's social life, organizing proms, playing hoops, and hanging out at the Great Court between classes. He was one of the best rebounders to have ever played at Drexel. "For me athletics was huge," Promislo said. "Looking back I marvel that we did as well as we did, since we were working in co-op right through December. Because of that, we often only had a few practices before the first game. I remember playing against Delaware at Convention Hall. I stole the ball and started running down the court. I was thinking, 'Wow, this is a very long way to the other basket!' "[9] Multisport phenomenon Bob Buckley added, "I was not supposed to play athletics because of my studies, but Coach Cozen saw me at PE and invited me to practice."[10] When Buckley's basketball career was over, he had scored 999 points! Today, Drexel's basketball court is named in honor of the great Coach Cozen, and the entrance to the basketball arena is known as Robert and Marlene Buckley Plaza.

The Semanik Years

In 1962 John Semanik became Drexel's director of athletics, and in 1965 his wife, Mary Semanik, became the women's director of athletics. John Semanik had graduated from Drexel Institute of Technology in 1956 and was the first alumnus to hold the position. His twenty-nine years as director saw many changes at the university, including the construction of the Physical Education Center, which greatly improved the facilities. The Semaniks also implemented the move to NCAA Division I, abolished football, created a focus on basketball, and ushered in Title IX legislation.

During 1965–66 and 1966–67, women's basketball posted back-to-back undefeated seasons. During the first of those two seasons, the Dragons outscored their opposition by almost twenty-eight points per contest. They allowed just under twenty-seven points per game on their way to a 7-0 record. The following season, the Dragons again dominated their opponents. Drexel averaged almost fifty-nine points per game while giving up just over thirty-two points. The Dragons were 8-0 during the 1966–67 campaign. Hall of Fame coach Lillian Haas served as Drexel's head coach for those teams and led the program from 1963 to 1992.

Physical Education and Athletic Center

Building and opening the 1975 Physical Education and Athletic Center (PEAC), later renamed the Daskalakis Athletic Center (DAC) is one of the Semaniks' greatest accomplishments. For its time it was a state-of-the art building, featuring a swimming pool and a separate diving well. The first win in the new gym is credited to the swimming and diving team. *The Triangle* reported, "Drexel inaugurated its new $8 million PEAC with a 57–56 swimming victory over LaSalle before 500 spectators."[11]

The building of the PEAC raised a serious question for the university: could Drexel sustain the costs of the new building and the cost of moving into NCAA Division I athletics while retaining all of its sports? The PEAC featured a much needed basketball arena. With that architecture in place, a commitment was made to compete in Division I with men's basketball as the flagship program. However, this came at the expense of football, and a decision was made to drop the sport in 1974. The Semaniks were in the middle of all of those turbulent and difficult decisions. The final analysis was dependent on finances and was ultimately a business decision. President Emeritus Chuck Pennoni reflected on this decision, "Frankly when we did away with football it was the right decision . . . we would not be good in the other sports otherwise."[12] Bob Buckley, who also played football at Drexel, agrees, "It was not a mistake to cut football . . . it was very expensive for the university and we did not think we could have a very good football team at that time."[13] Looking at that decision now, it definitely looks like the right one, given how many athletic programs are losing considerable amounts of money in college football, the Title IX problems it creates, and the fact that Drexel does not even have its own football stadium. President John Fry argued elegantly in a 2016 *Wall Street Journal* op-ed, "Not having a football program turns out to be a major strategic advantage for Drexel." Said Fry, "At Drexel we recognize the benefits of sports but are not burdened by the distractions that come with maintaining a football program."[14]

In 1992, the year the Semaniks retired, Drexel established the John and Mary Semanik Awards honoring Drexel's top male and female athletes. The wall that dedicates the lobby to the Semaniks contains a prominent spot to feature these athletes. President Fry commented during the Semanik naming ceremony in 2015 that the family atmosphere in Drexel athletics was started by the Semaniks and is "a legacy that continues today." Mary also endowed the first women's coaching position in the history of the program, the Mary Semanik Head Coach of Woman's Lacrosse.

Title IX at Drexel

In 1896 the modern Olympic Games were reinstituted in Athens, Greece, but women were not invited. At the same time at the Drexel Institute in Philadelphia women were not only welcomed to study but also had the opportunity to play sports. Over the years, Drexel has consistently fielded women varsity teams, even though until recently the university's enrollment was mostly men. In the 1970s it was still common for athletics to be "segregated" by gender. In the PEAC, the south side of the building was reserved for women's offices and locker rooms and the north side for men. If you wanted to check out a towel, there were different towels marked for men's and women's use.

In 1972 Title IX legislation became a federal law that prohibits discrimination based on sex in educational programs. The law does not apply solely to sports, but it has received its most meaningful exposure in how colleges apply the legislation to athletics. As a result, Title IX has significantly advanced the opportunity for the participation of women and girls in organized school sports. Drexel Athletics has always had a proud tradition of broad-based participation and the 1972 Title IX legislation put a national spotlight on those efforts. Title IX was slow to arrive for most schools and their athletics programs. In Mary Semanik, however, Drexel had an administrator that embodied women's athletics. Not only was Mary an exceptional athlete, perhaps her most notable recognition came from *Lacrosse Magazine*, which named her to the All-Century Women's Lacrosse Team for the United States. But she was also an accomplished coach and administrator, having started at Drexel in the 1950s as a teacher and coach for multiple teams.

In 1979 *The Triangle* published a piece entitled, "Does Drexel Comply with Title IX?" Even as a private school, the law applies to Drexel because many students enroll who receive federal financial support. Noted *The Triangle* report, "Title IX compliance is in the hands of Vice President of Student Affairs Dean Joblin. It is his contention that at Drexel, there is definitely an equal athletic opportunity available to the women. The main point to this success is that there is a separate program offered to both men and women. There are separate departments, with separate and equal department heads. Each program has its own and equal facilities."[15]

The idea that separate programs signals progress is related to the fact that there was a belief that women's sports had to be protected, and that Title IX could not be applied if women's programs were administered through men's programs. Over time this notion was replaced with the idea of an integrated approach to have men and women be part of the same program, to create one identity as the Dragons, rather than the Dragons and the Lady Dragons. This process, however, has been slow. For example, it was only in the 1990s with the appointment of Lou Marciani as athletic director that the two athletic director titles, men's and women's, were combined. While the legislation of Title IX had its own trajectory, Drexel was fortunate to have had outstanding women coaching and administrative role models in Mary Semanik and then in her mentee Laura White. In 2015 White was appointed chair of the NCAA Men's and Women's Tennis Committee, the first Drexel athletics administrator in program history to act as the chair of any NCAA sport.

Drexel has been long recognized as a national leader in Title IX gender equity, diversity, and shared leadership among men and women. The

March 2002 *U.S. News and World Report* ranked Drexel athletics number one nationally in gender equity. In 2005, the Women's Law Project reported Drexel ranked among the top five of Pennsylvania's Best Large Schools for Athletic Equity in Opportunities. Drexel is among the few schools that have "done a very good job at providing equitable athletic opportunities for women,"[16] according to the report. And in 2008, the NCAA, which oversees 1,200 member institutions and over 300,000 student athletes, awarded Drexel University a Top 5 Award for Overall Excellence in Diversity. While much work remains in this area, Drexel athletics has been singled out for its efforts in being a national leader in Title IX.

Parallel to these developments have been recent successes of women teams. For example, Drexel's field hockey team under coach Denise Zelenak has had multiple NCAA appearances, Colonial Athletic Association (CAA) championships, and wins over national programs including Duke, Cal, and Stanford. In 2009, field hockey defeated fifth-ranked UConn in the NCAA tournament to advance to the Elite 8. Our women's soccer team, formed in the 1990s, gained international exposure by playing a rare game against the Democratic People's Republic of North Korea. Our women's rowing and basketball programs continue to have national relevance in their sports, and women's softball, swimming and diving, and lacrosse all field competitive programs.

The Greatest Games Ever Played in Drexel Athletics

College sports are often about the experience of very special moments that can last a lifetime. Over the years Drexel athletics has had its share of such highlights. Following is a compilation of the greatest games ever played in Drexel athletics.

The 1961 Undefeated Field Hockey Team

In 1961 the women's field hockey team registered its only undefeated and untied season in Drexel history. Coached by former All American and Drexel Hall of Famer Helen Callas Reiner, the Dragons won all eight matches that season and outscored their opponents by a 25–12 margin. Callas Reiner was a multisport standout and played on the basketball team, the field hockey team, and the softball team, before graduating from the school in 1957. Helen was one of the first great field hockey players at the school and was a starter on the 1957 U.S. women's national team. Helen still to this day attends field hockey games and cheers on the Dragons! Not surprisingly she was also a member of the cheerleading squad during her days as a student athlete at Drexel, which she said, playing and coaching, "Drexel gave me a start in life. I owe everything to Drexel!"

Women's Basketball

Chuck Pennoni suggested the 2013 WNIT championship was one of the greatest games ever played in Drexel history. "If you look at all of the teams—Florida, Harvard, Auburn, Utah, Iona and Princeton—that this team had to go through to win the postseason title and the fact that it is the only postseason women's basketball championship in Philadelphia, you have to pick that team and that event."[17] Drexel women's basketball coach Denise Dillon would not disagree. "The atmosphere was electric, the crowd was fantastic," Dillon said, recalling the game at the DAC. Playing from behind with less than a minute to go, basketball standout Hollie Mershon took over. She scored what proved to be the game-winning basket with twenty-one seconds remaining and sank both ends of a one-and-one to put Drexel ahead by three. Utah had one last chance, but a three-point shot at the buzzer hit the rim and the DAC went wild as

The Drexel women's basketball team celebrates its first ever WNIT national championship in 2013, after Utah's desperate three-point attempt at the DAC fell short. (Drexel University Athletics.)

*Crew team members, c. 1915. (Drexel University Archives. PC 3 Early
photographs of the Drexel Institute of Art, Science, and Industry.)*

Drexel won 46–43. "That was a great memory,"[18] Dillon said, as she and
the team rejoiced in an hour-long net-cutting ceremony on the floor of
the DAC.

The women's basketball team's epic win over Old Dominion at the
2009 CAA championships was another great moment. The Monarchs were
riding a fifty-two-game winning streak in CAA championship play and had
won sixteen consecutive CAA titles before the Dragons burst their bubble.
The team's monumental win over James Madison University to win the CAA
championship that same year and advance to the NCAAs for the first time
in program history is another milestone. That was a huge win and the first
postseason CAA title for the Dragons in any sport. The five-overtime win
in 2007 over Northeastern at the DAC, behind standout Gabriela "Gabi"
Marginean, was memorable for all who witnessed the four-hour marathon.
Drexel finally prevailed, winning 98–90, in the longest game in NCAA
Division I women's basketball history. "We were two points from a hundred-
point game and there would have been free cheesesteaks for everyone."
Marginean laughed. "I fouled out in the beginning of the fifth OT. I was
happy we won, but I almost had a triple double—forty-seven points,

Drexel rowers celebrate the announcement of winning the 2013
Dad Vail Regatta team championship on the grandstand located at the finish line
on the Schuylkill River. (Drexel University Athletics.)

twenty-two rebounds, and nine turnovers."[19] With the scoring total of forty-seven, she set the Philadelphia women's record for points in a game.

Drexel Crew

Drexel rowing has progressed a long way since its inception as a varsity sport in 1958. A January 1959 *Triangle* article promises a "workout on the river" to "anyone, frosh or upper classman, who wants a sport which requires a lot of energy, stamina, and conditioning." Drexel rowing's longevity rests on the shoulders of many excellent coaches, none more worthy of mention than Dr. Thomas "Doc" Kerr, the first rowing coach for Drexel. According to alum Ron Madden, Boathouse Row folklore is that "Doc" purchased an old eight-oar shell needing much work and brought it to his backyard in East Falls, where he restored it himself. Then he had eight Boathouse Row clubs donate one oar apiece and—presto—Drexel rowing was born! The mystique of the Dad Vail Regatta is part of the fabric of the history of Philadelphia rowing and the close-knit culture of rowing itself. In the year 2013, the seventy-fifth anniversary of the Dad Vail, the stage was set for all time feverish competition. Six eights qualified over two days of heats for the grand finale: Virginia, Michigan, Florida Institute of Technology (FIT), Drexel, Grand Valley, and Michigan State. That year, Drexel had entered twelve boats in the Dad Vail and advanced six crews to the Saturday afternoon finals, a first. Head coach Paul Savell, a former national champion at Wisconsin, had assembled a strong and deep team for that year's Vail. Under his tenure, Drexel won the 2010 Henley Women's Elite race in England, finished fifteenth at the 2015 IRA national championships, and won a 2013 title at the men's collegiate division of the prestigious Head of the Charles. The Drexel Dragons men's eight was fast, very fast . . . it had podium speed, but winning a title had eluded the Dragons in the past. Could it be that on the seventy-fifth anniversary of the Dad Vail that the fastest boat on the river that weekend is the team with "Dragons" on their blades and "Pride" written on their hearts? Yes!

Men's Basketball

Hoops standout Bob Buckley thought that a number of games might qualify as the greatest, "The month in 2005 when our basketball team went on a tear to post wins over St. Joe's, at Villanova, at Syracuse, and at Temple would be my pick." The Dragons also won at Creighton that year, which coach James "Bruiser" Flint thought was the greatest game he ever coached for Drexel. "The atmosphere was over the top,"[20] Flint said. Drexel had a nation-leading thirteen road wins that remarkable 2006–2007 season, but the bubble burst when the NCAA selection committee left the Dragons inexplicably out of March Madness as an at-large selection. The men's hoops team also posted a seismic win at Louisville in 2012, the first Cardinals loss in their new plush arena, the KFC (Yum!) Center.

Drexel's all-time baseball leader in triples, Sean Joyce, thought the 1996 men's basketball win over Memphis in the first round of the NCAAs in the famous Pit in Albuquerque, New Mexico, was a great moment, because it put Drexel "on the map." Malik Rose and the Bill Herrion–coached team came into the regional as the twelfth seed and disposed of the fifth seed and sixteenth-ranked Memphis Tigers for a NCAA March Madness Cinderella win. Anyone who watched the upset will never forget it. Malik Rose, who later won two NBA championship rings with the San Antonio Spurs, reflected on the 1996 game. "That game was so much fun," Rose said. "I remember we had so much anger built up inside of us. That whole week the players and fans from Memphis talked so much trash. Everywhere we went there, they were yapping. At the mall, at the hotel, around the arena, yap, yap, yap. By the time the game rolled around we had so much anger built up in us Memphis had no chance. We jumped on them from the tipoff and continued until the final horn blew. Still one of the best wins in my life!"[21]

The 83–80 men's win in 1987 at Penn's Palestra over then eighteenth-ranked Navy with "the Admiral," David Robinson, playing center for the Midshipmen and dropping forty-four points on the Dragons was another Drexel moment. The Palestra, where the game was played due to high ticket demand, is an iconic building and the Eddie Burke–coached Dragons

Malik Rose ('96) graduated from Drexel University with All-American honors after leading the Dragons to their only NCAA tournament win, over the University of Memphis, in 1996 in Albuquerque, New Mexico. (Source: Drexel University Athletics.)

notched an iconic win over Navy that day. Standout guard Michael Anderson, who was the first Drexel alum to play in the NBA, powered Drexel. The *Triangle* headline read, "Drexel Drydocks Navy." Guard Todd Lehman was quoted as saying, "It was the biggest basketball game I have ever played in my life!" Vice President for Student Affairs Arthur Joblin summarized the day as follows, "wonderful, wonderful, wonderful!"[22] As big as that game was, however, Michael Anderson felt the 1986 defeat of Hofstra in the ECC championship game at the Towson Center in Maryland was even greater. That win propelled Drexel to its first ever NCAA bid.

Men's Lacrosse: Mother's Day, Sunday May 11, 2014—Franklin Field

In 1941, Drexel Institute of Technology fielded its first lacrosse team under head coach Maury McMaines. Herman "Eppy" Epstein coached the team from 1948 to 1968 and made a particularly strong impression on the lacrosse team during his twenty-one years as a head coach at Drexel. He also served as assistant football coach and an associate professor of physical education. The latter was fitting because, at the core, Eppy was a teacher. His legendary methods ranged from highly theoretical discussions of strategy and positioning, to whacking an errant player across the backside with the lacrosse stick that he always carried for impromptu demonstrations of technique. Another coach who made a significant impact on the Drexel men's lacrosse team was Chris Bates. Bates's organizational and leadership skills served as the foundation to propel the Dragons into the national spotlight. He spent ten years as the head coach at Drexel (2000–2009) after serving four as an assistant (1995–1999). He won two Colonial Athletic Association regular season championships. Chris also led his team to the program's first ever win over a number one–ranked team when the Dragons knocked off Virginia in Charlottesville in 2007. Drexel freshman Colin Ambler scored his only two goals of the game in the final ten seconds. "The Virginia upset was a signature win for our program," Bates said. "Yes, it shocked the lacrosse world and got an enormous amount of publicity, but it was more important for our team, our athletic department, and our university to believe in the possibility of what our program could truly become. There was so much effort by so many people to build the foundation of a top Division I program. This game validated a lot of work over the years and provided the foundation for our program to springboard and become a consistent national contender. It was truly a great day to be a Dragon!"[23]

While Bates, who left Drexel to become the head coach at Princeton, was an offensive innovator, Drexel's current coach is one of the best defensemen ever to play. National Lacrosse Hall of Famer Brian Voelker took the program to new heights, and the 2014 season will go down as one of the best in school history. For the 2014 Drexel men's lacrosse team to reach the NCAA, it had to first prove its mettle in the CAA championships to qualify for the NCAA tournament. A CAA semifinal overtime win versus Towson at Vidas Athletic Complex set up the CAA final at thirteenth-ranked Hofstra. A win against Hofstra, a lacrosse powerhouse that had been to the NCAA national championships seventeen times, would gain Drexel its first trip to the eighteen-team NCAA tourney. Near the end of an amazing game, Drexel's goal in the third overtime gave the men's lacrosse team its first CAA title and automatic NCAA bid. And, perhaps just as important, the Drexel men's lacrosse team was now seriously "road-tested" for their first-round NCAA championship matchup with fourth-ranked Penn at Franklin Field on Mother's Day. The Dragons closed the first half with three goals in a span of 11.2 seconds to turn a two-goal deficit into a one-goal lead heading to halftime. What started as a gorgeous afternoon to showcase Philadelphia lacrosse on a national stage turned into a coming-out party for Drexel men's lacrosse as the Dragons won their first ever NCAA lacrosse tournament game, 16–11.

Drexel University Athletics Today

Drexel athletics has grown to become a vibrant and dynamic part of the campus that touches upon the pulse of our university's heartbeat. The recent

The Drexel University spirit team consists of cheerleaders, dancers, and Mario the mascot, all of whom are an integral part of the fan experience at all men's and women's home basketball games. (Drexel University Athletics.)

growth of athletics at Drexel only rivals that of the university as a whole. Today, over 450 Drexel student athletes compete in eighteen varsity sports; fourteen hundred students compete intercollegiately in thirty-four club sports; and two out of three students participate in intramural competition. In addition, over 700,000 students and members used the Daskalakis Athletic Center in 2015 for recreational programming, including aerobics classes, cardiovascular fitness, and strength and conditioning workouts. In 2015, Philly.com voted the Drexel Rec Center the City's best gym. The modern incarnation of the "Sports Fans of the 1950s" is the DAC Pack, composed of students who celebrate Drexel pride and spirit, which has grown to become one of the largest and most visible student organizations at Drexel.

Anthony Drexel's vision to welcome men and women to participate in education and athletic pursuits laid a foundation for a modern Drexel athletics department, one that is completely Title IX compliant. From A. J. Drexel's vision of education for all, a dynamic, competitive, and inclusive athletics department has evolved that celebrates athletic and academic excellence as well as recreational participation within the context of higher education. In 2016 Drexel's student athlete graduation success rate was 93 percent (national average 82 percent), its overall graduation rate was 82 percent (66 percent national average), and its total cumulative GPA for all student athletes was 3.28. This unprecedented development that has taken place at Drexel athletics reflects an integral part of a campus that is motivated by the modern student's expectations to engage in a healthy lifestyle and to be part of a community—a neighborhood within Drexel.

NOTES

1. *The Triangle*, April 29, 1955.
2. Helen Callas Reiner personal communication with Eric Zillmer, January 17, 2016.
3. *The Triangle*, April 29, 1955.
4. Vince Vidas personal communication with Eric Zillmer, April 2, 2015.
5. Judy Vidas personal communication with Eric Zillmer, January 16, 2016.
6. *The Triangle*, January 23, 1959.
7. "Remembering Don Yonker," *Soccer Journal*, November–December 1998, 14–15.
8. Igor Lissy personal communication with Eric Zillmer, January 14, 2016.
9. Dan Promislo personal communication with Eric Zillmer, January 18, 2016.
10. Robert Buckley personal communication with Eric Zillmer, December 22, 2015.
11. *The Triangle*, February 22, 1975.
12. Chuck Pennoni personal communication with Eric Zillmer, December 22, 2015.
13. Robert Buckley personal communication with Eric Zillmer, December 22, 2015.
14. John Fry, "We're Glad We Say No to College Football," *Wall Street Journal*, January 3, 2016.
15. *The Triangle*, November 16, 1979.
16. *Gender Equity in Intercollegiate Athletics: Where Does Pennsylvania Stand?* (Philadelphia: Women's Law Project, November 2005).
17. Chuck Pennoni personal communication with Eric Zillmer, December 22, 2015.
18. Denise Dillon personal communication with Eric Zillmer, January 15, 2016.
19. Gabriela Marginean personal communication with Eric Zillmer, January 20, 2016.
20. James "Bruiser" Flint personal communication with Eric Zillmer, January 15, 2016.
21. Malik Rose personal communication with Eric Zillmer, January 15, 2016.
22. *The Triangle*, January 23, 1987.
23. Chris Bates personal communication with Eric Zillmer, January 15, 2016.

Fight on for Drexel,
We've got the stuff we need to win this game
We're gonna fight on for Drexel,
Take the Dragon on to fame.
Fight on for Drexel,
The gold and blue is on another spree.
We're gonna fight, fight, fight, fight for Drexel U,
On to victory! (Four "D" yell and repeat chorus.)
"Four 'D' Yell" Chant
D-D-D-D
R-R-R-R
E-E-E-E
X-EL-X-EL
DREX-EL
DREX-EL
Fight—Team—Fight!!!

—"DREXEL FIGHT SONG," WRITTEN BY TODD GROO, '41,
AND GAY V. PIERCY, '39

7

Greek Life at Drexel

Michael Kelley and Anthony M. Noce

FRATERNITIES AND SORORITIES have been a consistent facet of student life at Drexel since the school's earliest days. Greek letter organizations, which have been in existence since the American Revolution, were present at most major colleges by the turn of the twentieth century. The earliest fraternal organizations at Drexel, about which little is known, were either primarily literary or supper clubs, possibly modeled on the secret societies of the Ivy League. Drexel's first known fraternity, founded in 1900, was Lambda Upsilon Delta (LUD), which described itself as "the only secret organization connected with the Drexel Institute." The last-known mention of LUD came in a list of student organizations from a 1908 issue of the campus magazine, the *Drexel Echo*. After LUD, Tau Rho Delta was established in 1905 and closed in 1915. Alpha Phi—the first fraternity known to have organized a campus-wide dance—was established in 1909 but had a short lived existence, closing in 1911. None of these early attempts at creating a fraternity or sorority at Drexel survived World War I.

In 1919 Drexel launched its co-operative education program, one of the first of its kind. Located at the nexus of a major transportation network, Drexel attracted commuter students who returned home after school to save money and fulfill familial obligations. Drexel also began attracting students who needed housing. Except for Van Rensselaer Hall, which opened in the 1930s, Drexel until 1967 had no student housing. Fraternities provided a safe and affordable housing option. Five fraternities and three sororities were

Freshmen students wearing Drexel dinks and name buttons.
(Drexel University Archives. PC 10 Chronological photographs.)

founded at Drexel as local organizations between 1919 and 1932 to fill the student housing void.

The first fraternities to be established in 1919 were Kappa Sigma Delta (KSD) (later, Pi Kappa Phi) and Phi Kappa Beta (later, Tau Kappa Epsilon). These fraternities shared a meeting room in Curtis Hall, whose namesake, Cyrus H. K. Curtis—founder of Curtis Publishing Company and a member of the Drexel board of trustees—was an honorary initiate of KSD. Alexander Van Rensselaer, second president of Drexel's board of trustees and the husband of Sarah Drexel Van Rensselaer; and Anthony J. Drexel Paul, the grandson of Anthony J. Drexel, were also honorary initiates. Kappa Phi Delta (later, Sigma Alpha Mu) was founded in 1921, followed by Alpha Upsilon Mu (later, Lambda Chi Alpha) in 1924 and Delta Sigma Alpha (later, Theta Chi) in 1927.

Drexel's first sororities were also established in the period after World War I. Phi Delta Mu was established in 1921; it became the Alpha Delta chapter of Sigma Sigma Sigma in 1926. Omega Delta Epsilon was established in 1922, and it became the Nu Nu chapter of Alpha Sigma Alpha in 1925. Kappa Delta Gamma, established in 1923, became a chapter of Delta

Sigma Epsilon national sorority in 1928, which was then merged into Delta Zeta in 1956.

Unlike the somewhat insular and secretive Greek organizations established prior to World War I, the fraternities of the new wave were prominent on campus. KSD was especially active; among its early initiatives was establishing the student newspaper that would later become *The Triangle*. Starting in the early to mid-1920s, fraternities began holding semi-formal dances in the Great Hall of Main Building, the first for which there is a record being the KSD Annual Tea Dance in 1926. Fraternities also put on elaborate original musicals. In a reflection of what was popular in the era, KSD's first musical was a minstrel show in 1932 reminiscent of Al Jolson's *The Jazz Singer* (1927) and *Mammy* (1930), including performers in blackface. Historical records suggest that the early minstrel shows evolved into Broadway-style musical shows written, produced, choreographed, and performed by the fraternity members. The "Pi Kapp Show" produced by Pi Kappa Phi ran continuously from 1939 to 1970 (with a break for the World War II Years) and produced over forty original shows, with titles such as *Graduation or Bust* (1947), *It's Still Moonshine* (1950), and *The Emperor Wears Bermudas* (1960). Some of the original show programs and recordings from the musical scores are housed in the Drexel Greek Archives.

Pi Kappa Phi show, 1940. (Drexel University Archives. PC 11 Academic photographs.)

An Inter-Fraternity Council (known as the IFC) was created in 1924 with faculty member "Doc" Hansen serving as the first advisor, and an Inter-Sorority Council was established in 1926. The IFC served as the liaison between fraternities and the school administration (still its most important function), and helped put together such things as a football league and the skit competitions known as "Keno" held every homecoming weekend.

Unlike the sororities established in the 1920s, all of which quickly became chapters of national organizations, Drexel's fraternities had no ties to national organizations or governing bodies until 1933, when Kappa Sigma Delta became the Alpha Upsilon chapter of Pi Kappa Phi National Fraternity. Three other fraternities followed suit: Phi Kappa Beta became the Alpha Tau chapter of Tau Kappa Epsilon National in 1939; Delta Sigma Alpha affiliated with Theta Chi National in 1940; and Alpha Upsilon Mu affiliated with Lambda Chi Alpha National in 1941. By contrast, Alpha Pi Lambda (known as "Apple Pi") was established in 1935 as an independent local fraternity with no national affiliations, as it remains today. Apple Pi quickly established itself on campus by holding a gala homecoming dance featuring the Don Brill Orchestra, in the same year the fraternity was established.

World War II resulted in a steady decline in fraternity membership across the country, and Drexel was no different. Only one sorority was established during the war: Sigma Omicron Pi (later Delta Phi Epsilon), in 1942. However, near the very end of the war, the Servicemen's Readjustment Act of 1944—the G.I. Bill—resulted in a wave of new college students and a revival of campus Greek life. As Regis Kubit, a Theta Chi brother and electrical engineering major from the class of 1955 recalled, "There was one thing about fraternities—there was competition, but we all stuck together. We all stuck together. And they were the social life at Drexel."[1] By 1950, with the addition of Phi Tau Delta (later Sigma Pi) in 1948 and Delta Kappa Rho (later Phi Sigma Kappa) in 1949, Drexel had eight fraternities, five of which were chapters of national organizations, and four sororities.

An example of the extravagance of the fraternity social events was in 1948, when Sigma Alpha Mu (known as "Sammy"), threw a "Grand Finale" gala in 1948 featuring Joe Grady and his seventeen-piece orchestra, known as the 950 Club. *The Triangle* described the event with the headline, "Sigma Alpha Mu sets a precedent at Drexel for Social Activities."

Between 1950 and 1971 five more fraternities and two more sororities were established, but only four of the fraternities survived. The fraternities were Phi Omega (later Delta Sigma Phi) in 1953, Alpha Beta Delta (later Tau Epsilon Phi) in 1954, Delta Iota (later Pi Lambda Phi) in 1962, Beta Nu in 1963 (closed in 1968), and Sigma Alpha Theta (later Sigma Alpha Epsilon) in 1966. The sororities were Phi Mu in 1954 and Omega Phi (later Phi Sigma Sigma) in 1959. Through the 1970s the twelve fraternities and four of the six sororities thrived. Delta Phi Epsilon and Sigma Sigma Sigma were dormant until 2004 and 2011, respectively.

Greek Housing

Between World War I and the late 1930s, fraternities and sororities leased houses in Powelton Village to provide housing for their members. In the early years, fraternities moved frequently and leased houses on an annual basis depending upon their housing needs. As the fraternities became more established, they began to seek more permanent housing. As the wealthy industrialists who built magnificent homes in Powelton Village left the city, these large homes were perfectly suited to house Drexel's fraternities. Pi Kappa Phi moved into the house at 3401 Powelton Avenue in 1939 (currently owned by Lambda Chi Alpha) and maintained the lease on the property throughout the war years by taking up a collection among the alumni. In 1939 Apple Pi purchased the "castle on the corner" at 216 North Thirty-Third Street. The house was built in the 1890s for Frederick A. Poth, a wealthy brewer and West Philadelphia development magnate, by architect A. W. Dilks, an apprentice of noted Philadelphia architect T. P. Chandler. The four-story, sixteen-room mansion still serves as the official residence of Apple Pi, and was added to the National Register of Historic Places in 1985. In 1946 Pi Kappa Phi purchased the house at 3405 Powelton Avenue, where it still remains today; 3405 Powelton was built by Joseph Wilson, the same architect who built Drexel's Main Building and what is now Ross Commons. Lambda Chi Alpha purchased 3401 Powelton Avenue in 1947, known as the George Burnham House, another property on the National Historic Register.

In 1952, TKE followed the lead of the other fraternities along Powelton Avenue by purchasing and moving into a historic Georgian-style mansion at 3421 Powelton Avenue, originally built for publisher Christian Febiger in 1898. Sigma Pi moved into TKE's former residence at 210 North Thirty-Fourth Street, which is today the home of both the Pi Kappa Alpha Fraternity and the Alpha Sigma Alpha sorority. SAM purchased the house at 3411 Powelton in 1958, and with that purchase the "Greek Row" along Powelton Avenue was complete. Throughout the 1950s and 1960s fraternities purchased homes along Thirty-Fourth Street south of Powelton Avenue and further expanded the "Greek Village" neighborhood. From the 1960s through the 1980s, the sororities shared the "PanHel" house, which was located at 208 North Thirty-Fourth Street.

While social life was a key contribution of the Greek system, the importance of fraternities and sororities as providers of student housing was paramount. At an institution like Drexel in the postwar years providing low-cost technical education was the top priority. Greek life helped to humanize the experience. David Paul was an electrical engineering graduate in the class of 1966, and a Sammy member—he remembered the importance of fraternities at an institution like Drexel:

> The lion's share of the actual classmate population were commuters. And, in fact, a lot of the people in the fraternity were commuters as well. But they would spend a lot of their day in the fraternity house. When they weren't in the classroom they were in the fraternity house, and wouldn't go home until late. So, I loved the fraternity house. I met so many people, and developed so many friendships and so many bonds. It was a true gift to be able to be in the fraternity house. And I thought I had a definite advantage, in that, basically, I had a built-in family where I lived. Whereas, if I had lived in an apartment or on campus in housing, I never would have achieved, you know, that kind of—that kind of situation, where fraternity brothers actually—we looked out for each other.[2]

Steve Plotkin, a 1963 graduate of the commerce and engineering program, recalled,

> In those days, you could live in the fraternity house as a freshman . . . admitted freshman . . . so I started school living in the Sammy House, 3411 Powelton Avenue. And they gave us rooms. And there were a number of other freshmen there—maybe ten or twelve— living in the house, with brothers. And after a period of, I think it was the first two or three quarters, then you'd become eligible to pledge, if they invited you. And I was invited and I became eligible, so I pledged. And you go through the usual hell in those days, and it was all very nice, good fun—nothing terrible, nobody died . . . [laughter] . . . and became a brother. And so that's how I got into the fraternity and I stayed in that fraternity house—except for my co-op periods—for the better part of four years.[3]

Regis Kubit's experience was similar, and speaks to the informality of admissions, and the need for students to be self-reliant when it came to managing their campus lives. Kubit arrived on campus in the late summer to find that there was no student housing for men:

> So, I signed up to go to Drexel. I don't know what was like a— maybe a Friday or something. So I said, "OK, where's the dorm?" . . . "We don't have a men's dorm. We only have a ladies' dorm." You'd have to stay in a rooming house or one of the fraternity houses. So they gave me a list of the fraternity houses and we went to, I guess, three of them and nobody was there. Nobody answered the door. And I got to the Theta Chi house and knocked and somebody answered the door. And they took house freshmen. And the guy says, "We have one room left." So I took that. That's how I became a Theta Chi. . . . Everybody here . . . nobody had any money, number one. So everybody was kind of, you know, all in the same boat.[4]

Murray Loew, a Sammy from the class of 1963, also recalled the importance of Greek life in keeping up with the grind of challenging classes: "The fraternity had all sorts of activities. Athletic, social . . . and, even when it came to, say, studying for exams, which was very helpful to do together, and at some point, the first-floor library of the fraternity house . . . was redone very nicely. We put in a big blackboard. And that was great, because when the time came to study for a physics test or whatever, all the people taking that course would gather in that room with the blackboard and work on problems together, and so on."[5]

Social Life and Expansion

Drexel's fraternities in the 1950s and 1960s were a generally positive force on campus. In 1952 Theta Chi, which was known as the athletes' fraternity, changed their "Hell Week" (the intense period of pledging before initiation) to "Help Week," during which they assisted in various community projects, for which they were honored by the Philadelphia Chamber of Commerce. At the same time, however, as one Theta Chi brother who graduated in 1956 remembered his experience with the fraternity, Pi Kappa Phi continued to put on annual musicals and Sammy continued with their annual "Sammy Week" charity event, capped by the social event of the year, the "Grand Finale" dance in the Grand Hall. Starting in the late

Students in the Great Court, with Ryder clock in the background, 1979. (Drexel University Archives. PC 12 Clubs and organizations photographs.)

1960s Tau Epsilon Phi created the annual TEP Distinguished American Award. Among the recipients were General Omar Nelson Bradley (former chairman of the Joint Chiefs of Staff) and scientist Jonas Salk.

In the 1950s Drexel's social life focused on the Great Court of Main Building. Regis Kubit, a Theta Chi brother and electrical engineer from the class of 1955, reflected: "All the fraternities had a spot in the court. And ours was the right-hand bottom of the steps, the right-hand corner . . . right there where you came down the steps and then you could go down into the auditorium. The Theta Chis hung out there. I think the TKEs hung out on the other corner, and the Lambda Chi, everybody had their spot. . . . And we were there because you could meet all the girls going up the steps."[6] A generation later the Great Court tradition continued, and it spilled out onto the "Green Beach." A Pi Kappa Phi member recalls these traditions, and the importance of the school-wide "lunch half hour," when no classes were scheduled:

> When everyone got together for lunch . . . every fraternity and sorority had their own meeting spot. . . . [There were] banners hanging down from the third-floor railing, when rush was going on, [and] everyone would have a banner painted really colorfully, very creative. They would list the rush events—the whole room was decorated. . . . In the courtyard outside of the main building, between that and what's now Lebow, that was of course Thirty-Second Street at the time, it was open . . . in front of Commonwealth Hall . . . there was basically grass and in the summer that was what was called the Green Beach. All the food trucks were lined up along Thirty-Second Street, and everyone was there and you would think you were at the beach—everyone had their spot with their group—a lot of camaraderie.[7]

Members working on the Pi Kappa Phi house,
1981. (Drexel University Archives. PC 12
Clubs and organizations photographs.)

By the late 1960s there were signs
that Drexel Greek life was changing with
the antiestablishment sentiment of the
era. The fraternities' focus on hosting
elaborate shows and concerts gave way
to the baby boomer generation and the
counterculture associated with the 1960s
and 1970s "Woodstock" generation.

The mid-seventies ushered in a new
growth in fraternity and sorority life.
The movie *Animal House* (1978) was
about a fictional fraternity that had no
morality. While actual fraternities, in-
cluding those at Drexel, did not demonstrate the intense, raucous behavior shown in the film, in many ways, many of the characters in the movie
were present somewhere in the fraternity system. Throughout the seventies
social life on Drexel's campus thrived in the fraternities. On any given
night, throngs of hardworking and dedicated students would gather at one
of the fraternity houses for a well-deserved nightcap or two, such as "Joe's
Bar and Grill" at Phi Sigma Kappa on Monday night, "Danny and Friends"
at Lambda Chi on Tuesday, "Dunes 'til Dawn" at Apple Pi on Wednesday
nights, the "Speakeasy" at Pi Kappa Phi, or "Hoosgow" at Sig Pi on Thursday night, and you could always find a band party on Friday nights at
TKE to kick off the weekend.

A Pi Kappa Phi member recalled the popular 1970s tradition of the
"May 10th Party":

> It started back in the '60s sometime. . . . May 10 every year the fra-
> ternities would get a permit from the city to close Powelton Avenue
> from Thirty-Fourth to Thirty-Fifth Street. All the cars would come
> off, the city would close off the street, and we'd pull up beer trucks
> with taps on the side, and on Pi Kappa Phi's porch we'd have bands
> playing all day long, and all night long, and it was just a big party,
> and it was wall to wall people, and it grew and grew and grew . . .
> 1979 was the last year of the May tenth party . . . some of the disc

jockeys on the radio knew about the party by then and they were advertising on the radio, it wasn't just Drexel, it was people from the city: "free beer and music, let's go!" That was the last block party that we had; it got out of control.[8]

Tough Years, and a New Era for Greek Life

Mirroring a national trend, during the 1980s nearly every fraternity at Drexel was placed on some kind of suspension or probation at least once, some as many as three or four times. The tumult of Greek life mirrored that of the larger university, which since the late 1980s had seen decreasing enrollments that by the 1990s threated Drexel's solvency. As university administrators struggled, a chapter of the traditionally Catholic Alpha Chi Rho was established, in 1992. As a new president, Constantine Papadakis, came in to revive the university in 1995, a chapter of the traditionally Jewish Alpha Epsilon Pi was established. Both perhaps suggested a return to a more values-based Greek life, as did the indefinite suspensions of Sigma Alpha Epsilon in 1997 (for hazing violations), and of Sigma Pi and Tau Epsilon Phi in 1999 (for undisclosed disciplinary violations). One fraternity member looking back remembers:

> In the late '90s through the early 2000s the administration at the time did not view fraternities well, and they were on a mission to kind of shut down fraternities. Almost every fraternity . . . at some point in time was closed down, for either a hazing violation, an alcohol violation . . . things that would have not been an issue in the '70s, '80s even early '90s all the sudden were issues now . . . they just saw . . . these guys are having parties and we're going to get in trouble so let's shut them down, and that led to a lot of people in the fraternity didn't really like Drexel too much during that period of time.[9]

At the turn of the twenty-first century, however, with the university growing again, there were increasing signs of a newly flourishing Greek system. One of the largest fraternities in the country, Sigma Phi Epsilon, established their PA-Beta Beta chapter at Drexel in 1999, and both Pi Kappa Alpha and Phi Kappa Psi opened chapters in 2001. In 2008, sensing that there were signs of a decline in membership, the alumni advisors to the fraternities and sororities formed the Drexel Inter-Fraternity Alumni Association (DIFAA). DIFAA was established to "serve as an advocate for undergraduate chapters of fraternities and sororities to university administration and the larger community, and to enhance the academic and social mission of fraternities and sororities at Drexel University." This was a welcome change, and marked a new era of cooperation between the Greek system and the university.

Drexel's fraternity and sorority alumni are the most active and engaged alumni affinity groups among all of its alumni. Many Drexel trustees who are Drexel alumni are members of fraternities and sororities. Each chapter has at least ten alumni who take an active role as advisors of their chapter. Drexel has always also maintained several chapters of multi-cultural Greek letter organizations who play an important role in keeping with Drexel's diversity and inclusiveness mission. Drexel today has twelve fraternities, six sororities, and ten Multicultural Greek Council fraternities and sororities, with more than 1,200 brothers and sisters. The Greek system is viewed as an asset to the university—fraternities and sororities provide student social life opportunities, and their retention rates, average grades, alumni engagement, and donations are higher than any other group on campus.

Looking back from 2016, it's almost impossible to imagine a time when the university relied on fraternities and sororities for its housing and for its social life. It's clear the university has changed a great deal; and yet, the traditions of Greek life at Drexel University remain strong, even if repurposed for a new era.

NOTES

1. Regis Kubit, interviewed by Robert Sieczkiewicz, university archivist, January 17, 2013. For additional materials on the history of Greek life at Drexel University, see "Drexel Fraternity and Sorority Life History," available at http://drexel.edu/studentlife/get_involved/fraternity_sorority_life/about/history/; *Drexel Echo*, *The Dusak*; *The Triangle* Collection, available at http://sets.library.drexel.edu/triangle and Drexel University Archives.

2. David Paris, interviewed by Robert Sieczkiewicz, May 1, 2013, Drexel University Archives.

3. Steve Plotkin, interviewed by Robert Sieczkiewicz, May 14, 2013.

4. Regis Kubit, interviewed by Robert Sieczkiewicz, January 17, 2013.

5. Murray Loew, interviewed by Robert Sieczkiewicz, June 7, 2013.

6. Regis Kubit, interviewed by Robert Sieczkiewicz.

7. Anthony Noce, interviewed by Scott Gabriel Knowles, December 15, 2015.

8. Ibid.

9. Ibid.

The "Jail House," The Lexerd, 1983. (Drexel University Archives.)

"Cavanaugh's Opened Doors"

Resident or commuter, faculty, staff, alumni or locals, everyone went to Cav's.

Come in late at night and you could run into Bernie Parent or any of the other Flyers stars from the '70's.

You knew where you were welcome by which door you were allowed to enter.

Ken McBride played the piano every Friday night in the restaurant. The bouncers were old and you needed enough money for dinner to get in.

The middle door led to the Old Man's Bar—open 24 hours for the shift workers at The Bulletin. *Students were never allowed in that door.*

The Jailhouse door was ours. Wednesday nights before Apple Pi's Dunes till Dawn. $2 pitchers and $1 for a whole pie.

Each fraternity had their chance to work the door and the bar. All you needed was your Drexel ID to enter. We did our homework and solved all the world's problems at the Jailhouse.

There were break-ups and make-ups, tears on our pillows and Karaoke before it was even popular. We danced on the bar without worry—no cellphones or internet back then.

We were all the same. Many of us were the first in our families to attend college and we were here to make the most of it.

But the most important door at Cavanaugh's was the back door on Ludlow Street. Day or night, whenever you knocked, owner and Theta Chi brother, Bill Pawliczek '61 would answer.

If you needed a place to study, a meal or a bed, Bill would let you in no questions asked. Many of us learned more at the Jailhouse than in class.

Thanks for the memories Bill, for the many doors you opened for us.

—CINDY LEESMAN, BS '83,
ASSOCIATE VICE PRESIDENT, ALUMNI RELATIONS

The Creative Impulse

Theater, Dance, Music, and the Artistic
Collections of Drexel University

Virginia Theerman

FROM ITS BEGINNINGS as a technical institute in 1891 through to the modern research university of 2016, Drexel has always balanced its priorities among art, science, and industry. Though known mainly for its engineering programs even today, the university continues to grow in the arts, particularly the performing and fine arts. Music, theater, and dance are a large part of the Drexel experience, open to all students regardless of major. Large holdings of fine and decorative art are also available to the entire university student body through the Drexel Collection and the Robert and Penny Fox Historic Costume Collection. This access to the arts, both in practice and in observation, was an extremely important part of Anthony Drexel's vision for the university, and remains central to the university's educational mission today.

The dramatic arts are intertwined with general performing arts history at Drexel from the beginnings of the university. The 1897 edition of *The Lexerd*, Drexel's yearbook, mentions "The Thespian Thirty" as a long-standing tradition of the mere five-year-old university and describes the production of two plays per year as the usual.[1] By 1916, a separate Young Men's Society and Young Women's Society made up Drexel dramatics, though World War I and the influenza epidemic of 1918 greatly reduced numbers and forced them to combine. In 1925, the Dramatic Club joined up with the Inter-Collegiate Dramatic Association, and then reorganized yet again in 1927 as the Rouge and Robe, an honorary dramatic fraternity accessible for entry via a

Students with their work in the Department of Fine and Applied Art, c. 1900. (Drexel University Archives. PC 3 Early photographs of the Drexel Institute of Art, Science, and Industry.)

point system earned through the actions of the Dramatic Club. In 1935, the Rouge and Robe became part of Alpha Psi Omega, a national dramatic fraternity, and in a slightly confusing twist the Dramatic Club took the name of the Rouge and Robe.[2]

From 1947 through 1955, the Rouge and Robe partnered with Drexel's glee clubs and orchestra to produce operettas, including the *Pirates of Penzance*. During this time, Alpha Psi Omega and Rouge and Robe also produced two three-act plays and three one-act plays over the course of the academic year. However, interest in these clubs seemed to be waning. By 1963, both dissolved, and a new club rose up in their place: the Drexel Players. After several years of changing performance spaces, the Mandell Theater was built in 1973 as part of the new MacAlister Hall and became the permanent home of Drexel Players' productions.[3]

In 1979 Dr. Alfred Blatter created the broader Department of Performing Arts, including the creation of minors that formalized the academic aspects of the theater productions. The 1980s and 1990s brought further formalization to the department, including mixed casts of student and professional actors and the permanent hire of a technical director for the Mandell Theater. Today, the expansion of facilities to the URBN Annex Black Box Theater has allowed for the establishment of the Co-Op Theater Company, a resident theater company that produces ten shows a year, as well as the Mandell Professionals in Residence Project, which brings professional actors to Drexel as both colleagues and teaching professionals for young, aspiring theater professionals.[4]

The performing arts department has also benefitted over the years from the presence of dance programs at Drexel. The study of dance dates back to the early years of the university, when students practiced Delsartean dance exercises as a part of early physical education. Women at the university had their own gymnasium on the fourth floor of the Main building, and photography dated to around 1911 shows them completing these dance-like exercises in bloomer outfits. Though a formalized program in dance would not evolve until later in the twentieth century, the university has had a long history of formal dances hosted by various Greek life organizations, the YMCA, as well as the engineering and business societies. In 1978 the student dance ensemble was formed as an extracurricular activity open to all majors at the university by audition. The former archery gallery in the Rec Center was given over for a rehearsal space, and the new Mandell Theater was used for performances.[5]

In 1992 after the resignation of the director of the ensemble, performing arts director Blatter looked to cut the dance program in order to balance the departmental budget. Work-study student and dance ensemble senior Jan Sherman, charged with writing the memo to the president of the university about this choice, went into action. She was the current president of the Student Government Association, and together with an incoming freshman student and aspiring dancer named Dianne Certo, petitioned university president Richard Breslin to maintain the program. He used funds from his discretionary account to save the program and hired dance artist-in-residence Miriam Giguere as the director of the ensemble. In 1992 the ensemble had fourteen dancers and no daytime classes, but by 1996 the ensemble had doubled in size and demand for a minor had started.[6]

In 1997, several students in the dance ensemble came together to create a petition for more studio space and a full-time faculty hire. These students also encouraged *The Triangle* to run a feature piece about the lack of support for dance at Drexel, and six of their parents called in to demand more university funding. These combined efforts, although unorthodox and somewhat unappreciated by the administration, were effective. Additional studio space was created and dubbed the Ellen Foreman studio within Mandell, and in 2013 the former women's gym on the fourth floor of the Main building was also allocated to dance, now housed within the Westphal College of Media Arts and Design. Dr. Giguere and the growing staff developed a dance major at Drexel, focused on the niche field of the intersections between dance and health inspired by the 1997 merger with MCP Hahnemann University.[7] Within the major, established in 2008, students can work toward three goals; either dance/movement therapy, dance in education, or physical therapy, allowing for a diversity of career options within the dance field.[8]

Today, the dance department at Drexel comprises three main ensembles open to all majors, as well as a dance major and minor with courses serving 350 students across the university every quarter. The Dance Ensemble and FreshDance Ensemble each produce two yearly concerts choreographed by faculty, visiting professionals, and students. The Fresh-Dance ensemble is composed entirely of freshman at Drexel, allowing them an opportunity to experience the program as a united incoming class. The smaller Youth Performance Exchange Touring Ensemble takes Drexel Dance out into the community, working with youth across Philadelphia.[9] Even students who are not enrolled in dance classes or within the dance ensembles can still be a part of dance at Drexel through the annual Performance Charrette program. This collaboration invites students of all backgrounds to contribute their creative skills toward a weekend production of a multimedia performance/design.[10] The mixing of skill sets and majors speaks to the Drexel tradition of multifaceted students who look outside of their major and choose to be a part of other Drexel groups, whether in theater, dance, or a musical ensemble.

Music has always been an integral part of Drexel. The original main building auditorium was offered as a rehearsal space for the Philadelphia Chorus at its opening, and the the Drexel Chorus was founded in 1893. There was also an early Department of Evening Classes in Choral Music.[11] Even after this department was dissolved, recreational music education remained a constant throughout Drexel history, including the Drexelians, a band organized in 1927 to play more contemporary dance music.[12] Drexel still today houses one of the finest organs in Philadelphia, installed through the gift of Cyrus H. K. Curtis, noted publisher, in 1928.[13] The 1930s brought the organization of men's and women's glee clubs. Highly influential was the work of Wallace D. Heaton Jr., who served as the music director at Drexel from 1942 to 1979.[14] He led the Varsity Singers, a group of student singers at Drexel that toured the Northeast and even made a trip to Europe for performances.[15]

In 1979, Dr. Alfred Blatter became the head of the Music Department, and broadened its scope to create the Department of Performing Arts.[16] Throughout many evolutions, including student groups, the ROTC band, glee clubs, and other groups of musically inclined students, Drexel has fostered the musical community. Today, that community includes five different choral ensembles. One of these groups, the University Chorus' Chamber Singers, led by performing arts department head Steve Powell, performs music from the Renaissance at the annual Madrigal dinner. This performance, now in its twenty-sixth year, combines a traditional Renaissance feast, a musical performance, and theatrical sketches.[17] Student ensemble bands at Drexel include the concert band, fusion band, guitar ensemble, jazz orchestra, Mediterranean ensemble, pep band, percussion ensemble, rock ensemble, and the university orchestra as well as

Members of the Varsity Singers pose in front of the Main Building. (Drexel University Archives. PC 10 Chronological photographs.)

Antoinette and Ray Westphal, pictured here with the famous Rittenhouse Clock in 2003, met as students at Drexel and never forgot the university. In addition to naming the College of Media Arts and Design, they contributed to the restoration of the A. J. Drexel Picture Gallery. (Office of University Communications.)

student-run a cappella groups.[18] Support for students in the music programs comes from performing arts scholarships, as well as from the Moss Memorial Fund, a fund set up in memory of Dr. Myron Moss, scholar of African-American composers, as well as devoted professor and band director within the Drexel music program.[19]

The Westphal College of Media Arts and Design has also evolved majors in music industry as well as entertainment and arts management, in addition to minors in music and performing arts.[20] Westphal is the home of the Mad Dragon Music Group, which includes an award-winning independent record label, Mad Dragon Records, as well as the branches Mad Dragon Media, Mad Dragon Live, Mad Dragon Publishing, and Mad Dragon Artist Management.[21] Westphal also holds the Audio Archives, which contains 6,200 master tapes from Sigma Sound Studios, an early Philadelphia recording studio. These tapes include recordings of bands popular in the Philadelphia music scene of the 1960s, '70s, and '80s, including well-known artists such as David Bowie.[22] The value of this resource to current students is immeasurable, providing historical context, musical inspiration, and a window on the creative process of other artists.

Although the archive of Sigma Sound Studios was only acquired in 2005, Drexel has a long history of collecting creative works with the intent of educating and inspiring students of the present and future. In 2013, "Highlights of the Drexel Collection," an exhibition in the new Pearlstein Gallery in the URBN Annex, put the long history of collecting at Drexel on display. Showcased were the many collections of Drexel, including the Audio Archives, the Drexel University Archives, and the Drexel Collection, among others.[23] With incredible foresight for the education of his future students in mind, A. J. Drexel had set aside funds for the purchase of decorative and fine arts from the inception of the university in 1891. Among the early purchases made by Drexel president James MacAlister were textiles, fine china, silver, and many other examples of European art and craftsmanship. This collection would become known as the Museum of the Drexel Institute, a repository for works of art that the students were able to view and use as inspiration in their studies.[24]

The collection of historic dress, first suggested in 1898 by Howard Pyle, director of the School of Illustration, would grow through generous donations from Philadelphia society as a subcategory of the Museum of the Drexel Institute. In the 1940s the accumulation of many fine examples of textiles and historic costume would lead to the creation of the separate Drexel Historic Costume Collection.[25] This costume collection would be run by Mary Brenneman Carter from 1954 through the 1970s, who would establish systematic management and create official protocols in the style of museums of the day. Working with Mrs. Anne Lincoln, a prominent businesswoman and the founder of Nan Duskin specialty shop of Philadelphia, Carter would petition designers of New York City and well-known persons throughout the world to donate to Drexel.[26] Their most significant acquisition in this period was a coral-encrusted raffia gown designed by Hubert de Givenchy for Her Serene Highness Princess Grace of Monaco, donated by the princess in 1969.[27]

Following Mary Carter's retirement, the collection entered a dormant period, although growth through donations would continue and ultimately build a collection of nearly 14,000 garments, textiles, and objects of dress. In 2008 a professional curator, Clare Sauro, was hired to take over the collection. She would supervise the construction of a new state-of-the-art storage facility and coordinate the move from Nesbitt Hall to the URBN Center, the new home of Westphal College.[28] An initial gift of $1 million from Robert and Penny Fox earmarked for collection development and support has now been supplemented with an additional gift of $2 million following the incredible success of the 2015 inaugural exhibition "Immortal Beauty: Highlights from the Robert and Penny Fox Historic Costume Collection."[29] The collection continues to grow and to serve as an educational tool and place of inspiration for students across the fashion design, design and merchandising, history, film, and museum leadership programs.[30]

The original Museum of Drexel Institute, now known as the Drexel Collection, today is housed on the third floor of the Main Building, where its holdings can be seen on rotating display, as well as in other gallery spaces on campus. The initial purchases made by James MacAlister have been joined by the art collection of A. J. Drexel's father, Francis Martin Drexel; the painting collection of Lankenau Medical Center trustee and president John D. Lankenau; and clocks and watches donated by the wife of publisher George W. Childs. Mrs. George W. Childs's donation includes the famous David Rittenhouse Astronomical Musical Clock, a masterwork of craft, which tells the time, month and day, the location of the planets, esoteric astronomical phenomena, and plays ten separate musical chimes.[31] Today, the Drexel collection holds more than 6,000 works of art, including European prints and drawings, Japanese woodblock prints, paintings, sculpture, furniture, silver, porcelain, and clocks and watches. Overseen by Lynn Clouser, assistant director, the collection maintains its mission to pursue the preservation, proper management, and documentation of this educational collection of fine and decorative arts.[32]

Since its inception, Drexel University and its esteemed founder A. J. Drexel have supported the arts as a valuable part of the modern education. Though the performing arts programs and various collections of fine and decorative arts have waxed and waned over the 125 years of Drexel history, the dedication to their preservation and the dedication to the student of the future have constantly been present. While always holding true to the balance of art, science, and industry, Drexel has markedly increased its options for students in pursuit of creative work into the twenty-first century, offering a wide array of artistic collections, diverse course work, and varied student ensembles for the inspiration and aspirational work of its students.

NOTES

1. *The Lexerd* (Philadelphia: Drexel University, 1897).

2. Samantha Wend, "Timeline and History of Theater at Drexel," overview guide and timeline of the history of Drexel theater, research notes (Philadelphia, 2015), 1–7; Edward D. McDonald, *Drexel Institute of Technology 1891–1941: A Memorial History* (Philadelphia: Haddon Craftsmen, Inc., 1942), 263–67.

3. Wend, "Timeline and History of Theater at Drexel."

4. "Mandell Theater," Westphal College of Media Arts and Design, available at http://drexel.edu/westphal/resources/MandellTheater/. "Mandell Professionals in Residence Project (MPIRP)," Westphal College of Media Arts and Design, available at http://drexel.edu/westphal/resources/MPIRP/.

5. Miriam Giguere (director, dance program) conversation with the author, January 2016.

6. Ibid.

7. "Drexel University College of Medicine History," Drexel University College of Medicine, http://drexel.edu/medicine/About/History/.

8. Miriam Giguere conversation with the author, January 2016.

9. "Dance Overview," Drexel University Performing Arts, http://drexel.edu/performingarts/dance/overview/; "Dance," Westphal College of Media Arts and Design, available at http://drexel.edu/westphal/undergraduate/DANC/.

10. "The Performance Charrette," Westphal College of Media Arts and Design, available at http://drexel.edu/westphal/undergraduate/DANC/PerformanceCharrette/.

11. Holly Frisbee and Phoebe Kowalewski, UR.04.006, Department of Performing Arts Records, Bulk, 1957–1967, Drexel University Libraries Drexel History Finding Aids, available at https://idea.library.drexel.edu/islandora/object/idea%3A5090.

12. McDonald, *Drexel Institute of Technology 1891–1941*.

13. Thomas A. Greene in conversation with Dean Disque and William Sylvano Thunder, "The Drexel Organ" (a short history of the donation of the Drexel organ, Philadelphia, August 12, 1948), 1.

14. Frisbee and Kowalewski, UR.04.006, Department of Performing Arts Records, Bulk, 1957–1967.

15. "Varsity Singers, European Tour Performance between 1957 and 1963," letters and leaflet records of Varsity Singer activities (Philadelphia, 1957–1963).

16. Miriam Giguere conversation with the author, January 2016; Frisbee and Kowalewski, UR.04.006, Department of Performing Arts Records, Bulk, 1957–1967.

17. "Chamber Signers," Drexel University, available at http://deptapp08.drexel.edu /chorus/chamber_singers.htm.

18. "Music Overview," Drexel University Performing Arts, available at http://drexel .edu/performingarts/music/overview/.

19. "Moss Memorial Fund," Drexel University Performing Arts, available at http:// drexel.edu/performingarts/about/moss-memorial-fund/; "In Memoriam: Myron 'Mike' Moss," Drexel University Performing Arts, available at http://drexel.edu/westphal/news /archive/2012/2012_07_23_Myron_Moss/.

20. "Music Industry," Westphal College of Media Arts and Design, available at http:// drexel.edu/westphal/undergraduate/MIP/; "Music," Westphal College of Media Arts and Design, available at http://drexel.edu/westphal/minors/MUSC/.

21. "About Mad Dragon," Mad Dragon Music Group, Drexel University, available at http://www.maddragonmusic.com/about/#mad-dragon-music-group.

22. Alissa Falcone, "How Did Drexel End Up with Rare David Bowie Recordings?" Drexel University, October 6, 2014, available at http://drexel.edu/now/archive/2014 /October/Bowie-Archives/.

23. "Highlights of the Drexel Collection," Westphal College of Media Arts and Design, available at http://drexel.edu/westphal/news/archive/2013/2013_04_15_Grand _Exhibition_of_Drexel_Holdings/.

24. "The Drexel Collection," Drexel University, available at http://drexel.edu /DrexelCollection/.

25. "The Robert and Penny Fox Historic Costume Collection," Westphal College of Media Arts and Design, available at http://drexel.edu/westphal/resources/FHCC/.

26. Clare Sauro (curator, FHCC) conversation with the author, January 2016.

27. Clare Sauro, "Immortal Beauty" press kit (information on the collection as distributed to the press before upcoming exhibition, Philadelphia, 2015), 1–3.

28. Clare Sauro conversation with the author, January 2016; and Clare Sauro, "FHCC Brochure" (brochure of information on the collection, Philadelphia, 2015), 1–2.

29. "Drexel's Fox Historic Costume Collection Receives $2 Million Gift from Robert and Penny Fox," Westphal College of Media Arts and Design, available at http:// www.drexel.edu/now/archive/2016/January/Fox-Gift/.

30. Clare Sauro conversation with the author, January 2016.

31. "Curator Pick of the Month: August 2015: Tall-Case Astronomical Clock," Drexel University, available at http://drexel.edu/DrexelCollection/view/Curator-Pick/.

32. "The Drexel Collection."

Drexel Institute College Bowl team, 1963.
(Drexel University Archives. PC 8 Events photographs.)

I had applied to graduate school, I was ready to go to graduate school, and then the G.E. College Bowl *happened, which was a national quiz program in New York. They would bring two different college teams in each week, have a quiz contest, and the winner of the contest would come back for another week. You could win up to five times, and then they retired the team and brought in two new teams. This was on television, on CBS; in fact I think it was the same theater that they just refurbished for Stephen Colbert and his program, and Drexel was asked to send a team and so they went around to ask the professors, "Who would be your obvious players?" and they went 0-20, because nobody they suggested would go on the team. Meanwhile, all of these ringers are going into the thing, just because we said "that's a great idea!" and we took this test, it was a long test, and then they started weeding us out and started practicing with us and finally we won, and that changed my whole life. We ended up winning five games. We went up against Mississippi State, Simmons College in Boston, Texas Tech, Knox College (the Quaker college in Illinois), and West Virginia University. They weren't powerhouses, well, Knox was a good school, but we had people coming from all areas. We were all retreads essentially, and with this knowledge, however we got it—because none of us could ever figure out how we ended up knowing this stuff—we just did very well. We had different areas covered. One guy was a chemist, one guy was a mathematician, I was an engineer, but I was beginning to get more interested in history. I became the expert on art from reading a book, I didn't know anything before that; but you could flash a painting in front of me and I could tell you who painted it, and if you gave me enough clues I could tell you when, too. When we won, the university went crazy over the victory. The experience of winning the College Bowl changed my life.*

—RICHARD ROSEN

9

The Past and Future of the Library
at Drexel University

DANUTA A. NITECKI

DREXEL'S LIBRARY is one of the university's longest operating departments. Created in 1891 and first located in one room in the Main Building, the library reflected a shifting emphasis, from conserving and protecting books, to enabling and encouraging faculty and students to use those books. Throughout its history, Drexel's library has followed the objectives of providing students and faculty a reliable place to read, collecting publications and other information resources to support education and research, and providing expert guidance to find them.

In this chapter I highlight the past and suggest a future for the Drexel Libraries,[1] as perceived from the early twenty-first century and in the context of four strategic directions the library is pursuing to meet the challenges of the foreseeable future: (1) ensuring access to authoritative information, (2) building learning environments, (3) strengthening connections to scholarship, and (4) modeling a responsive library organization.

Context for Creating a Library for Drexel

The focus from information acquisition to access that began to transform libraries in the late nineteenth century continued through the twentieth century. This transition reflected recognition of the need to provide effective

Main Building Library, delivery desk, 1901. (Drexel University Archives. PC 3 Early photographs of the Drexel Institute of Art, Science, and Industry.)

and personalized service as well as instruction in the use of the library and reference materials. It became accepted that books should be classified according to subject and not according to fixed shelf locations. Each book was to be listed with an adequate bibliographic description and this information was to be made easily available to users by author and subject. Cooperation with other libraries was seen as advantageous for borrowing materials. Hours were extended and facilities improved to provide a comfortable work environment for students from early morning to late evening on weekdays and for some hours on weekends. Financing the library became an accepted responsibility of the parent institution. Placing books on reserve for use by students in a particular course was a new practice. Book catalogs of materials held by individual institutions or by groups of libraries were published to facilitate the sharing of resources.[2]

The library for the new Drexel Institute embodied this vision, and it also served as the laboratory for the country's third library school, founded in 1892 by Drexel's library director Alice B. Kroeger.[3]

A student of the renowned Melvil Dewey (known especially for his development of a decimal classification system used by libraries to organize their collections by subject), Kroeger brought innovative ideas to Drexel. She directed both the library and the accompanying professional training program for library workers until her sudden death in 1909 at the age of forty-five. During its first year, the Department of the Library and Reading Room built a collection of nearly 8,000 volumes of books, periodicals, manuscripts, photographs, and slides, primarily through gifts and donations from Anthony J. Drexel and his business partner George W. Childs. A cataloging specialist, Kroeger was a member of the American Library Association's Catalog Rules Committee, established in 1901 to create the first code of rules for cataloging, and which later helped the Library of Congress to be an agency to distribute printed catalog cards.[4] Standardizing cataloging rules and methods laid the foundation for cooperation among libraries, most notably through interlibrary loan services.

TABLE 9.1: DREXEL LIBRARY DIRECTORS	
Directors of the library as well as the library school program:	
1891–1909	Alice B. Kroeger
1909	Mary Salome Cutler Fairchild (acting director)
1910–1912	June Richardson Donnelly
1912–1914	Corinne Bacon
Directors of the library during the temporary suspension of the library school:	
1914–1917	Elizabeth V. Clark
1917–1922	J. Peterson Ryder
Directors of both the library and the library school after its reestablishment:	
1922–1936	Anne Wallace Howland
1936–1949	Marie Hamilton Law
1949–1958	Harriet D. MacPherson (and Harry Dewey as librarian of Drexel Institute)
1958–1962	John F. Harvey
Directors of the library after its separation from the library school:	
1962–1964	Robert Johnson
1964	Frances Wright (acting)
1964–1989	Richard L. Snyder
1989–1990	William L. Page and Lucille Jones (acting co–directors)
1990–1995	Eileen Hitchingham
1995–1998	William Page (interim)
1998–2005	Carol Hansen Montgomery
2005	John Wiggins (interim)
2005–2008	Jane Bryan
2008–2009	Dorothy Schwartz (interim)
2010–	Danuta A. Nitecki

Twenty librarians have succeeded Kroeger as director (Table 9.1), and I am the current dean of libraries, charged with reinventing the library for the first part of the twenty-first century. The campus strategic plan through 2009 had only historic mention of the library, and awareness of the library's potential to contribute to the university's ambitious plans to become a major academic enterprise was low.[5] Some even questioned the need for a library. In a 2005 profile of Drexel's president, Constantine Papadakis, the *Wall Street Journal* reported that he was "averse to raising the annual budget for Drexel's library" and admittedly exaggerated to make a point that "spending too heavily on books, periodicals and the buildings that house them is a waste in the digital era."[6] That same year, however, Papadakis issued a letter to distribute an article describing the library's "fast-track migration to an electronic journal collection," authored by the dean of libraries Carol Hansen Montgomery,[7] in which he notes:

Our electronic library initiative met with some resistance but the initial challenges have been eclipsed by the benefits, both academic and financial. . . . The timeliness of library services has increased, and Drexel has been able to offer library resources to geographically scattered students on our two new health sciences campuses and in our online courses. Integration with online courseware, instructor's Web sites and the library's reserve system has raised the level of service and convenience for faculty and students, and the breadth and currency of information available to our researchers have vastly increased. . . . Each year, college students and faculty become more technologically savvy, and their expectations for information services increase. Because of our early commitment to electronic holdings, Drexel is well positioned to meet the needs of this "wired" population in the years to come.[8]

With his presidency in 2010, John Fry introduced a new strategic planning process. I was invited to create a plan for the library and given the absence of a shared library vision at the university, I initiated a "future search" process that culminated in a three-day conference involving nearly sixty stakeholders representing students, faculty, administrators, support staff, external friends, library staff, and information specialists. The outcomes included an improved understanding of the potential of, and challenges for, the library in advancing Drexel's mission; recognition of the value to collectively advocate for the library; and enthusiasm for the library as a place for connectivity.[9] From the many ideas generated in the planning process, we articulated four strategic directions that have since guided our tactical plans,[10] and which continue the library's evolution, from an organization that manages space and books, to one that facilitates learning and the creation of new knowledge. Each of the strategic directions are discussed in turn below.

Ensuring Access to Authoritative Information

Since access to information had long required the close proximity of readers to physical publications, accreditation assessments have traditionally counted volumes to establish a library's worth and contribution to education and research. The electronic availability of information has at least partially replaced the physicality of collections; purchased ownership has been increasingly replaced by licensed permission to access textual publications as well as other formats, including audio, visual, and data. Pricing models provided by publishers and information vendors, as well as packaged deals negotiated for consortium members, have created a complex challenge for librarians to optimize expenditures to ensure access to authoritative information in support of learning, teaching, research, and service.

Having volumes on shelves was never enough to ensure that faculty and students could find what they sought for their work. Drexel's earliest librarians were among the leaders in devising cataloging practices to improve access not only to what was sought but also to browse adjacent spines to stimulate the exploration of related content. In the 1960s, Drexel began to develop a computerized serials list that, in collaboration with the University of Pennsylvania, evolved into a printed list of science and technology titles acquired by both institutions.[11] A major conversion, also in the 1960s, from the Dewey decimal to the Library of Congress classification system, enabled Drexel librarians to catalog 35 percent more titles in 1967–1968 than in the previous academic year.[12] To share the burden of cataloging, Drexel in the 1970s joined the Ohio College Library Center (OCLC) and other groups to share not only bibliographic records, but also the volumes themselves. To this day, the library continues to be an active participant in resource sharing programs such as E-Z Borrow, OCLC WorldCat, and reciprocal library use for researchers with the University of Pennsylvania. Contemporary librarians also extend their expertise to communities beyond campus by improving electronic discovery of and access to local Philadelphia-based resources such as recordings of WHYY's *Fresh Air with Terry Gross*.[13]

Building local collections is a major expenditure in terms of both purchase costs and staff time spent selecting and processing appropriate titles. Acquisition funds come primarily from the university and are allocated by subject groupings. Library director Richard Snyder (1964–1989) included in his annual reports a calculation of the library's budget as a percentage of the university's budget, which went from 3.46 to 3.3 percent between 1961 and 1967 (though the library budget went up in absolute terms in those same years). The contemporary library receives a total budget that is approximately 1 percent of the university's total budget. Approximately half of the library's budget goes to build collections and to maintain licensed access to electronic resources, with the latter increasing in cost at approximately 7 percent annually—far more than inflation or tuition.

Snyder argued for new space in part on the basis of the library's anticipated growth in its collections; in his 1970–1971 annual report he acknowledged that "the cry has changed from predicting to nagging," and that efforts to initiate a building program made in fall 1967 were to no avail. Yet a new impetus for increasing library space was provided by the

Pennsylvania Department of Public Instruction's review of the library as part of its larger review stemming from the request to change the name of Drexel from an institute of technology to a university. Snyder described the challenge libraries have faced to build physical collections adequate to meet increasing demands for information:

> Although Drexel had made notable strides in its collection building, the Department's review questioned the adequacy of the collection size to support a University offering Ph.D. programs in eight engineering and science fields. The paucity of the collection was known to the Library staff, for it had been found wanting compared to several existing professional guidelines. An extended period of inadequate Library support and a rapid change in the role of Drexel from an undergraduate to a graduate and research institution had taken its toll. In the mean time, the optimum density of volumes per square foot had long since been passed. . . . Obviously a new building was required for collection, service, and staff to continue essential rapid growth. The President therefore verbally authorized action on a building program, late in 1969.[14]

Under Carol Montgomery's leadership, a major paradigm shift in collections was reflected in the library's 2004–2006 strategic plan. Montgomery described a vision and roadmap for Drexel's twenty-first-century library as an "information hub." The primary goal was to "migrate from a print to an electronic paradigm as quickly as possible" by acquiring serial back files, increasing purchases of electronic books, purchasing collections rather than individual items whenever feasible, evaluating and implementing efficient and innovative user-mediated document delivery services, and leveraging existing relationships with information industry and society vendors.[15] The trend she established to "go digital" early among academic libraries has resulted in current collection expenditures that go almost exclusively (98 percent) for licensing access to electronic resources.

The library has also been responsible for preserving and making available Drexel-related materials through its role as the university archives. Though periodic news items refer to exhibits featuring a special collection received or discovered, there has not been a strong focus on building the archives, and the library does not formally coordinate other archive collections across the university. The university's acquisition of a medical school in 2002 came with a rich archive, reflecting the history of the College of Medicine and its predecessor institutions (primarily the Woman's Medical

College of Pennsylvania and Hahnemann University); the medical college's Legacy Center is especially strong on the histories of women in medicine and of homeopathic medicine, dating back to the mid-nineteenth century. Similarly, Drexel's affiliation with the Academy of Natural Sciences (ANS) extends the university's association with the nationally significant ANS historic archive and specialized collections. Though these are managed independently of the library, cooperative efforts have improved access to collections through inclusion of bibliographic records for the cataloged collections of ANS in the library's online catalog.

On the horizon is the expected increase of data sets created by Drexel researchers. Beginning with Montgomery's strategic goal to develop unique archival digital collections, University Archives has maintained an institutional repository (IDEA) used primarily to preserve digital theses and dissertations. Initiatives are underway to offer faculty guidance and opportunity to meet increasingly common requirements from federal funders to make research data available to others. IDEA is expected to be one of several venues within an envisioned federated system of repositories that will preserve and facilitate global access to research data sets.

Building Learning Environments

Shortage of library space has been a repeated observation throughout Drexel's history, coupled with the evolving role of the library as a place. Several *Triangle* articles during the 1930s described facility changes to increase use and circulation, including a men's lounge and a dormitory library for use by female students. Reports in fiscal year 1931–1932 indicated that as many books were circulated in one month as had been circulated in an entire school year a decade earlier.[16] By June 1956 university president James Creese announced the groundbreaking for a five-story 70,000-square-foot new library to anticipate the "spectacular growth at Drexel in the next fifteen years."[17]

Harry Dewey in 1957 documented a report on the proposed new library building in which he noted that "the most important distinction between the concept of librarianship today and that of a hundred years ago is the modern idea of service to readers as against the old idea of the library as a storehouse of books."[18] Dewey worked with architects and consulted with faculty, students and staff, inviting comments and receiving nearly a thousand suggestions—all part of his belief that "a building made for young people to use should include the ideas of young people. Without your enthusiasm this plan cannot go forward."[19] He was first to establish a

Drexel Library, view of south exterior with car-lined Thirty-Second Street, c. 1959.
(Drexel University Archives. PC 5 Buildings and campus photographs.)

"philosophy" for the building, having formulated needs and expected design elements from this feedback. His proposed innovative ideas for Drexel's first library building included open stacks, the arrangement of collections by subject divisions with librarians in subject reading rooms providing reference service, the availability of headphones ("found in only the newest and best libraries"),[20] and television and movie rooms. Dewey envisioned that the "library can be like a large supermarket, embodying the best features of that institution: self help, multiple check-out gates, and a book arrangement whereby most of the reading areas could be on one floor."[21] The $1.7 million contract estimate for the building, which was to house both the library and library school, was funded by subscriptions from companies seeking Drexel assistance in training workers. One hundred twenty subscriptions were received from corporations with an estimated rate of giving of $240,000 per year.[22] By fall 1959 the new library (now the Korman Center) was fully open with a dedication ceremony attracting librarians internationally for a symposium.

Within a few years, faculty were complaining of overcrowding, to which library director Robert Johnson admitted, "We've just about reached the building's capacity in seating students" with unexpected increase in enrollment of library science students.[23] Articles in *The Triangle* over the next several years complained of noise, broken equipment, and a desire for more study rooms and extended hours. Expectations were voiced for a college library to "provide the student body with the proper facilities and atmosphere for studying."[24] When library items started to go missing with increasing frequency, a "tattle tape" security system was added in 1972. By 1973 predictions for a new library building were announced, motivated by the Middle States accreditation recommendation to relocate the library school, as well as the recognition that there was inadequate support for Ph.D. programs. The W. W. Hagerty Library opened in 1983 and yet by 1988 librarians at the University of Pennsylvania were complaining of too many Drexel students using their library. As the university faced grave financial challenges, a 1991 faculty editorial in *The Triangle* listed evidence of the library's decline such as a discontinued article-copy service, cuts in journal subscriptions, winter holiday closure, and reduction of science reference staff. In 1992 library director Eileen Hitchingham characterized the Hagerty building as "deteriorating around us."[25]

Technology-based services and equipment began to appear over the last quarter of the twentieth century. In 1976 the library offered Dialog, a fee-based computer-assisted bibliographic search service, of which modest use was made. The Visualtek Read/Write system to enhance partially sighted students' reading experiences was purchased through Student Affairs in 1981. The library offered Exels (Executive Library Services) in 1986, a first-of-its-kind service among Philadelphia academic libraries that produced copies of database searches identifying journal articles for businesses for annual membership and fees. A CD-ROM for business indexes and journals was offered in 1987, as was a self-serve online computer system with Dialog. A new automated catalog system went online in spring 1993, after nearly twenty years of planning.

In her 2004 strategic plan, Montgomery forecast that "the current role of the physical library will change . . . [to] play a larger part in the social, cultural and intellectual life on campus . . . to learn, exchange ideas, collaborate and socialize," making the library the campus "Information Hub."[26] She referenced it as "the logical place to create an environment that facilitates the 'one-stop-shop' concept." Contemporary library trends were proposed, including addition of a café in Hagerty Library, food service within the Hahnemann Library, increased study spaces, improved technologies, a leisure DVD collection, and the reduction of multiple reference desks to one. In 2007 the top floor of the Hagerty Library became an extension of Drexel's new law school, and to achieve full accreditation, access was restricted to law students. The loss of study space for undergraduate students was addressed in 2011 by building the Library Learning Terrace, a dedicated space adjacent to the dormitories designed for students to arrange their own learning environment; librarians and other staff join students for specific programs or consultations, but along with physical collections, are uncharacteristically not present "just in case"[27] they might be needed.

Since 2010, there have been numerous initiatives to assess library space needs and conditions, including a discussion with more than two hundred students over plans for the Learning Terrace; engagement with students to identify and document "learning environments" around campus; visioning sessions for imagining a future library, facilitated by architects; and designing a renovation plan in 2013 to add over two hundred seats without altering the footprint of the Hagerty Library.

Understanding the relationships that physical environments have to learning is a nascent interdisciplinary field of study that addresses spaces beyond classrooms in support of informal learning. Drexel offers a laboratory for such study, having been the site for ethnographic research on what students do in the library,[28] and what faculty think of a library,[29] as well as for development of a tool to quantify the proximity of learners as an indicator of learning behaviors.[30] Many students have voiced their desire for a library as a place to "focus" without distraction; observations indicate the benefits of natural light for studying; faculty schedule meetings with students in the library; and staff use the library to test different digital formats and systems. Drexel students make heavy use of the library, often commenting that there are no places available to sit. The library currently includes technologically equipped places for students to explore data visualization, understand 3-D printing, record oral histories, and quietly read or borrow a laptop anytime from a kiosk, (the first program of its kind in Philadelphia). The library is an "information exploratorium" where learning and the creation of new knowledge occurs through intentional personal discovery and shared experiences. Librarians also have promoted this role in support of Drexel's promotion of civic engagement through enabling installation of a self-checkout kiosk in the Dornsife Center for local community members to borrow an iPad, loaded with over sixty-five applications for literacy training, news, job hunting, and entertainment.[31]

Drexel's library was a pioneer in establishing a website on campus and in 2014 contributed programming expertise to create an award-winning educational Web environment at the Legacy Center, to engage high school students with digitized archival sources.[32] The library website has evolved into a virtual place to identify services and resources, reserve study rooms, conveniently link to licensed electronic resources, as well as chat with information staff who guide navigation to find materials. Cyberspace has become the library's most active learning environment.

Strengthening Drexel's Connection to Scholarship

A major currency of scholarship is publications—researchers share the outcomes of their work through peer-reviewed articles, others read and cite them, and reputations and rankings emerge through bibliometric analyses of citations. Becoming part of this cycle starts with learning how to identify and evaluate existing publications, and librarians guide novice academics in how to do so, starting with their first undergraduate research papers. Instruction on "how to use the library" became "bibliographic instruction" that helped students develop information literacy and critical-thinking skills for lifelong learning. Librarians at most universities have taken responsibility for teaching students these skills and at Drexel they collaborate with other units, such as the writing center, to integrate focused units into the curriculum. Faculty sought lessons for their students even more as search systems and the organization of publications changed and increasingly sophisticated and varied automated products emerged to utilize digital resources.

In recent years, Google's efforts to create a universal digital library have simplified the search for information. Understanding how information is organized and retrieved has become less necessary to finding something. However, to evaluate what is found and to know the relative value of uncovering authoritative information, requires some basic understanding of information sources and organization, which librarians offer. In the past few years Drexel librarians have shifted strategies from drawing people into instruction sessions to providing personalized consultations, especially for more advanced researchers, offering online instruction, sharing customized guides online, and partnering with faculty to educate students in their literacy skills and ethical practices. Librarian expertise bridges systems and human experience, contributing to improved designs and communications.

As Drexel strives to become a comprehensive research university, evidence of faculty productivity and comparative impact of their research strengthens the university's connections to scholarship and its competitiveness for recruitment and retention of the best minds. Librarians have applied their knowledge of publishing and information science to work with

Thomson Reuters and campus programmers to build a central database identifying faculty academic achievement. A faculty portfolio program begun in 2013 offers faculty and other researchers help in managing curricula vita data and preparing reports customized for internal reviews and grant applications, while also establishing authoritative data for comparison with other institutions. Furthermore, Drexel librarians are joining other innovative information professionals to design ways to curate and increase discovery of research data output and documentation for future use, improve faculty productivity, and meet funding regulations for managing data.

A library as a place of connectivity also celebrates scholarship. Throughout Drexel's history, exhibits, speakers, and receptions were some of the traditional ways to bring attention to collections of publications and other artifacts of intellectual output. Since 2010, the library has toasted the end of each academic quarter with an informal social gathering open to all faculty and professional staff. This "ScholarSip" tradition includes a short faculty presentation of interdisciplinary research that triggers conversation among attendees from across their many departments and diverse disciplines—an enjoyable way to build community and nurture Drexel's intellectual life.

Modeling a Library Organization

Libraries have typically been hierarchically organized around functions. Drexel's library departments were organized around administrative services, technical processes, user-facing service units, and, in some years, subject areas such as science, technology, and business. A reorganization in 2010 created a new system, intended to be more responsive to change, and to foster leadership and growth among library staff. Working with the library dean, three directors form a strategic leadership group (SLG), with each having library wide responsibilities while also directly supervising program managers. SLG members' responsibilities represent the library's priorities to (1) continually improve the quality of service, (2) develop partnerships to advance scholarship, and (3) design and implement effective business practices and learning environments. SLG along with ten program managers constitute a managerial leadership group that provides operational advice and coordinates the implementation of library policies and procedures. A library advisory group with broad faculty and student representation also advises the library dean.

Matrix management and routine meetings, both staff-wide and of leadership groups, strengthen the engagement of personnel with the library's efforts to advance the university's mission. Staff development is further encouraged with available funds for each employee to participate in training programs or professional services. Client comments via an online opinion site, letters, and *Triangle* stories have consistently praised library staff for their helpfulness and expertise.

Library decisions are increasingly made based on evidence and with an overall strengthened capacity to respond to change. To continue transforming the twenty-first-century library, the future will likely require a greater diversity of expertise and professional backgrounds. Drexel's library history has shown that such change can be done with a relatively small staff by providing them opportunities to expand their skills, and by redefining positions as they open up. The library has recently added staff with expertise in accounting, data analysis, communications, project management, licensing, teaching, and research. Our staff also increasingly reflects the ethnic and cultural diversity of the clientele served.

A Look to the Future

Originally the laboratory for students of librarianship, Drexel's library increasingly welcomes study and advice from all disciplines, to improve its support of Drexel's education and research activities. Operationally challenged in acquiring and housing a physical collection, the library balances ownership with licensing and resource sharing to ensure timely access to information essential to faculty and students. Though not bound by physical walls, the library will continue to provide focused and diverse learning environments. As an organization, the library will continue to benefit from a culture of responsive learning and adaptation, a committed service-based workforce, and strategic and managerial leadership positioned both among its staff and across the university. Its value to the university's future is acknowledged in the library's inclusion in early drafting of the president's upcoming campaign. The library's exciting challenge will be to continually translate its once unquestionable but at times neglected purpose to meet the evolving nature of scholarship and higher education Drexel offers in decades to come.

NOTES

1. "Drexel Libraries," used at least since 1960, is the name (as a singular noun) for the organization that currently consists of four physical library sites: W. W. Hagerty Library, Hahnemann Library, Queen Lane Library, and the Library Learning Terrace. To

avoid confusion throughout this essay, "library" will be used to refer to the entire system. The libraries of Drexel's law school and Academy of Natural Sciences are not part of the Drexel Libraries.

2. Sharon Gray Weiner, "The History of Academic Libraries in the United States: A Review of the Literature," *Library Philosophy and Practice* 7 (Spring 2005): 58.

3. E. J. Humeston, "Library School Profile: Drexel from the Nineties to the Sixties," *Journal of Education for Librarianship* 5 (1964): 61–68.

4. J. C. M. Hanson, "The A.L.A. and L.A. Catalog Rules," *Bulletin of the American Library Association* 2 (March 1908): 9–11.

5. *Plan for a Time of Transforming Opportunity: The University's Strategic Plan through 2009*, Drexel University, available at http://www.ece.drexel.edu/reports/strategicplan/DrexelStrategic_plan_04-09.pdf.

Mention of the renovation of the W. W. Hagerty Library also appears in *The Future Is Drexel: 2007–2012 Strategic Plan*, 50, available at www.drexel.edu/~/media/Files/em/publications/Strategic_Plan.ashx.

6. Bernard Wysocki, "How Dr. Papadakis Runs a University Like a Company," *Wall Street Journal*, February 23, 2005.

7. Carol Hansen Montgomery, "Pioneering an Electronic Journal Collection at Drexel," *Emerging Trends in Academe*, June 2005.

8. Letter from Constantine Papadakis to Drexel Colleague, July 5, 2005, UR.01.015 Constantine Papadakis administration records, Drexel University Archives.

9. Danuta A. Nitecki et al., "Evaluating a Future Search Conference for an Academic Library's Strategic Planning," *Library Leadership and Management* 27 (2013): 1–21.

10. "Drexel University Libraries Strategic Plan: 2012–17," brochure available at https://www.library.drexel.edu/sites/default/files/Strategic%20Plan%20Brochure%20PDF.pdf.

11. 1968–1969 Library Director Richard Snyder's Annual Report.

12. 1967–1968 Library Director Richard Snyder's Annual Report.

13. "Libraries Consult on Project to Provide Access to 40 years of WHYY's 'Fresh Air with Terry Gross,'" WHYY, available at www.library.drexel.edu/libraries-consult-project-provide-access-40-years-whyys-fresh-air-terry-gross.

14. 1970–1971 Library Director Richard Snyder's Annual Report.

15. Carol Hansen Montgomery, *Vision for the 21st Century Libraries: Drexel's Information Hub Strategic Plan 2004–2006*, Draft 5, August 2004.

16. 1931–1932 Report, UR 5.2.16.6, Drexel University Archives.

17. Jim Spillane, "New Library on Drawing Boards; Ground Breaking Expected Next Year," *The Triangle*, June 1, 1956, 1.

18. Harry Dewey, *A Report to the Faculty, Staff, and Students on the New Library Building Proposed for the Drexel Institute of Technology* (Philadelphia: Drexel Institute, 1957), box 25, UR 5.2, Library Records, Drexel University Archives.

19. Jan Beymer, "Drexel Library Nears Construction Stage: Suggestions Invited on Proposed Library; Reading Rooms, Air-Conditioning in Plans," *The Triangle*, April 26, 1957, 3.

20. "Plans for Library Nearing Completion; Study, Movie, and TV Rooms Provided," *The Triangle*, October 11, 1957, 1.

21. "Library Will Be Reality in Two Years," *The Triangle*, October 26, 1956, 2.

22. "Library Contract Awarded: Will Open by Fall '59," *The Triangle*, February 7, 1958, 1.

23. Joe Child, "Inefficient Library Facilities Plague Faculty and Students," *The Triangle*, November 8, 1963, 9.

24. Bob Raywood, "Noise Annoys," *The Triangle,* May 1, 1964, 5.

25. Letter from Eileen Hitchingham, dean of library, to Dave Noyes, director of facilities, December 14, 1992.

26. Carol Hansen Montgomery, *Vision for the 21st Century Libraries*, 9.

27. On the "bookless" library, see www.library.drexel.edu/library-learning-terrace.

28. Michael Khoo, Lily Rozaklis, and Catherine Hall, "A Survey of the Use of Ethnographic Methods in the Study of Libraries and Library users," *Library and Information Science Research* 34 (2012): 82–91.

29. Danuta A. Nitecki and Eileen Abels, "Exploring the Cause and Effect of Library Value," *Performance Measurement and Metrics* 14 (2013): 17–24.

30. W. Michael Johnson et al., *Peer Engagement as a Common Resource: Managing Interaction Patterns in Institutions* (Ann Arbor, MI: Society for College and University Planners, 2015).

31. On the laptop and iPad lending kiosks, see www.library.drexel.edu/laptop-ipad-lending-kiosks.

32. "Innovative New Legacy Center Site Provides Opportunity to Interact with Collections Online," Drexel Libraries, available at www.library.drexel.edu/innovative-new-legacy-center-site-provides-opportunity-interact-collections.

In 1983 Hagerty announced that every student at Drexel had to have a computer. I was on the committee to select the computer. And we had narrowed it down to an IBM XT computer . . . that was going to be the thing. The computer was going to be sold to us for one thousand dollars. And they were ready to end the deal and that was going to be the end of the search for the computer for Drexel. The added advantage at the time was that "no one was ever fired for choosing IBM" as their computer. So IBM was a solid choice for everyone involved. IBM started literally nickel-and-diming us, except it wasn't nickels and dimes. The computer was a thousand dollars, but it needed a separate memory option that was another two hundred fifty, then we needed some cables that were fifty apiece, Then there was another thing, I mean every time we looked around, it was going up. Soon it was close to two thousand per student. . . . Everyone started getting shaky about the deal.

I went up to Lowell on an accreditation visit . . . somebody walked into the room and said, "There's a telegram for Dr. Eisenstein." I stepped out of the room to take the telegram. The telegram said, "Don't come home, call me first," and it was signed by Bernie Sagik, who was at that time the vice president for academic affairs. So I got to an office and I called Bernie up, and he said, "There is a new computer that Apple has come out with." I was familiar with the Apple and the Apple 2. I knew all that, but they weren't acceptable to us. He said, "No, this is something totally new, totally different." He said, "I don't know anything about it but I know it's really new, it's really hot." So he said that there was a guy by the name of Mike Murray—who by the way was at that time sales manager for Apple Corporation—he was gonna be at a hotel near Logan Airport in Boston the next day. He said that I should go to room such-and-such at this motel, this airport motel, and he'd show me this computer.

So I stayed over one more night, went to the motel. When I came in and there were about three or four people in the room. They had a sheet over the computer, and the guy pulled the bedsheet off to show it to me. It was as I found out later the original Macintosh. I was the first person outside of Cupertino to see that computer. . . . He was there to show it to the people at MIT, and then he was going to Brown University to show it to them. So we just happened to catch him on that. And for the first time I saw icons on a screen, a mouse. I had never seen a mouse, nor had I ever seen graphics like that before. I had no idea . . . I had never thought about a font in my life. It was absolutely fascinating to me, and I thought, you know, this is it, this is the deal.

So I went back to the selection committee and I said, "Listen, you have to forget the IBM. This new computer from Apple is the one you have to get. They are going to make it available to us for a thousand dollars—that's all inclusive." And first question was "Is it compatible with the IBM computer"? Well, no. Was there software for it? No. Were there any programs for it, like a word processor? Not yet. So the committee justifiably kept saying, well, what's the name of this? What's it like? I couldn't tell them. I had to say you just gotta trust me on this. So they took a vote and unanimously voted to adopt the unknown computer that turned out to be the Macintosh. So that's how we got the Macintosh; the secondary effect of that was in 1984 enrollment in the electrical and computer engineering department swelled to over four hundred students, entering students, where we previously had 120, 130. All of them were interested in computers. My whole entire department those early years, I had just become department head in '80, so this was three years, four years, into department head. I had to add faculty like mad, computer faculty. I had to transform people who had been teaching circuits and electronics into computer people. . . . And as it emerged the engineers were probably the, not the last ones [to adopt the computer], but they were probably not the ones that were most aggressive in using the computer. The ones that hit on it first were all the people in humanities, particularly the design people. They just latched onto that. The humanities loved the easy word processing, and the ability to get stuff out so quickly and edit, revise. That was all unheard of.

—Bruce Eisenstein

10

One Hundred and Twenty-Five Years of Computing and Information Education and Research

DAVID FENSKE

F IVE YEARS AFTER the end of his nineteen-year tenure as dean of
what was then known as Drexel's College of Information Studies,
Guy Garrison in 1992 delivered a significant Lazerow lecture on the
history of his library school. The lecture was later revised and extended, pictures were added, and it was republished as the book, *A Century of Library
Education at Drexel University: Vignettes of Growth and Change* (2012).[1] This
chapter extends Garrison's work into the twenty-first century, when what
had been the library school became known as one of the early "iSchools,"
and later, the College of Computing and Informatics.

Since the first class of ten students entered Drexel's library training program in 1892, the university has been a leader and early adopter in library
science, information science, and now computer science. The first library science program was founded by Melvil Dewey at Columbia University in
1887; Drexel's program is often referred to as the second such program in
the United States, though there is some confusion on this point, as the Pratt
Institute's library school was founded in 1890.[2] The major events in the history of library and information studies at Drexel are summarized in
Table 10.1. The major landmarks are accreditation by the American Library
Association (ALA) in 1949 (making Drexel the longest continuously accredited program in the United States), the creation of the first Ph.D. program
in information studies in 1974, the creation of an undergraduate program
and the renaming to the College of Information Studies in 1984, the

TABLE 10.1: MILESTONES IN THE HISTORY OF LIBRARY AND INFORMATION STUDIES AT DREXEL UNIVERSITY

1892	A certificate program in library science is organized under the direction of Alice B. Kroeger; school and library occupy second floor of Main Building of Drexel Institute of Art, Science, and Industry.
1922	Drexel Institute's School of Library Science introduces a fifth-year bachelor of science degree in library science (B.L.S.).
1949	The School of Library Science is accredited by the American Library Association Board of Education for Librarianship. The degree has been continuously accredited ever since.
1954	The B.L.S. degree program is upgraded to the M.S. degree; a special track for employed librarians is provided with evening and Saturday classes offered.
1959	The school is renamed the Graduate School of Library Science.
1962	The school moves into the newly constructed Drexel Library Center.
1963	The school moves into the Rush Building. A second master's program is offered, the M.S. in Information Science.
1970	The two graduate curricula are merged, forming the M.S. in Library and Information Science; a third area of specialization, Educational Media, is added to the program.
1974	Ph.D. program is launched.
1978	The Graduate School of Library Science is renamed the School of Library and Information Science. The B.S. in computer science degree is launched in the Department of Mathematics in the College of Science. The M.S. in computer science degree is launched around the same time.
1983	The Department of Mathematics is renamed the Department of Mathematics and Computer Science.
1984	The B.S.I.S. (bachelor of science in information systems) is initiated as a five-year co-op-based program. The School of Library and Information Science is renamed the College of Information Studies.
1985	The B.S. in computer science is accredited by CSAB and has been continuously accredited ever since.
1991	The Multidisciplinary Information Systems Engineering (MISE) Center is created.
1992	The M.S.IS (master of science in information systems) program is created; the college celebrates its centennial.
1995	M.S.IS program is offered online; the college is renamed the College of Information Science and Technology.
1997	The multidisciplinary M.S.S.E. (master of science in software engineering) is launched.
1999	The online certification program in competitive intelligence is initiated. The bachelor of arts in computer science is launched.

(continued)

TABLE 10.1: MILESTONES IN THE HISTORY OF LIBRARY AND INFORMATION STUDIES AT DREXEL UNIVERSITY	
2000	The M.S. concentration in the management of digital information is offered online.
2001	The Institute for Healthcare Informatics and the Knowledge Management Collaboratory are launched.
2002	The B.S.S.E. (bachelor of science in software engineering) is initiated. The Institute for Healthcare Informatics and the Knowledge Management Collaboratory move into a new research facility in Rush Building. The Computer Science Department is split from the Department of Mathematics and transferred to the College of Engineering.
2003	The M.S. specialization in information/library services is offered online. The B.S.I.S. (bachelor of science in information systems) offers a four-year program with a one co-op option. The B.S.I.S. is accredited by the Computing Accreditation Commission (CAC) of the Accreditation Board for Engineering and Technology (ABET).
2004	The B.S.I.T. (bachelor of science in information technology) is approved.
2005	Drexel is one of the signatory colleges of the iSchool charter. The Master of Science in Library and Information Science creates six concentrations.
2013	The College of Computing and Informatics is formed from the merger of the College of Information Science, the Computer Science Department, and the Computer Security program from Goodwin.

creation of the iSchools charter in 2005, and the creation of the College of Computing and Informatics in 2013.

Library information science (LIS)—a term that developed in the late twentieth century that combines the original library science with the more recent information science—refers to a spectrum of interdisciplinary subfields: The practices in and of libraries, archives and preservation, the adaption and uses of information technology, the use and users of information including its dissemination, and the application of computer technology in these fields. LIS education is most often epitomized by the master's degrees involving variations of these terms, and information science by the Ph.D.s established in that field, starting in the 1970s.

During the last decade of the twentieth century, Richard Lytle, the dean of what by the end of his ten-year tenure (1987–1998) was the College of Information Science and Technology (CIST), in many ways set the

View through banner from conference room window at the College of Information Studies, 1987. (Drexel University Archives. PC 5 Buildings and campus photographs.)

trajectory for LIS at Drexel into the twenty-first century. Lytle focused on software engineering through collaborations with the Department of Math and Computer Science and the Department of Electrical Engineering. He moved CIST beyond its traditional strength in the master of science in library and information science (M.S.L.I.S.) by establishing the new M.S. in information systems (M.S.I.S.), and successfully implementing it as an online degree with the aid of an Alfred P. Sloan Foundation grant. Lytle also expanded the undergraduate program, which by the end of his deanship grew to such an extent that it practically overwhelmed CIST, a common problem in technology-driven fields.

The college has for more than three decades demonstrated a marked flexibility, diversifying its academic offerings as a means of adapting to change, and in the process blurring the lines between library science, information science, and computer science. This is perhaps most evident in its technology-driven degree programs, starting with the establishment of the bachelor of science in information systems in the 1980s, and, in collaboration with the Department of Computer Science, the B.S. and M.S. degrees in software engineering. Today, the two theoretical pillars of the College of Computing and Informatics are the Ph.D. in information science and the Ph.D. in computer science. The distinction between degrees with similar names and sometimes overlapping requirements—in part a function of the proliferation of new disciplines and interdisciplinary fields and subfields—presents a challenge in explaining their distinctions to university administrators and the parents of high school students, to name but two of the several befuddled constituencies.

The establishment of online degree programs in the late 1990s and their massive growth in the twenty-first century has been particularly important, providing the M.S.I.S. and M.S.L.I.S. programs a broader audience, and the college overall significant financial benefits. The success of the online M.S.I.S. was an important step in the establishment of what is now Drexel University Online, which offers online programs across the entire university, and is a crucial component of the university's financial stability and growth.

From 1999 to 2013 the CIST faculty grew from about twelve to forty-five, with a commensurate increase in college staff and administrators. There was during this period also a substantial amount of turnover—by 2013 only four of the faculty from 1999 remained. Each new faculty member came with new ideas and opportunities, and overall quality improved. Drexel's LIS program has been a fixture among the top ten in the country as ranked by *U.S. News and World Report*, but there has been a long-standing tension between the traditional LIS curriculum that is ranked and the increasing diversity of related degrees. In contrast to the *U.S. News* rankings, which are based primarily on surveys of professionals, in 2007 a consortium of universities organized as Academic Analytics produced a report of the leading information science programs based entirely on scholarly output and bibliometrics, and in which the CIST's twenty-four Ph.D. faculty scored quite well: fourth in journal publications per faculty; fifth in citations per faculty; and seventh in the percentage of faculty with a journal publication. Overall, the college ranked eighth nationally, between Pennsylvania State University (seventh) and Ohio State University (ninth).

With revenue from research grants, a base budget allocated by the university, and tuition revenue from online programs, budgetary complexity increased significantly. Before 2000, aside from two large (over $1 million), pedagogically connected grants (one from the Alfred P. Sloan Foundation for launching the online M.S.I.S. online, and another from the Kellogg Foundation for rethinking the curriculum), funded research in the college averaged less than $50,000 per year. By the 2010s, funded research expenditures amounted annually to several million dollars. The most important characteristic of funded research in the college was collaboration with other universities and other colleges within Drexel. More than half of the CIST's funded research was in partnership with virtually every other college and their faculties at Drexel, but primarily with the Department of Computer Science in the College of Engineering and with faculty in the College of Nursing and Health Professions.

While the Ph.D. program established in 1974 graduated an average of one student per year during its first decades, by 2010 it was averaging seven graduates a year—an increase directly connected to the increase in funded research. The Ph.D. is officially in information studies, though this is a term of an earlier era in library and information science. By 2010 most dissertations were on highly technical subjects—information visualization, data mining, semantic extraction, and related topics—that involved computing approaches to information problems, thus foreshadowing the evolution of CIST into the College of Computing and Informatics.

Any university administrator knows that funding research is one of the two most important tasks of higher education—the advancement of knowledge and the education of the next generation of professionals and scholars—and that research never fully funds itself. Since payrolls must be met, the obvious source of funds supporting the shortfall of costs from research and all of the costs of education comes from tuition revenue. In the years after 2000, there was a massive surge in the college's undergraduate population, primarily in the B.S. in information systems, and by 2015 an equally dramatic decline. The rise is easy to explain, the decline less so, since the job market in information systems and related fields has remained robust (indeed, graduates with the B.S. in information systems averaged some of the highest-paid jobs among all Drexel graduates). The most likely answer appears to be that high school students and their parents recognize and understand computer science as a field better than information systems—though all technical fields in undergraduate education typically experience rapid increases and decreases in enrollment.

While the growth of online degree programs was mostly a good thing, the downside was that a generation of administrators grew used to funding the total needs of the college from online tuition revenue and did not address any of the growth in the CIST's base budget—even tenure track lines were funded from online revenue, starting in about 2008. The college should be looking forward to a time when it can benefit from "responsibility centered management" (RCM), where the tuition revenue it generates from both online and traditional programs will largely be returned under a set formula and not redistributed at the discretion of university administrators. Yet RCM will not solve the fundamental tension between funding the advancement of knowledge (research and scholarship) and the costs of direct education.

Online education within CIST has also had significant peaks and valleys. In the early years, it was the M.S.I.S. that had by far the largest enrollment, but the M.S.L.I.S. (the online version of which was launched in 2000) became the college's largest master's program, in terms of enrollment, from 2005 to 2012—though thereafter its enrollment, following a nation trend, rapidly declined. New programs related to health care informatics have compensated for some of the enrollment declines in the M.S.L.I.S.

The tension within Drexel between the characterization of its "library school" and the reality that CIST was in fact much larger in scope and numbers than library science and practice, reflected larger trends. Starting in the 1980s, the library school deans of Drexel, Syracuse, Rutgers, and the University of Pittsburgh formed a "Gang of Four" that met periodically to discuss the growing diversification of their programs away from the traditional L.I.S. degree, the inclusion of new undergraduate programs, and the limitations of ALA accreditation. From the Gang of Four, the deans of Drexel, Syracuse, and the universities of Michigan, Pittsburgh, and Washington formed a Gang of Five in 2000, from which the notion of "iSchools" emerged. At the 2002 meeting of the Association of Library and Information Science Educators (the group that represents the faculties of all ALA-accredited programs) in Philadelphia, the Gang of Five went public in what we could say was an interesting, well-attended public meeting—and despite some concern, the iSchool Consortium grew.

The iSchool movement seeks to move beyond the confines of LIS to imagine that "the information field is widely recognized for creating innovative systems and designing information solutions that benefit individuals, organizations, and society. iSchool graduates will fill the personnel and leadership needs of organizations of all types and sizes; and our areas of research and inquiry will attract strong support and have profound impacts on society and on the formulation of policy from local to international levels."[3]

The iSchools Consortium has matured into an international organization with sixty-five institutions on five continents, it has applied for nonprofit tax status in the District of Columbia, has an elected executive committee, has retained an executive director (myself, David Fenske), and expects to include one hundred institutions by 2020. In 2016 the consortium sponsored its tenth iConference (intended to "pus[h] the boundaries of information studies, explor[e] core concepts and ideas, and creat[e] new technological and conceptual configurations—all situated in interdisciplinary discourses"), hosted in Philadelphia by Drexel, and the 2017 conference will be in Wuhan, China.[4]

In May 2013, a task force charged with reorganizing Drexel's disparate computing- and information-related programs recommended the creation

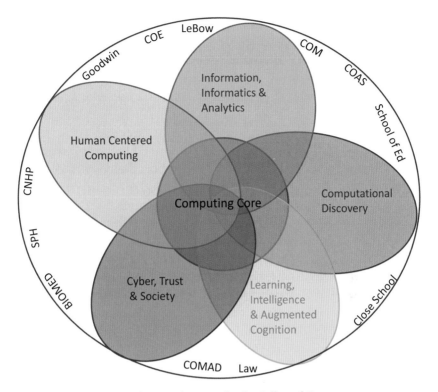

*Schematic showing the vision for the College of Computing
and Informatics and Drexel University.*

of a College of Computing and Informatics (CCI) through the combination of CIST, the Department of Computer Science in the College of Engineering, and the Computer Security program in the Goodwin College. The idea behind CCI, aptly summarized in figure 10.1, is that it will serve as the home for the university's core computing faculty, yet also serve as an interdisciplinary hub for faculty engaged in related research in the university's other colleges and schools. Provost Mark Greenberg accepted the report, authorized the formation of CCI, and asked me to form the transition team and to become the founding dean.

The vision for CCI is massive and the effort at actually creating the new college has only barely begun. My story thus cannot be concluded, though significant national trends can be noted. There are now a significant number of colleges nationwide engaged in the new approach reflected in the creation of CCI—the task force report mentioned five such colleges and there are at least three more in formation as this essay is being finished. All are members of the iSchool Consortium. This happens to be the case because the applied areas of computer science and its variants, and information science and its variants, have begun to significantly overlap, demanding a new approach, the importance of which is reflected in the following quote from the National Academies 2012 report *Continuing Innovation in Information Technology*:

> Imagine spending a day without IT. This would be a day without the Internet and all that it enables. A day without diagnostic medical imaging. A day during which automobiles lacked electronic ignition, antilock brakes, and electronic stability control. A day without digital media—without wireless telephones, high-definition televisions, MP3 audio, cable- or Internet-delivered video, computer animation, and video games. A day during which aircraft could not fly, travelers had to navigate without benefit of the Global Positioning System (GPS), weather forecasters had no models, banks and merchants could not transfer funds electronically, and factory automation ceased to function. It would be a day in which the U.S. military lacked precision munitions, did not have the capabilities for network-centric warfare, and did not enjoy technological supremacy. It would be, for most people in the United States and the rest of the developed world, a "day the Earth stood still."[5]

NOTES

1. Guy Garrison, *A Century of Library Education at Drexel University: Vignettes of Growth and Change*, rev. ed. (Philadelphia: W. W. Hagerty Library, 2012).

2. Drexel's library school is referred to as the second established in the country in "Drexel University's Plan for a Time of Transforming Opportunity: The University's Strategic Plan through June 2009," 5. Pratt in fact refers to its library school as the first in the country; see "About the School of Information," available at www.pratt.edu/academics/information/about-the-school/. At the very least we can say that, between 1887 and 1892, the first three library programs in the United States were founded, at Columbia, Pratt, and Drexel.

3. "About," available at ischools.org/about.

4. "About the iConference," available at ischools.org/the-iconference/about-the-iconference/.

5. Committee on Depicting Innovation in Information Technology et al., *Continuing Innovation in Information Technology* (Washington, DC: National Academies Press, 2012), 1.

Bill Hagerty (Drexel president, 1963–1984) had a grand vision for Drexel. He wasn't the most participative of managers, so to speak. A lot of people thought that he was, perhaps, a benevolent dictator. You know, Bill had a lot of ideas and he just went ahead and did them. There wasn't a lot of consulting with the faculty, but that isn't to say that Bill didn't have people he asked, because I was one of them. The fact is, that Bill had a vision that Drexel Institute would become Drexel University; and, for a lot of reasons, he set out to build up the business school. It moved into Matheson Hall, and the day they opened it was the day I started, January 1, 1965.

We ran a couple of conferences and had papers we issued out of the conferences. Mainly, individuals who were involved either came from engineering to work with us or wrote papers for different professional groups. . . . I had gotten an acceptance to give a paper at the Institute of Management Science in Vienna. So, I went to see the dean, Jim Parrish, and I said, "I got this invitation, can I go?" He opened his desk drawer—he was a very deliberate guy with a strong southern accent—and he said, "I've got five hundred dollars for you, take out whatever you need." They didn't even have a system for me to report my expenses, he just said "go ahead." . . . The fact of the matter was, we had to build a faculty to support our accreditation, besides gerrymandering some of the courses, and the business school just began to boom in the number of students that were applying.

—Milton Silver, LeBow College of Business

From the Business Department,
to the Secretarial School,
to the LeBow College of Business

DANIEL JOHNSON

BUSINESS EDUCATION at Drexel began in the aptly named Business Department, established as one of the original units of the institute in 1891. Some hint of what might have been taught in the department comes from Anthony Drexel's reported admiration for the "commercial schools of Europe which aim to train young men to *do* business rather than simply *record* business."[1] Drexel's Business Department was part of a trend of new business colleges established in Philadelphia after the Civil War. The Union Business College had been established in 1865, and the first degree-granting business college in the United States had been founded in 1881 by industrialist and entrepreneur Joseph Wharton at the University of Pennsylvania.

In 1896 the Business Department became the Department of Commerce and Finance, the curriculum for which was structured along tracks divided by gender, as was common—there was, for instance, the Ladies Department at Union Business College. According to Drexel's course catalog, the men's track was designed to provide "fundamental training for the activities of business," and a coeducational track was intended "to prepare young men and young women for positions as *commercial teachers*" trained not to do business themselves, but to inform others of business practices and customs. This gender division was explained in terms of employers' demands: "while young women are not excluded from this special field of educational work, there is a greater demand for young men."[2]

Secretarial School, accounting class. (Drexel University Archives. PC 3 Early photographs of the Drexel Institute of Art, Science, and Industry.)

By 1914 the Department of Commerce and Finance had become the Secretarial School, which was equally open to men and women. The early twentieth-century notion of secretarial work, as the school's materials noted, "demands a sound cultural foundation and thorough knowledge of general subjects." A secretary should, for example, be "able to control properly correspondence, transportation, and methods of communication," along with being well acquainted with general subjects in order to best represent their company.[3] The philosophy of Drexel's secretarial education recognized that:

> all technical education is composed of two parts, direct vocational subjects and underlying general subjects; and while the greater amount of time is given to the vocational branches directly concerned with the work of a secretary, it is also recognized that to be of most value these branches must be firmly based on sound general training. Modern industry demands thorough, all-round equipment. The secretary who uses poor English, who is inaccurate, and who is unable to express to others the work in his or her charge, is not so equipped.[4]

This approach to education was best exemplified by courses in English and rhetoric required of secretarial students. While Rhetoric I revolved around simple sentence structure, clarity in writing and speaking, and basic grammar, Rhetoric III consisted almost entirely of the study of novelists such as Aldous Huxley and Nathanial Hawthorne, in hopes of instilling in students an "appreciation of prose writing, and a power to apply its art to concrete solutions of daily problems in writing and speaking."[5]

Reflecting a move away from vocational education, in 1922, the Secretarial School became the School of Business Administration. The change was described at the time as a fundamental recognition of the new national economy:

> Of the many changes that mark the contrast between the life and customs of the Nineteenth and Twentieth Centuries, none is more striking than specialized training and knowledge of which the young man requires before entering upon his life work. Formerly the young man who was obliged to earn his living could begin work and make a fair degree of progress with a meager educational equipment. Today, however, as a result of the tremendous economic development, methods of transacting business have become so interrelated and complex that a reliable knowledge and understanding of these methods can no longer be acquired by general and indiscriminate inquiry.[6]

The school was also cognizant of "a more radical change in the life and customs of the past century and . . . the entrance of women into the fields of activity formerly occupied by men."[7] As such, Drexel offered "comprehensive and unusual advantages to aspiring women."[8] Business education for women, especially in the immediate aftermath of the passage of the Nineteenth Amendment, was promoted as a recognition that the American woman's

> sphere has so broadened that today she participates in the discussion and determination of the most important political, social, legal, economic, and domestic questions. . . . She therefore has a right to demand the kind of education which will fit her for these increased responsibilities, and enable her to meet intelligently the readjustments that must take place as a result of new rights, duties, and obligations for which she has continuously and so courageously fought.[9]

In 1945 the School of Business Administration was expanded to become the College of Business Administration, in order to take advantage of "the location of the Institute in one of the largest industrial and business centers, and the cooperation of Philadelphia's leading business and industrial organizations." Three courses of study in the college—in commerce and engineering, business administration, and retail management—were designed specifically to be integrated with the institute's co-op program. Course content remained largely the same, but classes were reorganized to extend from six to eighteen months, to provide time for students to intern at department stores, mail-order houses, brokerage houses, accounting firms, credit and financial institutions, insurance companies, and real estate agencies.[10]

Milton Silver, a retired professor and former head of the Department of Management, recalls that the commerce and engineering program (C and E, now known as Business and Engineering) proved especially successful as a multidisciplinary approach to business education. "We had a conglomeration of programs, but the one that stood out was the C and E program . . . we were able to convince employers, mainly the government, that C and E was about the same as industrial engineering, which was not taught in the engineering school."[11]

Department stores in Philadelphia such as Lit Brothers offered co-op opportunities to many C and E students. The career of one alumnus of the college, Earl Lestz, started in a co-op in inventory management at Lit Brothers, from which he moved on to executive positions at Federated Department Stores, and ended up in Hollywood, controlling the entire inventory and back lot for Paramount Studios. For his accomplishments at Paramount, Lestz was awarded a star on the Hollywood Walk of Fame.

Planning for a doctoral program in business began in 1971 (shortly after Drexel made the transition from an institute of technology to a university), and was finally created in 1981, largely through the work of finance professor and director of graduate studies John Clark (whose wife, Margaret Clark, later provided the endowment for two annual awards given to Ph.D. students in honor of her late husband). Harry Collons, who was then dean of the business college, explained that developing a "small, high quality" Ph.D. program in business administration would be "the main thrust of the university's development over the next five years."[12] Both Collons and university president William Hagerty emphasized that the program would not seek to replicate doctoral programs at other schools, but would instead build on the "strengths and traditions of Drexel" by implementing a co-op program, allowing Ph.D. candidates to apply their theoretical knowledge to real-life situations.[13] In 1980, when the Commonwealth of

Drexel representatives sharing information about the co-op program in Retail Management, 1938. (Drexel University Archives. PC 11 Academic photographs.)

Pennsylvania approved its Ph.D., Drexel was one of only one hundred schools in the nation that had obtained accreditation from the American Assembly of Collegiate Schools of Business for both its undergraduate and graduate programs. Paul Dascher, Collons's successor as dean, called the doctoral program "the first of its kind in the United States," as students not only had to complete a co-op before beginning their dissertations, but were also required to gain a significant amount of teaching experience.[14]

The business school again witnessed a minor name change in 1974, with the addition of a simple conjunction. The College of Business *and* Administration shared many of the same qualities as its previous two incarnations, while outlining new goals for its graduates. As the Secretarial School had aimed to produce competent and reliable employees, the newest evolution of business at Drexel strove to train future managers. The college created a new undergraduate concentration in management,[15] and the co-op program was restructured to provide students some experience in supervising and managing employees. The co-op was also reevaluated to ensure that students had the opportunity to excel in entry-level positions, and to hopefully get hired by co-op employers after they graduated. The new focus on management reflected a recognition that the education of students for positions of leadership in business is the joint responsibility of both the college and the industry. The college provides the broad academic background needed for intellectual growth, a knowledge of all phases of business, and specialized instruction in some one field. Industry, on the other hand, through Drexel's cooperative plan, provides the highly specialized training characteristic of the individual company or industry, together with the experience essential in the process of developing executives and administrators.[16]

In 1984, the university required that all students own a personal computer. As President Hagerty explained this decision,

At the very time that a new and more highly sophisticated level of technology is needed, at the very time when worldwide population

College of Business students in class, 1986.
(Drexel University Archives. PC 11 Academic photographs.)

pressures cry for immeasurably greater levels of production in all areas—a great wave of disillusionment about the applications of scientific knowledge has begun to sweep no small sector of this country—and this—amazingly enough—in the generation that has profited by the greatest technical advances in the entire history of the human race. . . . [This is why] technology permeates all aspects of Drexel education and it is the products of such a technological university who will be equipped to face and master the future which stands before them.[17]

For business students in particular, Hagerty noted that "the computer is a very basic fact of life."[18] By the 1980s, all business students were required to take a general course in computer programming, and in 1984 a new concentration in computer systems management was established.[19] As the course catalog explained of the new concentration,

Modern organization is extremely information dependent. Complex decision making environments, computers, and quantitative models and methods have heightened the need for specialists involved in all phases of information collection, processing and reporting. The computer system management field of concentration prepares the student for careers in the design, implementation and management of information systems oriented towards the management or decision making processes in the organization.[20]

Overall the period from the 1970s until the early 1990s, before the presidency of Constantine Papadakis, was a dynamic one for business education at Drexel. Richard P. Freedman, an associate professor of legal studies, recalls:

> Beginning in the late 1970s and through the early 1990s, under the direction of Dean Paul Dascher, the College of Business and Administration came into its own. Through the leadership of Dean Dascher, the reputation of the college grew to a point that when business students answered questions about where they were studying business, the questioner's automatic response wasn't "Isn't Drexel an engineering school?" New cutting-edge courses and programs were implemented, high-quality faculty were hired and the college flourished. In the early 1990s, the college, as well as the university, fell victim to a severe decrease in the number of enrolling students. After Dean Dascher left, there were a number of deans hired to lead the college, but as qualified and talented as those deans were, they could not overcome the enrollment issue. The college's reputation and ranking suffered. It wasn't until later in the 1990's, after Constantine Papadakis was hired as the president of the university, that the college began to climb back to the status it previously held.

Along with the rest of the university, the business college, most notably during Pamela Lewis's tenure as dean, from 1997 to 2000, began its resurgence. First, in 1999, Bennett LeBow—founder and chairman of the Vector Group holding company, a 1960 graduate from Drexel's electrical engineering program, and a West Philadelphia native who could only afford college because of the co-op program[21]—provided a $10 million gift to the business college, which was subsequently renamed the Bennett S. LeBow College of Business. Second, the business college began making strides in one of the new fields emerging at the end of the millennium, online learning—a reflection of Papadakis's overall strategy for increasing enrollments and projecting a technologically advanced identity for the university.

Drexel introduced its online masters of business administration (M.B.A.) program in the fall of 1998, the university's second online graduate degree, followed by the masters in information technology.[22] Drexel marketed the online M.B.A. directly to corporations, forming agreements to train employees of companies such as Metropolitan Life Insurance.[23] In 2000, LeBow College began offering what it called the nation's first "Techno-M.B.A." program. A hybrid graduate degree, the Techno-M.B.A. "combined traditional core business courses with a strong emphasis on e-commerce, information systems, and information-technology management."[24] The program emerged from Drexel's partnership with eCollege.com, a software company that provided the university with around-the-clock technical assistance. Students in the Techno-M.B.A., who lived as far away from Drexel as Ireland, were identified by a webcam that scanned their irises.[25] The Techno-M.B.A. has evolved into the current "M.B.A. Anywhere" program, which the *Financial Times* ranked as the fourteenth best online M.B.A. in the world in 2014.[26]

In 2002, George Tsetsekos, who had come to Drexel in 1988 as a finance professor, became LeBow's dean. Tsetsekos shared Papadakis's focus on growth, and managed to increase the college's faculty by more than fifty percent, to triple the number of Ph.D. students, double the number of students getting master of science degrees, and increase the number of undergraduates as well.[27] In 2010, Bennett LeBow made a second gift of $45 million for the construction of Gerri C. LeBow Hall, the new home of the business school.[28] President John A. Fry announced the donation by LeBow as the largest ever single gift to the university, which would significantly reduce the cost of the $92 million building.[29] R. John Chapel, a business school alumnus from 1967 best known for his work in mergers and acquisitions, also helped out with the new building with a $1 million gift to build the R. John Chapel Dean's Suite—building upon an earlier $2.5 million gift to establish a dean's chair in leadership.[30]

Gerri LeBow Hall is a twelve-story classroom and conference center designed by Robert A. M. Stern and Philadelphia's Voith & Mactavish, and it marks the entrance to the university at Thirty-Second and Market Streets (where Moses Ezekiel's 1904 statue of Anthony Drexel is now also located). LeBow Hall, which replaced Matheson Hall (a 1965 building from Drexel's "orange brick" era), is home to the College of Business, the new School of Economics, as well as five academic centers: corporate governance, strategic leadership, teaching excellence, research excellence, and experiential learning).

Through the Dana and David Dornsife Office of Experiential Learning, LeBow students are offered opportunities to work on class projects assisting local and global companies. In one such project, students helped a family-owned, Italian olive oil company expand its product distribution to

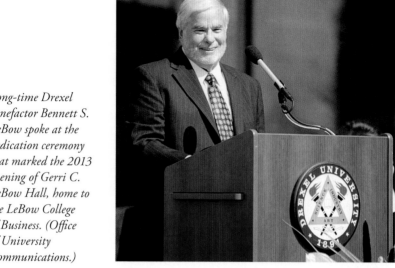

Long-time Drexel benefactor Bennett S. LeBow spoke at the dedication ceremony that marked the 2013 opening of Gerri C. LeBow Hall, home to the LeBow College of Business. (Office of University Communications.)

Japan. Meanwhile, most of the fifteen active student organizations housed within LeBow College (including chapters of national organizations such as the National Organization for Business and Engineering, and DECA, which is dedicated to facilitating students' business networking) allow for even further experiential learning opportunities.

Capping off a remarkable period of faculty growth, enrollment expansion, new programs, curricular reform, and institutional advancement through major gifts and construction, Tsetsekos announced that he would resign as dean in 2012, and has returned to the faculty as the George Francis Professor of Finance. Today, with Frank Linnehan as dean, LeBow College comprises 2,800 undergraduate students spread across twelve majors, as well as 1,020 graduate students pursuing an M.B.A., M.S., or Ph.D. The college is also the home of the School of Economics, which was created from the Department of Economics in 2013, and the Goodwin College of Professional Studies, which was transferred into LeBow in 2015.

The internationalization of business and the growth of transnational corporations, the Great Recession and the transition of the United States from a manufacturing to a service economy, and the digital revolution have all fundamentally transformed the needs of business in the twenty-first century, and business schools must remain nimble enough to seize on new opportunities. The remarkable transformation of Drexel's business education program—from the Business Department, to the Secretarial School, to LeBow College—is a reflection of such nimbleness. With the addition of a new partner school in the form of the Close School of Entrepreneurship, and the growth of the economics program in the form of a new school within the college, LeBow is now better positioned than it has ever been to identify and exploit future opportunities.

NOTES

1. James MacAlister and Seymour Eaton, "Department of Commerce and Finance," *Drexel Institute of Art, Science, and Industry Course Catalogue*, 1897, 9.
2. Ibid., 11–12. Italics in original.
3. Hollis Godfrey et al., "Secretarial School," *Drexel Institute of Art, Science, and Industry Course Catalogue*, 1915, 4.
4. Ibid., 5.
5. Ibid., 24–26.
6. "The School of Business Administration," *Drexel Institute of Art, Science, and Industry Course Catalogue*, 1925, 78.
7. Ibid., 4.
8. Ibid., 5.
9. Ibid., 4–5.
10. "College of Business Administration," *Drexel Institute of Art, Science, and Industry Course Catalogue*, 1947, 51–52.
11. Milton Silver, interviewed by Scott Knowles, November 5, 2015.
12. Larry Marion, "A Ph.D. in Bus. Ad. Soon?" *The Triangle*, October 29, 1971, 1.
13. Ibid.; Mawuna Gardesey, "A Ph.D. in Business," *The Triangle*, November 7, 1980, 1.
14. Ibid.
15. "College of Business and Administration," *Drexel University Course Catalogue*, 1975, 51.
16. Ibid., 41.
17. William W. Hagerty, *Drexel University: A Ten Year Overview 1963–1973*, folder 8, box 16, UR 03.013, Annual Reports Bulk 1945–1989, 25–26, Drexel University Archives.
18. Ibid., 25.
19. "College of Business and Administration," *Drexel University Course Catalogue*, 1984, 60–67.
20. Ibid., 62.
21. Susan Snyder, "Drexel to Receive $45 Million Gift for New Center for Business School," *Philadelphia Inquirer*, November 16, 2010.
22. James M. O'Neill, "Schools without Boundaries: Convenient to Study and Inexpensive to Set up," *Philadelphia Inquirer*, October 8, 1998, F1.
23. O'Neill, "Schools without Boundaries."
24. Martha Woodall, "Drexel 'Techno-MBA' Program to Provide All Courses Online," *Philadelphia Inquirer*, February 10, 2000.
25. Paul Eisenberg, "Drexel: Moving into Phase Two," *Philadelphia Business Journal*, August 11, 2000, 19.
26. "Financial Times Ranks LeBow Online MBA in Top 15," *DrexelNow*, March 10, 2014.

27. "George P. Tsetsekos Completes 10-Year Tenure as Drexel LeBow Dean," LeBow College of Business, Drexel University, available at www.lebow.drexel.edu/news/george-p-tsetsekos-completes-10-year-tenure-drexel-lebow-dean.

28. "Bennett S. LeBow Commits $45 Million for New Building," LeBow College of Business, Drexel University, available at www.lebow.drexel.edu/news/bennett-s-lebow-commits-45-million-new-building.

29. Snyder, "Drexel to Receive $45 Million Gift for New Center for Business School."

30. "R. John Chapel Jr. '67 Pledges $1 Million to Drexel LeBow," LeBow College of Business, Drexel University, available at www.lebow.drexel.edu/news/r-john-chapel-jr-67-pledges-1-million-drexel-lebow.

I had taught anthropology and sociology for one year before arriving as an instructor in what was then the social science department at Drexel. The department was an amalgamation of history, political science, sociology-anthropology under the leadership of Stan Wasson, and was housed in Matheson Hall. I had completed my master's and most of my coursework for the Ph.D. at Bryn Mawr College and thus, while I was full-time I would not be tenure track until the doctorate was finished—hence the instructor title. There were a few of us in that position in different parts of the humanities and social sciences, which was part of the business college.

The majority of the students taking these courses were the first generation to go to college and had selected Drexel because it offered degrees that could lead to careers and upward mobility. They also were predominantly commuter students living with their parents and using the money from their co-op jobs to pay most of their tuition. They were extremely serious about their majors and highly motivated to do well. At least in these early years, most were white and male and very local to Philadelphia and the inner suburbs. While some took their liberal studies courses as a necessary evil, many found them a break from the courses in their majors and as part of the '60s and early '70s as involving subjects that also had reality. I remember some very lively discussions and arguments among the students and with points in the books. I encouraged this if they based the discussions on the course material and if they could prove me "wrong." Given the times, this was a challenge from an "authority" figure and a woman. Some of these discussions carried over from class to my office.

In my department the tenured and tenure-track faculty were supportive and willing to do mentoring of new faculty informally. Stan Wasson opened his home for dinners and conversations once or twice a year, as did other faculty. Even department meetings explored how to handle topics like the civil rights protests. It was an exciting time to be a young faculty member.

As we moved into the '70s, I was able to create a variety of additional courses—some still offered, such as The Human Past, Societies in Transition, Women in a Changing Society (changed by administrative request to Women and Men), Worldviews, Science, Magic and

Religion, and some special topics courses like Anthropology through Science Fiction. One I remember was on Native Americans, and we had several books including Bury My Heart at Wounded Knee. *I taught this in a room on the third floor of the Main Building, every seat was filled, and students sat on the window ledges and on the floor. It was possible to organize a trip in private cars to New York to go to museums, have lunch and dinner together, and then drive back. We went to hear speakers at other area colleges, and I had an occasional class at my house in University City. It is not surprising that I am still in touch with some of the students from these years. It was an exhilarating time to teach and to learn.*

—Barbara Hornum

12

Pilot '71

From Home Economics to Design, Media,
and Beyond in the Westphal College

David Raizman

I N THIS ESSAY I trace the evolution of Drexel's College of Home Economics into what is today the Westphal College of Media Arts and Design. I focus in particular on an experimental curriculum introduced in the late 1960s, Pilot '71, that eventually transformed the university's design programs. The adoption of Pilot '71 is but one demonstration of the steady pace of change that has taken place in design-based education at Drexel, and elsewhere, since the end of World War II, and that has continued into 2016, the year of Drexel's 125th anniversary.

Home Economics and Design

The shift from home economics to design after World War II was a gradual one at Drexel. In 1945 the College of Home Economics (CHE) offered degree programs in costume design, dietetics, general home economics, and home economics education. It also provided part of the coursework for a program in retail merchandising that was located in the School of Business Administration. In 1947 retail merchandising moved to CHE, was renamed fashion and textile merchandising, and in 1967 renamed again, to design and merchandising.[1]

By 1951 CHE had the largest enrollment in home economics programs at any private college in the country.[2] Regardless of which major a student selected, all home economics freshmen were required to take a common first

School of Domestic Science and Arts, domestic science laboratory, 1914. (Drexel University Archives. PC 3 Early photographs of the Drexel Institute of Art, Science, and Industry.)

year curriculum that included courses in the liberal arts and sciences as well as introductory courses in nutrition and clothing,[3] and two courses in "art appreciation and design." These first-year courses were designed to fit "not only to the needs of homemakers . . . but also [to] prepare young women for responsible positions in institutional administration, in textile manufacturing, in the many areas of food technology, and in home economics education."[4]

With a student body composed entirely of women, food preparation laboratories in the Main Building, and an early childhood center (known as the Grace Godfrey Home Management House) housed in a building next to Van Renssalaer Hall (the women's dormitory), CHE's degree programs all reinforced women's traditional domestic roles, providing the skills and background necessary for the responsibilities of homemaking.[5] What tied these roles to design was that child development, nutrition, *and* aesthetics all contributed to the cultivation of healthy, well-adjusted families living in tastefully decorated and efficiently managed homes and wearing attractive, appropriate clothing. It is thus not surprising that Drexel's three design majors—costume, fashion and textile merchandising, and interiors (added as a degree program in 1953)—were all located in CHE.

The required freshmen courses in design used the textbook *Art Today*, first published in 1941. The revised 1956 edition added numerous illustrations of postwar modern art, architecture, and textile patterns. Its chapters were less concerned with exercises intended to develop high levels of competence in drawing or painting than with fostering skills of visual discrimination and an appreciation of different materials and processes.[6] Students learned to discern principles of visual organization, practiced some still life and figure drawing, and later were expected to apply those understandings to real life choices in dress, interiors, or visual merchandising.[7] The commitment to postwar modern art and design in the 1956 edition of the textbook connected the arts with new developments in technology: "Change in the arts is as much a part of this dynamic age as is change in science."[8] *Art Today*'s chapters encouraged students to make "art effective

School of Domestic Science and Arts, model laundry, c. 1918. (Drexel University Archives. PC 3 Early photographs of the Drexel Institute of Art, Science, and Industry.)

School of Domestic Science and Arts, costume design, c. 1916. (Drexel University Archives. PC 3 Early photographs of the Drexel Institute of Art, Science, and Industry.)

in daily living" and stressed that visual appeal was as important in design as utilitarian requirements. The textbook also makes clear the relationship between design and home economics, with the first chapter, titled "Art in the Home," emphasizing that art grows from the universal "need for shelter and protection."[9]

By the time of the 1956–1957 Drexel catalog, the introductory statement for CHE noted a stronger emphasis on "professional education" through the cooperative education program, while retaining the traditional commitment to home management.[10] Rather than being hidden under the generic rubric of "home economics for business" as they had been previously (along with programs in institutional management, medical technology, home economics education, and briefly a collaborative program in nursing), career-oriented programs in fashion design, fashion and textile merchandising, and interior design were individually named and more prominently placed in the *Bulletin*—and all programs required cooperative education. Drexel's home economics education thus sought to reconcile the competing demands of career preparation, a woman's traditional homemaker role, and the liberal values of a holistic education, with the latter two objectives maintained through a required common freshmen curriculum.

In 1962 Marjorie Rankin (a graduate of the master's program in clothing, textiles, and household art at Cornell University's College of Home
Economics) was appointed CHE dean. An advocate for change and the
continued vitality of home economics, Rankin oversaw the growth and expansion of CHE's career-oriented programs, including those in the fields
of applied design and nutrition, as well as medical and institutional technology. The college enrolled over six hundred full-time students and was
growing rapidly, to almost nine hundred students in 1966. As part of this
expansion, CHE in 1965 was divided into three departments: nutrition;
human behavior and development; and the largest, design, which accounted
for more than half of the total college enrollment for that year, and had
nine full-time faculty—all women except for one male instructor, Wade
Jolly, who joined CHE in 1947.[11] The Department of Design, chaired by
Professor Mary McCue Epstein, housed programs in fashion design, interior design, and design and merchandising, and, beginning in 1975, offered
course work in graphic design and photography.[12]

Pilot '71: A New Curricular Initiative

Under the direction of Dean Rankin and design department head Mary
Epstein, CHE initiated a pilot program in the fall of 1967 for thirty-eight
freshmen design majors—named Pilot '71, for the year in which incoming
freshmen in the program would graduate. Though Pilot '71 was not mentioned in the 1967–1968 university bulletin, CHE's introductory narrative
section acknowledged an "atmosphere of change" in education, noting that
a greater emphasis on individuality was challenging the institution of the
family.[13]

A 1966 press announcement for Founder's Day (an annual event held
at the end of the fall term, celebrating Anthony Drexel's legacy) called Pilot '71 a "radical re-orientation of the thinking of the College" that "will
make possible a new generation of students who can address themselves to
the inventive development of new solutions."[14] In a 1968 lecture to the faculty of the College of Home Economics at Virginia Polytechnic Institute,
Rankin elaborated that Pilot '71 constituted a shift from an "applied" to a
"theoretical" approach, in response to the "trend toward women being gain-
fully employed outside the home." Seeking to address the challenges to both
home and family during the cultural upheavals of the 1960s, Rankin offered
a revised definition of home economics as "the use of Art, Physical Science
and Social Science to create an enhancing matrix for individual life."

Professor Elliott Barowitz conducting a critique of freshman design projects in Drexel's Main Building, fourth floor, c. 1967–1968, the first or second year of the College of Home Economics Pilot '71 program. (Drexel University Archives.)

Notably absent in her lecture were the words "home" and "family," in favor of the "individual."[15]

Despite Dean Rankin's apparent hopes that Pilot '71 might provide a reformulation of home economics to maintain its relevance in a changing world, it was not the overarching and inclusive discipline it had once been. The shift was apparent in 1974 when CHE was renamed the Nesbitt College of Design, Nutrition, Human Behavior, and Home Economics.

To create and implement Pilot '71, two new faculty members were hired into CHE, Elliott Barowitz in 1966 and James Hallahan in 1968. Both were men, and had neither industry experience nor an educational background in the applied arts. Both had instead studied painting at the Rhode Island School of Design (RISD).[16] Barowitz modeled the Pilot '71 curriculum on RISD's two-year foundation program.[17] The two painters refined and expanded the existing foundation in design to include three design studios and two courses in drawing in the freshmen year,[18] three additional courses in the sophomore year titled "Mix Media" (later Mixed Media), and two classes in painting in the junior and senior years.[19] This new art and design core replaced the home economics–based common freshman-year curriculum that had existed since the end of World War II, substituting an enlarged "art-based" foundation for one grounded in home and family.

The new foundation, around which the design curricula were built, retained content in the humanities (including art history, which became a series of three required survey courses covering the Western canon), social sciences, and sciences, while adding considerably to the design component. Pilot '71 thus articulated a new approach in which art was a unifying principle. The underlying belief was that design and art were fundamentally alike; both were based upon principles of visual organization that could be applied to Drexel's programs in fashion, interior, or apparel (later product)

merchandising.[20] The specific skills and practical differences that distinguished these three programs were less significant than the visual language
that tied them together. Once acquired, a student with a foundation in color,
two- and three-dimensional visual expression, and organization could "design" anything.

According to at least some of the students in the program, Pilot '71 was
empowering: it introduced them to a new, aesthetic way of thinking, and
created a dialogue by which the students could define themselves as artists
and individuals.[21] The course descriptions in the catalogs from this period
reveal the nature of these foundation courses and their objectives. Lacking
precise reference to either fashion or interiors, they stressed awareness of materials and abstract formal relationships, such as a "general concern for the
non-referential qualities of design" and the investigation of "design problems dealing with aesthetic discipline, special design goals, and material limitations, emphasis upon spatial and two-dimensional relationships in black
and white."[22] For one Mix Media course the description reads: "an investigation of a selected range of materials focusing on creating three-dimensional
objects in various scales and environments. Essentially non-functional, non-
referential, and non-permanent objects." The description for a third Mix
Media course, based upon performance-based media, added "the use of projected images, i.e. sound, photography, film, drawing, and painting."[23]

The terms "nonfunctional" and "nonreferential" indicate that the foundation of an art-based design education was an informed, creative, more
open-ended approach to problem-solving in design, dealing with abstract
relationships in two- and three-dimensional space (and time) that later

Open Faculty meeting with students in Mix Media studio,
Department of Design, College of Home Economics, Nesbitt Hall,
1971. Pictured (left to right) are Professors Elliott Barowitz,
Dennis Will, James Hallahan, Keith Newhouse, and students,
including Renee Weiss (Chase) at far right, The Lexerd, 1972.
(Drexel University Archives.)

would be applied to the professional fields of fashion or interiors. The studio was the laboratory for such investigations, and each student's solution to a specific design exercise was presented in terms of a dialogue or "critique" where faculty and other students discussed and exchanged observations about their design decisions. The two members of the pilot program I spoke with recalled both the demanding as well as exciting nature of the new foundation studio courses. Surprised and perplexed at first by the absence of any obvious relationship between their new course of study and the applied major they had selected, they became fully immersed in something new, exhilarating, and engaging. The "culture shock" of creative and individual freedom they experienced and the sense of liberation they felt led to a confidence that they would be successful as designers.

A Wider Context

The model that Barowitz and Hallahan developed for Pilot '71 reflected a broader trend, and was employed not only at RISD but at many art and design schools in the United States, including both Temple University's Tyler School of Art and the Moore College of Art and Design in Philadelphia, where foundation courses institutionalized a fundamental and underlying connection between fine art and applied design. For instance, Tyler's traditional orientation toward the fine arts included ceramics, but by the mid-1960s also comprised new programs in studio craft (jewelry and metalsmithing, weaving and textiles) and graphic design. Regardless of their area of specialization, all students in the fine or "allied" arts were required to take foundation courses in design during the freshman and sophomore years focusing upon "principles of organization."[24] At Moore, which focused more on art education, all freshmen took the same required courses in two- and three-dimensional design, color, and drawing, all oriented around the fine arts, and could major in fields ranging from painting to textiles and illustration. Moore's catalogs from the 1950s used the analogy of a spoked wheel to describe a fine arts foundation at the center, with areas of specialization as the radiating spokes, increasingly distinct and separated from one another.[25]

The origins of the fine arts foundation model instituted at Drexel through Pilot '71 can be traced to the Preliminary Course (*Vorkurs*) at the Bauhaus school in Germany, located first in Weimar (1919–1924), then Dessau (1925–1932), and finally in Berlin (1932–1933). The school's closure in 1933 by the Nazi government resulted in an exodus of faculty and students to Switzerland, England, and the United States. The presence of Bauhaus faculty at American colleges and universities, such as Josef and

Anni Albers, first at Black Mountain College in North Carolina and later at Yale University, and Laszlo Moholy-Nagy at the New Bauhaus (later the Illinois Institute of Technology) in Chicago, helped introduce and spread the fine arts foundation as a standard approach to design education. As at Drexel, the foundation faculty at the Bauhaus consisted primarily of fine artists; and as with Pilot '71 and similar programs elsewhere, the Bauhaus *Vorkurs* emphasized underlying aesthetic principles that governed the design of print materials, textiles, metalwork, and furniture.[26] There was as well a liberal element in the course work, encouraging freedom of thought intended to develop individual creativity and open-ended solutions to formal problems of composition and color harmony.[27] Also similar to the ideals of Pilot '71 was a presumption that design and art were fundamentally alike, that the specific skills and practical differences which separated them were less significant than the visual language that tied them together in a spirit of personal discovery, experimentation, and cultural unity.[28]

Bauhaus-inspired foundation courses emphasized personal growth, hand-eye skills, and the ability to "think" visually or formally, seeing, for instance, interiors as three-dimensional spaces occupied by relationships among three-dimensional forms, and garments as abstract forms moving in space. The expressive freedom advocated in the foundation courses (as well as in required painting and sculpture classes) was tempered by technical and other constraints (such as costs, functional requirements, and materials), a form of "creative problem solving" that produced a lively dialogue between the possible and the practical. The foundation fostered a belief in the fluid relationship between fine and applied art, based upon the values of individual creativity and shared aesthetic principles. These values were contemporary with, and no doubt connected to, the rise of abstract nonobjective avant-garde art after World War II in New York City and internationally, which emphasized personal discovery and formal explorations, a particular kind of visual thinking that found its purest form in the fine arts.[29]

Growing Pains

Pilot '71 became the common core of foundation courses for design students at Nesbitt College in 1969, and occupied center stage as the number of design majors grew and as new design majors were introduced. In 1984 Dean Rankin retired and Dr. J. Michael Adams was named as her successor. In 1986, the Department of Design split into two new departments: fashion and visual studies, including all of the faculty teaching the foundation courses; and interiors and graphics, comprising the interior design program and faculty in graphic design (which became a separate major in 1988) and photography (which became a major in 1990).[30]

I arrived as the head of the Department of Fashion and Visual Studies in fall 1989, just as tensions between faculty in the foundation program (referred to as visual studies) and the degree programs were emerging.[31] Among the issues I recall were how to compensate for the increasing lack of sewing skills among fashion design majors, in part a result of the elimination of "home economics" courses in their junior and senior high schools. To address this problem faculty in the fashion design program recommended moving the Construction Skills course earlier in the curriculum, introducing a specific technical component;[32] another battle concerned the elimination of the second of two required painting courses to make room for a new course in computer-aided design (CAD) for fashion, displacing part of the fine arts orientation of the foundation program. Also, amid enrollment declines across the university, some faculty in the applied programs felt there was a need to introduce courses relevant to the majors earlier in the curriculum, in the hope of retaining career-oriented students who were impatient to be immersed in their chosen field. These and related issues posed a threat to the integrity of the foundation core and the central, unifying role of the fine arts in the curriculum; as mentioned above, this threat was exacerbated by the introduction of computer-aided design, not only in fashion, but in the other design majors as well, including graphic design.[33] The result of these pressures was a slow erosion of the fine arts–based foundation through the elimination of fine arts courses, the introduction of choices rather than requirements, and the movement toward specialized variations on foundation course content for specific majors, rather than maintenance of the unified model initiated by Pilot '71.

In 1994 the program in film and video production, including the management of Drexel's radio and television stations, moved to Nesbitt College from the College of Arts and Sciences, and performing arts (comprising music, theater, and arts administration) followed in 1997.[34] In 1998 a new program in digital media was added to the college as well. In 2001 the Department of Performing Arts created an innovative music industry program, which included a Drexel recording label, Mad Dragon Records. These additions created a larger but also more diverse group of students and faculty,[35] and they shifted attention toward popular media and away from fine arts.

Faculty in the newer media-based programs lobbied to be exempt from parts of the fine arts foundation, or asked that it be treated as a "menu" from which students could pick and choose courses relevant to their professional needs; meanwhile, the foundation itself adjusted to changing

circumstances, with younger faculty adapting content to the needs of particular majors. The acquisition and introduction of new programs that
diluted the fine arts–based foundation continued into the new millennium,
as Nesbitt College became in 2001 the College of Media Arts and Design,
and in 2005, following a donation by tax software company founder Ray
Westphal in honor of his late wife, a CHE alumna, was renamed the Antoinette Westphal College of Media Arts and Design (AWCoMAD). New
departments and programs included entertainment and arts management,
product design, television, and television management. The subdivision of
the digital media program into three more specialized majors in animation
and special effects, game production, and interactive digital media all represent an increasingly dynamic, and challenging, atmosphere of change.[36]

In 1967 the number of full-time college faculty at the time the pilot
program was initiated was nine, of whom two had backgrounds in fine arts.
In 1989, full-time faculty devoted to the design-based programs was thirty,
of whom eight were fine artists. In 2015, full-time faculty numbered 126 in
five departments; the number of fine artists and art historians was sixteen,
the highest in history, but a smaller percentage of the total number of
faculty.

Visual studies faculty in the Department of Art and Art History have
embraced technology and tailored the introductory design courses to address new skills and interests, and have initiated stronger links with majors
such as film and digital media. Interdisciplinarity, encouraging communication and collaborations among programs, and overall flexibility seem more
important for the future of design education than the foundation as it
emerged in the later 1960s with Pilot '71.

The theory and practice of design and design education has also changed.
Terms such as "human-centered" or "user-centered" are now commonly
used to describe a design process in which aesthetics is but one of several
"stakeholders" in a dialogue that involves the importance of interactivity
and reconciling multiple points of view that include marketing, consumer
psychology, aesthetics, technology, user-interface, and environmental impact. While certainly not marginalized, the fine arts no longer occupy the
center in this new design paradigm.[37]

The Future

As a new academic year began in fall 2015, Westphal College could boast
national and international rankings in several of its design programs.[38] From
a foundation in home economics after World War II, to a fine arts–based

foundation beginning in 1967, and to the expansion into media and entertainment in the 1990s and beyond, the success of the Westphal College's programs has depended upon a dynamic and flexible approach to its curricula that acknowledges but no longer depends upon the fine arts–based design core that emerged in Pilot '71. And even this core has evolved and adapted to changes in technology and a greater degree of specialization. Yet Westphal College's most recent strategic plan calls for more interdisciplinary collaboration to find common ground among its programs, perhaps compensating for the lesser degree of commonality in the freshmen and sophomore program curricula, and searching for a new body of knowledge that might unify the college's diverse programs and student body.

Whether provided by a common freshman year, a sequence of foundation courses and the experience of critique, or by the excitement across disciplines of new technological and information tools such as CAD, virtual reality, and 3-D printing, Westphal College has been sustained by the shared excitement of exploring new ways of thinking among students and faculty alike. When I spoke with Renée Weiss Chase, professor of fashion design at Drexel, and her friend and classmate Lee Andes, both participants in Pilot '71, each remarked that the excitement and creative freedom that the new foundation generated for them and their fellow students in 1967 could now be felt by many of today's students in the relationship they share with emerging technologies. And when I spoke with Sibby Merkel Brasler, 1960 graduate of CHE's textile merchandising program, she remarked on the interest faculty took in her own personal and professional development, recognizing, encouraging, and developing each student's potential.[39] Pilot '71 marked a particular moment in our college's history—it was a link to the past as well as a bridge to the future, combining continuity with the embrace of change—but it also reflects a common spirit of student-oriented education that spans the history of the college, and of design education at Drexel.[40]

NOTES

My thanks to the staff in the Hagerty Library Archives for their interest and assistance with archival materials in the preparation of this chapter.

1. *Drexel Bulletin*, 1947–1948 (Philadelphia: Drexel Institute of Technology, 1948), 109 and *Drexel Bulletin*, 1967–1968 (Philadelphia: Drexel Institute of Technology, 1968), 84.
2. "History of the College of Home Economics, Drexel Institute of Technology," Founders Day text, 1967, 3, Hagerty Library Archives, Drexel University. Enrollment data from 1951 in the Drexel Institute of Technology *Bulletin* reported four hundred

undergraduate majors in the college's programs, not including graduate students or the part-time Evening College enrollment.

3. Students in all of the college's programs were required to take courses including Child Development, The Family (offered in sociology), Family Management, and Design in the Home; cf. *Drexel Bulletin*, 1955–1956 (Philadelphia: Drexel Institute of Technology), 127.

4. *Drexel Bulletin*, 1945–1946 (Philadelphia: Drexel Institute of Technology), 101.

5. See Carma R. Gorman, "An Educated Demand: The Implications of Art in Every Day Life for American Industrial Design, 1925–1950," *Design Issues* 16, no. 3 (autumn 2000): 45–66, especially 47ff.; and Carma R. Gorman, "The Changing Status of Design in Art in Every Day Life, 1925–1940," *Studies in the Decorative Arts* (spring/summer 2007): 145–65. On the professionalization of home economics, see Sarah Stage and Virginia B. Vincenti, eds., *Rethinking Home Economics: Women and the History of a Profession* (Ithaca, NY: Cornell University Press, 1997).

6. Ray Faulkner et al., *Art Today: An Introduction to the Fine and Functional Arts*, 3rd ed. (New York: Holt, Reinhart and Winston, 1956).

7. My thanks to Mrs. Sibby Merkel Brasler, 1960 alumna of the fashion and textile merchandising program in the College of Home Economics, former trustee of Drexel University, and benefactor of the College of Media Arts and Design. Sibby remembered her textbook from her freshmen year; other recollections emerged during my interview with her on November 17, 2015.

8. Faulkner et al., *Art Today*, v.

9. Ibid., xix.

10. Co-op had become an integral part of the degree programs beginning in 1944; cf. "History of the College of Home Economics, Drexel Institute of Technology," Founders Day text, 2, Hagerty Library Archives, Drexel University.

11. *Drexel Bulletin*, 1966–1967 (Philadelphia: Drexel Institute of Technology, 1967), 123. My thanks to Steven DePietro and his staff in the provost's office at Drexel for assistance with gathering enrollment information for this chapter.

12. Professor Epstein earned a bachelor's degree in home economics in 1937 from Hood College and a master's degree, also in home economics, from the Drexel Institute of Technology in 1948.

13. *Drexel Bulletin*, 1967–1968 (Philadelphia: Drexel Institute of Technology), 79.

14. "History of the College of Home Economics, Drexel Institute of Technology," 1.

15. Marjorie Rankin, "A Pilot Program in Home Economics: Changing an Applied Curriculum to Include a Theoretical Approach," lecture, Virginia Polytechnic University, 1968, 3, Hagerty Library Archives, Drexel University.

16. Barowitz earned a B.F.A. in painting from the Rhode Island School of Design (RISD), completed one year of study at Carnegie Institute of Technology (now Carnegie Mellon University) in Architecture, and an M.F.A. in painting from the University of Cincinnati after studying for one year at San Francisco Art Institute. Hallahan earned a degree in literature from the University of Connecticut, studied painting for three years at RISD, and completed a master's degree in art at the Teachers College of Columbia University. Barowitz retired from Drexel University as professor in 2002, while Hallahan left Drexel in 1972.

17. Elliott Barowitz, interviewed by David Raizman, November 17, 2015.

18. The three-term sequence consisted of courses in black and white, color, and 3-D design and remains in the present course catalog, available at http://catalog.drexel.edu/undergraduate/collegeofmediaartsanddesign/fineart/.

19. Sculpture was also required in either the junior or senior year, taught by an expanding fine art faculty with M.F.A. degrees, including professors Dennis Will and Keith Newhouse, as well as Lydia Hunn and Brian Wagner; elective, though popular courses in hand-weaving were offered by instructor Yvonne Bobrowicz, a graduate of the Cranbrook Academy of Art. Another requirement of the Pilot '71 curriculum was a course in basic photography, which also became a required part of the foundation beginning in 1969.

20. D&M students were required to take the freshman sequence of design courses, but not the sophomore sequence of "Mix Media" required of interiors and fashion majors. The curriculum added more requirements in art history. This difference persists in the current D&M major.

21. Renée Weiss Chase and Lee Andes, interviewed by David Raizman, October 15, 2015.

22. *Drexel Bulletin*, 1969–1971 (Philadelphia: Drexel Institute of Technology), 122.

23. Ibid., 123.

24. *Catalogue*, 1961–1963 (Philadelphia: Tyler School of Art, 1963).

25. *Catalogue*, 1952–1953 (Philadelphia: Moore Institute of Art, 1953), 35. My thanks to Ms. Virginia Theerman, senior design and merchandising major, for her assistance in gathering information from both the Tyler School of Art and the Moore College of Art and Design.

26. Architecture was the ultimate aim of the Bauhaus educational program, demonstrating the unity of arts; the school's first director was architect Walter Gropius. Gropius resigned in 1928 and a program in architecture was not introduced until after his resignation, under the directors Hannes Meyer and later Mies van der Rohe.

The literature on the Bauhaus is extensive; for an introduction see Frank Whitford, *Bauhaus* (London: Thames and Hudson, 1984); more recently, see Barry Bergdoll and Leah Dickerman, *Bauhaus 1919–1933: Workshops for Modernity*, exhibition catalog (New York: Museum of Modern Art, 2009). The complex, even contradictory institutional history of the Bauhaus is the subject of Gillian Naylor, *The Bauhaus Reassessed: Sources and Design Theory* (New York: E. P. Dutton, 1985).

27. Iohannes Itten, who directed the *Vorkurs* at the Bauhaus from 1919 to 1923, directed spiritual exercises with the students as well; cf. Whitford, *Bauhaus*, 51–59.

28. At the Bauhaus it was cultural renewal with utopian aspirations during the Weimar Republic; in the United States it was a youth movement, challenging authority, and believing in the power of art for personal and social transformation. The *Drexel Bulletin* for 1975–1976, mentions the college's programs in relation to "global and societal challenges" such as hunger, the disadvantaged, and the environment (86–87).

29. See Irving Sandler, *The New York School: the Painters and Sculptors of the Sixties* (New York: Harper & Row, 1978), 311.

30. Dean Adams created a new program in hotel restaurant and institutional management, preserving a link to home economics; according to Sibby Brasler, one of Dean Adams's motivations was to add more men to the student population of the college. In 1990 the nutrition program moved to the College of Arts and Sciences.

31. Sylvia Clark served as head of interior and graphic studies.

32. To strengthen the professional preparation of fashion design students, Professor Chase installed current industrial sewing and other machinery to replace the domestic machines that were being used.

33. The fine arts faculty in general were skeptical of the role of the computer in design and in design education. In a documentary film on the introduction of the microcomputer at Drexel, directed and produced by Professor Dave Jones in 1985, foundation

faculty questioned whether the computer was "too rational" to be an effective visual tool for designers and might not be capable of effectively translating ideas or visions onto paper; one faculty commented that the relevance of the computer to "art" was remote. See D. B. Jones, "Going National: Introduction of the Microcomputer at Drexel University 1985," Hagerty Library Archives, Drexel University.

34. A degree program in dance was added in 2008.

35. The Department of Architecture, formerly located in the Evening College, also became part of the Nesbitt College of Design Arts in 1987. Architecture remained a part-time, evening program until 1992, when a new "2+4" program was inaugurated under department head Paul Hirshorn. The curriculum, however, accredited through the National Architecture Accrediting Board, was almost entirely self-contained. From 1992 until 2000, 2+4 architecture students took introductory drawing taught by the visual studies faculty.

36. The full listing of AWCoMAD programs can be found at http://www.drexel.edu /westphal/academics/.

37. Klaus Krippendorf, *The Semantic Turn: A New Foundation for Design* (Boca Raton, FL: Taylor & Francis, 2006).

38. Published in September 2015, *College Factual* ranked AWCoMAD as the seventh best design and applied arts school in the country. This new ranking is in addition to *Business of Fashion*'s recent ranking of the fashion design program as the third best in the country and tenth best in the world, The Princeton Review's ranking of the gaming program as fourth in the country; *Design Intelligence*'s ranking of the interior architecture program as seventh in the country; Fashionista.com's ranking of the design and merchandising program as number three in the nation; and our graphic design program received "Highest Honors" recognition from *Graphic Design USA*.

39. Although not mentioned in this chapter's text, both Professor Chase and Mrs. Brasler mentioned the example and mentorship offered to them as students by Dolores Quinn, professor in the department of design from 1948 until her retirement in 1983. Ms. Quinn taught fashion design, visual merchandising, supervised the annual fashion show, and received three grants from the National Endowment for the Arts supporting her research in clothing for the physically handicapped. Professor Chase continued that work, publishing *Design within Limits* in 1990, now in its second edition (New York, NY: Fairchild Publications, 2003).

40. It is not surprising that several graduates of the college during the 1970s returned to Drexel as faculty and in administrative roles. Professor Renee Weiss Chase ('71) served as head of the fashion design program from 1986 until 2011; Karin Sundstedt Kuenstler ('73), associate professor of design, was head of the Interior Design and Graphic Studies Department (1996–2007) and now serves as associate dean for research in the college; and Roberta Gruber ('75), associate professor of design, directed the design and merchandising program from 1996 to 2007, since which times she has been head of the design department.

We had parties at the Drexel Lodge and at Cavanaugh's, and we had a lounge in our department where the students hung out with the faculty, so it was a close community. I used to invite a lot of the foreign students—back when I first started it was mostly Indian students in the graduate department. The American students figured after five years of school, or four years if they weren't from Drexel, they wanted to earn some money so they didn't go right to grad school; but we had a large population of Indian students, a few Chinese students, and more recently there were a lot Middle Eastern students. I used to invite them to my place for Jewish holidays, give them a cultural experience, and a lot of them still remember it; we're still friends and we stay in touch. We teased them. When I started here I was their big sister, eventually I became mom, and when I left I was grandma.

One Christmas party, the university Christmas party, it was the year the Macintoshes came out, '84 or Christmas of '83, I guess it was. President William Hagerty knew me because of his son. So we'd always tease when we'd meet. "Oh Mike's doing real well," and I'd say, "Really?" You know, he'd say, "Yeah, he got a big bonus," so I would say, "Well, look where he got his degree!" and "Where's the check to the department?" You know, we had this repartee. So I teased him at the Christmas party and I told him, I said, "You're letting faculty buy the Macintoshes, students buy the Macintoshes, why can't the staff?" We were not allowed to. He said, "Well we're afraid that they'll learn how to use them and then go for higher-paying jobs out in the industry . . . but you wouldn't do that! You can get one!" His secretary was right there, and I said, "Got that, Cathy?" and I brought in a check the next day. I wasn't going to let him take it back.

I had a fairly thriving business on the side typing Ph.D. theses with my typewriter, because we used the [IBM] Selectrics in order to get the Greek symbols; and you would have to take the page out of the thesis, type the Greek letter, put [the page] back, and the students couldn't correct them, but once they started with the Macintosh and the word processor, I went out of business.

—JUDY TRACHTMAN

Drexel, Urban Renewal, and Civil Rights

James Wolfinger

IN THE TWO DECADES after World War II, the Drexel Institute of Technology was swept up in large trends that roiled the economy, politics, and culture of the United States. Chief among these trends were the restructuring of Philadelphia's industrial economy, the implementation of urban renewal policies, and the growth of student activism and the black rights movement. Drexel emerged from the 1960s with a larger physical plant and a larger engagement, albeit not always a happy one, with its black students and the surrounding community.

Government spending during World War II reversed the terrible economic setbacks that Philadelphia experienced during the Great Depression. Across the city, as many as 40 percent of Philadelphians, and a staggering 50 percent of the African-American community, experienced unemployment. As late as 1940, 20 percent of Philadelphians remained jobless. But over the course of 1941 the federal government invested $130 million in Philadelphia industries, reinvigorating the city's manufacturing base. By the end of the war Pennsylvania had received $11.7 billion in defense contracts (the sixth largest total in the nation), with Philadelphia holding the lion's share of that total. Across the city one out of four workers found employment in the 3,500 plants, such as Baldwin Locomotive and Philco, that produced war goods ranging from tanks and radar equipment to military uniforms.[1]

The demand for workers led to significant growth in the city's population. Standing over 1.9 million in 1940, Philadelphia's population surged to more than 2 million in 1950, the high point in the city's history. The greatest growth came in the black population, which jumped from some 250,000 people in 1940 to 376,000 in 1950. Those numbers only continued to grow in the ensuing decades, hitting 529,000 black residents in 1960 and 654,000 in 1970. African-Americans moved from representing 13 percent of the total population in 1940 to 18 percent in 1950 and 34 percent in 1970. By 1950, African-Americans for the first time eclipsed the number of immigrants from foreign countries residing in the city.[2]

Black Philadelphians, who had historically experienced a hostile city, during wartime found a unique, but fleeting, opportunity to gain substantial employment in area industries. The number of black workers in manufacturing rose from 14,000 in 1940 to 54,000 in 1944, with Midvale Steel and Sun Shipyard being key employers. War's end, however, brought the end of government contracts, and prospects for Philadelphia companies and their employees quickly soured. In the months immediately after the war, Baldwin and Midvale laid off half their employees, Sun Ship contracted from 34,000 to 4,000 workers, and Cramp's Shipyard closed entirely. A few plants, such as Budd Manufacturing and the Navy Yard, prospered through the Korean War, and Philco remained a major manufacturer of electronics, but overall the economic outlook was gloomy.[3]

More than the evaporation of government contracts was at work, as it became obvious that World War II had only temporarily arrested Philadelphia's prewar industrial slide. In the immediate postwar decade, many textile manufacturers shifted their operations to the South; King of Prussia drew SKF, General Electric, and other industries to the suburbs; and Yale & Towne, Budd, and B. F. Goodrich left the city as well. The city's industrial areas, employers argued, were too cramped and too reliant on nineteenth-century transportation (railroads and water). As the companies moved, opportunity disappeared: 50,000 of the city's 350,000 industrial positions vanished in the 1950s (200,000 more would go by 1985) with the textile industry especially decimated by the loss of jobs.[4]

As industrial work left Philadelphia, so did the city's residents. Overall, Philadelphia's population dropped from its apex of 2.07 million people in 1950 to 2 million in 1960 and 1.95 million in 1970. Philadelphians of European descent accounted for much of the exodus. From 1940 to 1950, for example, West Philadelphia lost 24 percent of its Irish population, South

Philadelphia lost 27 percent of its Italian population, and North Philadel-phia lost 19 percent of its Jewish population. In part, they left for employ-ment opportunities in the suburbs: residents of suburban Bucks and Montgomery counties saw their wages rise by 46 percent and 26 percent, respectively, while Philadelphians' wages remained stagnant. They also left for new homes, new schools, and the widely acclaimed suburban lifestyle then in vogue.[5]

The subtext for this movement of the city's population, however, was the issue of race. Residential segregation hardened and related racial ten-sions grew across Philadelphia in the postwar period. In part, African-Americans could not move to the suburbs because they lacked the stable income necessary to buy a new home. But they also faced overt discrimi-natory housing policies, such as redlining that limited their access to mort-gages, and federal and municipal policies that placed public housing in inner-city neighborhoods, thus furthering the concentration of black Philadelphians and limiting them to areas with ever-decreasing employ-ment opportunities. When African-Americans did try to move into "white" communities in the city and the suburbs (Levittown, Kensington, and Ju-niata Park are three noteworthy examples), they met heavy, and often vio-lent, resistance. In the late 1940s and 1950s Philadelphia still had large European ethnic enclaves, but the familiar pattern of whites living in the suburbs and blacks in the city was becoming increasingly obvious.[6]

Philadelphia's political leaders, especially liberal Democrats such as Richardson Dilworth and Joseph Clark, who had swept out the old, cor-rupt Republican political machine, grew gravely concerned with the fate of their city. The same was true of their allies in the business community. An economy in decline, racial tensions mounting, and a population bleeding away from the city proper all spelled troubled times ahead. In response, they tried to forge stronger ties to the suburban counties, build a more robust transit system, and revitalize a number of urban communities, including Center City and West Philadelphia, through a redevelopment process called "urban renewal." These initiatives and others related to them came to be called the Greater Philadelphia Movement. Under the leadership of plan-ner Edmund Bacon, often known as the "Father of Modern Philadelphia," city planners and their political patrons rebuilt much of Center City, including Penn Center, Market East, Penn's Landing, Society Hill, and Independence Mall. The city also constructed the Schuylkill Expressway (I-76), Vine Street Expressway (I-676), and the Delaware Expressway (I-95). In West Philadelphia, these efforts were led by the West Philadelphia Corporation (WPC), a coalition of institutions of higher education and medical facilities that included the Drexel Institute of Technology, University of Pennsylvania, Philadelphia College of Pharmacy and Science, Philadelphia College of Osteopathy, and Presbyterian Hospital. Their urban renewal plan led to the demolition of many buildings and the development of University City in their place. Such projects across the city disproportionately displaced African-American homeowners and their businesses.[7]

African-Americans, confronting limited employment prospects, residential segregation, and urban renewal projects that negatively impacted their communities, at first attempted to cope with their problems through legal remedies. They pressured politicians, most successfully in the Democratic Party, to attend to their interests, which resulted in fair housing and fair employment laws, with the state's Fair Employment Practices Act of 1955 (drawing on the example of the WWII-era Fair Employment Practices Committee) being the most notable example. Such laws, however, proved to be inadequate tools for solving the problems confronting black Philadelphia. By the 1960s, they turned to a more radical, confrontational, politics led by Philadelphians such as the NAACP's Cecil B. Moore. Unwilling to quietly acquiesce to a de facto Jim Crow society any longer, black activists challenged the right of Girard College to exclude students based on race, pushed the Philadelphia school board to end its discriminatory policies, and protested against unfair employment practices at area construction sites. Anger about Philadelphia's discriminatory ways boiled over in 1964 when North Philadelphia witnessed an early example of the many urban uprisings that swept the United States in the 1960s. This activism and conflict generated a white backlash that led in 1972 to the election of Frank Rizzo, who vowed to restore law and order to the city. To many black Philadelphians, his promise sounded more like a threat to unleash the power of the state on African-Americans.[8]

As economic decline, urban redevelopment, and racial conflict roiled Philadelphia, Drexel could not help but become engaged in these larger events. The question was how the school would deal with these larger currents while staying true to its educational mission. City and university officials immediately after the war both recognized Drexel's tremendous importance to the Philadelphia area. Reports showed that Drexel prepared one-third of the engineers in the region, its co-operative education program benefited some five hundred businesses while simultaneously providing financial assistance to the school's students, and a number of students taught science and math in Philadelphia schools. Drexel officials asserted, and city leaders agreed, that the school was vital to Philadelphia's and Pennsylvania's economy, and, with its emphasis on technical and scientific education in the context of the Cold War, the nation's security.

Drexel, if it stayed in the city, could help lead the way in making Philadelphia one of America's "great industrial research complexes."[9]

Much, then, was at stake, in keeping Drexel in the city. The Philadelphia City Planning Commission assisted the cause by naming the surrounding community a redevelopment area in January 1948. This declaration
held the promise of public assistance to acquire land at low prices and clear
community roadblocks. It must be noted, however, that Drexel was repeat-
edly troubled by Penn's receiving more government resources and better
treatment, to the point that President James Creese wrote that in its dealings with public authorities his school found itself in "not an encouraging
situation nor does it seem to me a just one." Nonetheless, the city made the
political and financial circumstances in West Philadelphia favorable enough
that Drexel's board of trustees, recognizing the school's deep roots in the
area, decided by the late 1940s not to follow the lead of many concerns especially in industry leaving Philadelphia, and instead followed the course
of expanding their institution and redeveloping the surrounding community. Doing so required not just public assistance, but an internal capital campaign called the "Three-Quarter Century Fund" to raise some $18 million
needed to construct a dozen or more anticipated buildings. This massive
expansion made Drexel physically larger and more economically secure, reshaped a large swath of West Philadelphia, and heightened tensions with
the black community, both in the surrounding neighborhoods and on campus itself.[10]

With the changes facing Philadelphia in the postwar period, Drexel and
Penn spearheaded the creation of the West Philadelphia Corporation in
1959. The constituent organizations charged the corporation with "the
sound development of the general area in which they are located." To
accomplish its goal, the WPC promised to compile information on crime,
housing conditions, building code violations, schools, recreation, and traffic;
disseminate this information to the public and government officials;
develop land use plans; and acquire, improve, and resell real estate. Drexel
and its partners argued that West Philadelphia represented "one of the more
important educational, medical, research and cultural concentrations" in
the city, but that the community was showing signs of distress. "The inevi-
table aging of housing, the shifts in residential market demand, the increased
obsolescence and over-use of community facilities, including schools and
recreational areas, [and] the outmoded traffic and circulation patterns" all
combined to challenge West Philadelphia's vitality. Only a holistic approach,
the WPC argued, could attract and keep the educational, cultural, industrial, and commercial institutions necessary to save the community dubbed

University City—the eastern portion of West Philadelphia bounded by the Pennsylvania Railroad tracks on the east, Spruce Street on the south, Forty-Third Street on the west, and Powelton Avenue on the north. Drexel was responsible for developing Unit 5—an area bounded by Powelton Avenue on the north, Thirty-Second and Thirty-Third Street on the east, Chestnut Street on the south, and Thirty-Fourth Street on the west—for campus expansion. Beyond providing institutions with a "suitable" community, Drexel administrators also used the WPC to construct housing that faculty members could use—the first such private housing development in West Philadelphia in twenty-seven years, according to the *The Triangle*. In doing so, they were following a federal report that used Drexel as a case study on urban higher education and that had noted universities' "vital interest [in] rescuing their cities from the blight of crowding, slums, and residential migration." Drexel officials in particular expressed their desire to "maintain a high standard of residence" in the area. Drexel's efforts led to the number of faculty living on campus climbing from 10 percent in 1959 to 25 percent in 1964, and with the WPC also working to develop better secondary schools Drexel expected that number to go even higher.[11]

By the early 1960s, Drexel, Penn, and the other members of the WPC agreed that a focus on research would bolster University City. In 1963 the West Philadelphia Corporation established the University City Science Center (UCSC) to develop real estate that would be used for the new University City Science Institute. UCSC, simply put, would buy land and construct buildings that the science institute would then use to house scientists as they conducted and disseminated research. The WPC anticipated building some one million square feet of laboratory space that would become "a scientific research center for all of metropolitan Philadelphia." The UCSC would play a vital role in connecting "the best minds of the institutions of higher learning and those of industry," argued UCSC vice president Dr. Jean Paul Mather. It would "endeavor to generate pure and applied research activities, to draw together and train scientists and to provide the research and conference facilities necessary for those scientific objectives." The project grew fitfully at first, with initial projections of some 5,000 scientists and engineers working on government-funded and private employer contracts taking time to become reality. Drexel administrators made presentations to some three hundred companies in the mid-1960s, but it took until the late 1960s and early 1970s for UCSC to become financially stable, with organizations such as the Educational Council for Foreign Medical Graduates, International Utilities Conversion Systems, Kuljian Corporation, and the Foreign Policy Research Institute purchasing

(Left to right) James Creese, Elmer W. Griscom, Robert K. Hampton, and Herbert E. Hagaer at Drexel Institute of Technology "A Greater Drexel" display, 1963. (Drexel University Archives. PC 4 People photographs.)

space in the development's buildings. By the late 1970s, UCSC had become an economic engine for Philadelphia, with the *Philadelphia Inquirer* lauding the center for generating "two-dozen new for-profit businesses from technologies developed in its laboratories and having caused a dozen other businesses to remain in Philadelphia." And the *Wall Street Journal* reported that the UCSC had built space that housed 3,500 employees in 1975.[12]

The redevelopment of West Philadelphia undoubtedly brought value to the city and the WPC's member institutions in terms of employment and business development, but it also created problems for the community. Critics, such as African-American attorney John Clay, asserted that "Neighborhood residents feel that redevelopment is solely for the benefit of the institutions and their associated personnel [who were] grabbing land at the expense of the small homeowner." A series of investigative reports in the *Daily Pennsylvanian*, the Penn student newspaper, labeled redevelopment in University City "The Quiet War in West Philadelphia." Developers of University City did themselves no favors when they cautioned the public not to "get so caught up in the humanistic side that we overlook the fundamental value of redevelopment for all Philadelphians." Such a state-ment was aggravatingly patronizing to the area's black residents because they were the ones who bore the brunt of redevelopment, even though the school seemed to worry most about students living in Mantua and Powelton Village (mostly working-class communities with large black pop-ulations to the north of campus) being displaced from their apartments before the school's first dormitory for men could be constructed in 1967. One study (the numbers were always in question because census statistics did not align with official statements) found that redevelopment dis-placed 574 families, 90 percent of which were nonwhite. Not only did the institutions in the area not care about black interests, African-Americans argued, but redevelopment policies seemed to be designed to "prolong seg-regation and social inequalities [and] push them further back into the ghetto and destroy their respectability." One journalist found that many believed "urban renewal means Negro removal." Black residents, espe-cially in Mantua, presented plans to rehab their homes but were ignored. Only after conducting a number of protests, including a sit in at Mayor James Tate's office, did they receive some consideration of their interests.[13]

"Some consideration," alas, is the operative phrase. With over one hun-dred acres slated for redevelopment, negotiations settled in at between two and seven acres to be reserved for rehabilitation of pre-existing structures and the provision of low cost housing. This, despite the fact that govern-ment officials vowed, under the pressure of protests, that their policy was "the saving of every possible residential structure." Speculators knew better and bought as many properties as they could in the area. They drove up the cost of the project, which often had to rely on the use of eminent do-main and thus "fair compensation" for owners, leaving even less money for property rehabilitation and low-cost housing. To dampen down protests, the institutional backers of UCSC agreed to form a commission that would have community representation and the power to review all plans related to land acquisition and development. The commission would also ensure that an equal number of housing units would be built to match those lost to redevelopment, and that the institutions involved would assemble a fund of ten million dollars to further the commission's work. Within two years, the commission disbanded as black Philadelphians protested that they had insufficient representation and no funds had been raised.[14]

On campus, reporters found that the tumult of the times, brought home by the town-gown controversies generated by UCSC, made the student body "more liberal." It was a "slow process," one student said in summing up the situation in 1969, because "most Drexel students are still oriented toward getting the college degree and the well-paying job. I'm not opposed to either degrees or good jobs, but I do think that there are some other important things in life. A growing number of Drexel students are becoming aware that wars, and poverty, and air pollution, exist, and that these problems affect us all. Also, some students are aware that educational changes are needed at Drexel. So far, there aren't enough students to effect statistical changes, but I think the day is coming when students will stand up and demand a voice in their destiny." That student did not have to wait long for that day. Sparked by student concerns over a dorm to be constructed at Thirty-Third and Arch Streets, Drexel students joined with community members calling themselves the East Powelton Concerned Residents to protest the school's expansion. Newspapers, especially the *Free Press* ("an independent revolutionary newspaper"), covered the events extensively, as protesters used inflammatory rhetoric to challenge Drexel's "capitalist technical and industrial expansion" that furthered the establishment's "domestic imperialist policy" as it robbed ordinary people of the "basic human right to self-determination of community people for control over their own living environment." Protesters then called on Drexel administrators to treat them as equals, not an advisory body, as the school put together and carried out its redevelopment plans. To give their rhetoric force, protesters tore down fences at a construction site, created a people's park, and occupied two Drexel buildings, including the administration building. Penn and Temple students joined the fray, and soon President William Hagerty—who had refused to meet with the East Powelton residents or respond to their requests—agreed to meet with a coalition of students and community members and spent several hours answering their questions. The tenor of these discussions, once the anger dissipated (although it did not disappear), emphasized the community's understanding, "We need Drexel, we need to participate in Drexel—but we also need a place to live." Despite the protests, Drexel's expansion resumed, although the administration did admit that it had to review its plans because of "agitation and questions from the so-called EPCR group in the Community." Other protests focused on the work being done at UCSC. Members of Students for a Democratic Society from Penn and "other educational institutions holding stock in the Science Center," presumably Drexel, challenged scientific work at the center that developed chemical and biological weapons. UCSC's Vice President Mather indignantly responded that "those beatniks on the street can go climb a tree as far as I'm concerned. If pickets show up, I'm going to have them arrested as trespassers." Under mounting pressure, however, the UCSC as a whole took a different approach, agreeing to ban all research that furthered the "destruction or incapacitation of human life." Mather resigned.[15]

The "liberalization" of Drexel also found expression in the assertion of black rights and black identity on campus. Drexel had an exceedingly small number of African-American students in the postwar period, with only 36 in 1967 (0.7 percent of the student population), a number that grew to 302 in 1970 (3.4 percent—a jump apparently due to a statistical anomaly caused by the school beginning to report its Evening College enrollments in 1969). The climate was hostile enough that the student newspaper in the late 1940s and 1950s carried a number of articles showing students performing in blackface for talent shows. Provost Allen Bonnell gave speeches about how students' environments shaped their educational attainment but claimed that in 1964 the civil rights movement had opened access "for Negroes and other minority groups." African-American claims that "it's no use trying," Bonnell said, are just a "standard excuse [and] no longer valid."[16]

African-American students, given the increasingly dire circumstances in their communities, saw the world differently. They were doing their best to overcome difficult odds, and saw Drexel as the key to a professional career and a better life. Yet, by the 1960s, many students were writing that the school made them feel "invisible," that to succeed they were pushed into "dressing white middle-class, acting, and even talking white middle class." By "the second year at Drexel," wrote Regina Arnold in *The Triangle*, "you become bitter about the whole scene." Black students received sixteen hours a week of airtime on the school's radio station for "The Black Experience in Music," and the glee club had significant African-American representation. But overall, wrote one reporter, "No student organization makes any attempt to enfranchise the members of the Black student population." Even in 1968, wrote another reporter, Drexel had only a few black employees, and almost all worked in "menial jobs." There was no African-American history class, no black instructors, no authors, poets, or playwrights of color on campus. For many black students whose "experience has been sheltered, meaning you've dealt almost exclusively with Blacks," wrote one woman, "the transition that is made in coming to a place like Drexel University can be a living hell."[17]

Black students took a series of actions in the 1960s to try to make Drexel more accommodating to their needs. They formed the Afro-American society during the 1967–68 academic year, and used it to hold information sessions for African-Americans considering attending Drexel and to host public lectures on African-American history and black power. They pushed administrators to hire more black instructors and increase the number of

Afro-American Society members, 1970.
(Drexel University Archives. UR 12.8 Yearbooks.)

African-American students to 10 percent of incoming classes. They pressed for courses in black literature, philosophy, history, and politics, with an intent to examine the "philosophical implications but also the social, political and economic ramifications of revolutionary Black Thinkers." Drexel added a few such courses in the late 1960s and early 1970s, but did not establish a minor in African-American studies until the early 1990s, well after many other universities had done so. Early offerings of these courses had a majority of white students as well as white instructors, and conflicts between black and white students were common. "Emotions flew fast and heavy," as one reporter put it. Black Drexel students also opened the Black Liberation Activities Center to connect the school to the local African-American community.[18]

Such critiques of the school angered some white students and pushed the administration in halting ways to be more attentive to black needs. African-Americans, wrote Dave Walter in *The Triangle*, would profit from being more conservative, rather than "crawl[ing] before the Great White Father in Washington like a beggar demanding some pittance in order to stave off violent outbursts. . . . Education, industry, and perseverance are more important than marches and riots." An African-American should "study both the responsible and the militant leaders of his race," wrote another *Triangle* correspondent, implying that the two were mutually exclusive. Drexel's administration, although a "bastion of social conservatism" in some black students' estimation, did make efforts beyond the black studies program to address black student demands. Some outreach, such as Bach festivals and organ concerts, were, at best, out of date. Others, however, were more attuned to community needs. Most notably, drawing inspiration from the Afro-American society, the school developed the MAP (Motivate, Apply, Prepare) program to help West Philadelphia high school students understand what it took to enter Drexel and succeed. It supported Big Brother and Big Sister programs as well as reading clinics. And it also established the Office for Community Affairs to provide sports camps, children's plays, educational opportunities, and Christmas food baskets to families in Powelton Village. This may not have been enough—and the school at times complained of the "considerable inconvenience and expense" required to "be a good neighbor"—but Drexel, under pressure from its black students, was more attentive and engaged than it had been just a few years before.[19]

Like most urban institutions, in Philadelphia and around the country, Drexel struggled with large-scale changes reshaping the United States. The restructuring of the economy drained resources out of the city, just as the black population was growing. Urban renewal represented an investment in the future of Philadelphia, but came at the expense of some of the city's most disadvantaged populations. And the rising demands of the larger African-American community and Drexel's black students put pressure on the school to be more inclusive, more accommodating to the needs of minority students and their communities. Signs reading "Drexel Hates the Community" still appeared in the area, but the school was at least making more of an effort to deal with the realities of race relations in West Philadelphia and on campus. In all, the postwar period brought significant challenges to Drexel. In some ways, those challenges presented opportunities for physical expansion and economic growth that shaped the school for decades to come. In other ways, those challenges highlighted the racialized nature of Philadelphia's society and the limited way Drexel addressed those problems.[20]

NOTES

1. For the context of Philadelphia's broader post–World War II history, I draw liberally on James Wolfinger, "Philadelphia, PA, 1941–1952," in *Cities in American Political History*, ed. Richardson Dilworth (Thousand Oaks, CA: Sage/CQ Press, 2011), 501–6.

2. Roger Simon, *Philadelphia: A Brief History* (Harrisburg: Pennsylvania Historical Association, 2003), 134.

3. On African-Americans' historical experience in Philadelphia, see James Wolfinger, *Philadelphia Divided: Race and Politics in the City of Brotherly Love* (Chapel Hill:

University of North Carolina Press, 2007); W.E.B. Du Bois, *The Philadelphia Negro: A Social Study* (Philadelphia: University of Pennsylvania Press, 1899); Roger Lane, *Roots of Violence in Black Philadelphia, 1860–1900* (Cambridge, MA: Harvard University Press, 1986); John Bauman, *Public Housing, Race, and Renewal* (Philadelphia: Temple University Press, 1987); Matthew Countryman, *Up South: Civil Rights and Black Power in Philadelphia* (Philadelphia: University of Pennsylvania Press, 2006).

   4. Wolfinger, "Philadelphia, PA, 1941–1952," 501–6.

   5. On Philadelphia's suburbs, see James Wolfinger, " 'The American Dream—For All Americans': Race, Politics and the Campaign to Desegregate Levittown," *Journal of Urban History* 38 (May 2012): 430–51; Herbert J. Gans, *Levittowners: Ways of Life and Politics in a New Suburban Community* (New York: Knopf, 1967).

   6. Wolfinger, *Philadelphia Divided*, ch. 7.

   7. James Wolfinger, *Running the Rails: Capital and Labor in the Philadelphia Transit Industry* (Ithaca, NY: Cornell University Press, 2016), ch. 6; Gregory Heller, *Ed Bacon: Planning, Politics, and the Building of Modern Philadelphia* (Philadelphia: University of Pennsylvania Press, 2013); Scott Gabriel Knowles, ed., *Imagining Philadelphia: Edmund Bacon and the Future of the City* (Philadelphia: University of Pennsylvania Press, 2009); Bauman, *Public Housing, Race, and Renewal*.

   8. James Wolfinger, " 'An Equal Opportunity to Make a Living—And a Life': The FEPC and Postwar Black Politics," *Labor: Studies in Working-Class History of the Americas* 4 (Summer 2007): 65–94; Countryman, *Up South*; Abigail Perkiss, *Making Good Neighbors: Civil Rights, Liberalism, and Integration in Postwar Philadelphia* (Ithaca, NY: Cornell University Press, 2014); Thomas Sugrue, "Affirmative Action from Below: Civil Rights, the Building Trades, and the Politics of Racial Equality in the Urban North, 1945–1969," *Journal of American History* 91 (June 2004): 145–73; Wolfinger, *Philadelphia Divided*, conclusion.

   9. "Testimony by Dr. James Creese, President, Drexel Institute of Technology Before the Committee on Zoning and Municipal Development of the City of Philadelphia," June 20, 1962, Drexel University Archives; "Drexel: A Magnet to Draw Research and Industry," Drexel University Archives.

   10. James Creese to Mr. Lightwood, July 26, 1948, Drexel University Archives; "The Aims and Objectives of the Three-Quarter Century Fund," Drexel University Archives; "Drexel: A Magnet to Draw Research and Industry," memorandum on conference with Senator Myers and Mr. Lammer of the Redevelopment Authority, November 25, 1953, Philadelphia City Planning Commission; *Alumni News*, winter 1963, UR 6.1/24/9, box 24, Drexel University Archives.

   11. *The Triangle*, April 24, 1959, 1–2; October 19, 1962, 3, 7; November 20, 1964, 2; *Space and Dollars: An Urban University Expands* (New York: Educational Facilities Laboratories, 1961), 7; D.W.R. Morgan to Dr. Creese, July 31, 1961, Drexel University Archives.

   12. MacKenzie S. Carlson, "A History of the University City Science Center: Part 2: Planning the University City Science Center (1959–1965)," available at http://www.archives.upenn.edu/histy/features/upwphil/ucscpart2.html; *The Triangle*, May 25, 1962, 3; May 28, 1965, 1; November 20, 1964, 2; May 20, 1966, 4; October 12, 1962, 5; MacKenzie S. Carlson, "A History of the University City Science Center: Part 4: Building the University City Science Center (1969–Present)," available at http://www.archives.upenn.edu/histy/features/upwphil/ucscpart4.html.

   13. *Daily Pennsylvanian*, January 23, 1967, 1; January 26, 1967, 1; January 24, 1967, 1; *The Triangle*, April 22, 1966, 2; David Paul, *When the Pot Boils: The Decline and*

Turnaround of Drexel University (Albany: State University of New York Press, 2008), 22; MacKenzie S. Carlson, "A History of the University City Science Center: Part 2: Planning the University City Science Center (1959–1965)," available at http://www.archives.upenn .edu/histy/features/upwphil/ucscpart2.html; *Drexel Institute Register, 1967–68*, 22. On Mantua and Powelton Village, see Elijah Anderson, *Street Wise: Race, Class, and Change in an Urban Community* (Chicago: University of Chicago Press, 1990).

14. *Daily Pennsylvanian*, January 24, 1967, 1; MacKenzie S. Carlson, "A History of the University City Science Center: Part 2: Planning the University City Science Center (1959–1965)," available at http://www.archives.upenn.edu/histy/features/upwphil/ucscpart2 .html; MacKenzie S. Carlson, "A History of the University City Science Center: Part 3: The Approval Process, Displacement, Protests, and a Lasting Public Relations Disaster (1965–1971)," available at http://www.archives.upenn.edu/histy/features/upwphil/ucscpart3.html.

15. *Drexel Triangle*, October 24, 1969, 7; MacKenzie S. Carlson, "A History of the University City Science Center: Part 3"; articles in file clippings, box 24, Drexel University Archives.

16. *The Triangle*, June 25, 1971, 3; October 7, 1949, 1; June 6, 1952, 3; April 10, 1964, 4.

17. *The Triangle*, April 26, 1968, 8–9; September 20, 1972, 11.

18. *The Triangle*, January 26, 1968, 5; November 12, 1971, 4; January 12, 1968, 18; March 10, 1970, 6; January 17, 1969, 8; *Drexel University Undergraduate Catalogs, 1991–92*, 22.

19. *The Triangle*, October 14, 1966, 5; November 14, 1969, 8; April 26, 1968, 8–9; July 31, 1970, 1; September 20, 1972, 11; Drexel Institute of Technology, February 2, 1970, UR6.1/24/4, box 24, Drexel University Archives.

20. *The Triangle*, September 20, 1972, 11.

Emanuel Kelly portrait.
(Drexel University Archives.
PC 4 People photographs.)

Emanuel Kelly graduated with a degree in architecture from Drexel University in 1971 and received his master's degree in city planning and urban design from Harvard University in 1974. He returned to Philadelphia in 1976 and, along with Vincent Maiello, AIA, established the architectural and planning firm Kelly/Maiello, Inc. Over the course of his many years in the city, his firm has worked on a number of significant projects, including the Pennsylvania Convention Center, the Philadelphia Criminal Justice Center, the renovation and preservation of Philadelphia City Hall, and many others for local and state government, educational entities, and social service organizations. In addition, his firm has taken a special interest in community revitalization and designing affordable housing for all residents.

In 1993 Mr. Kelly became the first African-American to serve as president of the Philadelphia chapter of the American Institute of Architects (AIA); in 1995 he received the Drexel University Distinguished Alumnus Award, with special distinction for professional achievement and community involvement; and in 2004 the AIA elevated him to its prestigious College of Fellows, an honor awarded to members who have made contributions of national significance to the profession.

Mr. Kelly is a member of the Philadelphia Art Commission, having been appointed in 2000 by Mayor John F. Street, and he has served as a member of the Bureau of Historic Preservation of the Pennsylvania Historical and Museum Commission. Mr. Kelly's major Philadelphia projects have included the President's House, Independence National Historical Park, the Pennsylvania Convention Center expansion, West Philadelphia High School, and the Family Court renovations.

—Robert Sieczkiewicz, Kevin Martin,
Rebecca Goldman, and Zachary Mohn

The End of Urban Renewal

Area V and Drexel's Expansion into Powelton Village

JEANNINE KEEFER

IN 1948 the Philadelphia City Planning Commission designated the University Area as the fourth of nine redevelopment areas in the city. The primary resident was the University of Pennsylvania (Penn), but as the postwar period progressed, Drexel University played a more equal role with its larger neighbor. By 1966 Drexel planned to expand west of Thirty-Third Street and north of Lancaster Avenue into Powelton Village. James Wolfinger's chapter outlines the larger complex history surrounding Drexel's growing physical plant paving the way for this unpacking of a small portion of that narrative. Though Drexel was long present in the neighborhood with the Van Rensselaer dormitory and a few adapted structures anchoring it on the north at Powelton Avenue, the new campus plan and proposed structures on a strip of land labeled Area V, incited protest from neighbors and students alike. At stake were the loss of affordable, ideally situated housing and acceptable dormitory designs. By 1969, the dialogue surrounding Drexel's plans moved from being productive to adversarial with students and residents demanding compromise and inclusion in the planning and design of Drexel's expansion.

Between 1961 and 1965 Drexel began planning for Area V and became an institutional district and a redeveloper, clearing zoning restrictions and providing urban renewal funding. The firm of Nolen & Swinburne, likely chosen based on its redevelopment plans for Temple University and its working relationship with the planning commission and the Philadelphia

Most recent addition to the Drexel campus is the Library Center, which houses not only excellent collections in science, engineering, home economics, and industrial management, but serves as a laboratory for the Drexel Graduate School of Library Science, one of the oldest and largest library schools in the United States.

WHEN AN URBAN university must expand, it finds itself in a peculiar set of circumstances. It may be surrounded by residences that can not be bought or are prohibitive in cost. It can't retreat to the country because such a move would defeat the basic function of an urban university.

Clearly, expansion demands sound planning. How much must the university grow? How much additional space is required to satisfy this growth? Is the land available?

To find the answers to these questions, the Drexel Board of Trustees turned to professionals. Management consultants made a comprehensive study of the Institute's primary (student) and secondary (employer) markets. One important conclusion of this report was that Drexel, to serve these markets, would have to expand its facilities to accommodate 14,000 students by 1970—an increase of 85% over the 1957 enrollment.

At the Education Facilities Laboratories, Inc., consulting engineers translated this projected increase in enrollment into a need for square feet of classroom and laboratory space—137,000 square feet, a figure that does not include the space necessary for the R. O. T. C. program, physical education, student activities, or student housing.

The Board also had to assure itself of the availability of land for such expansion. "Redevelopment in the Drexel Area," as prepared for presentation to the City Planning Commission, was approved by the Trustees as a planning document in support of Drexel's claim to certain land areas needed for an enlarged campus.

Only after these preliminary studies did Drexel determine its needs. These needs are divided into two groups: immediate and long-range. This booklet sets forth Drexel's *immediate* needs—the facilities that Drexel must have now if it is to continue to serve as the industrial university for the Greater Philadelphia area.

Drexel Institute of Technology: A Look at Tomorrow. (Drexel University Archives. UR 3.18 Office of Development records.)

Redevelopment Authority, designed the requisite master plan. The Powelton Neighbors group approved a bill to establish the survey and planning of the University City Area III, but later opposed Drexel's application because they were not kept informed by the Redevelopment Authority as they had been promised. Though the Nolen & Swinburne plan (hereafter the 1970 Plan) was not delivered until late 1964, its known boundaries spurred residents to take actions toward proposing a convincing alternative to Drexel's administration before too much damage was done.

In 1962 the Powelton Neighbors contracted their own planner, Walter Thabit, to write a study of the neighborhood countering the planned expansion of Drexel and the incursion of the Redevelopment Authority. Several groups in this period resorted to working outside the system to improve their community. The Powelton Neighbors were preceded by a group called

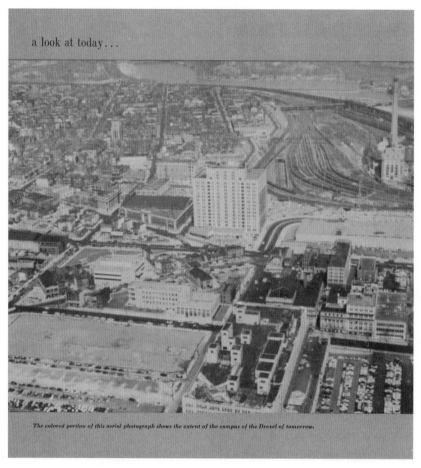

a look at today...

The colored portion of this aerial photograph shows the extent of the campus of the Drexel of tomorrow.

Drexel Institute of Technology: A Look at Tomorrow. (Drexel University Archives. UR 3.18 Office of Development records.)

the Powelton Village Development Associates (PVDA) and succeeded by the Powelton Civic Homeowner's Association (PCHA). PVDA successfully worked to revitalize the neighborhood by purchasing properties, rehabilitating them, then selling them back to neighbors.

These residents were not against Drexel's need to expand, but wanted more input into its physical manifestation. Thabit's document, *The Crisis in Powelton Village,* presented an alternative approach to institutional expansion. He encouraged Drexel to include the community in the planning process stating, "It would be far wiser if Drexel Institute were to fully and finally determine what it wanted, could afford, and made community sense,

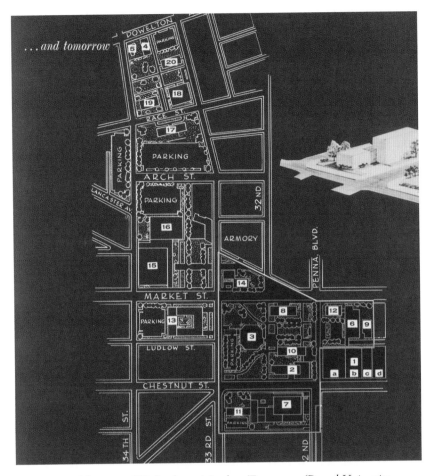

Drexel Institute of Technology: A Look at Tomorrow. (Drexel University Archives. UR 3.18 Office of Development records.)

publish its documented proposals in tentative form, and develop its final plans after getting community reactions."[1]

The document laid the groundwork for a dialogue between the residents, Drexel, the planning commission,[2] the Redevelopment Authority, and the city council. The concerns of homeowners clashed with strong institutional, political, and economic needs. President Hagerty's administration was conscious of issues facing their future including the relationship with Penn, the institution's role in the landscape of American higher education, and the politics they were willing to play to move expansion forward.[3]

The 1970 Plan continued the modernist planning established by Drexel in the early stages of their postwar expansion. Those structures built between 1950 and 1966 all conformed to a particular set of objectives described in the *University City Core Plan* of 1966: "The campuses of the University of Pennsylvania and the Drexel Institute of Technology will consist of super-blocks to provide a traffic free environment. Buildings will focus on the interior of the superblocks and on the walkways and courts that function as spines along which the institutions will develop."[4]

This design directive guided individual experience with the institution on a daily basis. It privileged the interior of the block rather than the edges where the institution interacts with the neighborhood and the city. Drexel's student village planned for Area V remained true to this directive and set the institution up for intense opposition in the future.

Drexel promoted its plans as a redeveloper in the first half of 1965 describing its expansion in three phases: (1) approval of the 1970 Plan, (2) approval of Institutional District Data, and (3) implementation of the Area V contracts. The City Planning Commission, the Redevelopment Authority, and the city council needed to approve steps one and two.[5] Residents would not be able to weigh in until months later during scheduled public hearings. They would be reacting to, rather than participating in, the planning and design process.

Construction on Kelly Hall, the first men's dormitory, in fall of 1965, marked the beginning of vociferous neighborhood resistance. In September 1966, the administration promoted its new plans including future dormitories and dining facilities on the north side of campus during a city council meeting of the Committee on Municipal Development and Zoning. The building and proposed identity of the campus were at odds with that desired by Powelton residents who "attacked" the plans during the meeting.[6] At this point the residents of Powelton were split into two groups. The Powelton Neighbors lent its support to Drexel, but the PCHA opposed the lack of community involvement in the expansion process, the splitting of Powelton into east and west, and the demolition of good building stock. PCHA hired a professional architect, Joseph Kuo, to draw up alternative plans to Drexel's expansion taking care to include all of Drexel's needs. The "Kuo Proposal" was presented to the planning commission during hearings, but the commission had already approved Drexel's own plans. The proposal eliminated the concentrated residential campus in favor of a more dispersed approach saving ninety buildings and suggested Drexel build up rather than out. But, this alternative proposal was dismissed by the administration.[7]

Prior to city council's approval of the 1970 Plan and Area V's establishment in 1968, the Redevelopment Authority began condemnation proceedings for 107 residential and thirty-nine non-residential structures to clear Area V.[8] PCHA then engaged a lawyer, Arsen Kashkashian, to attempt to halt Drexel's plans by claiming the expansion program violated the Housing Act of 1949. He argued that the act favored rehabilitation over redevelopment, sought benefits to the community as well as the institution, and did not allow a college or university to be a proper redevelopment area in itself.[9] The case did not stop expansion, but delayed it and forced the city and Drexel to seek alternative funding.

As mentioned before, there was no absolute agreement in Powelton on Drexel's plans. Some residents were in favor, some questioned the method but supported the larger project, and still others, specifically those living in the strip, were stuck in the middle battling with Drexel and the Redevelopment Authority via community action groups such as PCHA and later, the East Powelton Concerned Residents (EPCR, established in 1969). Because time had lapsed between property acquisition by the Redevelopment Authority in 1968 and demolition, the area became home to a new group of residents including Vietnam vets, poets, artists, drop-outs, drifters, and those interested in a communal way of life.[10] This new breed of resident was "concerned with getting public housing built and instituting subsidized housing in the area,"[11] two concepts staunchly opposed by the PCHA and embraced by EPCR.[12]

In the winter of 1968–1969, residents protested the construction of the new women's dormitory designed by Vincent Kling at Thirty-Third and Arch Streets. In December 1968 Judge Leo Weinrott issued an injunction to ban demonstrations by community members. Later in that month certain members of PCHA agreed to an out-of-court settlement with Drexel lifting the injunction against federal funds for Area V. Terms of the settlement allowed residents to remain in their homes if they could be rehabilitated to certain standards.[13] The settlement also provided for sixty to eighty new dwelling units, the rehabilitation of forty-nine existing structures, and improvements on seven vacant lots on Summer and Winter Streets, east of Area V. The university was to include PCHA in future expansion plans, and most importantly, the eleven people who formally brought the suit against Drexel were paid well for their properties.[14]

When the Redevelopment Authority did not take possession of all the properties in Area V, some residents still felt they had the opportunity to save their homes. The state supreme court vacated the injunctions against protesters on February 4, 1969, with a three-day construction moratorium ending the next day. That evening nearly sixty protesters, including members of the EPCR, began an all-night sit-in at Drexel's Main Building. On

February 5 demonstrations moved from the Main Building to the construction site where people lined up in front of the main construction gate, six people sat in the scoop of a bulldozer and four more perched on a crane to prevent workmen from excavating. President Hagerty issued the following statement: "We regret that the community organizations have taken this stand. However, Drexel still intends to follow through on its original offer. We have declared a moratorium on any demolition of housing north of Lancaster Avenue and we have commissioned a re-study of our development plans through Nolen & Swinburne."[15]

In late summer Drexel sought permission from the city to proceed with its work in Area V. The institution wanted to purchase just over eight acres including the properties granted a reprieve after protests the previous year for dormitories and dining facilities.[16] Kling's design for the first dormitory drew as much ire from residents as did its location. Neighbors felt the school could get more square footage in the form of a traditional high-rise building rather than that provided by the visual statement of the Kling design.

Students had little intersection with the residents of Powelton aside from the need for decent housing. The homecoming issue of *The Triangle* in October 1969 dedicated a considerable amount of space to enlightening students about the community and the current concerns in Powelton and Mantua. It supplied a very brief history of the issues and provided some solutions very similar to those suggested in other urban university situations: Drexel should stick to developing land zoned industrial, allow community groups access to Drexel's facilities, provide a permanent building for the mini-school (an experimental middle school supported by Drexel students and housed in a Drexel building at 3302 Arch Street), and work with the community, not only with programs, but also with physical development. Author Jay Lockman wrote, "Whether we realize it or not, Drexel exists in a community and has a neighborhood, and hence, has neighbors. That's who 'those people' are, and we'd better realize that our neighbors were here before we were. It's their community, and Drexel occupies a part of it."[17] Though Drexel had several programs in place to help residents and the community, the architectural threat, the threat of losing one's home, outweighed the goodwill these programs were able to generate.

Believing official channels of opposition were no longer going to help the cause of the average resident, EPCR and neighbors resorted to more physical and immediate demonstrations of their frustration and made plans of their own for an ice-skating rink and a park on the dormitory site.[18] Residents felt they had been defrauded when the area was declared a slum to make way for redevelopment, felt helpless against the plans and actions of the government and institutions, did not feel represented by previous groups such as PCHA, and wanted their voices included in the plans for the neighborhood.

EPCR picketed and removed construction fencing from the site at Thirty-Fourth and Cherry Streets on December 1, 1969. About one hundred members met the night before at the Powelton Elementary School to create plans to disrupt building in Area V. This time, however, Drexel students were involved in the planning and the movement. Student John Reiss claimed the school's housing program would do little to alleviate the great need for student housing and with such low density, the building would exacerbate the situation for both students and residents.[19] The protest spurred a meeting between EPCR and the Drexel administration, including President Hagerty. The community asked that dormitory construction be halted until negotiations could be held, but Drexel refused, stating their position had been publicly known since 1957. The fence was replaced and again torn down on December 3.[20] EPCR met to plan a large rally at the "Powelton Park" for December 6 and requested negotiators from Drexel attend the rally. Chic Construction Company, contracted to excavate the site, pursued legal action before the rally to obtain an injunction against the protesters. Judge Weinrott applied a temporary injunction against EPCR, four other groups, and three individuals. President Hagerty reiterated the dire need for the dormitory and the contractual responsibilities they had to the construction company, therefore the project would move forward as planned. He did state, however, that Drexel was willing and "anxious to meet with community groups in an orderly, reasonable manner."[21] But this move toward compromise would soon come to an end.

Residents booed as the sheriff read the injunction at the protest site on the sixth, then moved to the Student Activities Building on Chestnut Street to stage their rally. The sit-in lasted ten hours and ended only when Drexel police threatened to arrest those involved. On December 8, Drexel asked Judge Weinrott to issue an injunction against the Powelton protestors preventing them from conducting sit-ins in Drexel buildings. A hearing was to be held on the ninth to determine the permanency of the injunctions.[22] As December progressed encounters between Drexel and EPCR became a question of Constitutional rights and drew the attention of groups from outside Powelton. Judge Weinrott favored the institution stating, "Nobody is going to interfere with the construction of a dormitory at that site."[23] Residents claimed the judge was reactionary thus impeding a fair hearing, and in a few days construction fences were down again with no one claiming responsibility.[24]

Before Judge Weinrott made a final decision on extending the injunctions, he gave community lawyers one week to file their own briefs on the issue. In that time the NAACP and City Councilman Charles Durham, whose district included Powelton, joined the residents' cause.[25] Judge Weinrott and President Hagerty continued to draw the ire of the community and were burned in effigy at an EPCR meeting on December 15. Lawyers for EPCR filed a petition with the state supreme court to have Weinrott's injunctions struck down, claiming his conduct was unsuitable.[26] Though Judge Herbert Cohen would not hear the case until January 21, 1970, he introduced the issue of First Amendment free speech rights to the conversation. Despite attempts made at the end of 1969 to schedule a meeting between Drexel and EPCR to discuss the development of Area V, neither group could agree on ground rules. Drexel rejected demands to hold the meeting in Councilman Durham's office, to have it open to the press, to include more than five or six representatives, and to halt construction until talks were held.[27]

On January 2, 1970, *The Triangle* published the second of its two-part series on Area V, beginning with a recap of events from December of 1969. As a new participant in the crisis, the students were able to approach issues from a number of viewpoints as evidenced in the sit-in on December 6. "There were three groups—a silent majority . . . a small group who were concerned and who entered into discussion with EPCR . . . and a third segment of the Drexel student body who hung around hoping for blood."[28] Some students would lose off campus housing in Area V, some needed the planned housing, and others would neither suffer nor benefit from a residential campus. Two editorials encouraged Drexel to be flexible, proposing that "if some kind of workable plan for broad community involvement in Drexel can be arranged, we could be a model for all other institutions facing similar crises."[29]

Reaching out to the student community, EPCR attended an Interfraternity Council weekly meeting to plead their case in mid-January. Attending was Alan Johnson, Area V resident and architect, engaged by EPCR to help formulate alternatives to the Drexel plans. For the third time, the community tried to frame the discussion around the institution's designs for Area V. He suggested Drexel build on the site of the American Oncologic Hospital, follow Penn's lead and build twenty-two-story dormitories, move the proposed low-profile dining facility to the bottom of another building, abandon plans to close streets to traffic, and consider structures on the neighborhood scale of three to four stories.[30] As was the case with

Walter Thabit and Joseph Kuo before him, Johnson could not develop more concrete plans because Drexel would not share the necessary information.

Also present at the meeting was Hilburn Harbridge, president of PCHA. He reconfirmed PCHA support for Drexel following their 1969 agreement. As the official, incorporated nonprofit organization in Powelton, PCHA felt EPCR was an unorganized distraction rather than a functional conduit for change in Area V. PCHA's amicable relationship with Drexel and its settlement agreement assured them they would be included in Drexel's planning for Powelton, but only to the west of Area V.[31]

On January 19 EPCR sent a letter requesting a meeting with President Hagerty. It outlined a proposed location and timing of the meeting, who could attend, and a beginning agenda.[32] After a week of student opposition to the construction project, Drexel administrators agreed to a meeting on January 28.[33] President Hagerty called off the meeting at the last minute, leaving the groups, including Drexel and Penn students, to discuss their own next course of action. The result of that meeting was a march to the Great Court in the Main Building to begin a two-day sit-in on January 30. The protesters delivered the same list of demands as they had in the past: a moratorium on construction and demolition, a list of properties owned by Drexel, no more property acquisition, and meaningful negotiations to determine the future of the community.[34]

President Hagerty spent two hours talking with the group of two hundred people and answering their questions. He stated that Drexel had already postponed property acquisition and demolition in the area north of Lancaster, but construction of the dorm would continue. He announced that Nolen & Swinburne had been engaged to revise the expansion plans and that anyone could discuss those plans with the firm. The question, though, was who in the community would be given access to the architects and whether or not they would be consulted or asked to participate in the planning process.[35] In addition to this, the design of the dormitory spurred an internal revolt by female students who claimed the interior layout and the facilities would not meet their needs.[36] On the thirty-first a group of students met with Hagerty and emerged with a signed proposal for the community. It provided for a three-day moratorium on construction, for negotiations with five representatives each for administration, community and the students, and for the community to agree not to "molest" the dorm no matter the outcome of the negotiations.[37]

The second day of the sit-in was also the date for Drexel's first black student recruitment drive. According to the *Free Press,* this group was told by Assistant Vice President for Student Affairs Louis P. Murdock (Drexel's only black administrator) that Dr. Hagerty could not stay for the event because the SDS and the Weathermen had occupied the Main Building.[38] This statement diverted attention from the real issues that precipitated the protest. But, present at this meeting was Mrs. Edna Thomas, president of the Philadelphia Women for Community Action, one of the groups involved in the sit-in in the Main Building. Thomas publicly called on Murdock to tell the truth about the situation.[39] This incident suggests that Drexel did not want its relations with the community to dampen potential student enrollment, in particular by African-American students who might identify with the issues championed by the neighborhood.

The state supreme court voided the two injunctions against the community in the first week of February just before the construction moratorium was to end, clearing the way for another sit-in on February 4. Failed negotiations spurred faculty to issue a formal statement supporting any action within the law the administration might need to take against a protest.[40] Students blamed both sides citing that community relations and planning took precedence over the dormitory design.[41] Serving as the voice of reason, students proposed a planner be hired for each group to revise the expansion addressing the goals of their particular group and called on the school to "function as an urban university and realize that it does not exist in the woods by itself."[42] After the administration refused this proposal, students and community members resumed their sit-in until February 6, prompting Weinrott to issue another series of injunctions. Protests then moved to the construction site and continued throughout the spring of 1970, resulting in lawsuits, numerous arrests, and physical confrontations.[43]

In June of 1970 EPCR and its partner groups tried to be included in the expansion review undertaken by Nolen & Swinburne in association with PCHA and the West Philadelphia Corporation. Drexel vice president for community affairs J. K. Lee Smith rejected them on the grounds they were unwilling to respect any previous community agreements.[44] Twenty Powelton residents then occupied the architects' offices on July 9 demanding the firm stop planning for Drexel. The sit-in was suspended when Herbert Swinburne admitted there was too little community involvement in the process and asked that the EPCR coalition be included in the restudy of Area V.[45]

Conflict with the community continued into the fall over the clearing of the site of the Physcial Education building resulting in injunctions from Judge G. Fred DiBona against all parties prohibiting both protest and demolition. The injunction on demolition prevented Drexel from pursuing its building plans until the second half of the 1970s, when Myers Hall was begun.[46]

In the meantime, Drexel tried to convince students to live in the Kling dormitory with a mock-up of a typical room in Van Rensselaer Hall. Several inadequacies came to light, and though students remained unhappy with the built-in furniture, they proposed changes to make the room habitable. Design changes resulted in fewer rooms and thus higher cost for room and board, making off-campus housing in Powelton Village still more desirable.[47]

The Nolen & Swinburne housing study delayed progress, forcing Drexel to rethink the way it would expand. The study, delivered in March 1971, took nearly a year to write with the help of the Drexel Restudy Committee. It called for a meeting to join concerns between the community and the university and through a coordinated group "plan for support and commercial facilities on, or adjacent to, the Drexel campus, serving both university and community needs."[48] The report agreed with students, the community, and the Redevelopment Authority, calling for Drexel to be more flexible and willing to ease its adherence to the structure of the outdated 1957 plan.[49] On April 30, 1971, *The Triangle* gave students a brief history of the neighborhood conflict alongside three Nolen & Swinburne proposals for housing expansion. Despite mapping a path toward collaborative planning, the restudy was never approved by the board of trustees and never implemented.[50]

The Kling dormitory, dedicated as Calhoun Hall on October 28, 1972, did not mark an end of the tense relationship between Drexel and the community.[51] Despite an announcement in June 1971 that future expansion plans would include EPCR, tensions continued well into the mid-1970s. The Redevelopment Authority, displeased with Drexel's refusal to accept the housing restudy, severed its relationship with the university and took on the role of intermediary between the institution and the community. EPCR filed a lawsuit against the Redevelopment Authority and HUD, requiring the Redevelopment Authority to draw up its own plans for the area.[52] Drexel eventually negotiated an out-of-court settlement with EPCR. Many long-term residents lost their homes; others, tired of fighting, began looking for homes elsewhere; businesses looked to relocate. The vacuum left by so many choosing to leave was filled again by a new wave of squatters who were not part of EPCR, but just as reluctant to leave their new abodes.[53]

For the residents of Area V, the loss of a home was a complicated and troubling event. The conflict with Powelton residents, and later students, stemmed not only from the loss of property, but also from the proposed

designs for the campus and individual buildings. Residents declared they
were not against students living in their neighborhood, but wanted their
living spaces to be part of the urban fabric, not separated from it. Powelton's
two largest groups, PCHA and EPCR, not only vied for members, but also
disagreed on their approach to negotiation and protest. Unlike other areas
of the city where similar conflict was happening, Powelton was populated
with people from all walks of life and education levels, not just one socioeconomic or racial group. The mixed nature of the neighborhood not only
added to the area's vitality, but it also fostered differences of opinion. Drexel
students called for compromise and communication during the events of
1969–1970, but neighborhood opposition continued into the 1980s.

NOTES

1. Walter Thabit, *The Crisis in Powelton Village* (Philadelphia: Powelton Neighbors, 1962), 37.
2. Letter from Edmund Bacon to William Hagerty asking for the 1970 Plan and more background on Powelton plans, November 27, 1964, William Hagerty Administration Records, Drexel Archives.
3. The Redevelopment Authority needed the 1970 Plan to receive federal non-cash grants-in-aid. Memorandum as Requested by Dr. Hagerty, n.d., William Hagerty Administration Records, Drexel Archives.
4. Philadelphia City Planning Commission, *University City Core Plan* (Philadelphia: City Planning Commission, 1966), 17.
5. "Drexel's Expansion Plans Outlined as Part of Phla. Redevelopment," *The Triangle*, January 22, 1965, 1.
6. "Powelton Residents Attack Drexel Plans for Redevelopment," *The Triangle*, October 7, 1966, 1.
7. "Area Property Owners Request Halt to Drexel's Redevelopment Plans," *The Triangle*, October 13, 1967, 1.
8. "DIT Building Plans Go to City Council for Final Approval," *The Triangle*, January 27, 1967, 1.
9. "Area Property Owners Request Halt to Drexel's Redevelopment Plans."
10. Joseph Hanania, "The Squatters," *Philadelphia Magazine*, May 1976, 117.
11. "Powelton Village—An Urban Scramble," *Evening Bulletin,* November 9, 1969.
12. New groups included the West Powelton Concerned Residents, Philadelphia Youth and Young Adult Congress, West Park Community Council, Philadelphia Women for Community Action, Delaware Valley Association for Family Services, and the Philadelphia Community Union.
13. "Community Confrontation," *The Triangle*, December 5, 1969, 7.
14. Mike Kyle, "Another Side: PCHA," *The Triangle*, January 16, 1970, 5.
15. "Neighbors Bar Building of Drexel Dorm," *Evening Bulletin*, February 5, 1969.
16. "Drexel Seeks OK to put up 7 buildings," *Evening Bulletin*, September 3, 1969.
17. Jay Lockman, "Coming Home to Mantua-Powelton," *The Triangle*, October 31, 1969, 1.

18. "Neighbors Take Drexel Lot and Set Up an Instant Park," *Sunday Bulletin*, November 9, 1969.

19. "Drexel Tract to Be Picketed," *Philadelphia Inquirer*, December 2, 1969.

20. Douglas Gill, "Powelton Residents Wreck Fence on Drexel Lot for People's Park," *Evening Bulletin,* December 4, 1969. Gill's article gives a blow-by-blow account of the fence destruction on December 3.

21. Excerpt from letter from Dr. Hagerty to Mr. Greenberg as published in *The Triangle*, December 5, 1969, 7.

22. "Judge Bars Citizen Sit-ins at Drexel," *Evening Bulletin*, December 8, 1969. The December 6 rally was covered in the established press, but also initiated coverage by the *Philadelphia Free Press* on December 8 with a two-page spread dedicated to the piece, "Confrontation in East Powelton," authored by members of EPCR.

23. Harmon Y. Gordon, "Judge Issues Warning to Powelton Group," *Evening Bulletin*, December 10, 1969.

24. "The Land Belongs to the People: Drexel Fence Down Again in East Powelton," *Philadelphia Free Press*, December 15, 1969.

25. Nicholas W. Stroh, "NAACP Joins Fight to Block Dorm," *Evening Bulletin*, December 16, 1969.

26. "State High Court Upsets Injunctions Halting Drexel Protests," *Evening Bulletin*, December 18, 1969.

27. Nicholas W. Stroh, "Community, Drexel, Fail to Meet on Dorm," in *Evening Bulletin,* December 23, 1969.

28. "Community Confrontation," editorial, *The Triangle*, January 9, 1970, 6.

29. Ibid.

30. Mike Kyle, "EPCR Meets IFC," *The Triangle*, January 16, 1970, 5.

31. Mike Kyle, "Another Side: PCHA."

32. "East Powelton Asks Again," *The Triangle*, January 23, 1970, 5.

33. "The People Move on Drexel," *Philadelphia Free Press*, January 26, 1970. Much of the student opposition resulted from their displeasure with the actual design of the dormitory.

34. Harold Wilcox, Johns Wilson, and the Shadow, "Drexel Reoccupied: Off Drexel," *Philadelphia Free Press*, February 2, 1970.

35. Larry Marion and Jay Lockman, "From Sit-In to Negotiation," *The Triangle*, February 3, 1970, 1.

36. Nicholas W. Stroh, "Drexel Students Are Displeased by Interior of Design for Girls' Dorm," *Evening Bulletin*, January 22, 1970.

37. Wilcox, Wilson, and the Shadow, "Drexel Reoccupied."

38. SDS (Students for a Democratic Society) and its more violent splinter group, the Weathermen, were Leftist student groups active on college campuses.

39. Ibid.

40. "Faculty Report," *The Triangle*, February 6, 1970.

41. Al Rudnitsky, "Human Rights?" *The Triangle*, February 6, 1970, 8.

42. Jay Baumstein, "Ask for Answers," *The Triangle*, February 6, 1970, 8.

43. Jay Baumstein, "Community Groups Resume Sit-In," *The Triangle*, February 6, 1970, 1. "Seize The Land!" *Free Press,* February 9, 1970; William J. Storm, "12 Arrested Defying Ban on Drexel Sit-In," *Evening Bulletin,* February 9, 1970; Harmon Y. Gordon, "Judge Fines 3, Frees Nine in Drexel Protest," *Evening Bulletin,* February 14, 1970; "Drexel Dumps on People," *Philadelphia Free Press,* March 20, 1970.

44. Elaine Maguire, "Drexel Not Speaking to Community Coalition," *The Triangle,* July 10, 1970, 1.

45. Ken Moberg, Eddie Lowenstein, and Jack Wright, "Community Seizes Planner's Office," *Philadelphia Free Press,* July 19, 1970.

46. "A Pyrrhic Victory," *The Triangle,* July 17, 1970, 1.

47. Tom Kilkenny, "Dorm Mock Up," *The Triangle,* May 22, 1972, 1. Larry Marion, "New Dormitory To Include Proposed Revisions," *The Triangle*, November 20, 1970, 1, 3.

48. Jim Kitch, "New Plan for Drexel Expansion," *The Triangle,* January 22, 1971, 1.

49. "Drexel's Expansion Plans," *The Triangle,* June 4, 1971.

50. Joseph Hanania, "The Squatters," *Philadelphia Magazine,* May 1976, 229–30.

51. Gary Grobman, "Calhoun Hall Dedicated; Rain Dampens Protests," *The Triangle,* November 3, 1972.

52. Hanania, "The Squatters," 231.

53. Ibid.

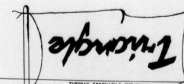

VOLUME XLVI   TUESDAY, FEBRUARY 3, 1970   NUMBER 49

"Dr. Hagerty, I would like to raise a point at this time. There seems to be a fundamental misunderstanding. The community is not asking to be consulted in an advisory capacity to further planning which Drexel carries out with full authority to carry it out. The community is asking to be met as equals with Drexel Institute in negotiations to jointly, as equals, plan for this neighborhood."
Gerry Goldin

"But that cannot really be decided until we have set forth what we consider to be the institution's objectives and needs. You have set forth your own concerns and needs. If these don't match, I agree that that is probably going to continue."
Dr. Hagerty

"If they can be made that way, we will proceed that way. I don't know whether they can be made that way or not."
Dr. Hagerty

from sit-in to negotiation

by larry marion and jay lockman

Drexel's first major sit-in ended Saturday evening at 6:00 p.m. after forty-six hours of discussion, negotiation, haggling and waiting. The issue at stake was Drexel's plans for expansion and in particular, the women's dorm now under construction.

Five area groups held an open meeting on Thursday, January 29, to plan an action against Drexel. They complained of a lack of response from Drexel to requests for negotiations, and a lack of good faith by Drexel administrators toward dealings in the community. After the meeting, the five groups, together with Drexel students and some Penn students, marched to the Great Court and sat down. It was 8:15 p.m.

After a short discussion, a steering committee presented five points of discussion to Dr. Edward McGuire, the senior representative of Drexel administration present. These demands included a moratorium on construction of the new women's dorm, an end to demolition in the community, publication of a list of all Drexel owned properties, including those listed under "straw" names, an end to Drexel acquisition of land in the community, and a start of "meaningful negotiations" with the community to develop a plan which meets the need of Drexel students and the area residents.

By the time this list was drawn up, the crowd had grown to 150 people, with about 50 Drexel students actively involved. The crowd spent the next few hours talking among themselves and with the various Drexel administrators who were on hand. The latter included Dr. Edward McGuire, V.P. for Student Affairs, Stephen Yale, Dean of Students, Louis Murdock, Asst. V.P. for Student Affairs, O.J. Eichorn, Dean of Men, Connie Goodman, Acting Dean of Women, John Dellinger, Asst. Dean of Men, and John Tully, Director of Public Relations. Most of these administrators ended up spending the night in the court with the protesters.

President Hagerty arrived at 10:00 p.m. and spent about two hours in speaking with the crowd and answering questions. During this time, Hagerty said that Drexel had already stopped demolition and acquisition of property above Lancaster Ave. He also announced that Drexel had hired Nolan and Swinburne, architectural consultants, to revise Drexel's expansion plans. He promised that anyone could discuss the revision of plans with the architects. The main disagreement between those who were sitting in and Pres. Hagerty revolved around whether Drexel's plans would be made with community "consultation" or with community "participation."

Hagerty left shortly after midnight, and the community and supporting students, settled down for the night. At this time, it was announced that the building would be closed, and no one outside would be admitted before it opened in the morning. Those inside were asked to

Continued on page 4, col. 3

President Hagerty meeting with students and Powelton Village community leaders in a debate over Drexel's expansion plans. (The Triangle, February 3, 1970.)

15

Drexel's Vietnam War

Jonson Miller

"THE DREXEL INSTITUTE with the single purpose of serving most effectively in the present crisis, has put its engineering school absolutely on a war basis."[1] This official statement during World War I is representative of the unity of purpose expressed by Drexel, its faculty, staff, and students during both world wars. The school provided national and local leadership and training for war industries and military officers during those wars. Drexel's Army Reserve Officer Training Corp (ROTC), a required program for all male students until 1969, continues to provide the army with officers to this day.[2]

In contrast to the unity of purpose expressed during the world wars, the Drexel community's response to the Vietnam War was disunited and conflictual—as it was in American society more generally. Yet Vietnam was not the first war contested by Americans. When the United States entered World War I, there was a more immediate and perhaps greater resistance than there was against the Vietnam War. Millions of American men refused draft registration, thousands of men resisted when called up, and some fled to Mexico to avoid the draft. Thousands of naturalized U.S. citizens renounced their new citizenship in order to avoid the draft, and people organized marches to protest the war.

In response to the antiwar movement during World War I, the federal government labeled all resisters "subversive" and linked them rhetorically to foreign enemy agents. Congress criminalized everything from

Students' Army Training Corps (SATC) group photograph on steps
of the Main Building, 1918. (Drexel University Archives.
PC 12 Clubs and organizations photographs.)

avoiding the draft to criticizing the war or the government. Paragovernmental and vigilante groups supported by the government attacked and even imprisoned war critics, and even innocent people unconnected to antiwar activities.[3] This was not a climate in which the Drexel administration was likely to tolerate antiwar sentiment on campus. By contrast, while many opponents of the Vietnam War, including those at Drexel, expressed concerns about a climate that suppressed free speech, dissent was not criminalized—it even flourished in both the alternative and mainstream media.

World Wars I and II were "total wars" in the sense that the federal government asked for the support of any and all institutions. Drexel provided new academic programs and professionalized old ones to support the war efforts. For example, during World War I, Drexel developed a professional dietetics program approved by the U.S. Army Medical Corps to provide dieticians for military hospitals and other institutions.[4] During World War II, Drexel participated in and provided regional leadership for the Engineering, Science and Management War Training Program designed to "meet the shortages of trained personnel in fields essential to the national defense" through twelve- to sixteen-week industrial and engineering courses for both men and women paid for by the federal government.[5] Students organized various drives and benefits throughout World War II, including scrap and blood drives, book drives for troops, war bond drives, and the purchase of

Students advertising the sale of defense stamps, 1942. (Drexel University Archives. PC 8 Events photographs.)

nine jeeps for the army.[6] The Korean War did not produce the dramatic changes at Drexel that World Wars I and II did, but still Drexel students supported blood drives for troops and clothing drives for Korean refugees. In contrast to the Vietnam War era, during the world wars and Korea many students were still eligible for the draft, a topic reported in *The Triangle* without alarm or dissent.[7]

The U.S. government did not attempt a total mobilization of the country during the Vietnam War. In fact, unlike Presidents Wilson, Roosevelt, and Truman in the earlier conflicts, President Lyndon Johnson tried to minimize the war's impact on Americans out of fear that too many demands, such as a declaration of war, war taxes, a general draft, or the mobilization of the reserves, would jeopardize support for his Great Society programs. And unlike during the world wars, the government never developed a program to deliberately build support for the Vietnam War among citizens and institutions.[8] Not having asked for support, institutions like Drexel did not give it. Not being mobilized for war, Drexel did not demand unity of its members.

Drexel and the Draft

Under the Selective Service Act of 1948, 2,215,000 of the 8,615,000 men who served in America's military between 1964 and 1973 were drafted into service. The law required all men over eighteen to register, but effectively drafted only men between the ages of eighteen and twenty-five who met the necessary physical requirements. Married fathers were rarely drafted. College students (as long as they earned at least a C average and scored sufficiently high on a Selective Service intelligence test) and workers in "essential" fields received deferments.[9]

During the Vietnam War, the work of processing draftees was carried out largely by local draft boards made up of citizens—mostly white, middle-class men who were World War II or Korean War veterans. Especially in the South, blacks were greatly underrepresented or even entirely absent from the draft boards that performed the important work of assessing deferments and conscientious objector claims. The composition of draft boards and the deferment structure led to the disproportionate drafting of minority and working-class white men. As historian James Westheider frames the issue, "In 1964, an eligible African American had a 30 percent chance of being drafted, whereas for a white, it was only 18 percent. . . . By 1967, almost one third of eligible whites were being drafted, but the figure for African-Americans had also risen to nearly 64 percent of those eligible for induction." Moreover, "draft-eligible men with less than a high school education appeared three times as likely to be drafted as those with a college education."[10]

Army colonel Harry G. Summers Jr., in his report to the army on why the Vietnam War went so badly for America, argued that "one of the most damaging aggravations was the decision to grant draft deferments for students." These deferments produced among troops the perception that it was a poor- or working-man's war, while the privileged avoided the sacrifices.[11] Deferments were automatic for college students, but even then, professors who opposed the war sometimes passed failing men to help protect them from the draft. Of course college protected students only until they graduated, who, unless they went into a protected profession or into graduate programs that enjoyed deferment status (as did President Bill Clinton and Vice President Dick Cheney), were again eligible for the draft until they turned twenty-six. Other men, like President George W. Bush, protected themselves from going to Vietnam after college by joining the reserves or National Guard. President Lyndon Johnson worried that mobilizing guardsmen or reservists for the war would be economically disruptive, so they too were largely kept out of the fight. The only guardsmen who served in Vietnam did so as volunteers.[12]

Male Drexel students were part of that small and privileged group of Americans protected from the draft. Most of the Drexel men who served in the war volunteered to do so or did so after receiving their commissioning as an officer after their service in four full years of the Army ROTC.

Librarian assisting ROTC officers, 1942. (Drexel University Archives.
PC 12 Clubs and organizations photographs.)

In 1969, the draft system shifted to a lottery that assigned a number to each day of the year. Men born on the day assigned number 4, for example, knew that they were up for the draft soon, while those born on day 365 had little to fear. Whereas the old system created uncertainty and drove men to find ways to avoid being drafted, the new lottery created certainty for many men that they no longer needed to take any action to avoid a draft.[13]

Debating and Protesting at Drexel

Just after the Gulf of Tonkin Incident, in which Secretary of Defense Robert McNamara claimed that North Vietnamese ships attacked U.S. navy ships in international waters, 85 percent of Americans supported some military intervention in Vietnam. American troops had already been serving and dying in Vietnam since 1961, but were categorized as advisors and support personnel for the Army of the Republic of Vietnam. When American involvement became explicit in 1965, the war was a popular one among Americans. Nonetheless, there was already some draft resistance and a 20,000-person antiwar rally in Washington, DC, that year. And American opposition to the war grew with each year. After the 1968 Tet Offensive, in which the North Vietnamese army and the National Liberation Front struck targets throughout South Vietnam, a majority of Americans believed that entering the war had been a mistake, though a majority also opposed withdrawal. Protests continued to grow and public support for the war continued to decline.[14]

In 1965, President Johnson sent "truth squads," consisting of government officials, to college campuses to respond to critics at "teach-ins." In 1967, the House Un-American Activities Committee and the FBI claimed that antiwar organizations were infiltrated by international communists in order to delegitimize large protests. While communists and other radicals were certainly among the organizers, they were not beholden to international communism. American law enforcement and intelligence agencies then began sometimes illegal surveillance and harassment of, and attacks on, the antiwar movement. Marxist opponents of the war, influenced by philosopher Herbert Marcuse, tried to prevent the truth squads from speaking, arguing that the views of the government were so heinous that it was necessary to deny them a platform altogether.[15]

Organized opposition to the war appeared on Drexel's campus in 1967 and continued through the end of the war. In June of 1967, sixty-four professors and thirty-seven students signed an open letter in *The Triangle*, endorsing Senator and Committee on Foreign Relations chairman Frank Church's *New York Times* editorial against the "stifling of dissent" when what was needed was vigorous debate about the war. The Drexel letter urged the U.S. government to find alternatives to "bringing about negotiations [with the North Vietnamese and Vietcong] by force" and the "devastation of all-out war."[16] Despite the wording of the letter, it was in fact a local event that drove Drexel professors and students to publish it. Two English professors, Joel Balshom and Marty Kellman, had been among the most vocal Drexel opponents of the war. Someone entered their locked office at night using a key and wrote derogatory and anti-Semitic statements on their antiwar posters. This was enough to upset the Drexel faculty. But they were driven also by what they perceived as President Hagerty's lack of concern about the event.[17]

Any stifling of debate or free speech did not prevent *The Triangle* from taking a decidedly antiwar position by 1967, a decisive year for the antiwar movement. The movement itself escalated in step with the American escalation of the war. In 1966, Americans kept 385,000 troops in Vietnam. In

1967, it was 500,000. Moreover, the number of American troops killed doubled between 1966 and 1967. By the end of that year, nearly half of Americans believed that entering the war was a mistake. It was also that year that Martin Luther King, Senator Robert F. Kennedy, Muhammad Ali, and other prominent Americans publicly called for an end to the war. Nonetheless, a mere 10 percent advocated immediate withdrawal. In fact, more Americans sought an escalation of the conflict in order to end it sooner.[18]

Initially at least, it was the Drexel faculty rather than students who drove antiwar activity on campus. Professors offered "teach-ins" to convince students to oppose the war.[19] Among the faculty, humanities, social sciences, and especially English professors were among the most active in the antiwar movement, though younger mechanical engineering professors were also active.[20] *The Triangle* published articles about the war, protests, and draft issues. The editors also used the paper to express concerns over free speech, publishing an editorial in 1967 defending dissent and denouncing "Red-baiting and other McCarthyist tactics"[21] and printing a photograph of "members of a local Marine Reserve unit beat[ing] up an anti-Vietnam War demonstrator in Houston."[22] In 1969, Drexel ROTC commander Colonel James Miles allegedly called antiwar protests treasonous. Sociology professor J. W. Smith used *The Triangle* to publicize and criticize these comments as attacks on dissent and free speech.[23]

Members of the Drexel community supported and participated in the National Moratorium Day on October 15, 1969—an organized boycott of work and school all across the country, as an alternative to yet another large and no-longer-newsworthy protest in a large city. Participants organized vigils, teach-ins, pamphleting, and other activities.[24] President Hagerty declined to shut down Drexel for the day, but he did urge students and professors who opposed the war to participate and develop a program of teach-ins and activities to "make some meaningful contribution to the resolution of the issues created by the Vietnam War." Not that they needed his encouragement, but a Student Mobilization Committee did exactly that.[25] *The Triangle* endorsed the actions and published front page articles promoting and reporting on the Moratorium Day events. The editors and the Student Congress called for Drexel students and professors to participate and "suspend normal business."[26] Hagerty also joined seventy-eight other college presidents in signing a letter to President Nixon and congressional leaders calling for a faster withdrawal from the Vietnam War.[27] The first moratorium was followed by the March on Washington in November, which a few Drexel students and professors attended.[28]

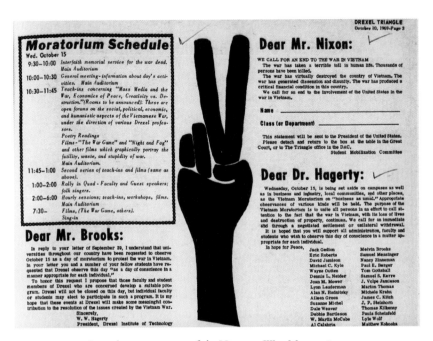

Drexel news coverage of the Vietnam War Moratorium.
(The Triangle, October 10, 1969.)

It isn't clear how active the Drexel community was in anti- or pro-war activities. Retired political science professor Michael Sullivan, who had joined the faculty in 1969, just before the Moratorium, recalled that most of the students were "apathetic," especially the business and engineering students. But there was more antiwar than pro-war activity.[29] Though *The Triangle* did not report directly on any pro-war activity, its reporters did cover a 1970 debate over a Drexel strike against the war that indicated at least some organized support for the war among ROTC cadets.

Though it is not clear how large or active it was, Drexel did have a chapter of the Young Americans for Freedom (YAF), formed nationally in 1960 with the support of William F. Buckley Jr., for the purpose of shifting the Republican Party toward more conservative positions, such as dismantling the New Deal and shifting from mere "containment" to the "roll back" of communism. The YAF supported the Vietnam War as an essential fight against communism—which they claimed was the greatest threat to American freedom—but did oppose the draft, which they saw as a violation of individual rights.[30] Although *The Triangle* had a decidedly antiwar editorial position, the paper in 1967, at the urging of the YAF, published a letter by Captain Booke M. Shadburne, a marine who had died in Vietnam earlier that year. He argued for a stronger military response, including blockading the major North Vietnamese harbor and cutting all supply routes into South Vietnam. He also described Vietcong murders and kidnappings of civilians. Yet Shadburne also advocated for abandoning the war altogether if the United States were not going to fight it properly.[31] Perhaps it was his conclusion that led the firmly antiwar *Triangle* to publish this letter.

After Kent State and the Invasion of Cambodia

By 1970, large demonstrations and continuing moratorium events were declining in the face of exhaustion by organizers and the withdrawal of troops under President Richard Nixon.[32] Withdrawals under Nixon should have been a victory for the antiwar movement, but the president's decision to secretly bomb and then invade Cambodia sparked renewed outrage. On May 2, protestors set fire to the ROTC building at Kent State University in Ohio and tried to prevent firefighters from putting out the flames. Two days later, Ohio National Guardsmen killed four student protesters and wounded thirteen others. The massacre fueled further protests, including a 100,000-strong rally in Washington, DC, on May 9. Though less apparent in news and memory, on May 14, police killed two students and wounded twelve others during rioting at Mississippi's Jackson State University. Antiwar organizers called for student strikes, and in agreement more than eighty university presidents shut down their schools for at least one day, sometimes for the rest of the spring term. Protests of some sort occurred at most colleges and universities.[33]

After a week of teach-ins, leafleting, and a vigil for the Kent State students, approximately 2,000 Drexel students met in the Main Building auditorium to debate joining the nationwide student strike. Several professors, speaking from the stage and the audience, took positions on either side. President Hagerty stated emphatically that Drexel would not close or change its schedule. Students also expressed a range of positions. ROTC cadets spoke out against the strike altogether. Student organizers called for a vote to support the strike by keeping Drexel open but allowing flexibility in classes so that student participants would not be penalized. *The Triangle* reported that the vote was "three to one" in favor of the motion, marking a peak in antiwar sentiment at Drexel, one that matched the growth of opposition by the American public in general.[34]

Drexel faculty and administrators expressed a range of positions in response to the vote, but expressed general support for allowing students to participate in events. The vice president for academic affairs, Ralph Crouch, who was perceived as particularly conservative regarding these issues, wrote to the faculty that it was "wrong to interrupt the educational process" regardless of whether or not one opposed the extension of the war to Cambodia; nonetheless, he urged students to make individual arrangements with their professors to make up any missed work. The Faculty Council, though it took no formal position, did encourage the faculty to avoid scheduling exams or other class activities that would unduly hurt the performance of students participating in the strike. Thirty-seven professors wrote a letter to *The Triangle* to say they were "outraged" at the extension of the war and the killing of the Kent State students, and they urged "unqualified support—both moral and professional—to our striking students."[35]

The vote against an outright strike, unlike at so many other schools, may have resulted partly from the fact that Drexel used a quarter system, which meant they were still in the middle of their spring term. For schools on semester systems that were already finishing up their terms, ending early was a more viable option for administrators who, regardless of their positions on the war, may have just wanted to avoid campus conflicts. Compared to most schools, Drexel's academic calendar would have experienced greater disruption from an extended strike or an early end to the school year.[36]

Media coverage of antiwar protests declined along with President Nixon's continued withdrawal of troops from 1970 up to the end of the U.S. role in the war in 1973. Similarly, interest in antiwar activity declined at Drexel, though strikes and protests continued at other schools in response to the occasional escalation of bombings of North Vietnam.[37]

Drexel's Army ROTC

ROTC programs, offered at more than 250 schools, including Drexel, produced as many officers for the military as did the service academies themselves during the Vietnam War. But the declining popularity of the war and new military policies led to a decline in ROTC programs. One exception was at historically black colleges and universities, where the army's efforts to increase the number of black officers led to an increase in ROTC programs, up from three to nineteen schools by the time of American withdrawal from Vietnam.[38] Yet ROTC survived at Drexel.

The predecessor of Drexel ROTC, the Student Army Training Corps (SATC), which also served Saint Joseph's University, was established in 1918 by Lieutenant James P. Lyons. During World War I, men joined the SATC as privates in the U.S. army and were periodically evaluated for their potential. Some were quickly shipped off as privates while others were sent off for training and then to more advanced officer schools. As a 1918 Drexel SATC pamphlet put it, "No attempt has been made to maintain the plan of the former four-year course . . . every other consideration has been subordinated to the aim of developing promising [officer] material in the minimum of time."[39] Rather than deferring service, joining the SATC may have been a good way to ensure that your enrollment at Drexel was short.

The SATC ended with World War I, but Lyons remained and established one of the army's 135 Reserve Officer Training Corps battalions to take its place as a peacetime institution.[40] Until the Vietnam War, male enrollment in two years of ROTC was mandatory. The army required a minimum two-year program, which did not obligate students to subsequent military service, but it did exempt them from the draft during those two years. Students then had to apply to complete two more years of advanced training that led to a commission in the army as a second lieutenant. Only 8 percent of eligible Drexel students did so.[41]

In 1965, the year combat troops entered the war, President Hagerty appointed a committee to review Drexel's ROTC policy. The Defense Department had come to see compulsory ROTC as too expensive and as producing more officers than needed. In 1962, Major General Frederick Warren, who oversaw Army ROTC, ordered all ROTC units to reduce their freshmen enrollments by 15 percent. He did this without consultation with the host schools, which generated concern in the schools about the extent of military control over ROTC. By 1963, universities began shedding ROTC programs, leading to a drop in enrollments and panic in the armed services about an officer shortfall. In response, the armed services proposed legislation to Congress to provide scholarships to entice students into ROTC. The resulting 1964 ROTC Revitalization Act decreased the number of hours per week of cadet training, provided the title of professor for the highest-ranking ROTC officer, and required that ROTC courses count for the equivalent credits of academic courses. The new law succeeded in increasing the number of cadets, but made school administrators uncomfortable with the mandated academic status of ROTC officers and their courses.[42]

President Hagerty's committee recommended maintaining compulsory ROTC, but reducing it to just the freshman year. The recommendation for maintaining compulsory ROTC was based on its role as a "unifying activity" for all Drexel men, its leadership training, the fact that freshman weren't ready to decide for themselves whether or not to enroll, and the fear that voluntary enrollment would lead to such a decline that Drexel would no longer meet the hundred-cadet minimum set by the army and would lose the ROTC program altogether. The committee also cited reasons of military preparedness and national obligation. The army relied on ROTC to supply nearly half of its officers, so Drexel had "an obligation to meet this need."[43] The two-year requirement remained until the end of the 1968–1969 academic year, when, in part because of the war, Drexel shifted to an all-volunteer program.

By the spring of 1969, with antiwar activities growing and more than half of Americans polled indicating their opinion that the Vietnam War was a mistake,[44] ROTC programs plummeted in prestige, faced outright hostility on some campuses, and saw their enrollments decline. Nationally, ROTC enrollment dropped by more than 25 percent between 1968 and 1969. The lottery draft system made ROTC less appealing, since men with higher draft numbers no longer needed to find a way to avoid the draft. On the other hand, men with low draft numbers sought out ROTC, especially the Navy ROTC, hoping to remain in school long enough for the war to end, or at least to give them some control over their placement in the military.[45]

In 1973, the year American forces completely withdrew from Vietnam, Drexel opened up ROTC to women through a separate "Women's Army," with the same scholarships and other benefits as men.[46] The armed forces had provided limited opportunities for women in ROTC since 1954, when ten Air Force ROTC programs began accepting women. The program ended in 1959 after attracting few cadets into what was clearly a second-class program that offered few opportunities in the air force, but was revived in 1969 after more officer positions opened up to women. In 1973 the army provided ROTC programs the option of allowing women to enroll; Drexel was one of the first to do so.[47]

Reconsidering the Vietnam War
Legacy at Drexel

American service men and women, especially those who served in the later years of the Vietnam War, sometimes experienced a tough transition when they returned home. Veterans had higher rates of unemployment than did nonveterans, even when controlling for age and race, and they voiced frustration that they "weren't allowed to feel proud" of their service in the face of widespread and vocal opponents of the war. Some veterans, such as Vietnam Veterans against the War spokesman and future secretary of state John Kerry, went on to join that opposition.[48]

America's failure in Vietnam, along with the Watergate Scandal and revelations of FBI attacks on the civil rights and other liberation movements, left Americans generally skeptical about the use of force in the world and distrustful of government up to 1980. But then-presidential candidate Ronald Reagan sparked a reevaluation of the war. While his positions had their roots in the war-time positions of supporters of war, he helped to reframe the meaning of the war, offering a vision of a professional military that fought a "noble cause," but was "stabbed-in-the-back" by unfairly critical media, antiwar protestors, and a political establishment that forced the military to fight with "one hand tied behind their back."[49] Much of Reagan's revisionism has been challenged. For instance, Vietnam War veteran and prominent revisionist Harry Summers places the blame on the lack of public support for Vietnam on a government that purposefully did not cultivate support for and did not clearly explain the purpose of the war.[50] Debate over whether or not the United States and South Vietnam could have won the war still produces a large literature.[51]

The 1980s brought a reconsideration of the meaning of the war, civilian-military relations, and the place of the Vietnam War veteran in American life. Drexel too experienced this reevaluation. In 1987 *The Triangle* published two side-by-side front-page articles dedicated to the veterans of the Vietnam War. The first article covered the October dedication of the Philadelphia Vietnam Veterans Memorial, located over the I-95 tunnels along Spruce Street, for the 646 Philadelphia-area residents who died in the war. Not only did *The Triangle* editors find the dedication newsworthy, but the author framed the story in terms of respect for and appreciation of Vietnam veterans. As the article's author, Adam Geibel, lamented, "It has taken nearly fifteen years (since America's withdrawal of troops in 1972) to recognize and honor the men and women from the Philadelphia area who served and died in that war." Geibel noted that the veterans who brought etchings of names from the national Vietnam War memorial ("The Wall") in Washington, DC, "made the trip on foot and in some cases, by wheelchair." Drexel ROTC cadets and instructors participated in the dedication.[52] Although the article did not say so, the memorial bears the names of at least four Drexel students:

- Richard W. Brooks III (Cedarbrook, PA): A 1966 graduate. Commissioned as army officer after completion of ROTC. Brooks was killed by a sniper in 1967 and posthumously awarded the Silver Star.

- George Albert Gray (Melrose Park, PA): Studied one term at Drexel, then enlisted in the army in 1966. Gray died in 1968 from wounds from small-arms fire while piloting a helicopter.
- Charles Thomas Hershey (Philadelphia): Took night classes, then enlisted in the army in 1967. Hershey died in Quảng Tín Province in 1968 and posthumously received the Silver Star.
- Frank John Nostadt Jr. (Philadelphia): Studied electrical engineering at night, but was drafted into the army in 1964. He is believed to have died in the 1965 Battle of Ia Drang, the first ground battle between American and North Vietnamese troops.[53]

The second article memorialized Brooks, who received his second lieutenant commission after graduating and serving in the ROTC. Waiting for him at home was his wife and a baby son he had never seen. On December 27, 1967, after being in Vietnam for just six weeks, a sniper shot and killed him while he was patrolling along the coast in Quảng Tín Province, which was, at the time, the northernmost province of the Republic of Vietnam (South Vietnam). This story is sad enough in and of itself, but the editors framed as a tragedy, not his death, but the response, or lack thereof. After noting the pain of the family Brooks left behind, the editors wrote, "But due to the political climate of the time their pain was assuaged even less than other generations who lost loved ones—there was no respect or honor offered."[54]

Lamenting the fact that Drexel's war dead from all of our wars have never received a memorial, and that, furthermore, "It would be almost criminally negligent to allow the memory of Brooks and his peers to be lost forever," the editors, with some anger, proposed naming a newly built and unnamed dorm after Brooks and dedicating it to all of Drexel's war dead. "Usually a worthy name is suggested and a large contribution check changes hands when a Drexel building is titled. Perhaps—just this once—the powers that be could pass up the financial opportunity and remember those who really sacrificed, not to a school or a nation or even a people, but to a higher ideal." Drexel did not take up the editors' suggestion. Instead we have Towers Hall. Despite the above, the editors were not uncritical of the war; it was primarily the treatment of our veterans that concerned them. As they wrote of Brooks,

> He died in an unpopular war, at a time his men and women who shared his uniform were unjustly vilified. Maybe the Vietnam effort was entirely wrong, though some Indochinese refugees might

effectively argue that point. Certainly our leaders—the politicians and the generals—were incompetent and caused needless grief and bloodshed.

A memorial to a Vietnam veteran might be cause for more thought and reflection than a memorial for the dead of any other war usually receives—not only to honor those who died for freedom but a warning to future generations of decision makers never to blindly accept the word of old politicians (who will never face snipers and booby traps).[55]

It is hard to imagine these articles or the editors' proposal appearing in *The Triangle* twenty years earlier.

Drexel, America, and Vietnam continued to change after the 1980s. Since then, the two countries have normalized relations and started engaging in trade. American veterans have traveled to Vietnam and met Vietnamese veterans. We can see the visible results of the war- and peace-time engagements of our two countries in the presence of Vietnamese and Vietnamese-American students. I have personally taught the grandchildren of refugees who fled to America during and after the war, grandchildren of veterans and victims of the war, and grandchildren descended from American troops and Vietnamese women. Since the 2005–2006 academic year, the number of Vietnamese citizens studying at Drexel has increased greatly; in that year, only four Vietnamese students studied at Drexel, but that number increased to thirty-five the next year and peaked at 223 in 2013–2014.[56] Conversely, Drexel students and professors have traveled to Vietnam as part of the university's study abroad program.[57]

In the age of the all-volunteer military that followed the Vietnam War, Drexel has adopted a policy of strong support for and recruitment of veterans. Drexel now has an Office of Veteran Student Services to provide support and services for veterans; participates in the GI Bill Yellow Ribbon program; and matches government funding so that veterans can attend school with no expenses. Veterans also get course registration priority to minimize any delays in their degree progress.[58]

Like the rest of the country, Drexel experienced debates over and protests against the Vietnam War, concerns about dissent and free speech in times of war, and challenges to civilian-military relations. Also like the rest of the country, the Drexel community reconsidered the meaning of the Vietnam War and American veterans of that war. At the same time, Drexel, through increasing relations with Vietnam and the inclusion of Vietnamese students in the Drexel community, is a participant in the changing and warming relations between former enemies who fought a war that unsettled American campuses, killed 58,000 and wounded 300,000 American troops, and killed millions of Vietnamese on both and neither side of the war.

NOTES

1. "Students' Army Training Corps" (c. 1918), UR 10.7, ROTC 1918–1969, 3, Drexel University Archives.

2. For the history of Drexel during the world wars, see Edward D. MacDonald and Edward Hinton, *Drexel Institute of Technology, 1891–1941* (Philadelphia: Drexel Institute, 1942) and Miriam N. Kotzin, *A History of Drexel University, 1941–1963* (Philadelphia: Drexel University, 1983).

3. Alex Goodall, *Loyalty and Liberty: American Countersubversion from World War I to the McCarthy Era* (Urbana: University of Illinois Press, 2013), 13–17, 20–22.

4. "War Courses for Women: Who Desire to Serve the Nation as Dietitians in Government Positions," War Courses for Women 2005-96-01, c. 1918, Drexel University Archives. "War Courses for Women: Who Desire to Serve the Nation as Dietitians in Military Hospitals," War Courses for Women 2005-96-01, c. 1918, Drexel University Archives.

5. *Engineering, Science and Management War Training Program, 1943–1944*, UR6.16, World War II Collection, 1943–1951, 2006-143-01, 2–4, Drexel University Archives.

6. "Give a Book for Victory Campaign," *The Triangle*, January 16, 1942, 1; "Drexel—A Wartime College—In Review," *The Triangle*, May 29, 1945, 2; "Drexel Home Front Strives for Victory," *The Triangle*, May 29, 1945, 2.

7. "Bloodmobile Unit Visits Drexel Next Thursday; Clothes for Korea Drive Needs Your Support," *The Triangle*, November 30, 1951, 1; "Blood Badly Needed in Korea; Bloodmobile Visits May 19; Pledges to Be Distributed Today," *The Triangle*, May 15, 1953, 1; "Deferment Test Set for December 4th," *The Triangle*, October 15, 1952, 2; "It's Getting Drafty," *The Triangle*, January 16, 1952, 4; "The Draft May Reach the Students," *The Triangle* May 15, 1953, 4.

8. Harry G. Summers Jr., *On Strategy: A Critical Analysis of the Vietnam War* (New York: Ballantine, 1995), 12–14.

9. Melvin Small, *Antiwarrior: The Vietnam War and the Battle for America's Hearts and Minds* (Wilmington, DE: Scholarly Resources, 2002), 33. James Westheider, *Fighting in Vietnam: The Experiences of the U.S. Soldier* (Mechanicsburg, PA: Stackpole Books, 2007), 31, 32.

10. Westheider, *Fighting in Vietnam*, 32–33.

11. Summers, *On Strategy*, 12–14.

12. Westheider, *Fighting in Vietnam*, 34–36.

13. Michael S. Neiberg, *Making Citizen-Soldiers: ROTC and the Ideology of America Military Service* (Cambridge, MA: Harvard University Press, 2000), 117.

14. Small, *Antiwarrior*, 4–9, 12–13, 16, 20, 26, 29.

15. Ibid., 24, 61–62.

16. "An Expression of Concern," *The Triangle*, June 2, 1967, 5.

17. Barbara Hornum, interviewed by Jonson Miller, January 26, 2016. Michael Sullivan, interviewed by Jonson Miller, January 21, 2016.

18. Small, *Antiwarrior*, 55, 58–59, 64.

19. Barbara Hornum, interviewed by Jonson Miller.

20. Ibid. Michael Sullivan, interviewed by Jonson Miller, December 10, 2015, and January 21, 2016. Richard Rosen, interviewed by Jonson Miller, February 15, 2016.

21. "The Freedom to Dissent," *The Triangle*, June 2, 1967, 6.

22. "Members of a Local Marine Reserve Unit Beat Up an anti-Vietnam War Demonstrator in Houston," *The Triangle*, July 28, 1967, 5.

23. J. W. Smith, "Letter," *The Triangle*, October 24, 1969, 7.

24. Small, *Antiwarrior*, 107.

25. W. W. Hagerty, "Letter," *The Triangle*, October 10, 1969, 3.

26. "All We Are Saying Is Give Peace a Chance," *The Triangle*, October 10, 1969, 1, 3.

27. Elaine Maguire, "Hagerty Signs Petition for Vietnam Withdrawal," *The Triangle*, October 17, 1969.

28. Michael Sullivan, interviewed by Jonson Miller.

29. Ibid.

30. John A. Andrew III, *The Other Side of the Sixties: Young Americans for Freedom and the Rise of Conservative Politics* (New Brunswick, NJ: Rutgers University Press, 1997), 5, 8, 215; David Farber, *The Rise and Fall of Modern American Conservatism: A Short History* (Princeton, NJ: Princeton University Press, 2010), 75, 104. The founding YAF "Sharon Statement" is available at http://www.yaf.org/sharon_statement.aspx.

31. Brooke M. Shadburne, "Letter: A Marine's View of the War in Vietnam, *The Triangle*, November 17, 1967), 10, 12.

32. Small, *Antiwarrior*, 120.

33. Robert Buzzanco, *Vietnam and the Transformation of American Life* (Malden, MA: Blackwell, 1999), 105–7. Small, *Antiwarrior*, 121–123.

34. Jay Lockman, "Student Body Votes 'Strike,'" *The Triangle*, May 8, 1970, 3, 5.

35. "V. P. Crouch," *The Triangle*, May 8, 1970, 4; "Faculty Council," *The Triangle*, May 8, 1970, 4. Faculty Members, "Letter," *The Triangle*, May 8, 1970, 4.

36. Michael Sullivan, interviewed by Jonson Miller.

37. Small, *Antiwarrior*, 139–57.

38. Westheider, *Fighting in Vietnam,* 49.

39. "Students' Army Training Corps" (c. 1918), UR 10.7, ROTC 1918–1969, 3, 6, Drexel University Archives.

40. *The War Records of Men Trained in the Reserve Officer Training Corps at Drexel Institute of Technology Who Served in World War II, 1941 to 1946*, UR 10.7, World War II, Drexel University Archives. Neiberg, *Making Citizen-Soldiers*, 26.

41. "Minority Report of the Ad-Hoc ROTC Committee," December 1965, UR 10.7, ROTC 1918–1969, Drexel University Archives. Neiberg, *Making Citizen-Soldiers*, 40.

42. Neiberg, *Making Citizen-Soldiers*, 51–52, 54–57, 87–88 91–92, 94–95, 104–8.

43. "Report of the Ad-Hoc ROTC Committee," December 1965, UR 10.7, ROTC 1918–1969, Drexel University Archives.

44. James S. Miles to Drexel Faculty and Administration, May 13, 1969, UR 10.7, ROTC 1918–1969, Drexel University Archives.

45. Neiberg, *Making Citizen-Soldiers*, 113–14, 116, 117–18.

46. Peter Gentieu and Joseph O'Brien, eds. *Drexel Review of the Corps*, 1973, UR 10.7, ROTC 1970–1983, Drexel University Archives. Joseph W. Powers to Faculty and Administration, July 5, 1973, UR 10.7, ROTC 1970–1983, Drexel University Archives.

47. Bettie J. Morden, *The Women's Army Corps, 1945–1978* (Washington, DC: United States Army Center for Military History, 1990), 122, 287–88. Neiberg, *Making Citizen-Soldiers,* 158–61.

48. Westheider, *Fighting in Vietnam,* 161–62, 165–66.

49. Buzzanco, *Vietnam and the Transformation of American Life,* 134. Gary R. Hess, *Vietnam: Explaining America's Lost War* (Malden, MA: Blackwell, 2009), 13–14, 133.

50. Summers, *On Strategy,* 12–14.

51. For examples of revisionist arguments for how the allies could have won the war or at least lost better, see the following: Summers, *On Strategy*; Lewis Sorley, *A Better War: The Unexamined Victories and Final Tragedy of America's Last Years in Vietnam* (New York: Harcourt, 1999); Michael Lind, *Vietnam: The Necessary War: A Reinterpretation of America's Most Disastrous Military Conflict* (New York: Touchstone, 1999). For examples of "orthodox" arguments for the impossibility of victory, see Marilyn B. Young, *The Vietnam Wars, 1945–1990* (New York: Harper Perennial, 1991); George C. Herring, *America's Longest War: The United States and Vietnam, 1950 to 1975* (Boston: McGraw Hill, 2002); and Nick Turse, *Kill Anything That Moves: The Real American War in Vietnam* (New York: Metropolitan Books, 2013).

52. Adam Geibel, "Vietnam Memorial Dedicated in Philadelphia," *The Triangle,* November 6, 1987, 1. Information about the memorial is available at at http://www.pvvm .org.

53. "Our Heroes," Philadelphia Vietnam Veterans Memorial, available at http://www .pvvm.org/images/pvvm-images/our-heroes/pdfs/B.pdf.

54. "DU Grade Remembered," *The Triangle,* November 6, 1987, 1; "Our Heroes."

55. "DU Grade Remembered," 7.

56. Student data from Drexel University's Institutional Research, Assessment, and Effectiveness. Includes the number of Drexel students of Vietnamese citizenship, whether international students or legal residents of the United States, from 2005–2006 to 2015–2016.

57. Office of International Programs, *Academic Year 2014–2015 Annual Report,* 16, available at http://drexel.edu/-/media/Files/oip/PDF/annual_report_2015_online.ashx

58. Office of Veteran Student Services, http://drexel.edu/studentlife/student_family _resources/veterans/.

The people working on The Triangle *were typified, by some other students, as sort of a combination of Greenwich Village and Haight-Ashbury. We had a reputation for being extremely liberal and all that stuff, and perhaps not even representing "typical Drexel students." That reminds me there was a counter-newspaper that ran for a while. Some students felt that* The Triangle *had been hijacked by a bunch of left-wing radicals and it wasn't reflecting what was happening at the college, so they started, I think it was called the* Drexel Billboard, *and on their masthead it said "School News . . . for a Change." The criticism was, if you look back at* The Triangle *going back to the forties and fifties, it was full of a lot of innocuous college stuff. It was accounts of the fraternity and sorority events, there was a lot of coverage of sports and the dances and stuff like that, and very little about society at large, politics, or anything like that. The people who ran* The Triangle *wanted to get into that sort of broader journalism, and it offended some people. There were some students, in the late sixties, that still wanted a nice school newspaper that reflected the school events . . . and they didn't want to tread into areas of possible controversy like politics and current events. I'd remind you, at this time the involvement in Vietnam was escalating. I'd also remind you that race relations were coming to an unfortunate clashing point. We actually had race riots in Powelton Village, and part of my feeling was, how could you go to a school within a few blocks of race riots and the sort of confrontation situations that they represent, and not be concerned about these issues?*

—ALEX TURFA, CHEMISTRY, DREXEL FELLOWS PROGRAM, '70

16

The University and
the Urban Metabolism

Environmental Engineering at Drexel

CHARLES HAAS

IN THIS CHAPTER I trace the history of environmental education and research at Drexel University, from its origins during the first decade of the founding of Drexel Institute—when courses were established covering public hygiene, ventilation, and hydraulics, reflecting contemporary concerns regarding water safety and quality[1]—to its formal foundation through the establishment of the Institute for Environmental Engineering and Science in 1963, into the creation of the School of Environmental Science, Engineering, and Policy (SESEP) in 1997, and the dissolution of SESEP in 2002. I conclude with a survey of the university's environmental education and research assets (located primarily in the College of Arts and Sciences, College of Engineering, and Dornsife School of Public Health), which suggests the potential for this to be a tremendous area for future growth.

Even at Drexel's founding, what we now recognize as environmental engineering, science education, and research, were present and were of major societal concern, especially in Philadelphia, located as it is at the lower end of both the Delaware and Schuylkill Rivers, which made the city the recipient of multitudinous amounts of waste that had been discharged into the rivers further upstream. Rapid industrial development and coal mining resulted in heavy pollution of both rivers as early as 1815.[2]

In the latter half of the nineteenth century, large cities such as Philadelphia were afflicted with periodic outbreaks of what are now recognized as waterborne infectious diseases. It is hard to imagine that in Anthony Drexel's daily walk from West Philadelphia to his office at Second Street he did not recognize the fetid condition of the Schuylkill River. In 1891, the year of the Drexel Institute's founding, a typhoid epidemic in parts of the city fed by untreated Schuylkill water afflicted 317 people and caused forty-two deaths. Two years earlier, a similar outbreak afflicted residents served by Delaware River supplies, about which the *New York Times* commented:

> The mere fact that water has been soiled by discharges of sewage ought to be enough to excite in the minds of intelligent people aversion and disgust sufficient to prevent the use of it for drinking and cooking. When to this reason for the rejection of it is added the proof that all water so polluted may carry and very frequently does contain the seeds of infectious and fatal disease, it is surprising that any civilized community should continue year after year to drink anything so repulsive and dangerous, or should hesitate about procuring at any cost a supply of water that is healthful and clean.[3]

The concept of discharging waste into rivers stemmed from the now discredited miasmatic theory of disease, which associated illness with odors. By the time of the Drexel Institute's founding, the germ theory of disease had been firmly established, and the scientific and engineering community recognized that simple dilution of wastes did not result in decontamination. By 1914, filtration and chlorination of water supplies for Philadelphia were complete, although sewage treatment by Philadelphia and its various upstream dischargers was not really completed until the 1970s.[4]

By the 1920s, there was at Drexel a set of "municipal engineering" courses that addressed issues of water, transportation, and city planning. As Samuel Baxter, an alumnus of Drexel's evening college who later served for twenty years as the first commissioner of the Philadelphia Water Department, described these courses, they "included surveying work for construction and land surveying, highway construction and maintenance, waterworks: all of the things relating to water from hydraulics to treatment, the same thing relative to sewage treatment. They also taught structures and city planning."[5]

Industrial growth affected air as well as water. In the late nineteenth century there were growing concerns regarding the pollution from burning coal, particularly the soft coal used for heating and industrial processes.

Ordinances to regulate the sootiness of smoke emissions were enacted in Chicago and Cincinnati in 1881, and in Philadelphia in 1904.[6]

In October 1948, in Donora, a borough of 13,000 people in western Pennsylvania, a massive smog incident killed twenty people and adversely affected 6,000 others. Across the Atlantic, four years later, a peak "fog" episode in London was credited as the main cause of 7,000 excess deaths.[7] Numerous other incidents of heavy smog—the formation of which was soon recognized as resulting from atmospheric reactions among various air pollutants[8]—occurred during the 1950s, overturning the perception of air pollution as solely an aesthetic problem. A decade later, the publication of Rachel Carson's *Silent Spring* (1962) awakened the public to damage from chemical use, particularly to the ecosystem, and therefore motivated attention to issues beyond human health.

In 1947, Los Angeles established the first air pollution control district in the United States,[9] and the city of Philadelphia followed in 1948, by establishing the Division on Air Pollution Control and the Air Pollution Control Board within its Department of Public Health. In 1954 the city prohibited open burning and restricted smoke emissions.[10] At Drexel, reflecting the same concerns with air quality reflected in the establishment of new city government agencies, the Laboratory of Climatology was established in 1954, having moved from Johns Hopkins University with Charles Warren Thornthwaite. It was located somewhat far from the main campus, in Centerton, New Jersey.[11] Thornthwaite and his colleagues published path-breaking work on a variety of topics, including methods to estimate evapotranspiration and water balances,[12] which are still used today.

Though the Laboratory of Climatology became independent of Drexel in 1959 (apparently in conjunction with Thornthwaite's consulting work),[13] it nonetheless had a formative influence on the university, serving notably as one of the initial professional homes for the amazingly dynamic Francis Davis, who would play a foundational role in the establishment of formal environmental education and research at Drexel, where he became an instructor of physics in 1947, among other things. As one biographer described Davis's activities, "While teaching, serving as a Meteorologist [for WFIL-TV] and carrying out funded research [for the city government and a variety of federal agencies] . . . he found time to earn his Ph.D. in 1957 from New York University with some courses taken at the University of Pennsylvania." Davis was promoted steadily from instructor to professor, became head of the Physics Department in 1963, and dean of the College of Science in 1970.[14]

The formal inception of an environmental science and engineering program at Drexel can be traced to a 1961 letter by Davis to Leroy Brothers, Dean of Engineering, in response to a proposal to establish a professorship in air pollution and atmospheric physics in the Physics Department:

> I would like to suggest that you consider broadening this to a Professorship in Environmental Engineering. We already have (Purdom) the nucleus of a staff which could do research and teaching in areas such as air pollution, water pollution, waste water treatment and disposal, hydrology, geology, food technology, cloud physics, weather modification, atmospheric electricity, air ionization, the effect of weather on human and animal behavior and health, weather and plant growth and disease, pollution control at the plant level, plant environment and its relations to the worker, etc., etc.[15]

Possibly Davis's proposal was related to newly available federal funds for related research, starting with the 1956 Federal Water Pollution Act and 1960 amendments to the 1955 Air Pollution Control Act (the first major federal air pollution statute).[16] The proposal led not only to a new professorship, but to Drexel establishing in 1963 the Institute of Environmental Engineering and Science (IEES), initially funded by the U.S. Public Health Service. Davis served as the first director of the institute, with Dr. Paul W. ("Walt") Purdom serving as associate director on a part-time basis, as he was also an employee of the Philadelphia Division on Air Pollution Control.

In 1963, Purdom became a full-time Drexel faculty member, in civil engineering, immediately launching a Ph.D. program through IEES, and later, an environmental science and engineering master's program with concentrations in air resources and in water resources.[17] Federal training grant funds were successfully acquired to support both M.S. and Ph.D. students. The IEES was one of the few units at Drexel in the 1960s to offer a Ph.D., and it thus attracted faculty interested in advising doctoral students.[18] The M.S. program in water resources was established as a full-time, nine-month program in 1964, and it included many courses that can still be found in the university catalog.[19] The M.S. concentration in air and radiation was created soon thereafter. Between its founding and 1982, IEES (the name of which changed through the years) awarded 459 master's degrees and fifty-two doctorates.[20]

Reflected in the degree programs created by Purdom was his professional background in both environmental engineering and public health.

Indeed, during his time at Drexel Purdom served as president of the American Public Health Association.[21]

Organizationally, IEES was housed within the College of Engineering and Science from its founding until 1967, at which point the science departments separated from the engineering departments to form the College of Science (to which Davis was appointed dean).[22] With Davis as its primary creator, IEES had been linked most closely to the physics department, though with close ties to civil engineering as well. Purdom in fact suggested that IEES would be more appropriately located in civil engineering.[23]

In 1967—one year after Barry Commoner, a biologist and one of the premier public intellectuals of the environment, established the Center for the Biology of Natural Systems at Washington University[24]—Drexel's IEES became the Center for the Study of the Environment (CSE), with Purdom as its director, in which capacity he had the status of a dean and reported directly to the vice president for academic affairs. CSE was thus the equivalent of a college or school, and its separate units (for instance, environmental engineering and science) were the equivalent of departments.[25] In addition to its science and engineering programs, CSE also maintained a two-year program in "environmental management" for "students who possess advanced degrees, a minimum of three years experience, and who show superior promise and leadership capability."[26] Little, if any, information remains about the size, curriculum, and number of graduates of the environmental management program.

By 1970, CSE was renamed the Center for Urban Research and Environmental Study (CURES) and expanded in scope to include four subsidiary institutes (in environmental studies, energy sources and systems, urban management, and population studies). In theory, linking environmental and urban issues, as was clearly the intention of CURES, it reflected emerging paradigms in which urban areas were viewed from an ecological perspective—as Abel Wolman did in his formulation of the notion of a "city metabolism,"[27] employing concepts from the nascent field of ecology[28]—and in which there was a greater recognition of the importance of the social sciences in understanding environmental problems.[29] In practice, at Drexel at least, the connection between urban and environmental issues failed to take hold. According to one faculty member who participated in CURES, all but the environmental studies were "ghost operations."[30] Indeed, by 1973 CURES had been disbanded and only the Environmental Studies Institute (ESI) survived.

By 1969, there were twelve "core" faculty teaching in the environmental science and engineering graduate program. These faculty had a very diverse program of funded research, including projects studying the oxygen demands of life in the Delaware River, flavor research on coffee, the pollution of subsurface water by sanitary landfills, studies of incinerator residue, the atmospheric diffusion of radon, and the odor components of industrial exhaust.[31]

The 1970s was a landmark decade for environmental protection, starting with the establishment of the Environmental Protection Agency and passage of the National Environmental Protection Act in 1970. A host of other important laws followed (Table 16-1), each defining a key area of emphasis for environmental protection. Environmental science and engineering programs at Drexel and other universities developed research and education foci that followed the emphases in federal policy. The decade also began with the first Earth Day, which raised public consciousness towards issues of environmental protection,[32] though its impact was blunted

TABLE 16.1: KEY FEDERAL LAWS ENACTED DURING THE 1970		
Date	Law	Key Features
1970	Clean Air Act	Required development of primary and secondary air standards and state implementation plans.
1972	Clean Water Act	Funded expansion of wastewater construction program. Required all dischargers to have permits, and mandated development of effluent and water quality standards.
1974	Safe Drinking Water Act	Required establishment of standards for drinking water and reporting requirements.
1976	Resource Conservation and Recovery Act	Set up requirements for solid waste management, and a "cradle to grave" management system for hazardous waste.
1976	Toxic Substances Control Act	Mandated pre-distribution testing of new chemicals in commerce, and established controls on PCBs.
1980	Comprehensive Environmental Response, Compensation and Liability Act	Set up processes for cleanup of oil spills, and for abandoned hazardous waste sites. Set up procedures for assessment of liability, and federal funding for cleanup.
Source: Neil S. Shifrin, "Pollution Management in the Twentieth Century," *Journal of Environmental Engineering* 131, no. 5 (2005): 676–91.		

as public attention focused on the Vietnam War and the killings at Kent State.[33] It is not clear that Drexel had any activities on the first Earth Day.

In the early 1970s Drexel also received a significant bequest in support of environmental education—two endowed professorships, one in ecology and one in environmental engineering—upon the death in 1967 of Leroy D. Betz, a 1916 alumnus. The actual receipt of the $2.6 million gift appears to have occurred in late 1971 or early 1972.[34] The first Betz chairs were Richard Speece, in engineering, and Wesley Pipes, in ecology. In 1973 Pipes was the primary force behind Drexel's hosting the third national conference of the Association of Environmental Engineering Professors, providing national visibility for Drexel's programs.[35] In 1982 he resigned the Betz Chair when he moved to the College of Engineering (and was later replaced by Professor of Bioscience James Spotila), and Speece left Drexel for Vanderbilt University in the late 1980s (and was replaced by myself, Charles Haas, when I moved to Drexel from the Illinois Institute of Technology in 1991).

With Ronald Reagan's election and presidency came a stasis during the 1980s in the development of new environmental laws, and a temporary decline in public support for environmental controls.[36] At Drexel, Walt Purdom continued as director of what had become ESI until his retirement from the university in 1982. Pipes served as acting director during the 1982–1983 academic year, during which time faculty successfully fought against efforts by the vice president for academic affairs to eliminate the institute.[37]

Instead of being disbanded, the university hired a new ESI director, Herbert Allen, previously a professor of environmental engineering at the Illinois Institute of Technology. Though Allen became a faculty member in the Department of Chemistry, and as ESI director he reported to the office of graduate studies, he participated primarily in the College of Engineering, since, as he noted, "We were de facto engineering as science ignored us."[38]

With Allen as the new director, Speece's move to Vanderbilt, Pipes's resignation from the Betz chair, and the departure of another core faculty member in 1988 (Irving Suffet, who went to the University of California at Los Angeles), the institute was in a transitional state—as was the entire university, as it lurched forward uncertainly after the twenty-one-year presidency of William Hagerty. Allen left Drexel for the University of Delaware in 1990 and was followed by two interim ESI directors, both from the Department of Mechanical Engineering: Bernard Hamel in 1990–1991 and Nicholas Cernansky in 1991–1992. In 1993, when the financial condition of the university had made its future existence uncertain, Michael Gealt from the Department of Bioscience was named the permanent ESI director.

In the early 1980s in ESI there were approximately one hundred graduate students (the majority part-time) and twenty-five faculty, eight of which were considered the "core," with the others having looser affiliations and connections. All of the faculty were in fact "borrowed" from other departments or else hired on temporary contracts. ESI's facilities consisted of a common set of offices and laboratories in the former Abbotts Building, which has since been demolished and currently serves as a parking lot.

By the 1990s, the era of readily available federal training grants had vanished and Drexel had a fully developed set of departmental doctoral programs, so the incentives that had attracted faculty to IEES in the 1960s had diminished for ESI. Moreover, during the university's period of financial stress in the era of President Richard Breslin (1988–1994), it became clear that ESI's reliance on the good graces of departments to "lend" faculty was becoming untenable.

In 1995 Constantine Papadakis arrived as Drexel's new president, and in 1997 Provost Richard Astro created three new schools—Environmental Science, Engineering and Policy (SESEP); Biomedical Science and Engineering; and Education—which were to each have their own tenured and tenure-track faculty, some of whom would be existing faculty transferred from existing units, and others to be newly hired by the schools. Each school had a director who had the equivalent status of a dean, and who reported to the provost. The creation of SESEP was an expansion of ESI, necessitated in part by the fact that none of the deans of Drexel's existing colleges wanted to absorb the institute.[39] ESI director Gealt became the first SESEP director, though he left in 2000 to become dean of the School of Engineering, Mathematics and Science at Purdue University Calumet (and has since moved on to his current position as provost at Central Michigan University).

Following Gealt's departure, bioscience professor Susan Kilham was named interim director, and a search for a permanent director was initiated. Yet before a new director could be hired, a new provost, Harvill Eaton, notified SESEP faculty that, as of the 2002–2003 academic year, the school would be disbanded and that programs and tenure lines were to go back to individual colleges. During its five-year existence, SESEP had hired six new faculty, all but one of which (Robert Brulle, now in the Department of Sociology) quickly left the university. The school's faculty had also developed three new bachelor's programs (one in environmental science and two in environmental engineering) and new master's and Ph.D. programs in environmental policy. All these new programs remain as of 2016.

Since 2002, Drexel's programs in environmental science and environmental policy have been organized within departments in the College of

Professor Peter DeCarlo (center), doctoral student Anita Johnson, and Post-Doctoral Researcher Michael Giordano with an aerosol mass spectrometer. This was used by them to sample in Antarctica, Nepal, and the Marcellus well fields in Pennsylvania. (Civil, Architectural, Environmental Engineering Department, 2014.)

Arts and Sciences, and the programs in environmental engineering have been organized under the Department of Civil, Architectural and Environmental Engineering (CAEE) in the College of Engineering. The location of environmental engineering in CAEE (for which I have served as department head since 2003) has proven highly favorable to the development of the program; in the period from 2005 to 2015, seven additional faculty were hired in water resources, water quality, air resources, risk assessment and life cycle assessment.

The location of environmental engineering in a department that also includes architectural engineering has also provided for the development of a robust program in indoor air quality and ventilation, which harkens back to some of the early courses developed by Purdom in IEES. CAEE has also been able to rebuild a program in air resources and pollution control. The thorough integration of environmental engineering into the College of Engineering was notably symbolized when Joseph Hughes became dean in 2012. Hughes's training is in environmental engineering, and he earned his Ph.D. at the University of Iowa under Gene Parkin, who had previously been an ESI faculty member before moving from Drexel to Iowa in the 1980s.

Drexel's acquisition of MCP-Hahnemann University in 2002 and the subsequent establishment of what is now the Dornsife School of Public Health has led to fruitful interactions with environmental engineering in the area of environmental health, reinventing synergies originally encapsulated by Walt Purdom. Ironically, the Dornsife School has moved into the Nesbitt Building at Thirty-Third and Market Streets, which had previously been the home of SESEP.

The evolution of environmental science has been more fitful. At the time of the breakup of SESEP, the environmental science faculty, who were primarily ecologists, moved into the Department of Bioscience and Biotechnology (now the Department of Biology) and the school's environmental chemistry component was never reconstructed. In 2011, Drexel acquired the Academy of Natural Sciences (ANS). A number of ANS faculty combined with the ecology faculty to form a new Department of Biodiversity, Earth and Environmental Sciences (BEES). BEES remains strongly centered in ecology and environmental biology, with some limited aspects of environmental chemistry and earth sciences.

The environmental policy component of SESEP has endured the slowest redevelopment. Brulle was transferred into the Department of Culture and Communication, which did not have a uniformly strong culture of graduate education and research (and which has since been divided into several separate academic departments). However, other venues in the College of Arts and Sciences, including the Center for Public Policy, have shown interest in environmental and urban policy.

Drexel as of 2016 has a more robust set of assets than at any time in its history to take advantage of the broad student interest, research opportunities, and social impetus to deal with newer issues such as climate change, sustainability, and energy, as well as the historical issues of air, water and land pollution, The spread of these assets amongst multiple organizational units remains a challenge. If the university retains its historic sense of nimbleness, these challenges can be overcome to address opportunities in the future.

NOTES

1. Drexel Institute of Art Science and Industry, *Yearbook of the Departments and Courses of Instruction* (Philadelphia: Drexel Institute, 1899).

2. Chari Towne, *A River Again: The Story of the Schuylkill River Project* (Bristol, PA: Delaware Riverkeeper Network Press, 2012).

3. "Typhoid and Polluted Water," *New York Times*, April 16, 1891, 4.

4. Adam Levine, "The Grid Versus Nature," in *Nature's Entrepot: Philadelphia's Urban Sphere and Its Environmental Thresholds*, ed. Brian Black and Michael Chiarappa (Pittsburgh: University of Pittsburgh Press, 2012).

5. "An Interview with Samuel S. Baxter," November 10–11, 1981, ed. Robert D. Bugher and Michael C. Robinson, available at www.phillyh2o.org/backpages/baxter.htm.

6. Chris G. Whipple, "Analysis of Emissions, Exposures and Risks of Toxic Air Emissions from U.S. Coal-Fired and Oil-Fired Power Plants: The Challenges Ahead," in *Urbanization, Energy and Air Pollution in China* (Washington, DC: National Academies Press, 2004), 171–87.

7. M. L. Bell and D. L. Davis, "Reassessment of the Lethal London Fog of 1952: Novel Indicators of Acute and Chronic Consequences of Acute Exposure to Air Pollution," *Environmental Health Perspectives* 109 (2001): 389–94.

8. A. J. Haagen-Smit, "Chemistry and Physiology of Los Angeles Smog," *Industrial & Engineering Chemistry* 44 (1952): 1342–46.

9. South Coast Air Quality Management District, "The Southland's War on Smog: Fifty Years of Progress Toward Clean Air (through May 1997)," available at www.aqmd .gov/home/library/public-information/publications/50-years-of-progress.

10. Philadelphia Department of Health, "History of Air Pollution Control in Philadelphia," available at http://www.phila.gov/health/pdfs/History_122010.pdf.

11. Marilyn Mathews, "DIT Pioneers World's Only Climatology Lab," *The Triangle*, May 6 1955, 3.

12. C. W. Thornthwaite and J. R. Mather, *The Water Balance* (Centerton, NJ: Drexel Institute of Technology, Laboratory of Climatology, 1955).

13. Kenneth Hare, "Obituary: Charles Warren Thornthwaite 1899–1963," *Geographical Review* 53 (1963): 595–97.

14. Gerry Wilkinson, "Francis Davis," Broadcast Pioneers of Philadelphia, available at www.broadcastpioneers.com/francisdavis.html. Wilkinson lists "the Air Force, City of Philadelphia, the National Science Foundation, the U.S. Weather Bureau, the Environmental Protection Agency and the Department of Defense" as agencies from which Davis received funding. This list is somewhat questionable as the EPA was not founded until 1970.

15. Francis Davis memorandum to Dean Leroy Brothers, September 25, 1961, Drexel University Archives.

16. Forswall, Clayton D. Forswall, and Kathryn E. Higgins, "Clean Air Act Implementation in Houston: An Historical Perspective 1970–2005," Rice University Environmental and Energy Systems Institute, February 2005, available at www.ruf.rice.edu/~eesi /scs/SIP.pdf; Curtiss M. Everts Jr. and Arve H. Dahl, "The Federal Water Pollution Control Act of 1956," *American Journal of Public Health and the Nations Health* 47 (1957): 305–10.

17. Paul Walton Purdom letter to Mark Hollis (World Health Organization), December 9, 1963, Drexel University Archives.

18. Wesley O. Pipes e-mail to Charles N. Haas, June 6, 2011.

19. Drexel University press release, January 23, 1964, Drexel University Archives. Courses from the M.S. in water resources that are still taught today include Water and Waste Water Treatment Unit Operations, Stream Analysis and Pollution Control, Hydrology, Sanitary Microbiology, Water Resources Management, Environmental Chemistry, Statistical Analysis, Human Physiology, Epidemiology, Environmental Health, Public Health Administration, and Radiological Health.

20. Drexel University, announcement of ESI director search, 1982–1983, Drexel University Archives.

21. "Association News," *American Journal of Public Health and the Nations Health* 60 (1970): 759–61.

22. Drexel University, *University Catalog 1965–6* (Philadelphia: Drexel University, 1965).

23. Paul Walton Purdom, memorandum, January 13, 1965, Drexel University Archives.

24. "Barry Commoner Center for Health and the Environment," Queens College, available at www.qc.cuny.edu/Academics/Centers/Biology/Pages/default.aspx?/.

25. Drexel press release, March 12, 1967, Drexel University Archives; I. M. Suffet, telephone communication with Charles N. Haas, December 16, 2015.

26. *Graduate Bulletin 1971–2* (Philadelphia: Drexel University, 1971).

27. Abel Wolman, "The Metabolism of Cities," *Scientific American* 213 (1965): 179–90.

28. Eugene P. Odum and H. T. Odum, *Fundamentals of Ecology* (Philadelphia: W. B. Saunders, 1959).

29. Garrett Hardin, "The Tragedy of the Commons," *Science* 162 (1968): 1243–48.

30. Drexel press release on appointment of Francis Davis as dean, July 29, 1970, Drexel University Archives; Paul Walton Purdom, memorandum to faculty, March 21, 1973, Drexel University Archives. Stanley Segall, telephone communication with Charles N. Haas, December 22, 2015.

31. Paul Walton Purdom, Environmental Engineering & Science Graduate Program, *Annual Report 1968–9*, Drexel University Archives.

32. Luther J. Carter, "Earth Day: A Fresh Way of Perceiving the Environment," *Science* 168 (1970): 558–59.

33. Ron Simon, "1970's One-Two Punch: Earth Day and Kent State," the Paley Center for Media, 2010, available at www.paleycenter.org/1970-s-one-two-punch-earth-day-and-kent-state/.

34. "L. D. Betz Gift," *Drexel University Alumni News*, January 1972.

35. Wesley O. Pipes, e-mail to Charles N. Haas, June 6, 2011.

36. Riley E. Dunlap, "An Enduring Concern," *Public Perspective* 13 (2002): 10–14.

37. Stanley Segall, telephone conversation with Charles N. Haas, December 22, 2015.

38. Herbert E. Allen, "Re: History of Environmental Stuff at Drexel," June 4, 2011.

39. Richard Astro, telephone communication with Charles N. Haas, December 17, 2015.

What I love about Drexel, what has really kept me here for all these years, is that this place has never felt that it's arrived. It's never felt that, "here we are, this is who we are, and this is what we're going to be, and why change it?" Drexel's never felt that way. Drexel is always about becoming, it's never about having arrived, and, in a sense, that striving, that sense that, "well, we're not the best, maybe we can get better, we can be something else, we can be different," it has driven us in positive directions, we've benefitted from it; and sometimes we take false stabs at things, but we tend to learn from our mistakes and move on.

I think that Drexel has always attracted a fair number of very bright, ambitious, creative, energetic people; and maybe it's because it's in Philadelphia, it's close to New York, it's close to Washington, and not everyone can live in New York and Washington. I think it's an attractive place for a lot of educated people, because of the proximity to the greatest centers of culture in the country, because of the nature of this city; it's an old city and it's walkable and it has the feel of a European city, and I think that appeals to a lot of people who go on to achieve degrees in higher education.

One of the most inspiring things I've seen here was when we were looking for the new president, the search firm interviewed faculty, and they had the faculty in a big room and they said, "What school would you like Drexel to be like most?" Somebody said, "We don't want to be another school, we just want to be a better version of Drexel." So, we like the work that we do, we like the colleagues we've developed, we like the culture we've built, but sure, we want to be better.

—Mark Greenberg, Distinguished University Professor, Provost Emeritus

The Humanities at Drexel

Paula Marantz Cohen

IN 1982, a combination of factors brought me to Drexel University. I had recently completed my Ph.D. in English literature at Columbia University with a concentration on the nineteenth century English novel. But I had also spent two years working in a major public relations firm on Madison Avenue. The job market for English Ph.D.s had entered a serious slump (from which it has yet to recover), and I knew that getting a job in academia, especially on the East Coast where my family lived, would be difficult. The ad for an assistant professor of Humanities-Communications at Drexel University made clear it was looking for someone with a foot in both the academic world and the so-called "real" world. I happened to fit this profile.

My interview at Drexel went well. I had an immediate rapport with many of the faculty and was impressed in general with the department, which was a mix of scholars in literature, philosophy, history of ideas, modern languages, and filmmaking.

The university had other combined departments at that time. History and political science existed as the Department of History-Politics, and the social sciences was a larger mash-up as the department of Psychology-Sociology-Anthropology. Cross-disciplinary scholarship, no less cross-disciplinary departments, was then a relatively new concept, but the idea had been implicit in Drexel's mandate since its founding in 1891 as the Drexel Institute for Art, Science, and Industry (the three terms are still on its triangular insignia). Although "Art" referred less to fine art and litera-ture than to the applied arts of engineering and the now-defunct field of home economics, an awareness of the importance of "art," however defined, was signaled from the beginning.

The hybrid, interdisciplinary departments also conformed to the school's integration of cooperative education into its curriculum (interspersing pe-riods where students work at real jobs with periods in the classroom). The concept of learning by doing conformed to progressive theories of experi-ential education introduced in the early twentieth century by John Dewey and Maria Montessori. Thus co-op connected, at least theoretically, to phi-losophy and pedagogy, important facets of the humanities. As with cross-disciplinarity, experiential learning would come back into vogue at a later date and give Drexel a boost as it gained stature in the late 1990s and 2000s.

That said, the hybrids in the humanities and social sciences were not for progressive pedagogical reasons but for purely practical ones. These dis-ciplines had a service function with respect to engineering, the school's principle focus, and therefore did not require delineation in the eyes of the administration.

Some headway with regard to humanities education occurred in 1956 when then president James Creese initiated the Disque Reading in Indus-try Program. (John Disque had been interim president before Creese and dean of faculty and of engineering). The goal of the program was "the study of the individual in his relationship to order in the universe, to the moral and ethical problems of the society in which he lives, and to the understand-ing of his own psychological nature."[1] The courses on the books for 1957 include an array of offerings in the history of ideas: two comprehensive In-troduction to the Humanities courses, two America and the Humanities courses, and two Western Ideas and Values courses. These courses were am-bitious in their scope and seriousness. For example, the first, Introduction to the Humanities, "required of all freshmen," is described as follows:

> First term: Hellenism: the good life and rational conduct; the "this world" focus; Athens, the City State; Fifth-Century ideas and val-ues; Hebraism: the good life and spiritual salvation; the "other world" focus.[2]

William Hagerty, who assumed the presidency in 1963, understood the importance of the humanities, albeit as an adjunct to science and technol-ogy. In 1965, he requested approval to offer a bachelor of science in humani-ties and science. In 1967 he named Dean Robert G. Hallwachs head of the

Humanities and Technology Program. In 1969, he created the College of Humanities and Social Sciences, which allowed for expanded hiring in these disciplines. Dean Hallwachs explained the mission of the college:

> Inasmuch as the special character of Drexel University is its emphasis upon applied arts and sciences, it is appropriate that Drexel's proposed College of Humanities and Social Sciences should provide the historical, theoretical and practical basis to equip students to deal with current and future problems of man and society. The new college is designed to meet an immediate need whose roots lie in a technological explosion, which has found man piercing the heavens, harnessing the atom, communicating and computing electronically, and unlocking the secrets of life itself while fumbling for solution of his human problems of war, poverty, overpopulation, pollution and racial tensions. The potential of a technological university, as indeed of a technological world, requires that the work of science and its applications must be more closely linked to the studies of Man. The programs of the proposed college will be designed to accomplish this end.[3]

This mission statement reflects a keen sense of the contribution the humanities can make to the education of college students, but it is also highly generalized—more rhetoric than substance. It is not surprising, therefore, that the humanities at Drexel, by being peripheral to its central mission, tended to be short-changed whenever other interests got in the way. In the minutes of a meeting of the Board of Trustees on May 13, 1965, President Hagerty notes that the Reading-in-Industry program in which "cooperative students during their industry periods away from school were required to read a list of books and submit reports" was receiving opposition from students and faculty. He announced that "it will be dropped to be replaced by a multi-pronged program which will provide Drexel contacts for the cooperative students which will be pleasant, of greater interest, and result in closer relationship between student and the school."[4]

I suspect that Hagerty sacrificed an excellent program under duress. Dave Jones, a filmmaker who has been at Drexel since 1977 and would be a department head of Humanities-Communications, head of the Film and Video Department, and dean of the Honors College, knew Hagerty and notes: "A lot of faculty in the humanities thought [he] was a bully and a boor, but they misread him. He wasn't good at small talk, and he was down-to-earth and practical. He was supportive of good ideas for the humanities that came to him."[5] Peter Herczfeld who came to Drexel in 1967 and is now Lester Kraus Professor of Electrical and Computer Engineering, has a less sanguine view of Hagerty's response to the humanities: "From my perspective the humanities program in the late sixties and early seventies was very, very poor. It used graduate students from Penn and other schools for the faculty positions. Hagerty [at this time] viewed the humanities departments as entirely service departments for the school. As the school was rising in size and reputation, he started to pay more attention to other colleges, including the humanities."[6]

Dr. Herczfeld recalls only one cultural event at Drexel during the 1970s—a poetry reading by Miriam Kotzin of the Humanities-Communications Department. (Dr. Kotzin is still a practicing poet and member of the English department faculty.)[7] Ray Brebach, another former department head of Humanities-Communications and a former head of the Faculty Senate who came to Drexel in 1978, remembers another anecdote that humorously encapsulates President Hagerty's attitude toward non-engineering disciplines. It seems he wanted to hire a math professor, recounts Brebach, but the candidates presented to him were all engineers who did math. "I know what a real math professor looks like," Hagerty is reported to have declared: "he has long hair and wears Birkenstocks."[8]

Still, the 1970s and 1980s held a great promise for many of us. In 1970, the Drexel Institute of Technology had become Drexel University, a formal title change that seemed to augur a structural and conceptual one. An energetic new dean of Humanities and Social Sciences, Tom Canavan, made two important changes in the college: he instituted a policy that allowed newly hired tenure-track professors to teach half-time loads for two years (four courses a term was the full teaching load), thereby giving them time to do their own research; and he allowed creative work to count alongside scholarly work as a basis for tenure and promotion (once again, it was both in line with Drexel's applied orientation and prescient of the direction that other universities would eventually take).[9]

In 1984, Drexel also became the first university in the country to ensure that all entering freshmen would have a microcomputer (the contract was with an emerging company called Apple), and mandated that the computer be integrated into all coursework, including the humanities. Dave Jones remembers talking to President Hagerty about the initiative in the Drexel bar (a congenial meeting place in Macalister Hall that was discontinued a few years later), and pitching him on the idea of making a documentary film on the subject. Hagerty agreed to underwrite the film, which was made and premiered at Drexel, with a thirty-year-old Steve Jobs in attendance. A particularly amusing sequence in the film shows humanities instructors, of which I am one, teaching each other how to use the computer. The film is a testament to the way Drexel operated at that time. A good idea could be realized with minimal hassle.

I should add that, even thirty years ago, Drexel was a stimulating environment in which to teach the humanities. Despite the school's homogeneous population (overwhelmingly white, male, and Catholic—a makeup that has since changed dramatically), the students were energetic and forward-looking. Many were first-generation college students and truly grateful to be getting an education. They were also open and unbiased in their response to ideas. My hybrid department provided the opportunity for cross-disciplinary conversation and collaboration. I and many of my peers liked Drexel's real-world orientation and the chance to make our subject-matter relevant to students who might not normally be exposed to it.

The Humanities courses themselves were conventional in some respects and highly original in others. There were survey courses in both world and American literature and courses in general areas like period studies, genre studies, and major authors. But there were also an array of special topics courses that allowed us to indulge our more esoteric research interests, as well as more practical courses in public speaking, technical and science writing, and business writing. In the late 1970s, a master's program in technical and science communication was initiated.

The History-Politics Department showed a similar duality. It offered standard survey history courses but also specialized courses in military and political history as well as world history, unusual for the time. That department would also begin to forge a strong History of Science and History of Technology Program through hires, beginning in the 1980s that fit well with Drexel's engineering focus. This program would eventually achieve a national reputation. International Area Studies, introduced in the Humanities-Communications Department in the early 1980s, later became part of History and Politics, and then an independent unit. It has been a robust program ever since its founding and has placed students in careers in the State Department, international business, and academia. The political science side of the History-Politics Department also became known for work in polling and the statistical analysis of political trends.

But there were also definite frustrations attached to being in the humanities at Drexel during the 1980s. Engineering was the university's preeminent discipline, and these students had a packed curriculum that left little room for electives. Much of the teaching in the Humanities-Communications Department was in the three-course freshman humanities sequence required of every Drexel freshman. For a period of time in the late 1980s and '90s, even the basic writing and literature courses were incorporated into the engineering curriculum. This began as a program funded by the National Science Foundation and referred to as E4 (that is, engineering taken to a higher power by integrating other course work into it) and evolved to include all engineering students. Valarie Arms, a member of the Department of Humanities-Communications, helped to design and lead the program. Although innovative in forwarding a team-teaching approach to the humanities, it essentially kept engineering student together for all coursework during their first few years of study and tried to connect all reading and writing to the engineering curriculum. Many of us believed the approach ran counter to the way the humanities should be taught. Dr. Arms would later initiate another program, "English Alive," that combined the online teaching of writing with face-to-face teaching. This model has now become standard in the delivery of many of our freshman composition courses.

The department itself, whose eclecticism had so appealed to me, also began to pose problems soon after I arrived. In the late 1970s and early 1980s, the department head, Martha Montgomery, had taken advantage of a buyer's market and hired accomplished and ambitious individuals in a variety of humanities fields. But these individuals, of which I was one, soon became frustrated by our subordinate status within the university and eager to make our department more central to its mission. Interestingly, the archives show that this kind of dissatisfaction had been a problem at an earlier point in the history of the institution. One of the rationales presented by President Hagerty for the creation of a B.S. in humanities and science in 1965 was owing to concern about "the loss of good 'liberal arts' faculty who have left Drexel because they have taught service courses to engineering students and have not been able to teach older students in their respective majors."[10]

In the 1980s, this discontent emerged more sharply, given the state of the job market in the humanities. Many of us had come to Drexel because there were no other jobs to be had, but we had trained at first-rate institutions, thought very highly of ourselves, and were not content to be marginalized. Our dissatisfaction made itself felt. The Department of Humanities-Communications became polarized, with one group, content with things the way they were, battling a newer guard that felt that they needed to have a more central role in the intellectual life of the university. I remember one faculty meeting in which one of the younger, more ambitious scholars was accused of trying to turn Drexel into Princeton. In the early 1980s, the Department of Humanities-Communications divided specifically on the issue of Drexel's culture: there was the desire of some to change that culture and of others to let things alone.

A major initiative launched following the resignation of Dr. Montgomery was the creation of a Future Directions Committee, chaired by Mark Greenberg, a scholar of William Blake, who later would become the founding dean of the Pennoni Honors College, dean of undergraduate studies, and provost. The Future Directions Committee created a new set of majors that included literature, applied philosophy, film and video, corporate communication, technical and science communication, and science, technology, and culture, the last a throwback in a sense to the humanities and technology program and the B.S. in humanities and science of the 1960s. The aim here was both to elevate the department in importance and to make its work conform with Drexel's particular technological focus. MIT was a model in this regard since it had been developing strong humanities offerings with a link to technology for some time. Greenberg, despite his graduate training in Romantic poetry, was one of the founders and the first president of the Society for Literature and Science. At this time we also hired Richard Burgin, who launched his well-known *Boulevard*, the first in what would be a series of high-profile literary journals attached to the university.

The department underwent changes in its title as well. Humanities-Communications morphed into Humanities and Communications, demonstrating that the integration of disciplines was beginning to dissolve (History-Politics similarly became History and Politics). Humanities

and Communications then became English and Philosophy in the late 1990s, with the film and video major migrating first to the Department of Performing Arts in the college and then to the College of Media Arts and Design (COMAD, which later became the Westphal College) across campus. A graduate program in arts management as well as an undergraduate major in

Dr. Mark Greenberg, August 12, 1986. Founding Dean of the Pennoni Honors College and Provost Emeritus. (Drexel University Archives. PC 4 People photographs.)

performing arts that have since split into various separate majors also migrated to COMAD. The communications component of the department moved in with the social sciences to form a new hybrid: culture and communication.

This last was a controversial move, as many on the English side of the curriculum felt that they would lose traction within the university in losing control of the practical communications courses. This did not prove to be the case. The English and Philosophy Department, as it was eventually renamed, still offers all freshman writing courses, and the English major has been able to recruit a small but formidable group of students who have vitalized the department and raised faculty morale. Philosophy, meanwhile, has begun to build its major and has plans to separate into its own department.

These changes had begun in the 1990s, first under the stewardship of interim president Chuck Pennoni, then more aggressively under President Constantine Papadakis, who was determined to make Drexel a more comprehensive university and hire in the humanities and social sciences. (There was initially much grumbling on the engineering side of the university about this). This effort was further accelerated under President Fry, who has made a point of supporting cultural and civic initiatives of various kinds and making clear that the university needs to have a strong profile in the humanities. The university under President Fry bears little relationship to the much more narrowly focused, more provincial and homogeneous institution that existed under President Hagerty thirty years ago.

Ironically, the changes under these two presidents happened as the university itself transitioned into a more traditional form. The College of Humanities and Social Sciences that had housed Humanities-Communications when I was first hired became the College Arts and Sciences. The Humanities-Communications major became the literature major and, eventually, the English major.

At the time of this writing, the move toward traditional departments in the humanities and social sciences within the College of Arts and Sciences continues. Psychology became a separate department with a graduate program in cognitive and brain science in the late 1990s, coincident with the acquisition of the medical school, while sociology, anthropology, and communication have each become separate departments, with the languages moving to the new Department of Global Studies and Modern Languages. As noted, History and Politics has recently split, and there are plans for English and Philosophy to do so as well. In the Westphal College, the Department of Art and Art History has recently established an art history major (there was previously only a minor).

One might argue that the old Drexel with its hybrid departments was more in step with our postmodern zeitgeist. Still, while the form of the humanities at the university has become more conventional, there remain strong cross-disciplinary and applied components—centers and programs that stress interdisciplinarity.

One such program that was launched in 1991 was an honors program for students with high SAT scores and GPAs. With an endowment by Chuck and Annette Pennoni in 2002, the Honors Program became the Pennoni Honors College. The program grew substantially, and the college came to house a collection of other units devoted to cross-disciplinary study and intellectual, cultural, and social enrichment (fellowships, undergraduate research, a custom-designed major, travel-integrated courses, intensive mentorship, cultural opportunities and media, and other programming supporting a humanities orientation). Following my two colleagues from the original Humanities-Communications Department, Mark Greenberg and Dave Jones, each of whom served as dean of the college, I now hold that position.

The Honors Program, though not exclusively devoted to the humanities, is a strong advocate for humanistic thinking and cross-disciplinary study. Courses are in seminar form and have a cross-disciplinary orientation. They appeal to Drexel's humanities majors, but they also allow students in the sciences, engineering and business to get exposure to courses that involve film and literature, art and philosophy, urban space and politics, and history of science and technology. The program has recently initiated one-credit courses in "Great Books" (one book per term, discussed for one hour a week) and plans to expand this to one-credit courses on great films, music, and art. The Honors College also houses the Symposium, a series of cross-disciplinary courses offered each year, open to all students in the university, which brings together faculty from a variety of disciplines to address a single theme from a variety of perspectives.

There is no doubt that humanities at Drexel has been a vexed area—but perhaps because of this it has also been a site of exploration and originality of a sort not seen in many other institutions of higher learning. Even as we have sought respectability—copying what our more prestigious neighbors have done—we have also maintained an integrity of our own. The History and Politics Department has been the site of a number of creative interdisciplinary programs, including a Science, Technology, and Society (STS) graduate program (now part of an independent Center for STS), which offers two tracks for a master's degree and an accelerated bachelor-master's. The Center for STS is also a think tank where faculty in anthropology, criminal justice, history, information sciences, philosophy, political science, public health, and sociology conduct original research on the impact of new technologies, medical categories, and scientific knowledge.

A thriving writing culture has also emerged within the Department of English and Philosophy. Drexel houses an unusual number of online and print publications devoted to student work, academic work, and high-level creative work by writers inside and outside Drexel. Many of our faculty are editors of literary journals: Miriam Kotzin, whose poetry reading is remembered by engineering professor Peter Herczfeld from the early days, has had a burgeoning literary career as a poet and novelist, and edits the online literary magazine *Per Contra*. Kathy Volk Miller, a well-published nonfiction writer, edits the nationally known *Painted Bride Quarterly* and has developed a popular internship for students who work with her as part of the Drexel Publishing Group. She has also spearheaded a master of arts in publishing that draws from a range of academic disciplines and technologies and thereby gives students a practical understanding of the current publishing landscape. The screenwriting major housed in the Westphal College and developed by former Hollywood screenwriter Ian Abrams is another example of an applied writing option; it has sent people to play and screenwriting positions in New York and Hollywood.

Other high-profile cultural media are centered in the Pennoni Honors College and include *The Smart Set*, a nationally known online journal; *Table Matters*, an online journal of food and drink; and *The Drexel Interview*, a television talk show featuring writers, artists, educators, businesspeople, and scientists of note, that airs on some four hundred stations including more than 150 PBS stations. There are at least a dozen high-profile poets, fiction, and nonfiction writers associated with the Department of English and Philosophy who, while teaching expository writing courses, are involved in improv, slam poetry, and Fringe Festival events throughout Philadelphia.

The growth of writing-related disciplines has paralleled in many ways the emergence of writing as a discipline (a major field in English studies nowadays is composition theory, and a majority of university hires are in this area). Once considered a purely service function, composition has now become a respected field, and Drexel has been at the vanguard in hiring a number of accomplished faculty in this area.

Many of the faculty are cross-disciplinary or applied scholars in fields such as translation, applied philosophy, and pedagogy. We have an unusual number of faculty in the humanities who write for general interest publications and can accurately be described as "public intellectuals."

In general, the university has become extremely congenial to the study of the humanities, but in a Drexel-specific way, attuned to the real world and in step with technological and scientific innovation. As former provost Mark Greenberg has explained: "Ironically, the early dominance of engineering, science, and business in shaping the university's reputation gave rise to opportunities for humanists to project a true comprehensive research university, as programs in the health sciences and law were added to round out the modern Drexel University."

First under President Constantine Papadakis from the mid-1990s to the early 2000s, and now under President John Fry, there is a real awareness that the kind of student we want to produce at Drexel will be culturally informed as well as skilled in particular areas. John Fry has been especially alert to the ways in which writing and reading can reach beyond the university itself; an "inside-out" program in which largely humanities courses are taught to students and community members has been a pioneering aspect of the curriculum. In addition, there are several initiatives underway that link Drexel programs with arts and cultural institutions in Philadelphia—both helping to make those institutions stronger and to give students greater access to them. President Fry understands that to rise to the highest positions in their fields and make the greatest contributions to their society, students need to know something about literature, history, art, philosophy, and the connections among these subjects and their relationship to other fields of study.

Drexel has emerged as a vibrant center for cultural expression and partnership, while continuing to pursue its original mandate: to train students to make concrete contributions to the world in which they live.

NOTES

1. Miriam N. Kotzin, *A History of Drexel University, 1941–1963* (Philadelphia: Drexel University, 1983), 121–22.
2. Ibid., 216–17.
3. Ibid., 176.
4. Board of Trustee Meeting Minutes, Approval of Humanities Program, May 13 1965, 10, folder 9, box 11, UR 2.1, Board of Trustees and Executive Committee Records, Drexel University Archives.
5. David Jones, interviewed by Paula Cohen, November 7, 2015.
6. Peter Herczfeld, interviewed by Paula Cohen, November 10, 2015.
7. Peter Herczfeld, interviewed by Paula Cohen, November 8, 2015.
8. Ray Brebach, interviewed by Paula Cohen, November 4, 2015.
9. David Jones correspondence with Paula Cohen, November 11, 2015.
10. Board of Trustee Meeting Minutes, Approval of Humanities Program, May 13, 1965, 9.

Pennoni Honors College students gather outside of the Lincoln Memorial
during the first inauguration of President Barack Obama in 2009.
From left to right: Angela Petro, Joshua Hulbert, Jenna Stayton,
Kathleen Monahan, Jay Giller, Madison Eggert-Crowe.
(Pennoni Honors College.)

In January 2009, I was selected for a Pennoni Honors College course that centered on a trip to the first inauguration of President Barack Obama. Eighteen of my peers from throughout the university were selected to take the course. In preparation for the inauguration, we listened to, read, studied, and analyzed historical inauguration addresses. We each authored a paper predicting the themes Obama would include in his address. As a political science major currently working as a co-op for a political action committee, this was an excellent opportunity to see what I was learning in the classroom and on co-op working at a national scale.

We spent four days in Washington, DC, ahead of the inauguration and visited many of the national museums and landmarks. The energy in the Capitol that weekend was like nothing I had ever experienced.

It was obvious that everyone there, not only we students, appreciated what a special opportunity it was to be there to celebrate the historic inauguration of the first African American president of the United States.

The inauguration day was undoubtedly the most memorable part of the trip. That morning, we woke up at 3:45 A.M. to begin our trek to the National Mall to find the best spot to watch the ceremony. We waited on the Mall for seven hours in subfreezing temperatures to ensure we would have a direct view of the event. It was inspiring and humbling to be one of the millions of people who had also gathered on the Mall to witness this momentous occasion.

I consider myself lucky to have spent such a historic event with my peers—a group of intelligent, interested, and engaged students. The setting offered us the opportunity to connect with faculty and students we would otherwise have never met. It is one of my fondest memories, and I am thankful I was able to experience that special part of history.

—MADISON EGGERT-CROWE

18

The Pennoni Honors College

Pragmatism in the Pursuit of Academic Excellence

Kevin D. Egan

THE HONORS PROGRAM at Drexel, which became the Pennoni Honors College in 2003, was founded during a time of crisis for the university. From the mid-1980s to the mid-1990s, Drexel suffered declining student enrollment and faced a financial situation that threatened its solvency. Proposals for an honors program espoused the values and benefits of academic enrichment, as well as support for Drexel's best and brightest students; in its realization, the program became a way for the university to attract and retain the kinds of students that would keep the institution on its feet and growing into the twenty-first century. In its formulation as a haven for successful students and a beacon of intellectual rigor, the program also emerged as a significant response to Drexel's period of crisis; later, the founding of the Pennoni Honors College would amplify the initial mission of the program by incubating new, university-wide programs and serving a broad scope of students.

The origins of the honors program lay in those two dovetailing impulses that would come to shape the Pennoni Honors College as it developed and grew: the drive to cultivate the university's best students through innovative and rigorous coursework and programming, and the pragmatic necessity to serve the breadth of the undergraduate body. An early report on the formation of an honors program notes that "high-level students" were being dealt with as "only one sub-group within the undergraduate student body as a whole." In fact, the reporting group stressed in this document that they "ultimately have in mind the welfare, interests, and importance of the *entire* body of Drexel undergraduates." Early conversations justifying the creation of an honors program reflect this sentiment and highlight the possibility of extending to the rest of the university successful pedagogical and programmatic techniques that were experimented with in the honors program. This became a productive tension within the college as the honors program evolved and as new units, built with the intention to work with all Drexel undergraduates, were incubated (some of which would remain in Pennoni Honors College while others were moved elsewhere).

While a university honors program did exist for a few years during the 1960s (actually more akin to an accelerated degree program), the conceptual foundations for what would one day become the Pennoni Honors College can be traced back to 1985. That year, as part of the ten-year planning process for Drexel's Nesbitt College of Design Arts, Dean J. Michael Adams asked professors Marjorie Kriebel and Charles Morscheck "to develop a statement of concept and possible structure for an honors program in the College that might be translatable to the entire University."[1] This charge, and Kriebel and Morscheck's work, laid the conceptual foundation for an honors program structured by academic excellence, interdisciplinarity, and curricular experimentation.

These initial efforts seemingly stalled out for a time. Then, in 1988, President Richard Breslin called for a group of faculty to develop a strategy to work with and guide scholarship students—primarily recipients of the Presidential and Dean's scholarships, two of the university's preeminent merit-based undergraduate awards. Out of this initiative came the Honors Mentors Group, which was charged with a two-fold task, "to address the needs of Presidential and Deans' Scholars and to move toward early implementation of a full-fledged Honors Program at Drexel University."[2] This charge is an early indication of the dual character that the honors college would take on; the call to "promote the interests" of scholarship students is a broad mandate to support scholarly development across the undergraduate body at Drexel—a thread running through the many units that have been birthed in the college—while the development of an honors program speaks to a more specific structure serving high-achieving students.

First chaired by sociology professor Arthur Shostak, the Honors Mentors Group created the Honors Task Force, which submitted a proposal to President Breslin in June 1989, and shortly thereafter, Kathleen Reed, professor in the College of Information Studies, was tasked with creating an honors curriculum. The task force proposal highlighted the need to work with the university's merit-based scholarship students, especially the aforementioned Presidential and Dean's scholars. The group "moved vigorously and creatively" to address students' "non-financial needs" as well as the needs of the university to retain high-performing students.[3] Consequently, one substantive change that came about quickly from the group's work was the change in "the scholarship program from one-year awards to ongoing support."[4]

Furthermore, the group emphasized the "conviction that the existence of a well-supported honors program at this University will act as an intellectual leaven for *all* University undergraduates, including those who are not members of the Honors Program."[5] This ethos of serving both select high-achieving students and the entire undergraduate student body carries on with the current dean of the Pennoni Honors College, Paula Marantz Cohen, who, in a 2015 letter to the *New York Times*, remarked that the purpose of the Honors College is to "widen the lens" of experiential and cooperative education for students at Drexel. In so doing, Cohen highlighted that while some "programs are open only to the highest-achieving students . . . others—involving research, fellowship mentoring and interdisciplinary coursework—are open to all."[6]

The report to President Breslin also noted that, with a curriculum deeply rooted in technical and experiential learning and punctuated by the cooperative education program, there were few opportunities for interdisciplinarity at Drexel. The development of an honors program that spanned the entire undergraduate student body presented itself as a potential supporting structure for interdisciplinary course offerings. Memos circulated among the task force members proposed interdisciplinary courses tackling broad themes that capitalized on Drexel's strengths, including "Technology and American Society" and "Technology and the World Community." These proposals were the initial seeds from which grew the Great Works Symposium—a yearlong interdisciplinary course series currently administered by the Pennoni Honors College.

After several years of investigation and deliberation, a proposal for an honors program reached the faculty senate and was approved by that body in February 1991. Economics professor Roger McCain was appointed as the program's first director. At its launch in September 1991, the program comprised thirty-three students.

By 1991, Drexel was suffering—enrollment was declining precipitously, and a number of upper level administrators were leaving the university, culminating in President Breslin's resignation in 1994. Drexel alumnus C. R. "Chuck" Pennoni stepped in as interim president. Mark Greenberg, the university's provost from 2008 to 2014 and the founding dean of the Pennoni

C. R. "Chuck" Pennoni, interim president 1994–1995 and 2009–2010 (photo 1995). (Drexel University Archives. PC 4 People photographs.)

Honors College, credits the provost in the 1990s, Denny Brown, with the vision and understanding of how an honors program could help attract and retain students. In light of the precarious situation in which the university found itself, a program that served its brightest students could have the added benefit of helping to keep the university afloat. As Greenberg put it:

You had classes with students who we would never admit to Drexel nowadays, who couldn't do the work, and students who we were still offering very good scholarships to, who were brilliant. And, imagine being a really good student, really smart, and you're in class with a bunch of kids who just don't get it. How long are you going to put up with that? Are you going to stay here? So we were losing the good students. And the future, everyone knew, was to keep those good students and add to that pool. So, Brown's analysis was, we have to do something for these smart kids to keep them here. Otherwise, we've had it.[7]

With its rigorous and selective course offerings and a budding sense of community for stellar students, the nascent honors program became a mechanism for recruitment and retention. Greenberg explained that it "was designed to separate out the brighter kids, give them special attention, special courses, and all of the things that would help them want to stay here, succeed, graduate . . . they were the future."

In 1995, Greenberg was appointed director of the original honors program—a job he took on reluctantly, only after talking to honors students who told him bluntly that "if not for this honors program, we're out of here." Under Greenberg's direction, and with the help of a university that began growing under the new president, Constantine Papadakis, the honors program expanded, from fewer than one hundred students in 1995 to approximately fifteen hundred by 2000. This growth was enabled in part by the fact that a relatively large proportion of freshmen were accepted as honors students—approximately 20 percent—which some considered not selective enough, but which others thought was important to continue to serve those at "the upper end of the scale."

It was during Greenberg's tenure as director that the honors program became the Pennoni Honors College, as a result of a 2003 gift from Chuck Pennoni, based on the belief that a named honors college would maintain the university's momentum and growth. With Pennoni's gift, the Honors College had the resources to expand its programming and reach more students. As Greenberg notes, "It's at that moment that the Honors College became the home for innovative programs, for interdisciplinary programs, some of which were only for students in the honors program, but some of which were for the whole university." The Pennoni Honors College served as an incubator for new programs and units, including the Center for Civic Engagement (now the Lindy Center for Civic Engagement), the Study Abroad Office, the Great Works Symposium, the STAR (Students Tackling Advanced Research) Scholars Program, the Drexel Interview television program, the *Smart Set* online magazine, the Drexel Fellowships Office, the Drexel Writing Program, and the Cultural Passport (a students' guide to Philadelphia's cultural institutions, including free passes). The diversity of these units speaks to the expansion of the original vision articulated by the Honors Task Force—the commitment to scholar development encompassed a constellation of programs promoting service learning, exposure to international experiences, intensive undergraduate research opportunities, and interdisciplinary education, among others. As Drexel was able to attract a higher caliber of student, these endeavors found a centralized home in the Pennoni Honors College and developed in tandem with the rapid growth of the honors program.

The Pennoni Honors College found itself again in the midst of a university undergoing rapid and unexpected transformation in the late 2000s. In 2008, Dr. Greenberg became interim provost for the university, and film professor Dave Jones stepped in as interim dean. In 2009, Papadakis, battling cancer, stepped down as president and was replaced by Chuck Pennoni, reprising his previous role as interim president. Papadakis died soon thereafter, and Pennoni made both Greenberg's and Jones's appointments permanent. Jones served as dean of the Pennoni Honors College until 2014, when he resigned and was replaced by Paula Marantz Cohen.

The original intentions of the Drexel honors program—to serve some of Drexel's best and brightest students; to develop and offer rigorous, innovative, and interdisciplinary courses; and to assist in scholarly development for all students who seek it—continues to thrive today across all units of the Pennoni Honors College. The college currently consists of the honors program, the Office of Undergraduate Research, the Fellowships Office, the Center for Interdisciplinary Inquiry, and the Center for Cultural Media.

Each of these offices and centers was created to serve a specific niche of the student population. As the largest unit within the college, the honors program currently works with approximately two thousand students through curricular and cocurricular programming. The honors program curriculum no longer comprises just honors sections of regular disciplinary course offerings, or additional coursework to constitute such courses as honors options for individual students; now, the program regularly offers unique and advanced courses on topics ranging from World War II comedy, to genetics in popular culture, to terrorism and torture. Additionally, the honors program provides cocurricular opportunities such as alternative spring break service trips and the honors living learning community, as well as numerous guest speakers and sponsored activities throughout Philadelphia's cultural landscape.

The Drexel Fellowships Office has taken up one of the central tasks of the originally proposed honors program by helping to develop student scholars who have not only been competitive in their pursuit of national awards but have won a number of these awards, including NSF Graduate Research Fellowships, Gates Cambridge Scholarships, Udall Scholarships, Goldwater Scholarships, and Fulbright Awards. The office helps students with the application process by providing intensive individualized advising, working with each student to synthesize and articulate her or his array of academic experiences in order to craft a compelling fellowship application. Furthermore, the office works with applicants, regardless of whether they win a fellowship award or not, via post-process advising, helping them to learn from the application process and preparing them to capitalize on future opportunities.

As the STAR Scholars Program has grown—providing over 150 freshmen an intensive, faculty-mentored research project each summer since its inception in 2003—the Office of Undergraduate Research was created to offer structural support for these research endeavors, to help prepare students with necessary research skills and to provide dedicated resources to further expand research opportunities to undergraduates. The Center for Interdisciplinary Inquiry was formed as a hub for undergraduate interdisciplinary education by tying together the Great Works Symposium and the custom-designed major. Finally, the Center for Cultural Media acts as an outward-facing broadcast and online outlet for cultural analysis, including online publications (*Smart Set* and *Table Matters*) and the *Drexel Interview*.

As these units continue to grow and evolve, Pennoni Honors College will continue to serve outstanding and high-achieving students across Drexel University, and to incubate new programs and initiatives in pursuit of that service.

NOTES

1. J. Michael Adams, internal memo to Marjorie Kriebel and Charles Morscheck, 1985.

2. *Executive Summary of Undergraduate Honors Students at Drexel University, a report to President Richard D. Breslin* (Philadelphia: Honors Mentors Group, June 30, 1989).

3. Ibid.

4. Ibid.

5. *Executive Summary of Undergraduate Honors Students at Drexel University*, 2.

6. Paula Marantz Cohen, "College Honors Programs in Various Forms," *New York Times*, August 24, 2015, A21.

7. Mark Greenberg, interviewed by Scott Gabriel Knowles, November 4, 2015.

Taki [President Constantine Papadakis], the first couple of years, he rolled up his sleeves, and rightfully so he focused on enrollment. That's where he focused his energies. He went through three people in enrollment management until he ended up with Joan McDonald, who did a very, very good job. And after he got enrollment under control, then he started to address some of the other issues such as philanthropy and facilities. There was a period where we opened and improved or built a new building every year with Papadakis. And Taki was bigger than life. He was very charismatic; when he walked in a room, he lit up the room. And he was very hardworking. I never found a person who worked harder than Taki.

We used to have great debates, when I went in as chairman [of the board of trustees], Taki would be very focused on growth. I always favored quality. I defined Drexel as a quality, urban, technology-based, cooperative education, private university. And so I would even go more so on the side of quality to kind of counterbalance Taki on his ambitions for growth. We had excellent, excellent, debates. He would say, "Let's go to dinner. I want to talk to you about something." And we would debate for hours. I would think I won the debate. I would go home, and the next morning he would call me and say, "Chuck, can we meet? I want to talk to you." I would say, "What did you do? Stay awake all night thinking of other things and points for your argument?" Which he did! He was tenacious. Taki was tenacious, no question about it. When he had an idea, he wanted to do something. He was the right person for the right time at Drexel.

—C. R. "Chuck" Pennoni

19

Drexel Gains a Medical School

STEVEN J. PEITZMAN

D
URING THE YEARS 1998 to 2002, Drexel University acquired a
medical school—really something like two conjoined medical
schools, though not twins—and did so in a manner daring and
unique in the history of medical education in the United States. The story
of how such a school came to need a new owner has its roots in medical
reforms of the nineteenth century in one of America's preeminent medical cities. How it came to find that new owner reflects Drexel University's
quest for growth and standing in the late twentieth and early twenty-first
centuries. The story also reveals something of the turbulent nature of the
health care business in Philadelphia in these recent periods. And finally, it is
a moral tale, even a tragedy, complete with the fall of a flawed leader suf-
fused with excess ambition, and a bold rescue, against daunting odds, by
another helmsman of a large and growing enterprise.

The predecessor institutions to Drexel's College of Medicine each
claimed singular qualities representing new ideas and new opportunities in
Philadelphia, a city long known as a center of medical knowledge and education. The Woman's Medical College of Pennsylvania (MCP), founded in
1850, was the first medical school in the world for women and the longest
lasting as such. Through the early and mid-twentieth centuries, roughly a
quarter of women medical school graduates in the nation were Woman's
Med alumnae. Hahnemann University's uniqueness stemmed from its

early days as a homeopathic medical school founded in 1848, before transforming in the twentieth century and gaining national prominence as an academic medical center. Homeopathy in 1848 was a popular alternative therapeutic system devised by German physician Samuel Hahnemann, based on the notion that diseases could be cured with minute doses of a medicine that would in larger doses produce symptoms of the illness in well persons: "like cures like." Such distinctive medical schools with defined missions arose in Philadelphia because it was the nation's dominant medical city, full of doctors of every background and belief. Both schools had long and ongoing records of inclusiveness, claiming diverse student bodies throughout their histories, and carrying that distinction forward in their new incarnation.[1]

Into the 1980s, Hahnemann and MCP had developed areas of excellence—some similar, others distinct—but also weaknesses. Hahnemann sustained its reputation on sound clinical training, though it maintained important research efforts as well, particularly in virology, immune responses to malaria, cytokines, and hypertension. Having left minute homeopathic doses far behind, its downtown hospital housed a stack of intensive care units and offered advanced "tertiary" care. Several star clinicians in oncology, orthopedics, cardiology, and internal medicine attracted many well-insured patients—though situated as Hahnemann was on the edge of North Philadelphia, indigent Philadelphians also filled its clinics and beds.

The Medical College of Pennsylvania remained the smallest of Philadelphia's many medical schools, located in a somewhat peculiar location (for a medical school), with the attractive East Falls neighborhood on one side of its campus, and poor areas of North Philadelphia on the other. As with Hahnemann University's medical school, no one doubted that MCP graduates received a solid education. In fact, MCP during the 1970s and 1980s gained a national reputation for curricular innovation and research in educational methods. Innovations included a medical humanities program, the use of "standardized patients" (well persons portraying patients to teach or assess clinical interviewing and physical examination), the first three-year residency program in emergency medicine, a grant-supported initiative to integrate women's health into the curriculum, several early computer-based teaching modules, and (launched in 1992), an ambitious alternative curriculum called the Program in Integrated Learning (PIL), built on self-directed and group learning of the basic sciences through the thorough exploration of case narratives. Most of these were firsts among Philadelphia medical colleges. MCP also developed well-funded productive research programs in such areas as lipid chemistry, the physiology of aging, neuroscience, infectious diseases, pediatrics, and biological psychiatry. MCP students, like those at Hahnemann University, cherished an ethos of mutual support rather than competition.

Both schools, however, suffered bruising presidential mishaps in the 1970s. Hahnemann's was the more damaging. A newly chosen president came from the world of business, indicating the increasing "corporate" mind-set entering American medicine. Wharton Shober (hired in 1972) proved, however, a disastrous exemplar of this shift. Though he advanced the institution in several ways, Shober ignored academic custom, bullied faculty, initiated a disastrous research project to learn if carbon dioxide inhalation might cure drug addiction (it did not, but led to several deaths), and—most bizarre—arranged to award an honorary degree to Anastasio Somoza, the former dictator of Nicaragua. Hahnemann's reputation also suffered in the late 1970s from allegations of high-level improprieties in obtaining government funding for a hospital expansion. The Medical College of Pennsylvania's misfortune was to import from the University of Wisconsin in 1977 a new president, Robert E. Cooke, a physician-scientist of high academic standing with putative connections in Washington. Cooke proved imperious and secretive, and after two years of strife, was ousted by a vote of censure of the faculty. Unlike the Hahnemann turmoil, the Cooke affair remained largely internal to the institution. But such fiascos impeded progress and may have inhibited fund-raising.

And both schools needed to raise funds: each faced fiscal peril in the 1980s. The Medical College of Pennsylvania had minimal endowment and a relatively small hospital that competed poorly for paying surgery patients with the major downtown centers, while it provided a great deal of care to uninsured or Medicaid-insured residents of nearby North Philadelphia. As potential major donors, very rich alumnae were few, perhaps in part because women—its graduates from 1850 until 1972—were long excluded from the most lucrative surgical specialties. In addition, the MCP class size of about 120, the smallest of the Philadelphia medical schools, limited revenue from tuition—though it was regrettably high. Hahnemann University also lacked a sizeable endowment, but in the 1970s entered classes of nearly two hundred, and its hospital *did* offer the sorts of specialty care that could generate dollars to subsidize the medical school. But many of its best-known practitioners were in private practice (though providing much teaching as volunteers), and little of their practice proceeds may have gone to supporting the medical school.

The Allegheny Corporation Jumps the Alleghenies

By the early 1980s, the Medical College of Pennsylvania, recovered from the dismal Cooke interlude and functioning well, but showing annual losses from its hospital, started to explore a merger with another hospital in the Philadelphia area that might improve the financial underpinning and add some educational resources as well. New president Walter Cohen, a prominent dental scientist with experience in academic management and philanthropy, came on board in 1986 with a primary mission of finding a strong partner. At the same time, Allegheny Health Systems, Inc. (AHSI, soon renamed the Allegheny Health Education and Research Foundation, or AHERF), parent nonprofit corporation of the successful and respected Allegheny General Hospital in Pittsburgh, was seeking a close medical school linkage. It did so to elevate its academic status, partly by bringing medical students to its floors, and also to protect its residencies. Residencies, funded largely by Medicare, are hospital-based, postdoctoral training programs that require a medical school relationship for accreditation. A strong medical school presence, the AHERF officers believed, would foster growth and standing in a city dominated by the University of Pittsburgh's medical system. The heads of AHERF and MCP readily saw mutual benefit and a "good fit" in a trans-Commonwealth alliance. Perhaps even at the outset, the CEO of AHERF, Sherif S. Abdelhak, had in mind building a major health care system that could encompass Pennsylvania's two largest cities, and even beyond. Generally referred to as Sherif, he was viewed by many as a visionary, even a genius. This assessment would in due course require revision.

A deal was agreed upon in December of 1987 and implemented in 1988.[2] It became quickly and painfully clear to MCP people that, in fact, an acquisition had occurred in the guise of a merger: senior management now reported to Sherif, and the AHERF board chairman headed the MCP board. The MCP dean for fourteen years, Alton Sutnick, a physician-scientist of high integrity and accomplishment, was deposed in favor of a senior faculty member considered perhaps more dynamic. But a welcome infusion of funds appeared, and AHERF officers improved MCP's fiscal management. Sherif ruled: he made the decisions and micromanaged, though at least not the curriculum or daily educational work. Characterized by faculty as "scary," he little tolerated opposition or dissenting opinion. His most remembered utterance was "don't cross me." No one did.[3]

Many at MCP feared that AHERF would ship the school to Pittsburgh. Such a move seemed logical. But in 1990 AHERF purchased a low-rise building on Queen Lane in the East Falls section of Philadelphia, very near the MCP campus on Henry Avenue. The structure and tree-shaded grounds had been occupied by a division of the Lutheran Church. After a complex and costly renovation, the Queen Lane campus opened in 1992, greatly expanding space available for education and basic science laboratories. The investment confirmed assurances from administration that the school was not heading west. Sherif Abdelhak wanted to firmly plant AHERF in the Philadelphia "market." Additions at the Queen Lane campus opened in 2006 and 2009.

Abdelhak pursued two main strategies to succeed in the east. One aimed to assemble a mass of hospitals in the Philadelphia area that could achieve "leverage" and thus favorable rates of reimbursement in negotiations with health insurers. The company bought the United Hospitals group in 1991; it comprised the prestigious St. Christopher's Hospital for Children and three suburban general hospitals. United had been losing money and had accumulated a large debt. In 1997 Sherif purchased the Graduate Health System which included Graduate Hospital, one of too many in Center City. It also came with a large debt: this acquisition seemed clearly unwise. The second strategy required buying numerous physicians' practices and putting the doctors on what were often very generous salaries, in order to procure referrals to the system's hospitals. Other hospital systems did the same, but the scheme never worked for any of them, and for AHERF it provided another sure way to lose money.

The Next So-Called Merger

Most relevant, however, was the addition of Hahnemann University and its hospital to the AHERF system in 1993. Hahnemann University at this time included the medical school (formerly Hahnemann Medical College), the School of Nursing, the School of Health Sciences and Humanities (formerly the School of Allied Health Professions), and the Graduate School. By the somewhat liberal Commonwealth requirements, requiring at least three distinguishable units, Hahnemann was able to secure university status in 1981. Discussions about bringing Hahnemann into the AHERF system, and merging the medical schools, occurred in 1989–1990. Neither faculty as a whole favored such a move: MCP faculty and students feared they would be further swallowed up by the much larger and aggressive Hahnemann University, and those at Hahnemann felt concern about losing *their* identity. Whether faculty opposition mattered or not, the union did not take place until 1993—as a fait accompli determined from above by the CEO. With Hahnemann's university standing, AHERF created AUHS, the Allegheny University of the Health Sciences, including the MCP Hahnemann School of Medicine. Even those averse to the newest merger could admit that it made some sense: MCP brought a more progressive, innovative education program and perhaps a higher level of research in the basic sciences; Hahnemann had the large center-city hospital.

Making one medical school out of two of different sizes, cultures, and organizational structures proved no easy task. There ensued a torrent of committees, task groups, and meetings. Generally, procedures followed the MCP ways of doing things. Hahnemann faculty were surprised and angered about this, and more so when most of the departmental chairmanships went to existing MCP chiefs. The offices of the president of AUHS and its medical school (Abdelhak) and of the dean (scientist and former MCP chair of anatomy Leonard Ross), however, would occupy the Hahnemann executive space at Fifteenth Street. Placing the top leadership downtown offended the MCP community. Distrust and hostility flourished, though as much as possible the educational work continued diligently. The new entering class size would be 225, one of the largest among American medical schools, but fewer than the sum of the prior MCP and Hahnemann numbers. Adding to the complexity of the MCP—Hahnemann merger under AHERF, in 1996 AUHS opened a School of Public Health, intended to focus on urban health problems, and to use some of the teaching techniques developed for the MCP problem-based alternative track. The School of Public Health had been proposed by Iqbal Paroo, the president of Hahnemann University before the merger. An eminent figure of international reputation, Jonathan Mann, was recruited to head the school, but after less than a year as director, he and his wife died in September of 1998 in the crash of Swissair Flight 111 in Nova Scotia, a tragic loss to public health and advocacy for human rights, and, of course, a blow to the new enterprise.

Enter a Dragon

In July of 1998, before the first entering class under AUHS jurisdiction could graduate, the parent organization, AHERF, became the most spectacular bankruptcy in the history of American health care. For while committees and chairs went about the unruly task of melding the two schools into one, AHERF continued to gather debt as its hospitals and practices hemorrhaged losses. The CEO and CFO hid much of this from view. AHERF had bought hospital systems burdened with debt, and private practices that never met expectations for referrals. Sherif Abdelhak's grandiose schemes had drifted into the realm of delusion, and the overly large AHERF board in Pittsburgh provided no oversight. The Philadelphia health care environment in the 1990s—too many hospitals, powerful insurers implementing "managed care," decreasing reimbursements by Medicaid and Medicare—was not forgiving of even small blunders. Allegheny University of the Health Sciences was also losing money, mainly through the medical school, and probably owing in large part to high salaries paid to "star" clinical faculty. The new School of Public Health also showed a deficit in its earliest years, though the schools of nursing and health sciences avoided substantial losses. At the time of its bankruptcy AHERF owed 60,000 to 70,000 creditors approximately $1.5 billion. AHERF's Philadelphia hospitals and AUHS went on sale. Tenet Healthcare, a for-profit hospital group, with headquarters in California, after a series of bids and withdrawals by other organizations, emerged as the likely purchaser.

Tenet considered the continuation of AUHS (really meaning the medical school) as essential to the value of the hospitals, and its purchase was contingent on finding an academic partner to manage it. That partner would be Drexel. Why did Tenet consider it critical that the medical school survive? The purchase agreement called for Tenet to convey $90 million in funds to support AUHS as well as $40 million in "receivables" from clinical practice plans. It is likely that senior Tenet officials believed that to compete in the crowded Philadelphia health care market, an outside, for-profit, company needed to claim academic status for its new hospitals, or at least the largest of these. In addition, a strong medical school connection would foster the attraction of top-tier clinical specialists. Finally, a medical school connection is required to maintain residencies, which are essential to an educational setting and also provide relatively low-cost clinical services.

Tenet, then, wanted a medical school connection in 1998. Why did Drexel? Or, to be more accurate: why did Drexel president Constantine Papadakis wish to bring Drexel University into the unprecedented, very untidy aftermath of a catastrophic bankruptcy, to manage, and later absorb, a mangled, orphaned school of medicine? We will return to this question later. Following the bankruptcy, whereas it was assumed that at least some of the AHERF eastern region hospitals would survive, the future of the medical school seemed less certain—many faculty fled, student applications declined, endowments had vanished, and losses continued. Nonetheless, a staunch group of faculty headed by surgeon Joel Roslyn and neuroscientist Donald Faber formed a Committee to Save the University, later renamed the Committee for the University (CFTU). Its members met with governmental officials, held open forums, focused on raising morale, and worked to help generate a restructuring plan. AUHS administration (mostly of the medical school), and secondarily, officers of the CFTU, entered into negotiations with Tenet Healthcare. As the actual date of the sale of AHERF assets approached in September of 1998, attempts were made to find an academic base, or home, for AUHS, including the medical school. Only Drexel showed sustained interest: Dorothy Brown, interim president of AUHS, met with Papadakis. City and state elected officials, fearful of the loss of thousands of jobs if the former AHERF hospitals and AUHS actually shut down, of course encouraged such conversations. These talks initially centered on the possibility of Drexel serving as manager of AUHS, which as of the time of the sale of AHERF assets (to occur on November 10, 1998) would be renamed MCP Hahnemann University (MCPHU). AUHS/MCPHU would in effect be transferred to a new non-profit corporation known as PHEC, Philadelphia Health and Education Corporation. President Papadakis went about selling this plan to his board and faculty.

It was not an easy sell, though Papadakis could be persuasive. In 1998 Drexel was itself rising out of stagnation: arriving in 1995, Papadakis confronted declining enrollment, shuttered classrooms, thin endowment, and a mediocre reputation. By 1998, he had made remarkable progress, but it seemed to some board members and many faculty an inopportune time, if not outright folly, to take on direction of a bankrupt medical university still recording deficits. Concerns arose among faculty and some administrators that the medical school would drain resources away from continued development of Drexel programs, and that managers would assume burdensome new responsibilities. There was not a lot of time to weigh the potential gains and risks, with the sale of AHERF assets to occur on October 21, and Tenet's purchase contingent on AUHS/MCPHU finding an academic manager. A hurried process of due diligence ensued, with reports looking at everything from libraries to fund-raising. On October 13, the Drexel board voted against the proposal. Pennsylvania governor Thomas Ridge and Philadelphia mayor Edward Rendell promptly began discussions with officials at other universities, and with Drexel trustees, since Drexel still seemed the most likely partner. Perhaps the trustees would reconsider. The bankruptcy judge agreed to defer the sale until November. And—perhaps most critically—the committee of AHERF creditors, seeing a Tenet purchase of the hospitals as the last hope for turning the physical assets into dollars, offered to make a contribution of $50 million to Drexel's endowment. Since a campaign was already underway to raise $125 million toward the endowment, the creditors' enticement could hardly be ignored. It was already understood that Tenet would reimburse Drexel for expenses entailed in managing the university. On October 24, the executive committee of the Drexel board attended an ad hoc workshop on medical education and the state of Philadelphia's healthcare industry. Present were several consultants including Jordan Cohen, a senior academic nephrologist and former medical school dean, and at this time president of the Association of American Medical Colleges. Governor Ridge and Mayor Rendell dropped by during a break to offer encouragement.

A special meeting of Drexel's board took place on October 26, at which the board chairman, Charles "Chuck" Pennoni, first asking the vice-chair to preside, made a presentation in favor of the proposal, ending with a quotation from founder Anthony J. Drexel: "The world will change and the Institute must change with it."[4] The board voted unanimously to enter into the arrangement with AUHS and Tenet Healthcare. The agreement called for Drexel to administer the MCPHU for a trial period of eight months, with the option for another two years. With consummation of the bankruptcy sale on November 10, and with startling coordination of a workforce, the red AHERF "A" logo vanished from all structures overnight. Relief and tempered optimism followed.

The agreement gave Drexel the right to subsequently "acquire full ownership of the University," no doubt Papadakis's intended eventual outcome.[5] At a special meeting of the board of trustees on April 25, 2002, a resolution to "assume control of PHEC as of July 1, 2002" passed unanimously, with "sustained applause." PHEC, it will be recalled, was Philadelphia Health and Education Corporation, the corporate name of MCPHU. A board vice-chair asserted, correctly or otherwise, that this was "the single most important decision that had occurred in Drexel University's history since its founding in 1891."[6] Dr. Papadakis was quoted as declaring the vote "the proudest day" of his presidency.[7] Jacqueline Mancall, a professor of information science and president of Drexel's Faculty Senate, on behalf of her colleagues expressed cautious support and acknowledged new possibilities, while also calling attention to very understandable concerns. Faculty worried about possible impacts on other Drexel programs, tenure, various disparities, and faculty governance given the large size of the medical school faculty. This next step in the Drexel-MCPHU relationship was referred to as a "merger," though MCPHU/PHEC became a subsidiary corporation of Drexel, with Papadakis president of both. The relationship included a "firewall," a degree of legal separation aimed at protecting Drexel from financial loss incurred by MCPHU, such as might result from a medical malpractice suit. Businessman and "deal maker" Manuel "Manny"

President Constantine Papadakis (center) at Drexel University College of Medicine on Queen Lane campus, 2003. Drexel University Archives. (Drexel University Archives. PC 17 University Communications photographs.)

Stamatakis as chairman of the PHEC board became a staunch friend of the medical school.

Here we return to the question of why President Papadakis wanted the medical school, and other AUHS schools, to become part of Drexel. He understood in 1998 that although the medical school might not prove profitable, health care overall was a rapidly growing industry, and particularly so in the Philadelphia area. The new relationship would allow Drexel to "tap into a growth industry" as he explained to a reporter for the *Chronicle of Higher Education*.[8] The move exemplified Drexel's entrepreneurial spirit. But more was at stake. The strategic plan for Drexel's growth in the late 1990s looked toward increased research and doctoral programs. Clearly, within Philadelphia, Drexel's leaders wanted Drexel to be seen as a peer of the University of Pennsylvania and Temple—both of which had medical schools. So did most major universities nationally. A medical school could help legitimize Drexel as a true university, not just, as commonly misperceived, a solid engineering school with a lofty name. Finally, Papadakis and board members understood the AUHS/MCPHU rescue as a service to the community, preserving historic schools, worthy educational programs, and thousands of jobs.

Drexel University College of Medicine

"It is difficult to describe the degree of disarray within MCPHU which confronted the new leadership on November 11, 1998, their first day in charge," wrote the author of a report on the early phase of the relationship, referring mainly to the medical school.[9] Financial losses had thinned the ranks of leadership and faculty, and eroded infrastructure and staffing. Endowments and grant monies were lost or difficult to trace. Several major departments lacked chairs. The dean, pathologist Barbara Atkinson, had announced her intent to leave, and former oncologist Warren Ross, a clinical management consultant previously hired, was named interim dean. Drexel teams tackled the most urgent tasks first, which included filling essential staffing needs, rebuilding badly designed and maintained information systems, and dealing with countless details of re-registration generated by the new name and corporate identity. An assessment of the clinical practices got underway to quickly improve their financial picture. A marketing plan was developed in linkage with Tenet. Longer-term planning looked toward ensuring financial stability that could foster investment and confidence that the institution had a future. As expected, the name of the medical school became simply Drexel University College of Medicine (DUCOM), though for over ten years the tagline "In the Tradition of Woman's Medical College of Pennsylvania and Hahnemann Medical College" appeared on stationery, a welcome homage to the past. In 2003, the first class graduated under the new name.

Throughout the dispiriting and frightening decline and bankruptcy of AHERF, classes continued and students and residents went about learning on the hospital floors, in operating rooms, and in office practices. In 1998 faculty psychiatrist and WMCP graduate Barbara Schindler was appointed vice-dean for educational and academic affairs. In recent decades, medical school deans mainly serve as managers of clinical functions and business operations, while an associate or vice-dean looks after curriculum and its delivery. Dr. Schindler provided steady guidance and supervision during and beyond the period of rebuilding. The distinctive elements previously mentioned were continued—the problem-based alternative track, medical humanities, standardized patients, and the clinical skills laboratory. A set of student-run free night clinics added another educational opportunity, which also provided community service. Several programs representing

WMCP/MCP's origin as the world's first medical school for women continued and grew. The Institute for Women's Health and Leadership facilitated advances in women's health and well-being through research and education. The nationally recognized Executive Leadership in Academic Medicine (ELAM) program helped women in academic medicine navigate their careers. Honoring both predecessor schools, the Archives and Special Collections on Women in Medicine and Homeopathic Medicine (renamed the Legacy Center) expanded its collections and services in new quarters at the Queen Lane campus. It remains an internationally recognized research center.

Of course, setbacks occurred for the reborn medical school. On December 18, 2003, Tenet announced that it would close MCP Hospital (MCPH).[10] Though smaller than Hahnemann University Hospital, MCPH at the historic campus on Henry Avenue in East Falls served as a major teaching site for MCPHU medical students and residents and was home to many clinical faculty. It had been losing money, and at this time Tenet itself was in some trouble for overbilling Medicare and faced large reductions in its revenue. It was seeking to sell or close poorly performing hospitals. The losses at MCPH were attributed largely to a "poor payer mix" (i.e., many poor patients on Medicaid). Many MCP-based faculty believed that the hospital was doomed by a recent strategy to gather potentially money-generating surgical specialty practices at Hahnemann Hospital, downtown. In the perverse medical system of the United States, caring for routinely sick poor people, not in need of hip replacements or cardiac transplantation, assures financial worries. Neighborhood activists, government officials, and a group of loyal MCP physicians and later a determined MCP alumna toiled valiantly to keep the hospital open, and won several reprieves. In June of 2004, regardless of neighborhood needs, MCPH finally closed, by then a pathetic remnant of what it had been. At one point, Drexel, fearing a grave loss of teaching resources (for a very large class size of about 225), had considered buying it, but chose not to do so.

DUCOM has established affiliations for medical student and residency education with over twenty hospitals, some as "regional medical campuses." To compensate for the loss of MCP Hospital in 2004, a fruitful connection was established with Abington Memorial Hospital, but its merger in 2015 with Jefferson University perhaps adds complexity to that affiliation. Historic Friends Hospital became a valued academic site for psychiatry in 2004. St. Christopher's Hospital for Children, owned by Tenet, is DUCOM's primary locus for pediatrics—though its additional affiliation with Temple University School of Medicine in 2007 was unsettling. Indeed, DUCOM neither owns nor controls a hospital. This circumstance is not unique among American medical schools, but entails uncertainty. Tenet Healthcare has proved over the years not always the perfect partner when its objectives (profit) and those of DUCOM (education, patient care, and research) diverged. DUCOM students go to other affiliated teaching hospitals in Reading, York, and Easton—and still to Allegheny General Hospital in Pittsburgh. Also on the roster are Monmouth Medical Center and the Kaiser Permanente health system in California. Virtually all American medical schools work with more than one hospital, and although DUCOM medical students enjoy many choices, perhaps they spread out more than is healthy for maintaining a sense of unity and allegiance. On the other hand, fourth-year students at all American medical schools travel itinerantly to clinical "rotations" at hospitals often far from home base to preview residencies.

In 2005, following months of self-study, DUCOM welcomed to its campuses an inspection team from the Liaison Committee for Medical Education (LCME), the primary accrediting agency in the United States and Canada. Despite the years of turbulence, the LCME final report of October 2005 offered far more praise than demerits. Areas of strength included "an exceptional concentration of committed, student-centered educators" and a "vibrant culture of educational excellence." A "growth in research" and "exciting culture of scholarship" had been noted.[11] As the only serious deficiency, the LCME team identified an above average level of student indebtedness and inadequate availability of financial support. Oddly, the loss of MCPH was not mentioned. In 2011, Chair of Pediatrics Daniel Schidlow was appointed interim dean, succeeding Richard Homan, an academic family practitioner. Schidlow became dean and senior vice-president for medical affairs in 2012. It was hoped that his experience as chief at Tenet-owned St. Christopher's Hospital for Children might promote more salubrious interactions with Tenet administration. Schidlow's humor and love of music bring a lighter touch to the office; and he has made it a point to spend more time than his predecessors at the Queen Lane Campus, often informally lunching with students when not dealing with weighty matters downtown.

The next survey of the College of Medicine by LCME occurred in 2013. Again, much was praised, but two cited areas of "non-compliance with standards" raised concern. The traditional curriculum track ("IFM" or "Interdisciplinary Foundations of Medicine") for the first two years, which most students followed, deployed too many lectures and did not foster "active learning."[12] This critique reflected recent trends in American medical education.

Two notable events marked the year 2014: the "firewall" came down, an action making the College of Medicine a school within Drexel like any other; and late in the year, work began on a new curriculum, in part to address the LCME findings. There will be one curriculum for the first two years for all students, to be called "Foundations and Frontiers." It will place dominant emphasis on self-directed and small-group learning. Hot subjects in medicine in 2016, such as medical informatics, patient safety, translational research, and population health, will gain more visibility. Clinical years three and four will undergo some adjustments. Already in place is a new arrangement by which each class is divided into four "learning communities" or "societies," their names borrowed from a sundry selection of Philadelphia landmarks—Liberty Bell, Athenaeum, Rocky Statue, and Physick House.

And so, now a full member of the university, the College of Medicine intends to justify its welcome by energetically bringing its teaching programs into the future, in a spirit of innovation worthy of Drexel, but also recalling the two predecessor schools and their bold efforts to spread new ideas in the agitated America of the mid-nineteenth century. As times changed, these schools each had to either discard a nascent mission (Hahnemann Medical College—no more homeopathy), or modify it (Woman's Med— admitting men). Perhaps owing to these needed evolutions their place in the medical world of Philadelphia became unclear, and their internal strength thereby lessened. Neither could survive the harsh financial stresses of late-twentieth-century medical economics in a city crowded with hospitals and medical colleges. That their first hoped-for savior, AHERF, would prove more devil than redeemer, could not have been predicted. Fortuitously, the combined MCP Hahnemann School of Medicine came up for grabs exactly when a strong and capable leader, Constantine Papadakis, appointed to make big things happen, saw an unexpected opportunity, though a dicey one, to help make Drexel University a university.

NOTES

Joanne Murray, director of the Drexel University College of Medicine Legacy Center, was a valued collaborator in preparing this chapter. The author wishes to also acknowledge the generous help of Anita Lai at the Drexel University Archives, and Margaret Graham and Matthew Herbsion at the Legacy Center of Drexel University College of Medicine. Valuable information was provided through conversations with former Drexel University senior counsel Carl "Tobey" Oxholm and former DUCOM faculty member and dean for assessment Burton Landau.

1. The best accounts of the two predecessor schools are Naomi Rogers, *An Alternative Path: The Making and Remaking of Hahnemann Medical College and Hospital of Philadelphia* (New Brunswick, NJ: Rutgers University Press, 1998); and Steven J. Peitzman, *A New and Untried Course: Woman's Medical College and Medical College of Pennsylvania, 1850–1998* (New Brunswick, NJ: Rutgers University Press, 2000).

2. The fullest account of the AHERF mergers, acquisitions, and collapse in the Philadelphia region is Judith P. Swazey, *Merger Games: The Medical College of Pennsylvania, Hahnemann University, and the Rise and Fall of the Allegheny Health Care System* (Philadelphia: Temple University Press, 2012). For a business-oriented analysis, see Lawton R. Burns et al., "The Fall of the House of AHERF: The Allegheny Bankruptcy," *Health Affairs* 19 (2000): 7–41.

3. For Abdelhak's attributes, see Swazey, *Merger Games*, 74–97. "Don't cross me" was uttered in response to a question at a faculty meeting on November 17, 1993.

4. Drexel University Board of Trustees, Minutes of Special Meeting, October 26, 1998, Drexel University Archives.

5. Details of the agreement are stated in "Summary of Relationship Among Drexel University, Tenet Health System, and Corporation Acquiring Operations of Allegheny University of the Health Sciences," Drexel-MCP Hahnemann University Merger Collection, Drexel University Archives.

6. Drexel University Board of Trustees, Minutes of Special Meeting, April 25, 2002, Drexel University Archives. See also Katherine S. Mangan, "Drexel Takes Over Medical School," *Chronicle of Higher Education*, May 24, 2002.

7. Mangan, "Drexel Takes Over Medical School."

8. Katherine S. Mangan, "A University Tries to Revive an Ailing Medical School," *Chronicle of Higher Education*, October 22, 1999.

9. "The First Seventeen Months of Operation of MCP Hahnemann University by Drexel University November 1998—April 2000," Drexel University College of Medicine Legacy Center (archives), "AHERF" folder, vertical file.

10. For the closing of MCP Hospital see articles by Karl Stark originally in the *Philadelphia Inquirer*, available at articles.philly.com: "Tenet to Close MCP Hospital Phila. Will Lose Longtime Facility and 1000 Jobs," December 18, 2003; "Drexel Looking at MCP Purchase. The University Medical College [*sic*] Hired Consultants to Study a Possible Takeover, Becoming the Third Potential Bidder," February 24, 2004. These are but a few of many articles by *Philadelphia Inquirer* writers including Stark, Andrea Gerlin, and Josh Goldstein covering the demise of the hospital.

11. Frank A. Simon report to Constantine Papadakis, October 15, 2005, summarizing findings of Liaison Committee on Medical Education survey and awarding accreditation for an eight-year term.

12. Barbara Barzansky and Dan Hunt report to John A. Fry, June 14, 2013, summarizing findings of Liaison Committee on Medical Education survey and awarding accreditation for an eight-year term.

I would never accept the job of a president in a situation where I would be a ceremonial figure, I like to roll my sleeves and work with my colleagues in the trenches, and I thought that Drexel was perfect . . . The academic fabric of the institution was intact [but] . . . the management was not doing so well.

I was thinking of how to bring the university to the level that it deserves—you have to remember that back in the '50s and early '60s Drexel was competing with MIT, and so it's not that we took the university to a new height, we took the university to a height where it had been before.

I like to study the history . . . of the institutions I led—I felt it was so important to understand where Drexel came from in depth. So I knew that the Drexel quality of education was preeminent in the United States after the Second World War, and also I knew Drexel had reached a height of about 8,500 full-time undergraduate students in the mid-'80s. And then over a ten-year period, and the two unfortunate presidencies, it lost half of its students—half. Half of its students to 4,500 full-time undergraduate students. Now we are back to 9,000 and we are still not full . . . in the next two, three years we will increase another 30 percent our full-time undergraduate enrollment, and we will increase our quality also at the same time. . . . I will never stop.

—Constantine Papadakis, 2003

20

Nursing and Health Professions

Two Schools Become One at Drexel

GLORIA DONNELLY, STEPHEN F. GAMBESCIA,
AND LAURA VALENTI

T HE HISTORY of the Drexel University College of Nursing and
Health Professions (CNHP) is a convoluted tale of change,
upheaval, and resilience that includes the upgrading of nursing
education, the emergence of health professions careers, the bankruptcy of
Allegheny University of the Health Sciences, the reemergence of MCP
Hahnemann University after bankruptcy, and finally, the merger of CNHP
into Drexel University. Since joining Drexel in 2002, CNHP has embraced
Drexel's high-tech, experiential, cooperative educational approach, while
maintaining a focus on producing competent and compassionate health professionals. From 2002 to 2016, CNHP grew from 1,250 to 4,900 students,
who now account for more than half of Drexel's online enrollment and
20 percent of its graduate enrollment. CNHP is known for its use of
cutting-edge educational technologies, interdisciplinary approaches, clinical
excellence, and the application of Drexel's cooperative education model,
particularly to its undergraduate nursing program (one of only two
cooperative education nursing programs in the United States) and its
bachelor's in health sciences (which may be the only cooperative education
program of its kind).

CNHP is also the home of the Stephen and Sandra Sheller Eleventh
Street Family Health Services Center, in North Philadelphia, serving 6,200
residents of public housing with primary care, behavioral health, physical

therapy, nutrition, and a wide range of integrative health services. Sheller Eleventh Street is one of four CNHP practices; the other three are in Center City and on Drexel's University City campus. CNHP aspires to best practices through its innovative education and research, and its high level of community engagement through patient-centered practices and real-world applications and outcomes.

Roots of the Nursing Education Programs

CNHP traces its roots back to both the Hahnemann Hospital Training School for Nurses, founded in 1890, and the nurse training program of the Hospital of the Woman's Medical College of Pennsylvania (later the Medical College of Pennsylvania, or MCP), founded in 1904. The nurse training program of Woman's Medical College was phased out in 1978. The Hahnemann Hospital nurse training program evolved to offer associate's and bachelor's degrees as part of the Hahnemann University School of Health Sciences and Humanities (SHSH). SHSH's Department of Nursing coexisted with Hahnemann's medical college and graduate school, later becoming part of the MCP Hahnemann University (MCPHU) after MCP and Hahnemann's merger in 1993.

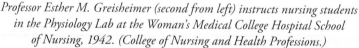

Professor Esther M. Greisheimer (second from left) instructs nursing students in the Physiology Lab at the Woman's Medical College Hospital School of Nursing, 1942. (College of Nursing and Health Professions.)

Roots of the CNHP's Educational Programs

The roots of the College of Nursing and Health Profession's current health professions programs lie primarily with Hahnemann University's medical school, the dean of which in 1967 appointed a committee to discuss the development of educational programs for the allied health professions. As a result, in 1968, a separate school focusing on allied health was created to accommodate the growing number of individuals entering emerging health services fields. The three initial degree programs in this new school were medical technology, radiologic technology, and mental health technology. Other health professions programs developed in departments in the medical school and were eventually moved to other schools within the Hahnemann University organization. Between 1965 and the mid-1990s there were many organizational restructurings and name changes for the emerging MCPHU schools and colleges.

Health professions programs proliferated at Hahnemann. In 1967, the first graduate art therapy education program in the world was added to the university's health professions offerings, and by 1974 there were concentrations in art therapy, dance/movement therapy and music therapy. In 1971, Dr. Wilbur Oaks, a Hahnemann alumnus and physician in the medical school, developed the first physician assistant program in Pennsylvania. In 1976, a master's in family therapy was established and embraced a mission and educational philosophy that included social justice and sensitivity to cultural diversity as fundamentals for educating and training couple and family therapists. The program's name changed to couple and family therapy and a Ph.D. program was added in 1998. Dr. Ivan I. Boszormenyi-Nagy, internationally known for his theories and approach to family therapy, was influential in the development of the couple and family therapy programs.

The 1980s were a decade of numerous name and functional changes to the health professions school, even though it was relatively new. Should the organizational entity be called a "college" or "school," and what programs should move to this college from the medical school? While university officials deliberated on names, structures, and the best grouping of programs, the health professions programs at MCPHU grew in enrollment and in the number of programs offered. As the school developed additional bachelor's degrees, it increased the number of faculty in the general studies program, particularly for courses in English, literature, history, sociology, medical ethics, and mathematics. By 1988, the school offered a bachelor's degree in biomedical science, providing an alternative to health professions students interested in a nonclinical track; and in 2006 it added what became a popular bachelor's degree program, in health services administration.

Training in physical therapy was introduced as a certificate program at Hahnemann in 1979 and developed into a master's level program in 1984 that was housed in a Department of Rehabilitation Sciences. In 1988 a Ph.D. program in rehabilitation sciences was established and its faculty continues to include internationally recognized researchers in pediatric rehabilitation, rehabilitation for women, and movement science. In keeping with national credentialing trends in physical therapy, the master's program transitioned to a doctor of physical therapy degree in fall 2000. The Department of Rehabilitation Sciences now offers a variety of postgraduate certificates in specialty physical therapy areas, such as hand therapy.

By 1986, MCPHU offered programs in medical technology, mental health technology, nursing, physical therapy, physician assistance, and radiologic technology, and graduated 340 health professions students that year. Programs in clinical laboratory science, medical laboratory technology, and respiratory therapy were discontinued by the 1990s. Since its merger into Drexel, CNHP has continued the practice of constantly evaluating the relevance of its programs to the needs of the health care system.

Bankruptcy, Merger, and Acquisition

In 1995, after the merger of MCP and Hahnemann by the Allegheny Health, Education and Research Foundation (AHERF), the Department of Nursing in Hahnemann's School of Health Sciences and Humanities was reorganized into the new School of Nursing, into which the nurse anesthesia program, originally based at the MCP Hospital, was also absorbed. By 1996, MCP and Hahnemann were renamed the Allegheny University of the Health Sciences (AUHS), which included four schools: medicine, nursing, health professions, and public health. In that same year, Gloria F. Donnelly, the founder and former dean of the School of Nursing at La Salle University, was appointed the first dean of AUHS's School of Nursing.

AHERF, including AUHS, declared bankruptcy in July 1998. By the end of the year Tenet Healthcare, a national for-profit health care company with more than 130 hospitals, purchased AHERF's eight hospitals, and later sold off or closed all but Hahnemann University Hospital and St. Christopher's Hospital for Children. AUHS (which was renamed MCP Hahnemann, or MCPHU) and the remaining hospitals emerged from bankruptcy by the end of the year. After much encouragement from government officials and Tenet, Drexel's board of trustees, with the encouragement of

President Constantine Papadakis, voted to have their university manage the MCPHU educational enterprise with an eye to a full merger.

In 2000, Drexel's senior management decided to merge the MCPHU schools of nursing and health professions into one organizational unit, the College of Nursing and Health Professions, with Donnelly serving as the first dean. In 2002, the merger transition team of Drexel University recommended that CNHP and the School of Public Health be fully merged into Drexel, becoming two of the university's eleven colleges and schools. The medical school, renamed Drexel University College of Medicine (DUCOM), remained a separate nonprofit corporation, though wholly owned by the university and finally merged into Drexel University proper in 2014.

During the post-bankruptcy transition period a series of organizational questions had to be answered. Should the physician assistant program be returned to the medical school? Should CNHP's psychology department merge with the existing Drexel psychology department, located in the College of Arts and Sciences (COAS)? Was the CNHP bachelor's in biomedical sciences duplicative of the premedical program in the COAS biology department? Should all health-related science courses and their associated faculty move from CNHP to COAS? Through a process of consensus-building among the CNHP health professions faculty and in light of their strong recommendation, the physician assistant program and, with only a few exceptions, all health-related science courses remained in CNHP. Eventually, CNHP's psychology faculty and programs merged into the COAS psychology department, and the CNHP chemistry faculty and courses moved into the COAS chemistry department. The CNHP biomedical sciences curriculum was revised to become a bachelor's in health sciences to avoid duplication with COAS programs and to provide a health-related undergraduate major for two groups of students: Those pursuing graduate clinical majors such as physician assistant or physical therapy, and those interested in nonclinical health careers.

In 2009, the nutrition science faculty and curriculum moved from the COAS biology department to CNHP's newly established Department of Nutrition Sciences, which now has bachelor's, master's, and doctoral programs, and coordinates the Eat Right Now Program, a federally funded project that provides healthy eating education to public school children in Philadelphia.

Since becoming part of Drexel, CNHP has phased out programs in medical technology and clinical science, emergency medical services, cardiovascular perfusion, and, most recently, radiologic technology (the only remaining associate's degree program). All faculty lines and budgets from these phase-outs were reallocated to support growth in existing or new CNHP programs. Finally, over a five-year period from 2002 to 2007, all CNHP curricula were changed from a semester to a quarter format to align with Drexel's calendar and cooperative system.

Embracing Drexel University's Innovative Educational Models

Drexel University now produces more bachelor's of nursing graduates than any other private American university, and CNHP's undergraduate cooperative nursing program is one of only two in the country. The nursing co-op program integrates work and learning through three six-month periods of fulltime employment during the five-year program, or one six-month work period during the four-year program. Health care employers in the Philadelphia region have responded favorably to the nursing co-op program, provided interesting co-op positions, and hiring Drexel nursing graduates.

In response to the national nursing shortage, CNHP became one of the country's leaders in accelerated nursing programs through its eleven-month program for career changers possessing a bachelor's degree in another field. The Accelerated Career Entry (ACE) nursing program admitted its first class in fall of 2001, and in response to enrollment demand added a spring cohort. Responding to continuing demand (and a continuing nursing shortage), a new part-time, twenty-four-month accelerated program was established in fall 2014 as a hybrid, with 50 percent of the instruction done online.

Estimates of future demand for health care professionals often neglect the growing need for health services administrators. CNHP has responded to this need by offering students four delivery options to earn the bachelor's in health services administration, the first of which was a part-time degree completion program for transfer students. An online option was later added. In 2004 a "Saturday Scholars" degree completion option was established, offering all-day Saturday classes for working students. The Saturday Scholars format has also been successfully used in the undergraduate program in behavioral health counseling. A traditional undergraduate program format, including the co-op, is also offered for both health services administration and behavioral health counseling.

Technology-Infused Education: Simulation

Since 2006 CNHP has developed and equipped an extensive "simulation learning lab"—4,600 square feet of space that can be configured into any type of clinical environment (for instance, an emergency room, patient room, labor and delivery room, and an environment to simulate home care). In addition, a simulated health assessment and primary care lab was designed with ten examination and/or counseling rooms, dual camera digital technology, classroom space with split screen plasma viewing screens, a faculty observation room, a standardized patient lounge, comprehensive simulation evaluation software, and archiving capabilities. Simulation experiences, now integrated into the majority of CNHP's nursing and health professions curricula, provide the opportunity for students and health professionals to experience complex clinical situations in a controlled environment without putting patients at risk. An interprofessional simulation program was established in 2011, in which students from both CNHP and medical students learn together through complex simulation scenarios jointly developed by CNHP and DUCOM faculty.

Through its continuing education division and its simulation certificate program, CNHP faculty and staff teach faculty from other schools how to integrate simulation into curricula. This certificate program has attracted nurse educators from not only the United States, but also Spain, South Africa, Guam, Canada, and the Middle East. Every year teams of Drexel nursing faculty visit South Africa and Baru Sahib, India, to share best practices in simulation and curriculum development with nursing faculty and students.

CNHP Practices

Since 1996, the CNHP has operated a nurse-led health center in North Philadelphia, situated among four public housing developments, with an interdisciplinary practice including nurse practitioners, nutritionists, physical therapists, dentists, and mental health specialists. Patricia Gerrity is the center's founder and director. Greatly expanded in 2002 through a $3.3 million federal grant for a new building, the Community Advisory Board named this much-needed health resource the Eleventh Street Family Health Services Center. In addition to providing access to what were once considered medically underserved individuals and families, Eleventh Street also provides faculty and students with cutting edge experiences in community health and in primary care practice, and is an integral part of CNHP's mission to teach students how to deliver culturally competent care, and to address health disparities.

Through a partnership with the Family Practice and Counseling Network of Resources for Human Development, Eleventh Street was accorded federally qualified health center status so that all primary, behavioral health and dental care would be reimbursed. Between 2002, when the first health center was built, and 2012, the patient base expanded to 6,200, with more than 30,000 visits each year. Sandra Sheller, an art therapy ('04) and family therapy ('05) alumna of the college, and her husband, Stephen Sheller, a Drexel University trustee and prominent Philadelphia attorney, took great interest in the work of Eleventh Street and decided to commit their personal resources to double the center's clinical space. Through a generous gift from the Sheller Family Foundation, a 17,000-square-foot, two-story expansion to serve our patients and increase space for Drexel students was added to the existing building. Renamed in 2015, The Stephen and Sandra Sheller Eleventh Street Family Health Services of Drexel University now includes unique spaces in which dance therapy, art therapy and music therapy are conducted; double the number of primary care examination rooms; additional classrooms and seminar rooms, a renovated and expanded fitness center and spaces in which to conduct sessions in the integrative therapies, such as mindfulness meditation and yoga.

Community risk assessment, health promotion and disease prevention outreach, a home visiting program, ongoing programs in fitness and nutrition, and the integration of behavioral health into primary care, are examples of the health center's comprehensive approach to working with the community on changing the life course of public housing residents and other clients. In the 2014–2015 academic year, Sheller Eleventh Street reported 32,000 patient visits in primary care, dental, and behavioral health care, and has received more than $50 million in external funding over the past fifteen years. The center was recently named by the Robert Wood Johnson Foundation as one of only thirty "Learning from Effective Ambulatory Practices" (LEAP) in the United Sates.

In addition to Sheller Eleventh Street, CNHP also operates Parkway Health and Wellness in Center City. The facility was opened in 2013 to provide interprofessional physical and behavioral health services, create new experiential education opportunities for Drexel students, and support translational research. Parkway Health and Wellness provides services and research in physical therapy and rehabilitation science, nutrition science, couple and family therapy, and the creative arts therapies (art, dance/movement and music). Parkway Health and Wellness is the home to both the Running Performance and Research Center, which performs running assessments and metabolic testing—and which was recognized in 2015 by *Philadelphia Magazine* as the "best place to fix your running form"[1]—and

Creative Art Therapy students at Hahnemann analyze clients' work, 1979.
(College of Nursing and Health Professions.)

Mother Baby Connections, which identifies and works with mothers at risk for postpartum depression and their infants.

CNHP physical therapists and nutrition counselors also offer services at practice sites at the Drexel Recreation Center on the University City campus. And finally, CNHP's Center for Family Intervention Science, also located in University City, serves as an intervention and research center for families and troubled adolescents. Dr. Guy Diamond, director of the Center for Family Intervention Science and the Couple and Family Therapy Ph.D. Program, is a noted researcher in youth suicide prevention who developed an evidence-based attachment therapy program for adolescents that is taught and used worldwide.

Leadership in Online Learning

Drexel's technologically oriented mission is reflected in CNHP's online educational initiatives. In 1999, shortly after Drexel began its management of MCPHU and in its efforts to successfully emerge out of bankruptcy, the School of Nursing offered its first hybrid course, with online content and monthly face-to-face meetings. As the demand for fully online courses increased, CNHP nursing faculty began to design and offer fully online degree programs in 2000. Since then, online degree and certificate programs have grown exponentially and now include full degree programs in undergraduate and graduate nursing, health services administration, hand therapy, post-graduate physician assistance, and numerous certificate programs. As of 2016, forty-five CNHP degree and certificate programs are offered online and the enrollment in these programs comprises more than 50 percent of Drexel's online enrollment.

Research Initiatives: Ph.D. Programs and Research Infrastructure

CNHP's strategic plan for the period 2012–2017[2] outlined strategic initiatives designed to establish research centers; align tenure and tenure-track appointments with research themes and cross school collaborations; establish external research partnerships; improve the research infrastructure to facilitate the development of proposals and develop a mentorship program for junior faculty interested in furthering programs of research. In 2015, for example, CNHP faculty submitted fifty-three research proposals, had fifty-two active research projects and total funded projects estimated at $11 million.[3] The college now includes twelve full professors and has increased the number of tenured faculty to twenty-eight since merging into Drexel. The research enterprise of the college will continue to grow in alignment with its Ph.D. programs in rehabilitation sciences, couple and family therapy, creative arts therapies, nursing, and nutrition sciences.

Conclusion

Through fiscal crises, name changes, reorganizations, and mergers, CNHP has evolved from a conglomeration of hospital- and medical school–based programs, to a strong and autonomous college within Drexel. CNHP's approach in educating health professionals for careers in clinical fields draws on a rich legacy of health care educational institutions combined with the unique features of a Drexel education. Since its merger into Drexel, the college has developed unique clinical programs and cutting edge clinical practices in sync with new trends in health care. Practice initiatives have expanded since the development of the Eleventh Street Health Center to include three additional practice sites. CNHP graduates are recognized for their competence, compassion and work ethic. Faculty and students work and learn in a variety of environments that emphasize evidence-informed

A College of Nursing and Health Professions education in 2015 goes beyond the classroom—relying not only on technology and simulation experiences, but including real-life experiences. The college's interprofessional and collaborative research is dedicated to the service, practice, and education of its students and the community that it serves through its own health and wellness centers. (College of Nursing and Health Professions.)

practice, interprofessional education and research, service to communities, and technology-infused education. There are many new initiatives on the drawing board as CNHP moves into the next decade, when health demographics and developing shortages of nurses, physician assistants, nurse anesthetists, physical therapists and mental health specialists will create new opportunities and increased demand for the graduates of the college.

NOTES

The writers of this chapter acknowledge the contributions of Drs. Willard Green, Michael Kennedy, David Flood, and the department chairs of the College of Nursing and Health Professions.

1. "Best Place to Fix Your Running Form," *Philadelphia Magazine*, available at http://www.phillymag.com/best-of-philly/awards/place-to-fix-your-running-form.
2. College of Nursing and Health Professions, *Strategic Plan 2012–17*, CNHP, 2012.
3. College of Nursing and Health Professions, *Dean's Annual Report 2014–15*, 66.

21

Drexel's Newest Schools

Biomedical Engineering, Science and Health Systems;
Education; Public Health; Law; Entrepreneurship;
and Hospitality and Sports Management

DONNA MARIE DE CAROLIS, MARLA GOLD,
AND LARRY KEISER

D URING THE LAST DECADE of the twentieth century and the
first two decades of the twenty-first, Drexel under both presidents
Constantine Papadakis and John Fry created a host of new academic programs, as reflected in the establishment of several new schools. The
first such school emerged out of the university's longstanding Biomedical
Engineering and Science Institute (BESI), established in 1961 as the first
of its kind in the United States. BESI was expanded to create the freestanding School of Biomedical Engineering, Science and Health Systems
(BIOMED), established in 1997 to take advantage of what President Papadakis saw as a unique niche that Drexel might occupy in the use of technology in healthcare and medicine.

Papadakis's vision of an emerging role for Drexel in medical and healthcare education was reflected in both the establishment of BIOMED and in
the university's takeover of the Allegheny University of the Health Sciences
(AUHS), starting in 1998. What is today the university's Dornsife School
of Public Health was established as a new unit of AUHS in 1996 and significantly enhanced when it, along with the rest of what had been AUHS,
was fully absorbed into Drexel in 2002 (the other schools, the College of
Nursing and Health Professions and the College of Medicine, are discussed
in Chapters 19 and 20). In that same year, a freestanding School of Education (previously a unit within the College of Arts and Sciences) was also

established, and in 2005 Drexel's School of Law welcomed its first students.

The law school was the last new school established under President Papadakis. Under President Fry, the university has established a new and innovative school of entrepreneurship, and Goodwin College (previously the "evening school"—one of the oldest units of the university) has been reorganized so that some of its programs now form the Center for Hospitality and Sports Management, which, as it reports directly to the provost, is the equivalent of a school or college.

This chapter covers primarily BIOMED, the schools of public health, education, entrepreneurship, and the Center for Hospitality and Sports Management, with briefer mention of the law school, more in-depth coverage of which is provided in Chapter 22.

Biomedical Engineering, Science and Health Systems

BESI was founded in 1961 by Hun H. Sun, an electrical engineering professor and pioneer in the use of engineering principles to design medical devices,[1] who joined Drexel in 1953 in the department of electrical engineering. Sun received his Ph.D. at Cornell University and his bachelor's degree from Shanghai Jiao Tong University (SJTU) in 1946, where he was a classmate of future Chinese president Jiang Zemin, whose son, Jiang Mianheng, would later get his Ph.D. in electrical engineering from Drexel. After Sun, Dov Jaron, an expert in the development of models to study cardiovascular dynamics and the interaction of mechanical cardiac assist devices with the cardiovascular system, was BESI director from 1980 to 1996.

When Papadakis created BIOMED in 1997, he appointed Banu Onaral, a faculty member in the Department of Electrical and Computer Engineering, as the founding director.[2] Onaral started at Drexel in 1981, and she specializes in information engineering with special emphasis on complex systems and biomedical signal processing in ultrasound and optics.

Onaral described the founding of the new school, capturing the interdisciplinary spirit of the enterprise:

In 1997 after strategic planning we turned it [the Institute] into a school which is not only a research institute but also is a department . . . it is basically a bridging, linking, leveraging, an orchestration . . . The thing that I think was very exciting . . . we

John M. Reid Professor of Chemical Engineering Margaret Wheatley (left)
works alongside doctoral candidate Lauren Jablonowski on tests of drug-delivery
tools in Wheatley's Microencapsulation Laboratory in the School of Biomedical
Engineering Science and Health Systems. (Office of University Communications.
Photo by Olsoncorp.)

went into areas that are now defined as truly cutting edge, we went
on our strengths which were in biosensing, bioimaging, bioinfor-
mation engineering, we built on those and we . . . bifurcated into
areas such as biomedical optics, bionanotechnology . . . Drexel took
leadership with our colleagues at Penn and other places in founding a regional nanotechnology institute. . . . These are not just research pursuits . . . we are very solutions driven . . . we are set on
the applied aspects, especially for health care and more recently for
home health care.[3]

In a reflection of BIOMED's solutions-driven approach, the school signed a
cooperation agreement in 2009 with the Med-X Research Institute of SJTU
to promote the advancement of learning through exchange and cooperation
in teaching and research. In 2011, Drexel partnered with the Wallace H.
Coulter Foundation to create a $20 million endowment for the Coulter
Translational Research Partnership program, which aims to accelerate biomedical discoveries, most notably a handheld brain scanning device used
by the military to assess injuries in the field.[4] At Drexel to date, "more than

40 projects—devices, diagnostics and drugs—have received money totaling about $5.54 million. . . . Of those, a dozen have been licensed, meaning management teams are raising venture capital for additional pivotal FDA studies."[5] Major labs and research groups within BIOMED today include: bioinformatics and computational bioengineering; biomaterials and tissue engineering; biomechanics, cardiovascular engineering; drug delivery; and neuroengineering.

Creating a School of Public Health

In 1993, the Allegheny Health Education and Research Foundation (AHERF) purchased multiple teaching institutions and hospitals in the Philadelphia area. In particular, AHERF acquired and merged the Medical College of Pennsylvania and Hahnemann University to form AUHS. In 1994, the AHERF board of trustees approved the plan to establish a new school of public health as part of AUHS, with the rationale being that it would foster the organization's mission of health promotion and wellness.

AUHS's School of Public Health (SPH)—the first such school in the history of Philadelphia—opened in the fall of 1996 with an inaugural class of twenty-eight students. The school had created an innovative, problem-based learning curriculum that focused on improving the health of people especially in the Philadelphia region through education, research and practice. Student master's theses, for example, were always linked to the health of surrounding communities. As founding dean William Welton put it, "Our students won't sit in a classroom learning about biostatistics and epidemiology, which are the traditional areas of public health. . . . They will get out and work with people from public housing, community agencies and neighborhood organizations in order to get a realistic picture of public health."[6] Philadelphia health commissioner Estelle Richman echoed Welton's enthusiasm for the program's orientation. "Philadelphia has never had a School of Public Health, and there has definitely been a void," Richman told the *Philadelphia Inquirer*. "The Allegheny program's approach is unique because it is very hands-on, unlike other schools of public health. Their students will concentrate on the people of Philadelphia, not only on diseases."[7]

In 1997 SPH, which at that point had sixteen faculty and fewer than fifty students, successfully recruited Jonathan M. Mann from Harvard—a world famous AIDS expert who had served as the director of the World Health Organization's AIDS program—to become the second dean. As dean, Mann planned to focus on "the city's public-health problems—drug abuse, teen pregnancy, AIDS, heart disease, preventable cancers and other

*School of Public Health students reflect on a study of collaboration between the
Philadelphia Department of Public Health and the School to improve population
health and train students, 2003. (Dornsife School of Public Health.)*

ills—the focus of the school's mission."[8] Tragically, Mann and his wife died
in the crash of Swissair Flight 111 in Nova Scotia in 1998, a serious loss to
public health and advocacy for human rights, and, of course, a blow to SPH.

In 1998, following AHERF's bankruptcy, the California-based Tenet
Healthcare Corporation acquired AUHS's facilities as part of a larger acquisition of Philadelphia-area hospitals, clinics, and other former AHERF
properties. AUHS's assets were then transferred to a new nonprofit entity
doing business as MCP Hahnemann University (MCPHU). In October
of that same year "a packed meeting of faculty and students" were told
by Allegheny administrators that "Tenet was planning to phase out the
school." According to a newspaper account of the meeting, the school was
"vulnerable because it is ringing up a $3.6 million deficit this year." Ad-
ministrators offered a positive note, however, that "other universities are
interested in us."[9]

They were right. At Tenet's invitation, Drexel University agreed to assume operation of MCPHU. Drexel managed the health sciences campus
for several years and its board of trustees performed due diligence to assure
that a formal merger of all academic units into one university would be fis-
cally sound. Looking back over the acquisition a few years later, President
Papadakis recalled that the "School of Public Health was losing a couple

million dollars a year when we took it over. . . . My first reaction was, close it down."[10] By 2001 SPH had one hundred students in its master's of public health (M.P.H.) and combined M.D./M.P.H. programs, and was no longer running a deficit. In 2002 Drexel's board of trustees voted unanimously in favor of merging MCPHU into their university.

Under Drexel, SPH got a new dean, Marla Gold, who was previously division chief of HIV/AIDS medicine at MCPHU, and prior to that, an assistant health commissioner for infectious disease control at the Philadelphia Department of Public Health.[11] Drexel committed significant funding for additional public health faculty and provided significant computer and information systems upgrades. Another benefit of the merger was the addition of colleges and schools within the university that provided new opportunities for collaboration in teaching and research. Drexel's particular strengths in engineering, technology, and business, afforded SPH access to an array of talented faculty and resources.

Given Drexel's stability, financial commitments, and leadership, the SPH was able to receive full accreditation in 2005. From 2002 to 2013, total school revenues increased by more than 700 percent and grant funding increased by more than 1,100 percent. Enrollment grew from forty-five to more than 450 students, and academic offerings went from one degree program to over ten degree and program offerings. In 2006, SPH professor John Rich was awarded a MacArthur Foundation "Genius" Fellowship in recognition of his work "addressing the health care needs of one of the nation's most ignored and underserved populations—African-American men in urban settings."[12] By 2010 public health students were racking up 70,000 cumulative annual hours of community service, and an undergraduate public health minor and major were added. The school also launched what became a renowned Autism Institute in 2012, under the direction of SPH professor Craig Newschaffer—the first of its kind to study autism through a public health perspective.

Ultimately, the school moved from 6,000 square feet of rented space near Hahnemann University Hospital in Center City to its own seven-floor building in the heart of Drexel's University City campus. Faculty diversity expanded, consequently attracting diverse students. In 2013, Gold stepped down as dean and in 2014, Ana V. Diez Roux, previously chair of the Department of Epidemiology and director of the Center for Social Epidemiology and Population Health at the University of Michigan School of Public Health, was appointed dean.

In 2015 the school was renamed the Dana and David Dornsife School of Public Health in honor of a $45 million gift from the Dornsife family.

This generous gift is providing the school the opportunity to establish a pioneering urban health collaborative, create three endowed professorships and four endowed scholarships, expand Drexel's global public health program, and establish a dean's strategic initiative fund.

The School of Education

Drexel has had a formal commitment to teacher education since the early 1930s. By 1981, due to declining enrollments, the university had narrowed its teacher training to four areas: home economics and early childhood at the undergraduate level, and library science and reading specialist at the graduate level.[13] The programs, with the exception of library science, were housed in the Nesbitt College of Design, Nutrition, Human Behavior and Home Economics.

In 1982, in response to a shortage in math and science teachers (both nationally and locally), Drexel collaborated with the School District of Philadelphia to create a "teacher-scholar" program, designed to attract high school students with outstanding math and science skills into the teaching profession. Once these students were at Drexel, they took more math and science than typical education majors.[14] The teacher-scholar program actively recruited capable students from low-income and minority families in keeping with the school district's guidelines that "applicants must meet Drexel standards [for admission], with priority given to poverty and minority students."[15]

Though the teacher-scholar program was located in Nesbitt College's Department of Human Behavior, it also relied on courses offered in Drexel's College of Science (such as those in mathematics, computer science, and the sciences). In 1986, the Department of Human Behavior, along with the teacher-scholar program, became part of the Department of Psychology in the College of Humanities and Social Sciences. Then in 1988 the teacher-scholar program was broken into two parts: an undergraduate major in teacher education, and a graduate certificate in teacher preparation, both located in the College of Science. An additional graduate certificate in environmental education was created in 1989, and the teacher preparation graduate certificate came to serve as the core of the master's degree in science of instruction, created in 1990.

In 1990 the colleges of science, and of humanities and social sciences, merged to form the College of Arts and Sciences (COAS), and the education programs (focusing on elementary education, secondary mathematics and science, and library science) were moved to COAS's Division of

Instruction. In 1997 the Division of Instruction became the School of Education (still housed within COAS), which in the same year was approved to offer a part-time Ph.D. program in educational leadership development and learning technologies. More programs followed, including those for instructional technology specialists, principals, and superintendents, and in teaching English as a second language.

The School of Education (SOE) became a freestanding unit, independent of COAS, in 2002, with Fredericka Reisman appointed founding director, followed in 2004 by William Lynch, who arrived after almost two decades of work at George Washington University, where he directed the Educational Computing Laboratory and founded a Center for Distance and Mediated Learning, among many other assignments merging technology, education, and professional development. Lynch recalls the challenge of coming into a school with "around 130 total undergrads, and 380 part-time graduate students—revenues were small and the budget was very small."[16] Lynch determined that the climate was right to expand the scope of degree offerings beyond teacher programs:

> I came from a university [George Washington] with a fairly large and diverse graduate school of education—I had been well aware that there was more to graduate schools of education than simply a focus on teacher preparation—especially among private universities. Private universities that wanted substantial schools of education had a diversity of products and of perspectives. The question is, would those markets be attracted to online education? We called a lot of people, including former provosts—consulted with them—to find out if there would be a market for online. People didn't know. We created an on campus and online version for a new higher education program masters. The original plan was to do parallel versions online and on campus—there was a very strong response to the online program— we never ran the on campus version. The conclusion that we came to was that perhaps Drexel had a strong investment in online education—and there were very few online competitors in this whole education array—If we did it well, people would in fact come. It proved to be true in every case that we tried.[17]

Following this successful launch of the online master's program in higher education in 2005, the SOE started master's programs and hired new faculty in global and international education, and educational administration. The school also initiated a bachelor's degree completion program in 2006 that

Drexel School of Education students working in a classroom at Chinatown Learning Center in Philadelphia, 2011. (Drexel University School of Education.)

Drexel School of Education students sipping tea at an accepted students day, 2006. (Drexel University School of Education.)

was primarily online with school-based field experiences. Master's degree programs in human resource development, learning technologies, and special education were developed and approved with their first students enrolled in 2007. By 2010 a growing program portfolio added blended and online formats at off campus locations, including the new doctor of education degree. Enrollments reached a peak of approximately 2,000 students. Looking back, Lynch recalls a strategic move that paid off for the university:

> President Papadakis offered a revenue sharing incentive to deans who started online programs, and that revenue is what built the School of Education. We invested much of that revenue in online education and expanded our faculty and staff—I felt obliged to reinvest it in quality—and one of my proudest accomplishments was the creation of a learning technologies group: instructional designers, media producers, and artists to work with faculty in the development and maintenance of our online courses. It was very, very successful—and that group eventually moved to Drexel eLearning—to provide those services across the university.[18]

In 2008, the SOE was subsumed under the Goodwin College of Professional Studies, to which Lynch was appointed dean. The two units had strong ties in regard to their capacity for working with non-traditional and adult learners. Goodwin College began as the Department of Lectures and Evening Classes in 1892, and went through a series of similar-sounding name changes, ending up as the College of Evening and Professional Studies in 1997. In 2001, as a result of a generous gift from builder and Drexel graduate Richard Goodwin, the school was renamed in his honor. In 2012 the School of Education and Goodwin College were again separated into freestanding units. In 2014 Lynch was succeeded as dean by Nancy Butler Songer—formerly the director of the Center for Essential Science at the University of Michigan—who inherited a school of forty-five talented faculty and a strong array of programs.[19]

The Close School of Entrepreneurship and the Lasting Impact of Anthony J. Drexel

There are few universities in the world that are named after an entrepreneur. Drexel University is one of them. The mission of the Drexel Institute at the time of its founding was to prepare students for their entry into an industrializing society. Anthony Drexel's spirit of entrepreneurship and innovation has been a mainstay of the Drexel University culture. Our research has an applied emphasis; our pedagogy consistently involves experiential methodologies—cooperative education being the cornerstone. And that pioneering spirit infuses Drexel's culture today. Just as Mr. Drexel recognized and predicted the skills needed for an industrializing society in the late nineteenth century, Drexel University today acknowledges the reality that entrepreneurship is a critical skill for the twenty-first century.

Continuing the revolutionary legacy of Anthony Drexel, Drexel University in 2013 underscored the need for entrepreneurship education by creating the Charles D. Close School of Entrepreneurship, based on a gift from the Charles and Barbara Close Foundation, with Donna De Carolis as founding dean. The Close School is a freestanding academic unit, outside of the traditional business school, that grants bachelor's and master's degrees. To truly appreciate the entrepreneurial spirit embedded and practiced at Drexel, this section provides a brief account of the progression of entrepreneurship as a research field and discipline in universities in general.

The development of formal curricular entrepreneurship programs at universities is a relatively recent occurrence. Historically, business schools, dominated by economics in the early twentieth century, took a functional approach to curriculum, with coursework and departments that largely centered on the traditional areas of accounting, finance, operations management and marketing. The discipline of management only appeared in curriculum during the 1950s; the result of works by Barnard (*Functions of the Executive*, 1938); Simon and March ("Behavioral Theory of the Firm, 1963"), Selznick, (*Leadership in Action*, 1957); Alfred Chandler (*Strategy and Structure*, 1962), Ansoff, ("Corporate Strategy" 1965), and Andrews, ("The Concept of Corporate Strategy" 1965). These scholars and practitioners, among others, laid the foundations for the discipline of strategic management, which focused on the overarching question of why some firms outperform others, and the role of the leader and top management in firm performance. Scholarly research in the field of strategy precipitated the evolution of courses and departments in strategic management in business schools beginning roughly in the 1970s.

In particular, business schools rapidly incorporated courses such as business policy, strategic management, and competitive strategy, in their curriculum. Simultaneously, scholarly research in strategic management gave rise to prestigious journals, such as the *Strategic Management Journal*, with a research agenda that included topics such as the role of the leader in firm strategy and performance, strategic diversification, and organizational structure and strategy. Interestingly, the scholarly study of entrepreneurship originated in the fields of economics, psychology, and sociology. In business schools, entrepreneurship during this period was viewed as a "subset" of strategic management and generally subsumed under management departments. In fact, a lively debate emerged among management scholars as to whether or not the field of entrepreneurship was indeed a research discipline in its own right or was an extension of strategic management.

During the 1990s and into the twenty-first century, entrepreneurship did in fact emerge not only as a standalone scholarly discipline in business, but also as a separate department within business schools. Similar to the development of strategic management as a separate and distinct discipline, so too evolved the prominence of entrepreneurship. Scholarly theoretical and empirical research motivated the establishment of journals and conferences dedicated to entrepreneurship and innovation. Concurrently, business schools began creating courses and eventually departments dedicated to the research and teaching of entrepreneurship.

This brief history of the evolution of entrepreneurship scholarship and pedagogy is noteworthy in one particular aspect that has significant relevance for Drexel: The fact that entrepreneurship was housed in a business school.

In terms of curricular offerings at Drexel before 2000, entrepreneurship courses typically focused on teaching students the elements of how to write a business plan. Business planning courses could be found in a variety of academic units across the university and these courses were tailored to the discipline of that academic unit. For example, there were versions of business planning and similar entrepreneurship courses in the Westphal College of Media Arts and Design, the School of Biomedical Engineering, Science and Health Systems, the College of Engineering, and other colleges across campus.

In 2000, through the generosity of Mr. Paul "Mel" Baiada and Mr. Charles Close, the Baiada Center for Entrepreneurship was created. Originally under the provost's office, the Baiada Center began to offer programming and business incubation opportunities for students across campus. In 2002 the Baiada Center became part of the business school, while always serving all university students through its evolving activities and annual business plan competitions. In addition, the Baiada Center engaged the entrepreneurial and business communities. In 2009, the Charles and Barbara Close Foundation, through a generous contribution, elevated the Baida Center to an Institute, solidifying its university-wide reach.

In the business school, there were elective courses in entrepreneurship but no major existed until 2004, when one was established as part of the

The Baiada Institute is a business incubator for student startups housed inside the Charles D. Close School for Entrepreneurship, with 1,900 square feet of co-working space and access to advisors to help with legal, financial and funding questions. (Office of University Communications. Photo by Halkin/Mason Photography.)

Department of Management, during the ongoing surge in entrepreneurial activity prompted in large part by advances in digital, communications and life sciences technologies and discoveries. Propelled by the innovations flowing from these areas, entrepreneurial opportunities increased and so did the number of entrepreneurs embracing those opportunities. The rising generation of millennial college students have demonstrated tremendous activity and continued interest in new venture creation. This generation seeks self-employment or desires to work in a new or growing venture; they are also more selective about the type of company they work for, demanding a fit with values and lifestyle. Thus a perfect storm for higher education was created: a demand for learning about entrepreneurship and what it takes to be an entrepreneur; and technological and market opportunities for new venture creation that spurs economic development and societal welfare.

The Close School is founded on two pillars. First, there is a difference between the terms "entrepreneur" and "entrepreneurship," the former being a person and the latter being a process. Most business schools teach the process and focus on teaching the functional areas as they relate to entrepreneurship. Understanding this differential leads to an entirely revolutionary approach to entrepreneurship instruction. The Close School curriculum is uniquely designed for students to experience what it is like to be an entrepreneur; to develop the outlooks and attitudes that define the entrepreneur. Specifically, entrepreneurship as a habit of mind, an innovative approach to life, career and profession.

Being a brand new school has its advantages. In particular, the Close School created thirty-five brand-new courses—a curriculum that includes courses designed for students to understand and experience being an entrepreneur. The school is able to integrate co-curricular programming from the Baiada Institute, which is now under the Close School. This enhances the learning from the Close School curriculum.

Anthony J. Drexel's approach to the institute that bears his name was eloquently articulated in his belief that "the world will change and therefore the University must change with it." The core assumption of this statement is rooted in an entrepreneurial approach to not only education, but to individual and organizational innovation. Drexel University's pioneering incorporation of cooperative learning within a college curriculum, coupled with the educational philosophy of preparing students for real life experiences, have remained the hallmark of the university's approach to pedagogy and research, perhaps most clearly expressed in entrepreneurship education.

The Center for Hospitality and Sports Management

In 2013, Goodwin College was reorganized to become primarily a center for the university's pilot First-Year Exploratory Studies program, for incoming freshmen who are undecided on majors. The School of Education, previously under Goodwin, once again became a freestanding unit, as did several other units (namely sport management, hospitality management, culinary arts and food science) that were brought together to form the new Center for Hospitality and Sport Management (CHSM), under founding director Jonathan Deutsch, a classically

Richard C. Goodwin, 2000. (Drexel University Archives.)

trained chef and author of the culinary textbook *Culinary Improvisation* who earned his doctorate in food studies and food management from New York University, and who among other things previously directed Drexel's hospitality, culinary and food science programs.

As President Fry commented about the establishment of CHSM,

> This change reflects the growing economic importance of tourism and leisure in Greater Philadelphia and across the nation, as well as Drexel's strength in producing accomplished and motivated professionals for those industries. . . . Drexel's commitment to the Center for Hospitality and Sport Management is very much in keeping with the Drexel spirit, and we look forward to seeing these programs thrive. As we attract even more outstanding students, we are hopeful that the program will grow into a college or school.

CHSM currently offers undergraduate degrees in culinary arts, culinary science, hospitality management, and sport management as well as minors in coaching leadership, culinary arts, food science, gaming, and casino operations. Graduate degrees are offered in sport management (both online and on-campus), food science, and hospitality management (online only). A certificate is offered in gaming and casino management. Accelerated degree programs, such as a combined bachelor of science and master of business administration, are available in culinary arts, culinary science, and hospitality management.

Through its focus on experiential learning and co-op opportunities, CHSM is positioned to fulfill distinct market needs in sport ticketing, restaurant management, arena management, food product development, recipe development, coaching, tour guiding, commercial kitchen design and layout, kitchen gardening, and hotel front desk operations.

As Deutsch has noted,

> Taken together, our programs support Philadelphia's largest industry and leading economic driver. . . . We have had strong programs in culinary arts, sport management, food science and hospitality management for decades. The Center for Hospitality and Sport Management is an opportunity to merge these offerings under one roof. We look forward to offering unparalleled experiential learning opportunities for students, serving as an event and program hub for industry professionals and conducting research that helps us improve the ways we do business in food, hospitality and sport.

Culinary Arts and Sciences students learn while doing in Drexel's Academic Bistro. (Office of University Communications.)

Moving Further into the Twenty-First Century

Drexel lies in the midst of one of the densest concentrations of higher education institutions in the country, and the new schools that have been established at the university since the turn of the twenty-first century are evidence that, even amid the many colleges and universities of the Philadelphia region, there are still unmet needs for new programs. In the case of the Close School of Entrepreneurship, the university created an educational niche that had previously not existed (at least not in the form of a freestanding school). What new market niches might emerge for new schools is of course an open question, but Drexel's past suggests that it will be ready to seize—or create—new opportunities.

NOTES

1. Kenneth A. Barbee, "H. H. Sun," available at giving.drexel.edu/areas/HHSun/.
2. "Remembering Professor Hun H. Sun," College of Engineering, Drexel University, available at drexel.edu/engineering/news-events/archive/2015/February/RememberingPro
fessorHunHSun/.
3. *The Drexel Interview*, Season 2, 2004–5.

4. "Drexel Biomedical Engineers to Help Upgrade Brain Injury Detection Device Used by Navy and Marines," *DrexelNow*, October 1, 2014, available at drexel.edu/now /archive/2014/October/InfraScanner/.

5. Available at http://drexelmagazine.org/2015/02/university-inc/#sthash.Ol0X08I8 .dpuf.

6. Noel Holton, "Classes to Start Today at Philadelphia's First School of Public Health," *Philadelphia Inquirer*, August 26, 1996, B3.

7. Ibid.

8. Huntly Collins, "Harvard Professor Named Allegheny Health School Dean," *Philadelphia Inquirer*, November 13, 1997, B2.

9. Karl Stark, "School of Public Health Could Be a Tenet Target," *Philadelphia Inquirer*, October 16, 1998, C1.

10. Huntly Collins, "Ready to Make a Difference: The New Dean Has Some Ambitious Plans for the City's Only School of Public Health," *Philadelphia Inquirer*, April 23, 2001, C1.

11. Marian Uhlman, "Drexel Gets New Dean of Public Health, *Philadelphia Inquirer*, August 19, 2002, C1.

12. See https://www.macfound.org/fellows/842/#sthash.6uTDmZVO.dpuf.

13. *Drexel University Teacher-Scholar Program: 1984 Self-Study Volumes I and II, Self-Study for PA Department of Education*, Nesbitt College of Design Arts, Philadelphia, 1984.

14. National Center for Educational Statistics, 1980.

15. *Drexel University Teacher-Scholar Program: 1984 Self-Study Volumes I and II, Self-Study*.

16. William Lynch, interviewed by Scott Gabriel Knowles, February 11, 2016.

17. Ibid.

18. Ibid.

19. William Lynch, Drexel University School of Education, 2014.

*The 80-foot-tall biowall in the Papadakis Integrated Sciences Building,
home to research and teaching in the College of Arts and Sciences, is North America's
largest living biofilter and the only such structure installed at a U.S. university.
(Office of University Communications.)*

The Future of Science

From Drexel Now

September 20, 2011

The Papadakis Integrated Sciences Building (PISB), designed by world-renowned Diamond and Schmitt Architects, has officially opened its shiny new doors.

The 150,000-square-foot structure at the corner of 33rd and Chestnut Streets is the new home of Drexel's Department of Biology, and an important step forward for scientific research efforts at the University. A special dedication took place Tuesday, September 20, with Drexel trustees, executive staff and the family of the late Dr. Constantine Papadakis, the new building's namesake.

"The Papadakis Integrated Sciences Building will play a major role in what might be a golden age in biology and life sciences teaching and research at Drexel," said President John A. Fry at the dedication.

In May 2009, Drexel's Board of Trustees unanimously approved naming the Integrated Sciences Building in honor of the late president for his legacy of innovation and excellence. The University community joined Interim President Chuck Pennoni and the Papadakis family for the ceremonial groundbreaking in November 2009.

This new facility will be Drexel's first building to be Silver LEED-certified; it is also anticipated to receive at least a 3 Green Globes® rating from the Green Building Initiative. The building houses 44 research and teaching laboratories for biology, organic chemistry and biomedical engineering, lecture halls, a 250-person auditorium and, perhaps most notably, a five-story biowall, which serves as a living air filter. Contaminated air is drawn into the water trickling behind the biowall. From the water, microbes in the plant roots take up and remove particulates and volatile compounds. Additionally, faculty and student researchers will study the wall for its potential health benefits. Drexel is the first university in the United States to have such a feature on campus.

The PISB aims to increase the quality and diversity of the student laboratory and classroom experiences, facilitating future leaders in the biology, biotechnology, environmental science, life science and pharmaceutical industries.

22

A Decade of Legal Education
at Drexel

Roger Dennis

TWO INTERRELATED phenomena have framed the history and development of Drexel's law school since its establishment in 2006. First, the demand for legal education significantly declined, especially as newly available data revealed that the salary levels for many young lawyers did not readily support the debt needed to finance a legal education. Second, the legal profession demanded law schools take on more of the practical training of new graduates.

In 2006 88,700 people applied to law schools in the United States, marking a 12 percent decline from the peak of more than 100,000 in 2004. There was a very modest increase during the height of the Great Recession as the entry-level job market for college graduates was very weak, but by the fall of 2014 there were only 55,700 applicants to law schools. In 2010 more than 52,000 students began their first year of law school, and by 2014 that number had declined to 38,000. Drexel's new law school thus faced hypercompetitive conditions as it recruited students, and it had to offer generous scholarships.

In response to client demands to control legal costs, employers wanted newly minted lawyers to be more fully formed professionals when they graduated law school. This meant that law schools had to bear more of the effort of training law students in a broad range of skills. This cost-shift from firms to schools coincided with calls within the academy that teaching legal reasoning, writing, and research—the typical core of traditional legal education—was no longer sufficient. Students ought to also have training in interviewing, counselling, negotiation, and investigation; experience client-centered legal drafting and problem solving; and they should know more about the business of law and about the businesses of their clients. A broader agenda for legal education had a significant impact on cost; skills-training classes tend to have lower enrollments than more traditional courses, and offering them thus meant a lower student-to-faculty ratio, again fundamentally affecting the economics of legal education.

My chapter tells the story of how these and other challenges were confronted during the Drexel law school's first decade of operation. It is the story of creating a program of legal education that supports the larger goal of growing an urban national research university. Drexel's new law school is committed to offering an intense, experientially-based program. The law school's curriculum focuses on areas of law that match existing university strengths. Its faculty are expected to produce scholarship appropriate for a national research university. The law school built programs that supported the university's high-level civic engagement strategy. The story of Drexel's law school is also one of how institutional planning and decision-making processes affect outcomes, how the decision-making style of a university president impacts the implementation of a major project, and the extraordinary institutional support that made it possible for the law school to meet its lofty goals.

The Institutional Context

Historically, Drexel's core programs were in engineering and business. Experiential education is part of the university's DNA; most undergraduate programs have traditionally been co-op based, meaning that, as part of their academic program, students obtain two or three full time, paying job experiences, for six-month periods, before they graduate. Linked to its co-op heritage, the Drexel brand is that it prepares focused, hard-working, job-ready graduates.

An important part of the context for the launch of the law school was Drexel's recent history of institutional transformation. In the mid-1990s the university faced an enrollment crisis as the demand for engineering education declined and Drexel's location in the center of a high-crime rust belt city that had been declining since the 1950s became very unattractive to its largely commuter-based student population. To meet the crisis Drexel began a program of university transformation. Drexel and its neighbor, the

University of Pennsylvania, led a neighborhood rebirth initiative that converted the University City neighborhood into a superb urban college town. Under President Constantine Papadakis, Drexel helped to create University City (a business district devoted primarily to neighborhood branding, security, cleanup, and economic development). The university increased its campus housing options, expanded its educational programs into hot areas such as digital media and computer and information sciences, and grew its arts and sciences offerings as well. Drexel also invested in advanced educational technology as a core strategy, becoming the first major university that was fully wireless. And, a significant part of Drexel's transformation was its acquisition in 2002 of the Allegheny University of the Health Sciences.

Drexel's strategy of change resulted in a doubling of the student population, increases in student quality, significant increases in sponsored research, major growth in endowment, and a generally enhanced institutional profile. From the depths of crisis, the university transformed itself into a well-ranked, comprehensive national research university.

Drexel's late president Constantine Papadakis was the visionary leader who drove the transformation strategy. He believed deeply in growth, and thus adding a law school to the university would be icing on the cake of a decade of remarkable change. Having a law school would increase university reputation. A legal education program would provide new opportunities for academic synergy. President Papadakis also believed the law school would be a cash cow that would quickly cover its direct and indirect costs, providing resources for other programs on campus. Using all of these arguments and the power of his outsized personality, Papadakis persuaded the university board of trustees, the academic leaders of the university, and the faculty as a whole that launching a law school was the next logical step for growing the university.

Planning for the Launch

Planning for the law school began shortly after the acquisition of Allegheny University in 2002, and from the beginning it was managed somewhat unconventionally. Typically, universities hire an experienced legal educator as the lead consultant, or a founding dean, as the first step in developing a new program of legal education. Drexel instead relied primarily on existing internal personnel. Early in 2003 Carl "Tobey" Oxholm III—the university's general counsel and a key figure in the university's growth strategy who had already had a distinguished career in private practice and public service—was designated by President Papadakis as the leader of the law school planning project.

Oxholm began consulting about law school development with prominent members of the judiciary and the bar, and formed an internal committee of high-level administrators and deans. These efforts were suspended in late 2003 as Drexel's senior management had to focus on the closure of one of the university's two primary teaching hospitals, but resumed early in 2005, with an aggressive goal of having an inaugural entering class of students in fall of 2006. The former dean of the University of Cincinnati Law School, Joseph Tomain, was hired as a consultant, to provide advice on the ABA accreditation process; and Arthur Frakt, former dean of the law schools of Loyola Marymount and Widener universities, became the principal consultant for faculty and staff appointments, and law school administration.

The internal university committee suggested that the law school have academic concentrations in health law, entrepreneurship, and intellectual property that would connect with other university academic offerings. To fit with Drexel's focus on experiential education, an intense externship experience (branded as a co-op) would be offered, for much more academic credit than was normal in American legal education, and available in both nonprofit and profit sites (at that time most law schools only offered externships at nonprofit sites). To ensure quality, the law school was to develop an aggressive oversight model of student experiences in the co-op. The financial plan for the law school expected losses in the early years, followed by breaking even on direct costs in the fourth year, and by the sixth year, $7 million in profits (based on direct costs), with a student population of 800 J.D. candidates, along with some non-J.D. programs.

During the 2005–2006 academic year the core administrative team and eleven tenured and tenure-track faculty were hired—a group unusually committed to the vision of the law school as both a leader in experiential education and a center for legal scholarship. The inaugural faculty developed the details for the first-year curriculum and governance rules related to faculty and students. An initial search for the school's founding dean was unsuccessful, so just before the law school opened Jennifer Rosato Perea, an inaugural faculty member who had extensive administrative experience at Brooklyn Law School, was appointed acting dean, and served in that role throughout most of the school's first year, until I joined Drexel as the founding dean (Rosato Perea then became dean of Northern Illinois University's law school, and is now dean of the DePaul University College of Law).

Three issues related to the law school's founding merit special attention, all of which show some of the complications attendant with the quick launch strategy encouraged by President Papadakis. First, unlike other new law schools, Drexel's was launched without a long term space plan. Papadakis's general approach to physical plant issues was that space needs should be met only at the last moment and when utterly necessary—yet even so, it was clear that some newly constructed space was needed to house the law school. Thus an ostensibly temporary "swing space" was built for the law school next to Hagerty Library, which included attractive classrooms, offices for faculty and administration and for the law library, with some modest space for student life activities. As additional faculty and a second and third year of J.D. students joined the school, more space was needed, especially for student life and library services. The result was a significant redesign, where the wall between the swing space and Hagerty's third floor was torn out and the law library expanded into Hagerty, resulting in reduced library space for the rest of the university, and significantly increased expenditures.

Second, planning for the law library was also affected by Papadakis's vision. The president believed that the modern library should collect almost all information electronically and need not have a large professional staff to serve the research needs of faculty and students. Thus much of the law library's collection was to be in electronic form, almost all print materials were to be off site at the Jenkins Law Library (a bar association library many blocks away from campus), space for students and faculty to do research on campus was to be minimal, and the library staff was to be unusually small as compared to other law schools.

Law library collections and staffing are subject to the accreditation standards of the American Bar Association (ABA), which require that libraries be an active and responsive force in the educational life of their law schools. ABA accreditation is essential to any law school, since students need to graduate from an accredited law school to be eligible to sit for the bar examination in most jurisdictions. The plan for Drexel's new law school called for sufficient faculty, a comprehensive curriculum, and appropriate support services for students, but the university would have had difficulty persuading the ABA that its planned law library met the needs of students and faculty. As a result, the plan to use the Jenkins Law Library was abandoned. A well-known leader in law librarianship, Christopher Simoni, was hired as library director and was charged with creating an ABA-compliant library plan. The model of a law library unusually committed to electronic resources remained, since this comported with accreditation standards, but some significant portion of the core collection was purchased in hard copy form. Content, rather than format, guided the collection development plan.

Third, Papadakis's belief that Drexel's law school would quickly become a cash cow was badly mistaken. The notion that law schools were cash cows has an honored history, arising in the 1950s and 1960s when most schools offered a narrow curriculum of core courses taught in large sections, and when most professors did not have intense research missions. Thus teaching loads were higher, there were fewer classes, and the cost of providing a program of legal education was relatively low. By contrast, today's law school curriculum is much richer, with many courses taught in small sections, and professors' research agendas and expectations are more intense, leading to lower teaching loads. Most law schools have student-to-faculty ratios in the range of ten or twelve to one, as compared to more than twenty-five to one in earlier decades. Moreover, the administrative staff needed to support student services, technology, marketing, and fund-raising has also grown. Finally, even before the hyper-competition for students began after 2004, schools were increasingly discounting their tuitions with more scholarships and fellowships. This was especially true in the Philadelphia region, which was already a crowded field for law schools.

The original plan for the law school envisioned a large and profitable part-time J.D. program and significant non-J.D. programs, even before full ABA accreditation. Yet a part-time J.D. program requires its own accreditation, which was not likely given the space constraints in the swing space building. And there were already three part-time J.D. programs in the region, two of which were at state-supported schools with significantly lower tuitions. As early as 2006 it was thus clear that the part-time J.D. was not feasible. The non-J.D. programs also came later than expected, since they are not permitted by the ABA until a school is fully accredited.

The university's board of trustees, Papadakis, and later President John Fry, have remained committed to their law school, allowing it to run substantial deficits every year since its founding. Drexel's senior leadership continues to believe that the law school enhances the reputation of the university as a whole. The law faculty have been productive, high impact scholars. They have contributed to interdisciplinary efforts in key academic areas such as public health and psychology. The law school's experientially based program has been viewed positively within the academy and practicing bar. Graduates are perceived as well trained and the law school's pro bono programs mesh well with the university's commitment to civic engagement. With this level of performance, the investment remains sensible.

The Curriculum

The major task facing Drexel's law school in its first years of operation was implementing a complex curriculum, designed so that students developed a client-centered approach to legal problem solving. The faculty believed that, in addition to understanding legal theory, doctrine, analysis, and modes of legal argumentation, students also needed to be effective written and oral communicators, legal researchers, fact investigators, transaction cost engineers, and counselors. Some of the skills can be taught in the traditional classroom and some can best be taught through experiential education.

The first year of a Drexel legal education looks very similar to the conventional law school curriculum, encompassing traditional courses in contracts, torts, criminal law, constitutional law, civil procedure and legal research and writing. Like most programs, students in their first year learn core doctrinal content and the basic skills of legal analysis and argumentation. Yet even within this established curriculum, Drexel faculty found opportunities to innovate. Many of the first-year doctrinal professors require students to participate in significant practical skills exercises such as drafting or oral argument. Students are exposed to skills training in interviewing, counseling, and negotiation through a weeklong workshop. The school is particularly focused on teaching legal research and writing in small classes, taught by tenured and tenure-track faculty, more credits of which are required than at many other law schools.

The second- and third-year curricula are a blend of traditional doctrinal courses, and opportunities for experiential education. The law school offers the full range of upper-level core courses (for instance, in evidence, business organizations, and tax law). Specialized courses in entrepreneurship, health law, criminal law, and intellectual property law support academic concentrations. Perspective courses are also offered, in areas such as legal theory and international law. As in the first year curriculum, many professors use simulations as major components of their courses.

Students are also required to take a clinic or co-op in their second or third years. The co-op is a non-paying, practice-based externship experience (of twenty-five or more hours a week) coupled with a classroom component in which students examine a range of topics on professionalism and reflect on how their assignments are furthering their learning agendas. Placements range across all practice settings—judicial, public interest, governmental, for-profit law firms of all sizes, and in-house corporate counsel offices. We have developed more than a hundred co-op partnerships and

to date more than seven hundred students completed co-op placements, acquiring 300,000 hours of experience working for organizations from Philadelphia to New York, Washington, Chicago, Tokyo, Dubai, Switzerland,
and Haiti.

The substance of the on-site portion of the co-op program is jointly established by the student and placement supervisor in a written learning
agenda. Students perform in role, completing tasks similar to those done
by newly licensed lawyers. But because the program does not permit co-op
partners to bill for a student's work, students can also be given some of those
traditional training opportunities, like second chairing a deposition, for
which clients are no longer willing to be billed.

The co-op program has been the single most cited feature students
report in deciding to attend Drexel. Surveys of participating students and
co-op supervisors reveal an extremely high level of satisfaction. Moreover,
from a general institutional marketing standpoint, co-op has embedded the
law school positively and promptly in the legal community. And, although
the co-op program is not directly related to placement efforts, a number of
students have obtained full-time jobs as a consequence of their co-op
placements.

Running the law school's co-op system requires the work of approximately two and a half full-time faculty members. There is an elaborate
matching process that requires students to interview with prospective sites,
and all sites are visited at least once a year by faculty. Supervising attorneys
undergo mandatory training on mentoring young professionals, for which
they receive free continuing legal education credits.

The law school built upon its co-op system by establishing field clinics,
currently located at the Defender Association of Philadelphia and the
Philadelphia Legal Assistance Family Law Unit. At the Defenders clinic,
students represent clients in preliminary hearings on felonies, argue motion, and try misdemeanor cases in municipal court. At Philadelphia Legal
Assistance, students engage in a broad array of activities, including representing victims of family violence in protection from abuse and custody
matters. Students handle a case from the initial intake through representation and will act as the client's lead counsel. Participating students commit
to a full academic year in a field clinic, while also taking a reflective seminar
on justice lawyering that examines the ways in which the legal system can
and should promote equality and fairness.

The third piece of the law school's experiential education program involves live-client clinics, located at the law school or with other university
outreach programs, and taught by law school faculty. Students work in these

clinics for a complete academic year and provide direct legal services to clients. Since opening our Appellate Litigation Clinic in 2009, students have successfully represented immigrants facing deportation, prison inmates seeking due process, and employees facing workplace discrimination. Their victories in the U.S. Court of Appeals include one Seventh Circuit case where they argued successfully on behalf of a community fighting the operators of a dump that fouled its air and water. Clients of the Entrepreneurial Law Clinic, opened in 2011 to provide legal services to startups in Philadelphia and elsewhere, have included the founders of CommonBond, whose success has been cited by the *Wall Street Journal* and the *Economist*. Through the Community Lawyering Clinic launched in 2014, students have helped residents of distressed neighborhoods adjoining the Drexel campus address a variety of legal issues and led workshops that educate residents about their rights in the workplace and the community.

To graduate from the J.D. program, students must provide fifty hours of pro bono service, working with practicing lawyers to serve the needs of low-income clients. Most students exceed the requirement, on average completing more than one hundred hours of service. In aggregate, our students have provided more than 100,000 hours of pro bono service to needy clients since the law school's founding. Though pro bono service is not credit bearing, it is an important component of the law school's commitment to experiential education. Students gain skills while being exposed to the ethic of service. Although students can find their own pro bono opportunity, most work in programs sponsored by the law school in collaboration with partnering agencies. This ensures that high quality service and education are simultaneously provided. As with the field clinics, the law school provides pro bono partners some funding, which enables them to offer high quality training and professional supervision to student volunteers.

A final component of the experiential education program is a commitment to practice-based cocurricular activities. Most law schools offer students opportunities to write for and manage a scholarly journal and to participate in interschool competitions that demonstrate mastery of appellate and trial advocacy skills as well as negotiation, counseling and other tasks. What makes Drexel's approach unusual is the percentage of positions made available in these activities, so that more than a third of Drexel's law students participate—a strategy that requires a considerable commitment of faculty time and financial resources. Besides the educational benefits robust cocurricular activities offer, these activities also enhance the law school's reputation. And the strategy has worked. The *Drexel Law Review* has hosted several symposia featuring nationally and internationally recognized scholars, resulting in widely cited publications. Drexel law students have also been unusually successful in interschool competitions.

Faculty Status and Research

A major current issue in legal education is the tenure and governance rights of conventional classroom teachers, clinical teachers, and legal writing teachers. ABA standards require that a law school be able to attract and retain a competent faculty, and they imply that full-time, doctrinal classroom teachers should be tenured or on the tenure track, and clinicians should have positions reasonably similar to those that are tenured. Meanwhile, there is no required model for tenure for legal writing faculty. Drexel's faculty sought to create a more egalitarian model in which all full-time faculty who were engaged in extensive scholarship would be tenured or tenure track regardless of what they taught, while faculty that did not have scholarly agendas would receive long-term contracts as "teaching faculty." Based on the law school's hiring experience, the subject matter of a faculty member's teaching is not linked to scholarly potential. As a major collateral benefit of this hiring model, Drexel was successfully able to compete in hiring for the very best clinical and legal writing faculty.

The commitment to a top-tier research program was an ambitious goal, particularly in light of the demands on the faculty to build a new institution. Scholarly activities have been supported through summer research grants, faculty development funds, and a generous research leave program. Law school faculty members have used these resources to publish highly impactful books and articles.

Responding to the Crisis in Legal Education

In the early years of the law school, in addition to the enormous effort it took to implement a new curriculum with an emphasis on experiential education, faculty and staff were also engaged in a wide range of other institution-building activities such as working with university administrators to resolve space issues, obtaining full ABA accreditation and membership in the Association of American Law Schools, developing administrative infrastructure, supporting students in obtaining employment, and assisting students in creating a wide range of co- and extracurricular activities. At the same time faculty were working under demanding expectations for scholarship. References to Drexel building the airplane and flying it at the same time were commonplace.

Amid the pressures of building a complex institution, the crisis in legal education compelled the law school to expand its range of initial offerings, primarily to diversify sources of revenue. First, in May 2014 the law school established a two-year accelerated J.D. course of study. Modeled on Northwestern University's program, students enrolling in Drexel's accelerated program begin their legal education in May and take six academic terms straight through, without summer breaks. These students take the same courses as three year students but graduate in two calendar years, saving an additional year of living expenses and shortening the number of years out of the work force. Very few law schools offer such an option, so Drexel faces less competition. The accelerated program has attracted thirty new students in each year that it has been offered.

Second, the law school also established in May 2014 a master of legal studies (M.L.S.), aimed at nonlawyers. The curriculum is focused on the huge and growing field of legal compliance for corporations and nonprofit institutions. Because compliance officials' skills and knowledge are very similar to those of lawyers, the law school is well positioned to meet the educational needs of the compliance sector. The law school decided delivering the M.L.S. online made sense as it facilitated a nationwide recruitment strategy, and the program now enrolls nearly one hundred students.

In fall of 2015 the law school jumped into international legal education when fifteen foreign lawyers joined the Drexel student body. Many law schools offer a master's of law (L.L.M.) in American law to foreign lawyers, most of whom, after getting this degree, return to practicing in their home countries. Drexel has excellent contacts with a number of foreign universities, and the law school used those connections to recruit a cohort of international L.L.M. students, and to attract foreign lawyers who wish to obtain an American J.D., which under ABA rules can be obtained in four semesters rather than six.

A Transformational Gift

Established law schools often obtain up to 20 percent of their budgets from donations, largely from their most successful alumni. For a new law school, the lack of alumni makes fund-raising a daunting challenge. Yet in this respect Drexel's new law school has succeeded spectacularly. In 2008, Earle Mack, a Drexel alumnus and former ambassador to Finland, provided a generous gift of $15 million to the law school, which was then named after him. Yet given the crisis in legal education and the financial realities of the law school, the university and Mack mutually agreed that a larger gift

Nationally recognized trial lawyer Thomas R. Kline made the largest gift in university history in 2014 to support the law school, which is now named in his honor. (Office of University Communications.)

was necessary, and the name was changed back to the Drexel University School of Law.

In September 2014 Thomas Kline—among the nation's most respected and leading trial lawyers and a member of the executive committee of the university's board of trustees—provided a transformational $50 million gift to what is now Drexel's Thomas R. Kline School of Law. Kline's gift, the largest in Drexel's history and the fourth largest in the history of legal education, is being used to support several key objectives. Most importantly, part of Kline's donation was an historically significant bank building in Center City, which is being renovated to house the state-of-the-art Kline Trial Advocacy Institute. The remaining portion of the gift will be used for programs in advocacy training, and student scholarships.

Conclusion

In Drexel's 125th year, the Kline School of Law is ten years old. Its history mirrors that of the larger university. Having faced enormous challenges, it has prospered. The faculty has built an innovative legal education program that is responsive to rapidly changing conditions in the profession. The law faculty members are high impact scholars, and the law school plays a key role in the university's broader civic engagement initiatives. All of this would not be possible without massive fiscal support from the university and from Thomas Kline.

"A Fulbright Scholar in China? No way. I don't think you should set your sights so high." My friend was well-meaning, but unaware of the global reach Drexel has developed for its students. I started learning Chinese through on-campus classes during my second year. The international area studies program not only expected students to learn a new language, but also encouraged time abroad. I was privileged to study abroad twice in Beijing, co-op as a student volunteer for the USA Pavilion of the 2010 Shanghai World Expo, and support a Great Works Symposium course studying World's Fairs on a class visit to the Expo. The time in China offered through Drexel made me a strong candidate for Fulbright, and I was honored to receive the student research grant in 2011. Through today, I'm amazed by the development of Drexel's global programs. Every few months there's an alumni gathering, a visit by faculty or sports teams, or study abroad students who reach to connect with other Dragons in China. My grandfather, a child of poor Italian immigrants to Philadelphia, took engineering classes at Drexel when it was comprised of just one building, half a century later it's amazing to see our university establish itself around the world.

—DANIEL TEDESCO, CLASS OF 2011

23

Drexel's Global Reach

Julie Mostov

AS EARLY AS 1965, Drexel president William Hagerty was a member of the National Citizens Commission on International Cooperation, and Drexel was a member of the Institute of International Education in New York, "created to catalyze educational exchange" with the idea of fostering greater "understanding among nations."[1] Yet the university was slow to embrace active educational exchange until later in the twentieth century.

There is evidence of intermittent outreach to international students from the 1960s, and early efforts to support international students in the 1970s. In particular, Gregory Barnes, a faculty member in what was then the College of Humanities and Social Sciences, in 1974 brought ten Iranian students to campus for English Language training, in 1978 and 1986 developed humanities courses specifically for international students, and in 1980 a training program for international teaching assistants. In 1988 Barnes proposed the establishment of the English Language Center (ELC), and became its founding director in 1989–90, working together with Barbara Hoekje, who would take his place as director in 2001. By 1990, the ELC had seventy students, and there were seven hundred-some international students at Drexel, the majority being graduate students.[2]

Also in the mid-1980s Vivian Thweat, a professor of French language and literature, convened a small group of faculty to found an interdisciplinary major in international area studies (IAS), following a national academic trend, and the availability of federal funding for such programs. Thweat made language proficiency, study abroad, academic achievement, and international career-building the hallmarks of Drexel's relatively small, but innovative IAS program.

In 1993 I gained two years of renewable funding from the International Research and Exchanges Board (IREX) to support Albania's philosophy and social theory faculty in their efforts to reintroduce critical thinking into their university curriculum after a long period of isolation, resulting from the totalitarian rule of Envir Hoxha. The IREX project paved the way for a series of projects in citizen diplomacy through 2007. In 1996, Richard Astro came to Drexel as provost and brought U.S. State Department funding for a high school exchange program in the newly independent country of Moldova. I took over this project, which expanded into additional citizen exchange programs in Serbia, Croatia, Montenegro, and Albania. Yet, as meaningful as these programs were to the participants, they did not make a significant impact on Drexel's internationalization. While individual faculty members in engineering, natural sciences and other disciplines included publications and funded projects with international partners in their research portfolios, these efforts were not recognized on campus as part of an international strategy.

The increase in Drexel's international student population grew with Philadelphia's attempt to look outward for investment and growth; it paralleled the city's hope to build exports, stop flight to the suburbs, recognize the draw of its educational institutions and research potential, and revive the city's cultural life. These efforts were also critical to the university's prosperity, and understood by President Constantine Papadakis soon after he arrived in 1995. Under Papadakis, Drexel joined the Board of the International House of Philadelphia and became the first university in the city (and country) to establish a sister city scholarship program with the International Visitors Council.[3] Papadakis and Drexel trustees such as Chuck Pennoni were founding members of the World Trade Center of Greater Philadelphia, and the university played a key role in various iterations of Campus Philly, a public-private initiative between the city government and local universities to support the recruitment and retention of international and domestic students in Philadelphia.

In 1997, when there were some eleven hundred international students at Drexel (accounting for almost 10 percent of the student population),[4] China's president Jiang Zemin (and father of Jiang Mianheng, who received his Ph.D. from Drexel in 1991) made his historic visit to Drexel to honor his son's professors and his old classmate from Shanghai Jiao Tong

University, engineering professor Hun H. Sun. At this time, according to newspaper reports of the events, Drexel boasted thirty-one Chinese professors and 250 Chinese students.[5] A chair professorship in Dr. Sun's name was launched with Jiang Zemin's visit and bestowed upon Sun's young colleague and cofounder of Drexel's biomedical engineering program, Banu Onaral. Onaral made the internationalization of Drexel one of her life missions, and she became one of the university's most articulate spokespersons for global engagement.

These early international pioneers at Drexel paved the way for what would become the university's strategy for international engagement. Drexel's potential role as a global actor came to life when the university's strategic plan for 2007–2012 facilitated the creation of the Office of International Programs (OIP) under Provost Stephen Director. Created "to establish the infrastructure necessary to take advantage of globalization," the OIP, which I directed as a vice provost, expanded to include the study abroad office[6] and a growing portfolio of programs, policies, and collaborations.

With the arrival of President John Fry in 2010, Drexel began to see its global engagement as part of a larger set of strategies under the theme of the "modern urban university," driving the growth of its neighborhood, city, and region. Global Drexel became an integral part of the university's commitment to make an impact outside of the campus, to gain greater visibility for the research and educational advances of the faculty, and to strengthen the appeal of the university to an increasingly diverse and academically capable student body.

As Drexel developed its global strategies, many universities were experimenting with the idea of building campuses abroad. Some had had a long history of satellite campuses for study abroad and others were creating new networks for recruitment or in the hope of producing revenues from countries eager to adopt recognized U.S. brands. Drexel decided that it would neither invest in bricks and mortar nor export its model abroad, but, instead, build mutually beneficial partnerships that would raise its visibility, complement its strengths, open up opportunities for experiential learning for students and research engagement for faculty, enhance recruitment and alumni engagement efforts, and reflect the university's commitment to collaborative strategies of knowledge production.

Thus, from the founding of the OIP in 2007, Global Drexel emerged with three guiding principles. First, the university would follow a partnership model of international engagement, building sustainable, mutually beneficial collaborations with selected world class universities in targeted countries, using alumni and faculty connections and key Drexel research strengths. Second, Drexel would seek to turn these partnerships into an increasing number of opportunities for student and faculty mobility, student exchanges, faculty-led international experiences, and research and co-op placements. And third, Drexel would enhance on-campus opportunities for internationalization and the appreciation and understanding of cultural difference through academic and co-curricular programming.

The earlier generations of international students such as Jiang Mianheng (now the president of Shanghai Tech University) and faculty pioneers in research and academic collaboration such as Banu Onaral were critical to this partnership model. The university was able to build collaborations with key universities abroad by leveraging the academic and professional strengths of our international alumni and the international profiles of our faculty. Thus, while Drexel was relatively late in terms of the development of a centralized international office or extensive campus internationalization efforts, it has been able to attract world class universities as partners and has joined the ranks of universities engaged in best practices in research collaboration and sustainable partnerships. Research and educational collaborations have burgeoned in strategic locations in China, Korea, Brazil, Chile, Turkey, Israel, India, and the African continent.

With its quarter system, year-round calendar, short intersessions, and co-op program, traditional approaches to internationalization, study abroad and faculty-led programs were difficult to apply at Drexel. Yet the university is at its best when able to use its differences to its advantage; as a place where things can change rapidly, and people are encouraged to run, not walk, with ideas, it has often turned challenges into opportunities. This ability to embrace change and be creative in the face of obstacles (along with new leadership ready to embrace internationalization) has been critical to Drexel's ability to transform itself over the last decade into a global university.

In just the last decade, Drexel's global offerings and international impact have increased exponentially, with growing numbers of students going abroad to study; engaging in research, service, or co-ops abroad; and with increasing numbers of faculty presenting their research and collaborating abroad. While the number and kind of these experiences have grown, Drexel has also enhanced efforts to promote global engagement on campus, to highlight the benefits of an international student body and international faculty, and to promote cross-cultural awareness and understanding with such signature programs as regular "cross-country conversations" and an annual student conference on global challenges. It has also embraced the use of online technologies to establish innovative global classrooms that link students on campus to classmates at partner universities across the globe.

President John Fry and Julie Mostov, Senior Vice Provost for Global Initiatives,
look at plans for an eco-friendly innovation center in Tianjin, Philadelphia's
Sister City, 2012. (Office of International Programs.)

Given Drexel's turn to local neighborhood partnerships, particularly, with John Fry's arrival, the university has also been exploring the ways in which to link its global and local narratives, developing service, research, and international experiences around the intersecting stories and challenges of the global and local, and bringing international partnerships into Drexel's planned "innovation neighborhood." This is how we bring the story of Global Drexel back into the larger theme of the school's 125th anniversary, the role of the modern urban research university and its link to Philadelphia.

As noted earlier, Drexel was an early supporter of the city's international sister city program, by offering scholarships to students from Philadelphia's sister cities. The establishment of OIP helped to expand that role and link Drexel more closely with efforts to increase foreign investment in Pennsylvania and Philadelphia. Drexel's reemphasis on its role as a driver of socioeconomic development for its neighborhood, city, and region coincided with the city's revived initiatives to gain greater recognition among world class cities. Thus, for example, a Drexel delegation, including President Fry and myself, joined Pennsylvania's governor in a mission to Brazil and Chile in 2013, and Philadelphia's mayor on strategic visits to sister cities Tianjin and

Tel Aviv (in 2012 and 2013, respectively). On all of these occasions, Drexel leveraged participation in the delegations to gain greater visibility for new or ongoing research and academic partnerships, while the city and commonwealth leveraged the university's presence to emphasize the significant assets in Philadelphia and Pennsylvania in the higher education and research sectors. An increasing number of players were beginning to realize that among Philadelphia's often overlooked economic and cultural strengths was its concentration of "eds and meds"—research institutions, hospitals, universities and colleges, along with the pharmaceutical industry. What better way to draw companies, investors, and foreign partners to Philadelphia than to include major universities in the global export and business strategies of government? Thus, both Drexel and the city embraced common strategies to enhance their visibility on the global stage.

These twenty-first-century collaborative efforts to link global Drexel with global Philadelphia can be seen on Drexel's part in three broad and intersecting set of activities. First, Drexel has taken a lead role in supporting efforts to champion the city's cultural, academic, and historic legacies and resources with audiences abroad. Second, the university has put itself at the table in strategic conversations and provided expertise, funding, and reputational presence to citywide organizations, associations, and networks promoting global Philadelphia. Third, Drexel has both welcomed and hosted a wide range of foreign delegations to Philadelphia and campus and carried the Philadelphia brand abroad as part of its own international partnership-building strategies. These engagements have been closely linked to Drexel's growing reputation as a part of the innovation and entrepreneurial ecosystem in Philadelphia, and sown the seeds of a vision of Drexel as a home away from home for global research partners in the planned innovation neighborhood.

Drexel became the sole educational sponsor of the Philadelphia Orchestra as that institution made a major effort to strengthen its economic position by retracing its historic linkages to China and, building on this legacy, to recapture audiences, excitement, and purpose in a series of "residencies" in that country, starting in 2012. The orchestra played a major role in the 1972 rapprochement with China, as a cultural ambassador, and has remained dear to the Chinese population and its millions of music lovers. Drexel seized this opportunity to support a major Philadelphia institution, be part of the cultural conversation in Philadelphia around how to remind the world of its exquisite treasures, highlight the university's new research and educational partnerships in China, and enhance recruitment. The residencies offered numerous occasions to gain name recognition through the association with the orchestra in China, and offer new university partners, friends, alumni, prospective students, and their families the special treat of attending orchestra rehearsals or concerts. Having played this role for three consecutive years, Drexel signaled to others in the city that it was ready to take an increasing role in public-private strategies to build the city's image as a world-class location. This recognition coincided with both Drexel's and the city's growing global outreach and its growing local voice in the economic revival of the university's neighborhood.

Drexel's OIP became a frequent participant at major city events to highlight international partnerships, sister city connections, business strategies, and programs hosted by international chambers of commerce, the Consular Corps, and individual consulates. While the University of Pennsylvania and Temple University remained players in some of these circles, Drexel began to take a leading role in many of these arenas. With Fry's attention to the urban university's role in propelling the city's progress and the OIP's readiness to host events and create forums for discussion on critical global themes, support a range of cultural activities, partner with other organizations, and engage in critical conversations around higher education's role in regional innovation, export and investment strategies, Drexel became an important player in Global Philadelphia.

The leaders of global Drexel serve on the boards of the World Trade Center of Greater Philadelphia, the Global Philadelphia Association, and the World Affairs Council, and participate in the research and strategic international efforts of the Economy League and other groups cooperating to position Philadelphia as a global city. Drexel was part of the city's successful efforts to gain recognition as a World Heritage City, participating from the start in conversations led by the Global Philadelphia Association. President Fry sat on the Steering Committee for this initiative and has provided financial support for promotional efforts. The OIP remains involved in follow-on activities and as we uncover the huge potential benefits of this global designation, Drexel faculty, staff, and students will play important roles in its successful advancement.

In line with its collaborative model of mutually beneficial partnerships, Drexel has also cultivated relationships with individual stakeholders in global Philadelphia, working closely with the Israeli Consulate and the Philadelphia-Israel Chamber of Commerce in highlighting research and innovation partnerships with Israel and its leading universities. The agreement signed in Jerusalem by the presidents of the Hebrew University, Drexel, and the Children's Hospital of Philadelphia to collaborate in pediatric translational research was one of the highlights of Mayor Michael Nutter's trade mission to Israel. Drexel also established a close relationship with the Italian Consulate, highlighting the enormous assets of Philadelphia as an innovation and research hub, home to world-class cultural institutions, and site of Italian-American heritage. At the same time, this partnership highlights Italy as an important leader in innovation, design, entrepreneurship, and sustainability. Recent joint efforts include a program highlighting climate proof cities and Italy's cutting-edge approaches to urban sustainability. Another example was a wine and cheese tasting highlighting key Italian industries and Drexel's growing culinary programs (including a related study abroad program in Rome).

In Philadelphia's successful proposal to gain world heritage city status, one of the key themes stressed (in addition to Philadelphia's association with struggles for independence, liberty, and democracy) was innovation. Philadelphia has regularly reinvented itself and rebuilt its economy in the face of global changes in technology and the market place. Its latest re-imagining—with health care and energy sectors and higher education as major drivers—puts an urban research university at the forefront of change. Recognizing this has been a key strategy for Drexel, and it is embedded in the strategic initiative to enhance the university's global impact. From research collaborations to strengthen urban sustainability to those exploring new materials for drug delivery or energy efficiency; from life-saving solutions in human performance and brain imaging to bio-fabrication and 3-D printing; and from studies of microbial risks to new methods for identifying correlations between poverty and environmental vulnerability, Drexel's approaches to international exchange and collaborative research embrace deep commitments to innovation and entrepreneurship. They are founded on shared knowledge production, creativity, and resilience; rooted in scientific exploration, critical inquiry, and mutual respect. This is the message that Drexel brings as it visits partner universities abroad and sends its students and faculty across the globe. It is also the message Drexel articulates when hosting international partners on campus and in Philadelphia.

As Drexel continues to reach out to stakeholders in the city to realize the promise of a vibrant innovation neighborhood, promote prosperity, and demonstrate the shared benefits of cooperation, the link between local and global will increasingly emerge as a critical theme. The OIP and Drexel's Office of University and Community Partnerships have recognized this by incorporating global-local connections for students, staff, and faculty into many of their programs, acknowledging the interplay between international experiences and Drexel's mission of civic engagement in Philadelphia. The two offices jointly created a "Drexel community scholar for global citizenship" position to encourage international students to facilitate local service immersion projects for domestic and international students and to link participation in neighborhood initiatives with cross-cultural understanding.

An increasing number of faculty-led study abroad programs have begun incorporating themes of social justice and civic engagement into their courses, highlighting challenges facing Philadelphia communities and communities abroad. Collaboration along the local-global continuum and recognition of the power of the university to shape conditions for positive growth remain constant themes, from efforts to attract international capital to research ventures and neighborhood projects, to university programs to increase job readiness, safe housing, and environmental security. There is enormous potential in university strategies to promote the parallel growth of global Drexel and global Philadelphia.

On this 125th anniversary, then, how do we see the future? As noted throughout this chapter, many of today's global challenges are related in significant ways to urban life. The role of the modern urban university will be inextricably linked to solving these problems through growing networks of collaboration and Drexel will find itself at the forefront of such initiatives in energy and the environment, translational medicine, cyber security and informatics, the eradication of health disparities, emergency response, and the intersection of technology and design. Drexel will continue to embrace and strengthen its partnership model, creating spaces where university and industry partners, community stakeholders, faculty, and students come together to find synergies, debate alternative strategies and policies, and generate sustainable solutions for a safe and prosperous world. Ideally, such collaboration will take place in state-of-the-art physical spaces—"collaboratories"—that will facilitate the gathering of stakeholders and encourage transformational thinking, experimentation, and communication across disciplinary and national borders.

The Drexel partnership model will grow into networks, both abroad and with us on campus, highlighting innovative solutions to global challenges facing our increasingly connected cities. The role of the flexible, responsive, embedded urban university will be more critical than ever as university networks engage in meeting the evolving needs of world populations. This ecosystem will be strengthened by the commitment to grow our international student body and reinvigorate our outreach to international alumni abroad.[7] At the same time, as Drexel increases the number of international students across the campus, it will need to include these students seamlessly into the fabric of university life, grow cross-cultural understanding on campus, and instill an appreciation among all students of their place in the world as global leaders and citizens. This is not a look twenty-five years in the future, but indeed, on the current horizon in programs already underway.

The following examples are just some of the ways in which Drexel has embraced this university role and will continue to do so looking forward:

- Drexel gained official observer status to the United Nations Conference of Parties (COP21) and sent a delegation of eight to the 2015 Paris climate talks. This delegation will be following up with a number of different forums on climate change and continued participation in the UN meetings.

- Two Drexel professors, Yury Gogotsi and MinJun Kim, won a multiyear grant from Korea's National Research Foundation (NRF) with collaborators from the National NanoFab Center (NNFC) on the campus of the Korean Advanced Institute for Science and Technology (KAIST), for a first-of-its-kind joint Nano Technology Co-op Center at NNFC, which provides exceptional opportunities in nanotechnology experiential learning for Drexel and KAIST students.

- Researchers in Drexel's School of Biomedical Engineering, Science and Health Systems have established a dual Ph.D. in biomedical engineering with Shanghai Jiao Tong University in China (one of Drexel's first international partners), built upon common research interests and collaboration, with a dual master's degree in the works.

- Drexel's professor Wei Sun has made significant breakthroughs in projects developing 3-D printing of stem cells and living cancer tumors through Drexel's joint center at the Shanghai Advanced Research Institute (SARI) of the Chinese Academy of Sciences, as has Professor Yury Gogotsi in developing a novel drug delivery system to shrink brain tumors with nano-diamonds, and both will be establishing new research collaborations with colleagues at the newly founded Shanghai Technical University (Shanghai-Tech) next door, whose founding president is Drexel alumnus Jiang Mianheng (Ph.D.,'91).

- Three additional joint projects with Drexel and SARI researchers in energy and the environment are seeing promising results and have provided opportunities for student engagement in China and Philadelphia. Professor Shannon Marquez is leading Drexel's

Dornsife Development Scholars program, engaging undergraduate and graduate students in co-ops and research projects in eleven countries in Africa in water, sanitation, and hygiene programs with partners World Vision.

- Professor Katie Gondor is spearheading a growing presence of students and faculty in research on biodiversity in Bioko Island, Equatorial Guinea, and Cameroon.
- Professor Owen Montgomery of Drexel's College of Medicine (DUCOM) and an interdisciplinary group of faculty from across the campus are building strong ties in maternal health care with Makarere University in Uganda.
- An interdisciplinary group of faculty led by Patrick Gurian and Charles Haas of Civil, Architectural, and Environmental Engineering (CAEE) has established ties with the India Institute of Technology in Delhi through a U.S.-India grant on microbial risk assessment.
- Another interdisciplinary team, drawing from CAEE, Westphal College of Media Arts and Design, the College of Computing and Informatics, the Dornsife School of Public Health (SPH), and the Office of Community Partnerships is working closely with colleagues from the Pontifical University in Rio de Janeiro (PUC-Rio) working on urban sustainability, linking their work with vulnerable neighboring communities in Philadelphia and Rio. They are enhancing this collaboration with global classrooms and face-to-face student projects.
- Drexel researchers from multiple disciplines, as well as the university's Academy of Natural Sciences, are beginning to partner with colleagues at the university in Cienfuegos, Cuba to look at responses to fragile ecosystems.
- Professors from DUCOM, SPH, and College of Nursing and Health Professions (CNHP) have established distinct research partnerships with colleagues at Ben Gurion University in Israel, funded by Stein Family Fellowship grants and continue to create a variety of opportunities for graduate students in Israel and Philadelphia.
- The SPH is establishing networks of universities in Latin America to address urban public health issues. Its researchers (together with faculty from the Kline School of Law) are building partnerships in public health (and law) at Shanghai Jiao Tong

University to create new arenas for comparative research and experiential learning.

- The Close School of Entrepreneurship is building links with entrepreneurship programs in Chile, Korea, China, Israel, and Turkey, and the LeBow College of Business's global classrooms are growing in popularity, creating models that are being duplicated across the campus and abroad.

- Drexel's study abroad office is continuing to support dual master's exchange programs with partners such as Politecnico di Milano, and to forge increased opportunities with partners across the globe. At the same time, Study Abroad and OIP have created a number of opportunities for students to think deeply about the experiences that they have had abroad and to link them not only to their studies and career goals but also to their appreciation of diversity and understanding of global-local challenges.

- The Global Engagement Scholar program at Drexel encourages students to engage in global initiatives on and off-campus and to reflect upon and share these experiences with others through an electronic platform. Students who fulfill all the requirements of this program gain recognition for this status on their transcripts.

- The establishment of the new department of Global Studies and Modern Languages, building upon the original International Area Studies program, is filling a critical role in supporting wider options for language acquisition, enhanced interdisciplinary explorations of global challenges, and enriched on-campus programming.

With all of these expanding research initiatives, burgeoning global classrooms, increasing numbers of faculty-led courses abroad, exchanges with partner universities, opportunities for global co-ops, and an increased focus on the local and global connections in our neighborhoods, Drexel is nurturing a global ecosystem vital to the role of the modern urban university of the twenty-first century. The university will continue to contribute to global Philadelphia, linking talent, creativity, discovery, and innovation with a deep commitment to cross-border partnerships and a keen understanding of how such collaboration can address social, economic, and technological complexities and turn wicked challenges into enormous opportunities, including "understanding among nations."

NOTES

1. Box 56, UR 1.8/56/8, National Citizen's Commission on International Cooperation, 1965, W. W. Hagerty Administrative Records, Drexel University Archives; UR 1.8/29/4, Letter to President Hagerty from President of Institute of International Education (IIE), 1965, W. W. Hagerty Administrative Records, Drexel University Archives. On IIE, see http://www.iie.org/en/Who-We-Are/History.

2. Available at http://www.drexel.edu/elc/about/25th-anniversary/. According to 1989 graduate admissions information, 234 graduate students confirmed their intent to enroll. These graduate students, from China, India, Japan, South Korea, Pakistan, Turkey, Taiwan, and Thailand, were largely enrolled in graduate programs in science and engineering, then business, and a few in information sciences and design. URI.10/20, "Memo from the Director of Graduate Admissions on International Graduate Admissions," October 31, 1989, Drexel University Archives.

3. Available at http://www.icontact-archive.com/c09d6xJ3viw2x6PD2onZRYXevdF BodzF?w=3. The International Visitors Council (IVC) is now called Citizens Diplomacy International (CDI).

4. International Student Brochure, UR.10.007, 10.1/53/#1441, Drexel University Archives.

5. R. Singer, M. Davis, and D. Leobet, "Jiang Charms at Drexel," *Philadelphia Inquirer*, October 31, 1997, A1, A19.

6. Drexel began sending students abroad in the late 1980s in small numbers, mostly through third-party provider programs, with the majority of students from the interdisciplinary international area studies major and the College of Business, with a small number from the College of Engineering through the global engineering network GE3. Study Abroad moved from unit to unit until it was adopted by the Pennoni Honors College (PHC) in the early 2000s and developed under Director Daniela Ascarelli and the PHC founding dean Mark Greenberg. It moved with Ascarelli to the Office of International Programs in 2008.

7. International students currently compose 14 percent of the undergraduate population and 17.5 percent of the graduate student population at Drexel (academic year 2015–16) Integrated Postsecondary Education Data System (IPEDS) Fall Enrollment Survey, Drexel University.

I remember thinking that the way A. J. Drexel started this university, and the way he did things, that it would have been of concern to him that within blocks of the university there was such poverty and hopelessness. That would have been antithetical to the way he would have approached things. He was a deeply civic person, and the way he established the university reflected the fact that he was a very inclusive thinker and doer. I think he would have been offended [seeing] the institution that is a place of privilege surrounded by a sea of poverty.

Mostly what I thought . . . for our students and faculty to participate with their neighbors in these kinds of really wonderful and joyous occasions like the things you see all the time over at Dornsife [Center for Neighborhood Partnerships] would be just great for the soul of the university. I thought from a cultural standpoint, a practical standpoint, and a mission standpoint that we were missing a huge opportunity.

I started driving around myself on the weekends and in the evenings and I said, "This is not good. It is not good at all." We've had a lot of problems, as you know, over the years. You can't insulate yourself from those problems by building a fence around an institution. I thought we had to attack the situation in a way in which I think we are now. I think we're seeing very good progress. And then of course getting the federal Promise Zone designation is a real help, because that draws in a lot of resources. Having the Dornsife and Lindy [Center for Civic Engagement]; we've raised close to fifty million dollars for some of these things already. I feel like we're off to a very good start, but if you ask me what the most gratifying thing is, it's how many faculty and how many students are deeply involved in this work right now, and how much it's making a difference for our neighbors.

—JOHN A. FRY, PRESIDENT, DREXEL UNIVERSITY, 2015

24

From the Physical to the Virtual with Drexel University Online

Kathy Harvatt

ONLINE EDUCATION, or e-learning, was little more than a concept as the twentieth century was coming to a close. Yet just two short decades later, e-learning has made its way into the mainstream of higher education, thanks to trailblazing institutions like Drexel University. In the early 1990s, under the progressive leadership of then president Constantine Papadakis (fondly known as "Taki"), Drexel began to envision a bright future for technology enabled distance education at the university, buoyed by a grant from the newly formed Sloan Foundation.

Well-known for its research in technology development and deployment, Drexel was one of ten universities nationwide handpicked by Sloan to explore the potential for asynchronous computer-based distance learning, with its College of Information Science and Technology (CIST) serving as lead investigator. By 1995 Drexel had started offering online courses, and in 1996 it unveiled a fully online degree program—a master of science in information systems, followed shortly by a master's in library and information science.

With the Internet still in its infancy, Drexel chose Lotus Notes as its initial course delivery platform, which at the time provided a convenient way to post what were basically lecture note handouts for students to read and respond to online. There was little if any meaningful interaction between and among students and their professors, which meant that in its earliest iteration, online learning was an altogether lonely process.

Still, in 1998, as the momentum for e-learning continued to build on the heels of the Internet explosion, President Papadakis, in his constant search for ways to grow the university's reputation and revenue, was determined to keep moving with this pioneering experiment. CIST, under the leadership of a new dean, David Fenske, agreed to continue his college's support for e-learning, and in 1999, Gloria Donnelly, dean of the newly created College of Nursing and Health Professions, had added her name to the list of "early online adopters."

As Donnelly explains, prior to 1998 the nursing college had been part of a separate non-profit subsidiary at the university—the Pennsylvania Health Education Corporation (PHEC)—which also included the colleges of health professions and public health, the medical school, and Hahnemann Hospital. And, according to Donnelly, it was hemorrhaging revenue:

> When Tenet Healthcare agreed to buy the hospital, Taki worked a deal with PHEC's creditors to create a $50 million endowment for merging the rest of us into the university. We were just coming off of . . . bankruptcy at the College of Nursing, so my faculty was eager to make the move. Like Taki, I saw online learning as the future of higher education, as well as a way for us to become financially healthy. It didn't take much talking to convince my faculty.

Donnelly's first grand experiment in 1999 was a master's course in nursing leadership, which was designed as a hybrid of sorts. "The class met in-person one Saturday a month and did everything else online, through an email discussion board. But when the students started asking why they had to meet on Saturdays, I thought why not just put the whole course online."

Around that time, interactive, Web-based learning management systems (LMS) like WebCT and Blackboard were entering the market, and after exploring her options, Donnelly and her faculty decided to go with Blackboard because of its more user-friendly design. But the university initially took a different tack when it chose to go with WebCT as its official LMS. "When that happened, I was already hosting a lot of our courses on Blackboard. So I asked John Bielec [Drexel's then vice president of Information Resources and Technology] what to do, and he told me that if we were satisfied with what we had, we should stick with it. The university eventually came around to our way of thinking, though, and Blackboard is now the platform we all use."

Creating the Drexel University Online
Business Model

Pleased with the university's initial attempts at distance learning, Papadakis spearheaded a feasibility study in 1998, aimed at identifying how the university might deliver a Drexel education to online students at a much larger scale. This study concluded that Drexel could achieve its objective by creating a separate, "offshore" operation to recruit and enroll online students, while using its acclaimed faculty and curriculum to provide them with a comparable academic experience.

But given other, more immediate campus priorities, the plan was shelved until 2001, when Papadakis proposed, and the Board of Trustees approved, a $4 million investment to establish a wholly owned, for-profit subsidiary called Drexel e-Learning (DeL), tasked with building the Drexel University Online (DUO) enterprise.

Under this arrangement, DeL would identify marketable programs, recruit qualified students, and help them through the application process. From there, the university's admissions office would take the reins, using its standard student selection criteria, while the individual colleges and schools would create, teach, and own the course content. Likewise, online students would pay the same tuition rate as their on-campus peers for the same education, a decision that proved to be a major selling point when it came to marketing the quality of Drexel's online programs.

To ensure DeL's success, the university recruited Dr. Thomas Samph—a former academic turned business entrepreneur—to head the company, reporting directly to Drexel's president. Samph asked his long-time business associate, Art Zamkoff, to join him in the venture, and to save money, the two of them set up shop in the back of the university's garage at Thirty-Fourth and Grove Streets. As Zamkoff remembers, "Those early days were all about austerity, because we wanted to spend our money on growing the business and showing the university a quick return on its investment. In fact, we even furnished our space with old, discarded office furniture that had been stockpiled in the basement there."

Once the two partners settled in, they turned their attention to building a rigorous business plan and hiring an experienced staff, with backgrounds in marketing and sales, customer service, technical support, instructional design, and project management. According to Zamkoff, "To get us off the ground, we hired two employees right off the bat; one to do our marketing and one to work with the deans on program development."

The university also made an important decision to focus the bulk of its online efforts around graduate programs, because as Zamkoff says, "They were not only less difficult to put online, but were also easier to promote among the qualified students we were looking to enroll. That meant conducting extensive research to figure out which graduate programs were potentially most profitable."

By that point the online master's in library and information science was becoming a "major breadwinner" for the university, a source of pride for Fenske, who noted that "We tracked ahead of all the national trends in library science for years, until around 2010, when the competition started closing in."

Using this program as an exemplar, DeL's executive team set out to enlist other deans who were willing to move their programs into the online space. As an incentive, Papadakis agreed to an even online tuition revenue split between DeL and the individual colleges. While Donnelly and Fenske were eager to remain on board, the dean of Goodwin College, Ali Houshmand, also agreed to offer undergraduate degree completion programs online, a move that encouraged other deans to follow suit.

According to Fenske, studies showed that the real cost of online education versus face-to-face was "a wash," given that the cost of instruction was pretty close to even in both models. "I had looked at the numbers and knew that we would have to reach a course section ratio of twenty-five students to one instructor to ever achieve the 20 to 40 percent year-over-year revenue growth rate the university wanted to see. But Taki was right, at least in the beginning, that graduate programs in information science, engineering, and nursing were potentially Drexel's biggest revenue generators in the online space."

Likewise, Fenske remembers the faculty's early resistance to teaching online, given that it was more time- and labor-intensive than teaching face-to-face. "That's why back then we paid them a healthy stipend for each course they developed, a practice that continued after DeL was created. And over time, the faculty who made the leap found that teaching online caused them to rethink how they taught in the classroom, as well."

Building the Online Learning Enterprise

In fall 2002, DeL enrolled seven students for CNHP's first fully online nursing program, as Samph and Zamkoff moved full steam ahead to grow the operation. As a result of the company's efforts, 2003 proved to be a seminal year in DUO's growth. Having added a healthy number of new online programs, significantly increased online enrollments, and expanded its operation to include 10 staff members, DeL also began to build its innovative channel marketing approach.

In the beginning, DeL had relied exclusively on direct-to-consumer student marketing in building DUO's enrollments, using a variety of approaches. Moreover, after the company acquired its drexel.com website domain from a group of students on the campus, who had purchased it for their own use, it became a major source of inbound student marketing and enrollment.

At the same time, however, DeL's original business plan had incorporated a five-year strategic goal of attracting at least 50 percent of Drexel's online students through what Samph and Zamkoff referred to as "channel partners," a concept they believed vital to business expansion. "We knew that many large corporations offered their employees some sort of tuition reimbursement, particularly for graduate programs," Zamkoff says. "So by cultivating these companies as partners, we were pretty sure we could enroll a lot of their employees."

Of course, as Zamkoff also recalls, "The channels didn't happen by accident. It took time to develop these partnerships, as well as an incentive for them to enroll students. So we offered them a tuition discount, came up with a simple memorandum of understanding, and put an experienced business development team in place, focused on building partners in our core program markets."

Within a couple of years, the partnership network had taken off in a big way and DeL was well on its way to meeting its goal of enrolling half of all DUO students through channel marketing. By 2005, Drexel's online enrollments had grown exponentially, to 1,500 across an ever-expanding portfolio of programs. In 2004, Tom Samph left DeL to go out on his own, and Art Zamkoff was appointed president. Around that time, Drexel's College of Engineering began offering a couple of its programs online, a significant step in expanding the DUO enterprise. By the end of 2005, DeL had also moved out of the garage and into a large office suite at a university-owned building on Thirtieth Street and Market Streets, in an effort to accommodate its growing staff (up from ten in 2002 to thirty in 2005) that included Nadine Ezzat and Will Wiebalck.

Now DUO's associate vice president of marketing, Ezzat began her career there as a search engine analyst, at a time when the DeL marketing team comprised only three dedicated individuals, who basically covered the spectrum. She remembers her job back then as something akin to a "jack of all marketing trades": "Being such a small team, we did everything from talking to prospective students, to placing media buys, to maintaining the website, to designing creative. It was hard to convince students and employers that online learning was equivalent to on-campus learning. But since we were one of the only brick and mortar schools with a large offering of quality online programs, a little bit of advertising went a long way, and we experienced phenomenal growth."

According to Ezzat, DeL's online student marketing efforts were pioneering as well, having early on adopted two leading-edge, Web-based tactics that not only produced excellent results then, but are still effective today: search engine and e-mail marketing.

At the time, Drexel's biggest competitors in the search engine arena were large for-profits, such as University of Phoenix and Capella University, that were spending massive amounts of money on paid search advertising, which in turn drove up their costs. But according to Ezzat, the reward was worth the expense, as this approach became DeL's "number one recruitment tool." So much so, in fact, that the DUO website received more than 750,000 visitors in 2005.

By the same token, DeL jumped on the e-mail marketing bandwagon from the very beginning, having recognized the growing importance of e-mail as a communication tool. As Ezzat says, "We definitely started a trend among our competitors, because as email marketing began to bring in a large number of enrollments for us, they quickly followed our lead."

Wiebalck, who is now Director of DUO's enterprise technology operation, joined the team in 2004, as a systems developer and one of only three members of the company's IT team, who did it all, from website construction and oversight, to help desk services, database management, and everything in between.

Given that there weren't all that many colleges or universities offering distance education programs at the time, Wiebalck saw his new job as a unique opportunity to build an IT infrastructure from scratch for a start-up venture, created with a unique company charter and mission. As he recalls, this structure promoted an entrepreneurial spirit that reflected the university's founding mission: "By having the flexibility to embrace innovative strategies like cloud computing, we were able to focus on solving business problems, which was very important in getting the operation up and running. It was also a tremendous chance for me to enhance and expand my professional skills. And today, the systems and processes we put in place back then are still the backbone of a very successful enterprise."

In 2004, DeL also added course developers to its team, in an effort to help the colleges improve the look and feel of their online programs—an essential strategy for building student retention rates, which were, as Zamkoff puts it, "abysmal."

"Although we were using a far more interactive learning management system, the teaching methodologies still needed an overhaul to take better advantage of the technology," Zamkoff says. "So while we were enrolling a large number of students, we were having a hard time retaining them, which is why President Papadakis threw his support our way when it came to upgrading the course design."

Having a separate DeL board of trustees, chaired by Drexel's president, was yet another essential factor in guaranteeing DUO's success. In addition to DeL's president, the original board also included deans Fenske and Donnelly, along with such prestigious members of Philadelphia's business community as Richard Hayne, Mel Baiada, Joseph Jacovini, and Richard Greenawalt—all of whom also served on the university's board of trustees. Zamkoff describes their meetings as "more brainstorming sessions than formal board meetings," a sentiment that Greenawalt and Baiada share in looking back.

As Greenawalt says, "There were no wilting lilies on the board then, and it's the same way now. We still don't want anyone to 'sell an idea' to us. Our meetings have always been a way to challenge new ideas and discuss them openly. And like [Drexel's current president] John Fry, Taki didn't flinch when there was a dialogue. They both set the stage for honest, robust discussions, and their leadership and constant involvement have been critical to Drexel's success in online education."

Baiada echoes that statement. "When you get five to ten smart, knowledgeable people into a room, the natural dynamic will be brainstorming and challenging each other's opinions. The early DeL board was no different."

Jacovini recalls that these lively conversations typically revolved around the marketing strategy, potential program offerings, and convincing deans and professors to participate. "We also spent a lot of time talking about the business model and whether we could monetize DeL over time. For example, could we sell our methodologies and services to other universities that were interesting in delivering programs online?"

As a mix of successful business professionals, who knew a lot about retail, marketing, call centers, and the law, this board was certainly well-equipped to debate these issues. But according to Greenawalt, "we didn't know if we were sufficiently technically knowledgeable. So down the road, we added Tim Foster, who because he had run large for-profit, online universities and colleges, knew the challenges and had the technical know-how."

Staying Ahead of the Competition

As online enrollments continued to increase, particularly with respect to graduate programs in nursing, education, information technology, and engineering, so did the number of online faculty. In fact, as Donnelly says, the virtual environment at Drexel has paved the way for recruiting outstanding faculty members, both in and out of Philadelphia: "I have nursing professors who teach from as far away as Alaska, simply because they can. And I count myself lucky because they are also recognized experts in their fields, who don't want to relocate, but do want to bring their tremendous experience into the classroom. In fact, given that the vast majority of our 5,000 nursing students are learning online, I have a hard time these days getting faculty to teach in-person on the campus."

Revenues from Drexel's online enterprise were also rapidly growing, thanks to DeL's highly successful channel marketing approach. Zamkoff knew, however, that enrollments would eventually begin to flatten, as the online market was becoming increasingly crowded with every passing year. "We were regularly adding new programs that we knew would attract prospective students, based on our extensive market research. But like any leader in any emerging field, you always have a target on your back, as the competition moves in to not only mimic, but also improve on your success."

To remain ahead of this competition, Drexel began to take a deeper dive into the issue of online quality standards for instructional design and delivery. In supporting that effort, the university created the Online Learning Council (OLC), comprising 80 administrators, faculty, staff, and technical support personnel, tasked with developing and deploying strategies for technology-enhanced teaching. The council also identified a cadre of OLC fellows, to provide faculty with peer-to-peer consultation around "best practices" in online teaching and learning.

Still, as the competition grew fiercer, enrollments began to slow by 2010. That same year Zamkoff left because of health issues, and Ken Hartman, DeL's senior vice president for marketing and business development, stepped in to fill his position. John Fry also became the university's fourteenth president, underscoring his support for online education in his 2011 inaugural speech, when he said "We must become more nimble in bringing our expertise and academic riches to the world through the 'disruptive innovation' of Drexel e-Learning and the scale of our growing Drexel Network."

In fulfilling this promise, Fry's five-year strategic plan formally identified online and hybrid education as one of four key areas of growth and development. And to address the ever-tightening competition for online students, Fry also began working closely with the university's trustees, along with DeL's leadership team and governance board, to explore new ways for invigorating Drexel's virtual campus enrollments.

Drexel University trustee and DUO board member Richard Hayne stated it well: "From my personal experience in business, and my board role with Drexel University Online, we know that our future is more about the clicks than the bricks."

Inventing DUO's Future

In 2013, Drexel hired Dr. Susan Aldridge to serve as both senior vice president for online learning and the new president of Drexel University Online. As a globally recognized expert in adult and distance education, Aldridge had successfully led efforts at her former university to expand enrollments, streamline business operations, and implement next-generation learning technologies. And with full support from both Drexel's president and DUO's board of trustees, she was tasked with transforming the online enterprise to better serve current and future students. At the time, the university was beginning to weigh the pros and cons of dissolving its wholly owned, for-profit subsidiary, Drexel e-Learning, and merging DUO into the university. But after two years of high-level discussions across the campus community, Aldridge and her DUO leadership team proposed an alternative business model—one that would create a non-profit entity, acting as a wholly owned/controlled "division" of the university.

According to Aldridge, the proposed model seemed like a more market-driven, efficient and effective solution, from both an administrative and an operational perspective, given shifting student demographics in an era of rapid change and intense competition. Moreover, this designation enabled DUO to receive philanthropic grants and major gifts for continued investment in both infrastructure and innovation.

As Aldridge puts it, "Non-traditional, adult students, such as those we enroll in Drexel's online programs, now make up nearly three-quarters of the college-going population. And their academic needs are very different from those of our traditional, on-campus students. So to serve them well, while also generating healthy tuition revenues, we were looking for a sustainable business model that was student-focused, resource-efficient, and easily adaptable."

The Drexel board of trustees embraced the proposed solution, and on July 1, 2015, the university transitioned its for-profit subsidiary, Drexel eLearning, Inc., to a non-profit entity officially known as Drexel University Online.

"This new hybrid structure is a unique model among institutions of higher education in the United States, which is definitely in line with our university's longstanding history of innovation and entrepreneurship," said President Fry. "By design, it not only allows for greater agility, it also stimulates greater synergy across the university, to sustain and build on our position as a national thought leader in technology-enhanced teaching and learning."

DUO board member Joseph Jacovini concurs, adding that this transition settles a longstanding point of discussion with respect to DeL's for-profit status. "For years, we debated the public perception around operating a for-profit business of this size within a non-profit institution. So by changing DUO's tax status, as well as its role, we've put that discussion to rest."

Under this new arrangement, DUO has moved beyond simply recruiting and enrolling online students, to working in partnership with the colleges to research and recommend market-responsive programs, while also designing engaging and accessible online courses. Likewise, DUO is developing high-tech, high-touch digital tools and support systems to facilitate online student success—from enrollment through graduation and beyond.

In 2015, DUO launched a free online course that allows prospective students to "test-drive" the virtual learning environment before they enroll, to determine if it is a good fit for meeting their academic needs. In early 2016 DUO unveiled an online student success course, which serves as an orientation for new students and a pre-term refresher for continuing students as they make their way through the program and on to the finish line.

According to Kimberly David-Chung, DUO's assistant vice president for student experience, these innovative tools and systems add considerable value by enhancing affinity and promoting persistence:

> While we know that the university's online programs and faculty are exceptional in terms of content and approach, we also know that online students need wraparound support to keep moving. So down the road, we want to use what we are learning now to develop a one-stop, high-touch cyber portal for them to use for quickly accessing ongoing services and relevant information, while also building a solid learning community throughout every phase of their student life cycle.

As envisioned, self-service access will run the gamut from course registration, financial aid, and tuition payment, to career development, student affairs, and professional networking. This portal will also act as a conduit to much-needed academic resources—including advising, writing assistance, tutoring, and peer mentoring—as well as to information about virtual events, webinars, and career opportunities.

For Jacovini, ideas such as these will enable Drexel to further seed its culture of continuous innovation. "Like my fellow Board members, I have always been of the mind that high-quality online education is a big part of this university's future. But as with any big thing, you have to constantly reinvent yourself if you hope to stay ahead of the field. It's all about identifying the next transformational steps and having the ability to quickly capitalize on them."

DUO also believes that this focus on continuous innovation puts Drexel in a prime position to take the lead in research and development around robust learning technologies that can be deployed online, on-campus, or a combination of both.

As a pioneer in online education, Drexel has certainly proven technology's transactional value as a flexible and highly scalable medium for delivering academic programs. But as the future unfolds, the university is highly invested in exploring technology's experiential value, for creating the active, authentic, and customized learning that today's students are coming to expect and tomorrow's students will actually demand.

In laying the groundwork for that shift in focus, DUO recently surveyed the global education market to examine trending technologies and their emerging impact on teaching and learning, in both fully online and hybrid classroom environments. Comprising dozens of interviews with faculty, administrators, and training officers worldwide, this survey revealed a wealth of promising practices, using an array of effective technologies—from virtual and augmented reality, to holograms, robotics, and wearable technology.

As Aldridge puts it, this research will prime the Drexel community to continue inventing the future of "connected" teaching and learning. "As our own Dave Fenske says, technology is no longer merely an educational enabler or even enhancement; it is the education. And given that technology research and development is such an integral part of our DNA here at Drexel, we are in a perfect position to explore new avenues for advancing that concept."

25

The Promise of a New Century

Drexel and the City Since the 1970s

SCOTT GABRIEL KNOWLES, JASON LUDWIG,
AND NATHANIEL STANTON

> If Anthony Drexel were to walk today from the Main Building
> where the Drexel Institute was founded almost 120 years ago,
> through our campus, and into these neighborhoods, would he
> be satisfied that we are fulfilling our mission as an urban
> university? What are the moral and practical obligations of
> an urban university like Drexel to its community? Is Drexel
> University a good neighbor to the surrounding communities
> of Powelton Village and Mantua?
>
> —DREXEL PRESIDENT JOHN FRY[1]

WHEN JOHN FRY rose to address the Drexel academic community at convocation in the fall of 2010, he turned away from the pep talk and platitudes that often mark such occasions. Fry used this opportunity, his first as Drexel's president, to describe a reality often overlooked throughout the previous generation—the neighborhoods bordering the university were suffering, and the university despite its immense intellectual and financial resources was not a consistent partner for positive change. Fry seized the moment to set forward an agenda aimed at fundamentally altering Drexel's relationship with its neighbors, and by extension with Philadelphia more generally. Drexel would become, Fry argued to the assembled faculty, staff, and students, "the most civically engaged university in the United States."[2]

Fry's words marked the first time a senior Drexel official had ever made such an unvarnished commitment towards engagement with the residents of Powelton Village and Mantua. Two years into the mayoralty of Michael

Nutter and the presidency of Barack Obama, Fry's speech fit in perfectly with the broader wave of enthusiasm for tackling urban problems in America, problems left alone for much of the previous thirty years, during which time Drexel itself had only unevenly engaged with the local neighborhoods. Neighbors still recalled the discord of the 1960s and 1970s, when urban renewal enthusiasm had brought the bulldozers to their streets, and when Drexel had been stopped in its development tracks by the organized actions of neighborhood groups like the East Powelton Concerned Residents.

Throughout the 1980s and 1990s skirmishes between students and neighborhood residents—sometimes taking on racial overtones—happened alongside more positive Greek organization-led neighborhood clean ups, and some university investment in community outreach programs. Drexel built nothing outside of central campus between 1977 (Myers Hall) and 1986 (Towers Dormitory), and then not again until 1999 (North Residence Hall)—long decades of quiescence compared to the robust "urban renewal" era of construction (and neighborhood tension) from 1963 to 1972. These interventions did nothing to stem the tide of gang activity, disinvestment, drugs, unemployment, and crime that damaged the quality of life in Powelton Village and Mantua.

Drexel had its own ups and downs throughout these decades, with a difficult era of plummeting enrollments and faculty-administration discord under the presidencies of William Gaither (1984–1987) and Richard Breslin (1988–1994). By 1994 the university tottered on the edge of bankruptcy. Following one year of crucial interim leadership under Drexel alumnus C. R. "Chuck" Pennoni, President Constantine Papadakis arrived in 1995. Papadakis proved himself to be a transformational leader who would oversee the reversal of the enrollment decline, while leading a remarkable period of growth in new schools and colleges. Papadakis's illness and death in 2009 brought sadness and uncertainty in the midst of a remarkable period of opportunity and change.

As John Fry spoke in 2010 he was reacting to each of these realities, and he was reacting to realities within the institution as well: an upsurge in residential student enrollments, a shift away from the vision of Drexel opening a campus in California, an increasingly successful research enterprise, a resurgent emphasis on health, urbanism, and the environment among the research units, and a realization that to survive Drexel would need to expand its physical footprint in a way not seen since the 1960s. This chapter reviews the parallel histories of Drexel, Powelton Village, and Mantua from the 1970s to the present—histories that intersect at various moments over those years, and became intertwined in 2010 with a strength that marks a critical break with the past.

Neighborhoods Challenged

Philadelphia's long-standing industrial dominance was coming to a slow and excruciating end by the 1970s. The steep decline of federal funding for defense industries was compounded by the departure of manufacturing firms on their way to the Sunbelt and beyond. Drexel found itself an increasingly outmoded technical school producing "a supply of well-trained scientists, engineers, and technicians" for a rapidly contracting regional industrial economy. In the Cold War quest to fit into the postwar economy, universities such as Drexel and the University of Pennsylvania (Penn) used federal urban renewal projects to try to literally reinvent the urban landscape and economy, creating new districts such as University City. The vision of techno-scientific urban landscapes was well intended, but ultimately, according to historian Margaret Pugh O'Mara "the residents recruited to University City were of a certain income level, extremely well educated, and almost all white." Conversely, "the persons displaced by University City renewal projects were almost always poor and black."[3]

The same dismantling of Philadelphia's industrial economy that thinned engineering and managerial opportunities for Drexel graduates also eliminated jobs on the factory floor as well. Philadelphia's postwar economic transformation was dramatic—with an overall slide from just over 2 million people in 1950 to less than 1.6 million today, accompanied by growth in the suburban metropolitan region and a massive shift from manufacturing to education, medicine, and services as the economic engines of the region.[4]

The neighborhoods of Mantua and Powelton Village were hit hard by deindustrialization. Once a country retreat out of the bustle of the city, by the late nineteenth century Mantua was a densely settled working class neighborhood. Population peaked at just over 19,000 people in 1950, and had dropped to 9,600 by 2010. The neighborhood went from 46 percent to 87 percent African-American between 1940 and 2010. In 2010 the poverty rate stood at 47 percent. These numbers could easily describe neighborhoods from Baltimore to Philadelphia, Syracuse to St. Louis through America's troubled years of deindustrialization and white flight to the suburbs.[5] Retail jobs also decreased under the pressure of rapid depopulation. Housing values in Mantua declined rapidly between 1960 and 1980.[6] As Drexel's leaders from the 1950s to the 1990s worked to keep enrollments stable amid the economic destabilization of the postwar era, Mantua and Powelton Village fought to keep their communities alive.

With crime and poverty rates on the rise, African-American community organizers set to work, led by two extraordinary individuals: Andrew Jenkins and Herman Wrice. Jenkins remembers an incident in 1966 that sparked his activism. Rival gang members shot the windows out of a store at Thirty-Sixth Street and Fairmount Avenue while his wife was inside. Jenkins explains: "Herman Wrice and I met on my porch . . . and we decided to begin to work with the gangs right after the shooting . . . we went and we met with various gang members and we tried to reach them but we found that many of them were too seasoned . . . so what we had to do was begin to work with a younger generation . . . around 13–14 years old . . . so that's how we began the Young Great Society."[7] Clearly resonant with Lyndon B. Johnson's "Great Society" language, the Young Great Society sponsored a constant schedule of youth activities intended to keep young Mantua teenagers out of the gang culture.

In 1967, a unification of six different community organizations in Mantua, including the Young Great Society, formed the Mantua Community Planners (MCP), led by Jenkins.[8] MCP's goal was to "develop and implement a positive social, economic, and physical plan for Mantua."[9] The timing of MCP's founding is a reflection of the degree to which neighborhood-level organizing was taking shape in reaction to urban renewal initiatives across the city. Penn and Drexel's expansion into Powelton Village was a catalyst, as were plans underway by City Planning Commission director Edmund Bacon and Redevelopment Authority director William Rafsky to hold a 1976 Bicentennial and World's fair in Philadelphia. The plan focused on the Schuylkill waterfront, the Pennsylvania Railroad yards north of Thirtieth Street rail station, and bordered Mantua-Powelton. MCP, especially Wrice and Jenkins, collaborated with the city's Bicentennial Corporation, even traveling to Washington, DC, when the city made its (ultimately unsuccessful) pitch to Congress for funding.[10]

Throughout these years Drexel supplied funds for community engagement, and created a vice president for community affairs position, held first by J. K. Lee Smith. Students, especially, took the initiative to participate in community-based programs. A student-organized Community Relations Commission was formed in 1968 with $10,000 in funding, and provided "arts and crafts courses including creative writing and drama for community residents."[11] Drexel athletic fields and gym facilities were opened to neighborhood children. Students volunteered as tutors in the Mantua-Powelton Mini-School, an experimental middle school at 3302 Arch Street, established by the Philadelphia School District.[12]

The pace of community engagement quickened throughout and in the aftermath of the 1970 Main Building "sit-in" (detailed in chapter 14), an episode in which students joined community members to protest the Drexel administration's plans for dormitory development in Powelton Village. *The Triangle* reported in 1971 that the Community Affairs office had created 42 programs, involving every college of the university, and spent approximately $900,000 in the five areas of education, housing, employment, culture and recreation, and recruiting. This included funding for direct investment in neighborhood schools; consumer education; a summer employment program that hired ten neighborhood youths to work in the Building and Grounds Department and in the library; seed money to start Powelton '76 (housing development organization); and a "Community Consulting Service" to provide "economically disadvantaged businessmen with the tools necessary for survival in . . . [the] competitive economy."[13] These efforts were aided by a moratorium on new construction in Powelton Village that Drexel abided by between the years when Calhoun Hall was opened (1972) and the construction of Myers Hall (1977).

Powelton under Siege

An influx of New Left activists and the spread of black liberation ideologies established Powelton Village as a center of antiestablishment politics by the 1960s and 1970s. In the land battles with Drexel during these years, the neighborhood often employed strategies in accordance with these ideological traditions. After accusing the university of only purchasing inexpensive homes in the neighborhood to allow them to deteriorate, several community members formed a cooperative to purchase and rehabilitate houses in the area, with the goal of selling them at low prices. After an ideological dispute with the rest of the cooperative, two members—Vincent Leaphart, a local handyman, and Donald Glassey, a graduate student from the University of Pennsylvania—left in 1973 to lead their own organization. Glassey spent one year transcribing the illiterate Leaphart's primitivist and anti-technology philosophy and collecting it into a manuscript called *The Guideline*, which acted as the foundational text for their new collective. They first called the group "Vinnie's Gang" before changing its name to Community Action Movement, and finally settling on MOVE.[14]

Throughout the 1970s, MOVE's dreadlocked members were infamous throughout Powelton Village for their profanity-laced sermons based on

Leaphart's philosophy, which they delivered to neighbors and passersby. During this period, Leaphart had begun calling himself John Africa, and all of his "disciples" adopted Africa as a surname. The squalid state of their Thirty-Third Street headquarters often drew the ire of the surrounding community, due to the smell emanating from the trash dumped in their yard, which attracted rats, and the several large, unvaccinated dogs living on the property. MOVE received national attention in May 1977 when fifteen members—armed with shotguns, rifles, pistols, and other weapons—confronted police officers gathered outside of their Powelton Village home. The standoff lasted for fifteen months, culminating in a gun battle that claimed the life of one police officer.

The high-profile incident's proximity to Drexel's campus—one fraternity house and several other student homes were among the buildings enclosed within the blockade established by the police department—caused many students' parents to call and write to the university's administration. In some cases, President Hagerty himself responded to letters from concerned parents, reassuring them that the school had instituted appropriate measures aimed at ensuring the safety of the student population.[15] Although no Drexel students were injured during the standoff, some Powelton Village residents questioned the university's role in creating the conditions that produced MOVE. Vice president J. K. Lee Smith replied that the university understood "the community's concern. However, it was at no time a catalyst in provoking action. This is an unfortunate human tragedy and we feel it inappropriate to criticize anyone. At this time, nothing constructive can come of criticism."[16] After the standoff ended in August of 1978, the remaining members of MOVE left Powelton Village to establish a new headquarters on Osage Avenue. Seven years later, the group was again involved in a standoff with the Philadelphia Police Department. The conflict ended when the police dropped a bomb on the MOVE compound, killing eleven members and destroying more than sixty houses in the neighborhood.

Even prior to the Powelton Village standoff, many within the Drexel population were uncomfortable with the prospect of the university's growing residential population, which was expanding further into Powelton Village and Mantua. Starting in 1975, Drexel undertook several efforts aimed at ensuring student safety in the area. This included the installation of new streetlights throughout Powelton Village, as well as the creation of a security squad, which began in 1975 with ten patrolling officers and two cars, as well as guards stationed at posts throughout the campus.[17] In 1979, Drexel hired nineteen additional Wells-Fargo security guards in an effort to tighten security measures.[18] In spite of these efforts to make the campus safer, the murder of a twenty-year-old student, whose body was found in Randell Hall in November, 1984, stunned the university community. An entire decade passed before a police investigation revealed that a former security guard had committed the crime. Drexel continued hiring guards from Wells-Fargo, and later Pinkerton Security, until 1993, when an increase in crime in the surrounding area compelled the university to create its own security force.[19]

Some within the university saw the progressive tightening of security measures as a defense against a somewhat hostile neighboring community. In one op-ed published in a 1991 issue of *The Triangle*, a student claimed:

> Our town watch program was first established to protect the streets and apartments of Powelton Village. Does anyone really believe for a moment that this program was designed to protect ourselves from other students? Not a chance. We go out on the streets to protect ourselves from Powelton Village residents . . . In my years here, I have never been physically accosted on the street by a drunk Drexel student. I have, however, been accosted by drunk Powelton Village residents. I have been violently approached by Powelton Village residents and have been asked for money and verbally insulted.[20]

Of course, many within the Powelton Village community were equally displeased with the recent influx of college students. Powelton residents, often through the Powelton Village Civic Association (PVCA), complained often of trash piles outside of fraternity houses, loud parties, drunken violence, and stolen street signs. Despite various student organizations leading and participating in neighborhood clean-up drives, in 1993 PVCA president Sue Minnis proclaimed that the problem in the neighborhood was "worse than ever."[21]

In 1984, after a racially motivated assault on a local Powelton resident by fraternity members from Lambda Chi Alpha, the Powelton Village Civic Association (PVCA) not only made demands for greater safety, such as the closure of the fraternity house until the next fall semester, but they further instructed Drexel to engage with the community rather than simply put out the fires of its students. The PVCA demanded "A full time adult resident in each fraternity/sorority directly responsible to a Drexel Vice-President," who was "to be the community's point of contact for fraternity/sorority problems."[22] These negotiating terms alone presented a significant advancement of the civic scope of the PVCA agenda from earlier

William Gaither, Drexel president 1984–1987. (Drexel University Archives. PC 4 People photographs.)

controversies. Additional demands included: "Drexel recruit 200 students, young and old, from surrounding areas by Fall semester 1984; maximum financial/academic support be afforded to them; that Drexel commit to maintain the level at 200 students throughout the year, every year," and for a "mini-mall shopping area to be established by 1 May 1985."[23] Rather than simply requesting a complete stop to Drexel activities, or suggesting a limitation of those activities, the community demanded not only that Drexel control the activities of its students, but for Drexel to enhance the local community's economic well-being. The community, led by the PVCA, saw the racially-motivated assault as the most recent of a long string of such attacks from students.

Many Powelton Village residents had reason to believe that William S. Gaither's inauguration as Drexel president in May of 1985 would usher in a new era of cooperation between the university and the community. Between his appointment and inauguration Gaither made two significant steps towards rehabilitating the university's relations with the community. The first was the successful negotiation with the PVCA, in February of 1985, for the construction of New Tower (Towers) Residence Hall, a dormitory located at Thirty-Fourth and Arch streets. During the negotiations, the university and the PVCA outlined the process by which the two parties would collaborate on future long range planning projects. This included agreeing to "a co-operative review process for all future Drexel development projects of Community Interest."[24] In a letter informing Graham Finney, chairman of the City Planning Commision, of the New Tower "Dormitory Agreement," Gaither and Peter Dodge, PVCA president, urged that both parties "set aside past differences and embrace the solution at hand."[25] Gaither also purchased a house in Powelton Village—a 120-year old Victorian on Thirty-Seventh and Hamilton—and moved his family into it before even assuming the duties of president. Dodge, whom the university invited to speak at Gaither's inauguration, stated: "The commitment he and his wife, Robin, and daughter, Sarah, made in moving here was just a revolutionary change

Harold Myers, Drexel interim president,
1987–1988. (Drexel University Archives.
PC 4 People photographs.)

in attitude and posture from previous
Drexel administrations. . . . It also was
a message sent throughout the Drexel
administration, by their president having done that—and the message got
through."[26]

With the community having seemingly found a new and powerful ally
in Gaither, it looked like the university and community would strive towards mutual cooperation and peaceful
co-existence.

In 1987, however, an employee filed a sexual harassment claim against
Gaither. In response to the media's coverage of the situation, several Powelton
Village residents protested outside the offices of the *Philadelphia Inquirer*,
which they accused of leading a "smear campaign" against the Drexel President. During the protest, Young Great Society co-founder Herman Wrice
lauded the work Gaither had accomplished in the community, including the
construction of a neighborhood health center dealing with pertinent issues
such as AIDS prevention and teenage pregnancy. The scandal, however,
would lead to Gaither's resignation in 1987, and the loss of a powerful ally
within the university administration.[27]

In the late 1980s and early 1990s, faced with high unemployment, high
infant mortality rates, and poor school performance, the neighborhoods
surrounding Drexel university began a conflict against a new, deadly enemy:
the urban crack-cocaine epidemic. Herman Wrice stood at the forefront of
the community's response to drug activity in the area, founding Mantua
Against Drugs (MAD) in 1988. Wrice framed the battle against drug
dealers as a battle "to the death," employing aggressive tactics in his organizations' efforts to reclaim the streets,[28] including organizing marches, circulating photos of known drug dealers, rehabilitating abandoned homes
and more direct methods, such as entering suspected crack houses and
smashing televisions and windows.[29] Wrice became a national celebrity for
his community work, but national press and even a visit from President
George H. W. Bush could not reverse the accelerating economic decline of
Mantua.

Years of Turmoil

Drexel celebrated its one hundredth anniversary in 1991, but the institution was in dire condition. Richard Breslin, a former Catholic priest, became Drexel's president in 1988. By 1991 freshman enrollment had dropped to 1,207, a decline of one-third since Breslin's arrival. This was a catastrophe for a tuition-driven institution with a small endowment. Competition in the regional higher education market was tightening, state funding for higher education was being reduced, and the regional economy was contracting badly—a wicked combination for the uniquely evolved technical institution that was Drexel University. At the same time, labor troubles surfaced with maintenance workers represented by Teamsters Local 115. With a university-wide wage freeze in effect, Breslin refused a wage increase to the union. A strike resulted, with the Teamsters parking trucks on "Thirty-second Street, on Chestnut Street, on Market Street blaring the same tune from morning 'til night, 'We Will Rock You,' by Queen"—a situation that lasted for months.[30] To save money the university skimped on heating and air-conditioning, and shuttered several buildings. "In the fall of 1994," according to David Paul, the decline in enrollments continued when the freshman class size fell to 949. "Total full-time university enrollment reached 7,288, a decline of 23 percent since the beginning of the Breslin administration and 28 percent since the resignation of William Walsh Hagerty."[31] Breslin resigned in 1994. Though board chairman George M. Ross praised Breslin's "stamina," the *Philadelphia Inquirer* quoted a faculty member who described "general delight around campus that [Breslin] . . . has resigned.

There is a general feeling that the university is in decline."[32]

C. R. "Chuck" Pennoni, a Drexel alumnus and chairman of Pennoni Associates, a consulting engineering firm that he founded in 1966, would serve as head of the board of trustees from 1997 to 2003. Following Breslin's resignation in 1994, Pennoni became Drexel's interim president. He recalls the first order of business for some of the trustees was

Richard Breslin, Drexel president 1988–1994 (photo c. 1988). (Drexel University Archives. PC 4 People photographs.)

to explore options for Drexel, which some felt was on the verge of bankruptcy, to be acquired by another university. "When I was asked to come in, the chairman and some of his executive people said 'Chuck you should talk to Penn about taking over Drexel, you should talk to Temple about taking over Drexel, talk to the state about maybe making it part of the state system.' "[33] Pennoni, however, saw things differently. He did not intend to see his alma matter go out of existence, nor did he plan to sit by idly as a figurehead in the "interim" role. He explains his response:

> So I didn't do any of that. I just stuck to what was happening at Drexel. Drexel hadn't given raises for three years and there were deficit budgets for about four years in a row . . . [They asked] "What's the problem with Drexel?" And I remember my answer. "There's nothing wrong with Drexel that good management can't correct." When I went on in 1994, there were seven union grievances against the university, there were five buildings that were closed, they were turning off the electricity on Friday, Saturday, and Sunday in order to save money. . . . even the buildings that were mothballed . . . when I went to look at them, they weren't closed properly and water was getting in. . . . So all these problems to me, you know a guy who came up through the ranks, an engineer in design and construction, all these problems were about managing people, hiring and firing, doing budgets and so forth, to me these were the types of things that needed to be attended to . . . I found some more money to give some raises by the end of the year and we had a balanced budget at the end of the fiscal year.[34]

With the precipitous decline in enrollments, the university had lowered its entrance requirements. Pennoni saw that "they were letting kids in that weren't qualified. They were doomed to fail. Because the goal was to just fill the seats. Drexel's reputation was in the tank. So you weren't getting the best student supply."[35] In 1995, Pennoni hired English professor Mark Greenberg to direct what was at that time a small honors program. With its specialized coursework and diverse, interdisciplinary programs, the honors program helped to attract and retain students who might have otherwise not thought of Drexel in those years (see chapter 18).

Perhaps most crucially, however, Pennoni went to work with the Board of Trustees in 1994–1995 to hire the next president of the university.

Resurgence: The Papadakis Years

Constantine Papadakis was among the candidates for Drexel's next president, and he quickly rose to the top of the pool. Chuck Pennoni met Papadakis in 1991 when Pennoni was serving as President of the American Society of Civil Engineers, and he had been out to the University of Cincinnati twice to speak to the engineering students when Papadakis was engineering dean.[36] The University of Cincinnati's urban location and emphasis on its co-op program made it a good training ground for an engineer aspiring to lead Drexel. Papadakis's personal narrative was compelling as well. "I came to the United States in 1970 with one suitcase, one coat, and my untested knowledge of English," Papadakis explained—an immigrant experience relatable to many Drexel students and alumni.[37] Most importantly, Papadakis, who went by the nickname "Taki," impressed the search committee (and everyone he met) with his energy. Pennoni recalls that "Taki was bigger than life. He was very charismatic, when he walked in a room he lit up the room."[38] Papadakis was hired in May of 1995, and was slated to start in November. In the meantime, projections of further deficits and enrollment decline for the coming school year led the board to move Papadakis's starting date up to August 1.[39]

To Papadakis the "fixed costs of the university were so high and the university size had dropped so low . . . my first effort when I came on board was recruit, recruit, recruit."[40] Enrollment management saw a shake-up, and a move away from what had been Drexel's "reliance on a single message—preparation for a career immediately following college." The co-op would remain central, but new attention would be paid to promoting the co-op as a gateway to graduate and professional training. "The ensuing enrollment management strategy focused on increasing the number and quality of students concurrently."[41] The A. J. Drexel Scholarship was established to recruit top students, and at the same time tuition increases were phased in every two years on entering freshmen. Papadakis's idea was to "start pushing the market and see how much we can push without a backlash."[42]

Papadakis's next move was to take control over the marketing of the Drexel degree. He explained his approach in a speech to the Philadelphia Public Relations Association in 2006:

> Along with Drexel's trustees, I had big plans for the university, academically. But we could not accomplish those plans if we couldn't communicate them. . . . That's why I moved very quickly to make

sure our public relations function reported directly to me. Prior to that, PR was part of our development office. It was just seen as a component of fundraising, and not much more. But in an organization as large and ambitious as Drexel, each of our goals relies on effective messaging. My first priority was to reestablish a Drexel brand that reflected the three components of our core identity— one, a commitment to technology; two, a tradition of co-operative education; and, three, engagement with our home, the city and region of Philadelphia. These three attributes—tech, co-op and civic engagement—differentiate Drexel in a region with 83 colleges and universities.[43]

The strategy worked. Between 1996 and 2003 freshman applications more than tripled, the freshman class expanded from 949 to 2,012 students, and the overall undergraduate population doubled. The expansion in tuition revenue drove a similarly astounding growth in teaching capacity, with the tenure track faculty growing from 295 to 391 in those same years, and the total number of employees expanding from 1,450 to 5,300.[44]

Ed Rendell, Constantine Papadakis, and George Ross during commencement (left to right). (Drexel University Archives. PC 4 People photographs.)

Papadakis's next goal was to add colleges and schools. The most ambitious venture along these lines was undoubtedly the takeover in 2002 of the Allegheny University of the Health Sciences (an institution composed primarily of the Medical College of Pennsylvania and Hahnemann Medical College), by which the university found itself with three new units: the Drexel University College of Medicine, the College of Nursing and Health Professions, and the School of Public Health (see chapters 19, 20, and 21). Other new units added in these years included the School of Education (1997, see chapter 21), School of Biomedical Engineering, Science and Health Systems (1997, see chapter 21), School of Environmental Science, Engineering and Policy (1997–2002, see chapter 16), Pennoni Honors College (2003, see chapter 18), and College of Law (see chapter 22).

The rapid pace of change, combined with Papadakis's adoption of a top-down corporate management style led to conflicts with the faculty. "We try to avoid using too many committees," he told the *Philadelphia Inquirer* in a 2007 profile. "If the faculty senate was taking three years to approve a program of study, then the window of opportunity would be closed. . . . We are down to the point where decisions are being made in two to three months." When he hired a provost without a national search in 2002, the faculty senate censured him. Papadakis downplayed the incident, noting that "since he had veto power there was no point in forming a committee and getting faculty and staff input. . . . I would veto every candidate until they get me the one I want."[45] Asked about the "corporatization" of the university, Papadakis replied, "I publicly say that the student is the customer—if the students were not here I would not need the faculty—the customer is the student who pays the tuition . . . the secondary customer is the corporation that hires our graduates."[46]

With the economy of Philadelphia transitioning in the late twentieth century to heavier reliance on anchor institutions such as universities and hospitals, Drexel's local prominence grew. Papadakis characterized the revitalized Drexel as an "engine of economic development" that had made "major contributions to our city," evidenced by the meteoric growth in students, personnel, co-op placements, and its saving an estimated 13,000 jobs by helping avert the implosion of the Allegheny health system.

And with the expanding student body it was necessary that the university also resume construction, moving again into discussion (sometimes conflict) with its neighbors in the Powelton Village and Mantua neighborhoods. In 1997 Drexel and Powelton Village residents created the "Powelton-Drexel Community Greening and Action Plan." This initiative won support from the William Penn Foundation and resulted in

Dr. Hun Sun, President of China Jiang Zemin, and Drexel president Constantine
Papadakis (left to right). (Drexel University Archives. PC 4 People photographs.)

renovation of the "Tot Lot" at Thirty-Fifth Street and Powelton Avenue.[47]
As the university geared up for the construction of two new dormitories,
Brian T. Keech, head of government and community relations, worked to
establish a more effective mode of communication with neighborhood
leaders. In 2005, Keech established a biweekly meeting in his campus office
with PVCA leadership to discuss upcoming projects, as well as perennial
community complaints about their student neighbors regarding trash
and noise. The PVCA described Drexel's plans to build the Race Street
Residences as a "significant test" of the 1985 Dormitory Agreement. An understanding was ultimately reached: Drexel would build the Race Street Residences in 2007 and Millenium Hall in 2009, Race Street between Thirty-
Third and Thirty-Fourth Streets would be closed to traffic and converted into
a pedestrian walkway, and a new two-and-a-half-acre public "Drexel Park"
would open at Thirty-Second Street and Powelton Avenue. Drexel reserved
the right to build a structure on the north side of Drexel Park up to seven
stories in height, "but not for residential purposes." Drexel also agreed
to no future "high density student housing" construction north of Powelton
Avenue.[48]

On October 30, 2007 Drexel University hosted a Democratic primary debate. (Drexel University Office of Government and Community Relations.)

In addition to provisions for the new student residence halls, the 2007–2012 Campus Master Plan called for a new recreation center, an "Integrated Sciences Building," retail development along Market and Chestnut Streets, and a hotel/conference center across from Amtrak's Thirtieth Street Station. In his second decade of leadership, Papadakis was eager to fill in the campus and expand Drexel's footprint when possible.[49] At the same time, Papadakis was looking beyond the Philadelphia region, first with an ambitious plan to vastly increase online education, and with a plan announced in 2008 to open a second Drexel campus— in Sacramento, California. These plans were underway when Papadakis contracted lung cancer, took a leave of medical absence, and then died in April of 2009.

A New Vision: John A. Fry and Drexel into the Twenty-First Century

After such a dizzying period of growth, the unexpected death of Papadakis left a mood of uncertainty over the university. Chuck Pennoni stepped in again as interim president, at the request of Board of Trustees Chair Richard A. Greenawalt (a 1966 Drexel graduate). Greenawalt led an arduous search process, soliciting input from the Drexel community as well as a dozen university presidents across the country.[50] John A. Fry was selected among 150 candidates and four finalists.[51] A native of Brooklyn, Fry earned a bachelor's degree in American Civilization in 1982 from Lafayette College and an MBA from the Stern School of Business at NYU. Fry had worked for eleven years in higher education and nonprofit consulting with KPMG Peat Marwick and then with Coopers & Lybrand's National Higher Education Consulting Practice—a role in which he spent considerable time advising the University of Pennsylvania.[52]

In 1995, Fry was asked by Penn president Judith Rodin to come on board as executive vice president—it was the same year Papadakis arrived at Drexel, and the two struck up a friendship. Like Drexel, Penn was facing its own crisis. A graduate student had been killed close to campus in 1994 and another was murdered in 1996. The fear of crime was met by "lingering community resentment caused by Penn's past expansion projects." The challenge was to decide "whether and how the University should take action to improve neighborhood conditions; and how to reduce the isolation of the campus from the community by creating a public environment with broad appeal."[53] The result was a multiyear series of efforts bundled under the heading of the West Philadelphia Initiatives. John Fry was at the center of it—looking back he recalls:

> When I arrived at Penn, they had obsessed over this issue of how to improve West Philadelphia. I remember distinctly being given a box of studies full of West Philadelphia plans. What did I know? A lot of the stuff looked good to me. Thoughtful, smart people had actually spent a lot of time on it, but it was clear to me that none of this had ever actually been implemented. . . . I remember thinking people have been sitting around for years thinking about this, we don't have any more time. . . . We started a series of different initiatives that resulted over a period of time in streets that were cleaner and safer and livelier, we formed the University City [UC] District, we started UC Bright, which was street lights on all the major corridors west of Fortieth Street. We started UC Green, which involved cleaning up of public spaces and turning them into pocket parks. . . . We started the mortgage assistance program to incentivize people to buy homes in West Philadelphia. . . . We cleaned up the Fortieth Street corridor. We did a lot of commercial development, residential and retail. By the time we got to 2001, we were in full motion, the biggest thing being the creation of the Penn Alexander school.[54]

The West Philadelphia Initiatives were broadly viewed as a success—a case study in university-led urban transformation. In 2002 Fry accepted the position as president of Franklin and Marshall College, where alongside academic and financial initiatives he also employed what he had learned at Penn, working to enhance the business district and neighborhoods surrounding the college.

Chuck Pennoni recounts the challenges Fry was facing when he walked through the door on his first day:

> Everything was a work in progress, you have California a work in progress, a law school a work in progress, a medical school that still hadn't achieved what we had hoped to achieve. The physical plant, it was a work in progress. Our whole enrollment management issue was a work in progress. Our focus on building up research was a work in progress . . . the College of Media Arts and Design . . . Athletics . . . We were taking everything, every one of those areas to the next level, including nursing and public health. So John had to come in and address each of these.[55]

Papadakis had left Drexel "in midstride," and as such construction projects like the Integrated Sciences Building (renamed after Papadakis) and Gerri C. LeBow Hall needed to be finished. The Sacramento campus—open only since 2009—required serious consideration (it closed in 2015). In 2011, Drexel forged an affiliation with the Academy of Natural Sciences (founded 1812), resulting also in the formation of a new unit in the College of Arts and Sciences: the Department of Biodiversity, Earth and Environmental Science (see chapter 4). To evaluate and set goals for the academic enterprise, Fry initiated a strategic planning process with the close involvement of the faculty, a break from the Papadakis management style.

Simultaneous to reviewing the situation within the university, Fry set to work on an ambitious plan to foster community engagement in ways that went beyond good relations in the service of easing dormitory construction projects—he was looking to join the neighborhoods in the process of fundamentally improving their economic conditions. The university substantially expanded its home loan forgiveness credit to $15,000, available for the purchase of properties in an area known as the Home Purchase Assistance Zone (encompassing the neighborhoods of Powelton Village, West Powelton, Mantua, and Belmont) and expanded its security patrol area.

The growth of the student population was once again affecting Powelton Village and Mantua. The 2010 census actually showed an increase in

*President John A. Fry (second from left) celebrated his inauguration in April 2011
with (left to right) C. R. "Chuck" Pennoni, interim president and Drexel
trustee; Associate Professor Barbara Hornum, then chair of the Faculty
Senate; and Richard A. Greenawalt, chairman of Drexel's board.
(Office of University Communications.)*

white population in Mantua to 8 percent, up from a low of 2 percent in
1990. This statistic most likely reflected the movement of students into
the neighborhood, seeking lower rents than those available in Powelton
Village.

Lucy Kerman, who had previously worked with Fry at Penn on the creation of the Penn Alexander School, joined Drexel in 2010 as Vice Provost
for University and Community Partnerships. One of Kerman's initial projects involved collaboration with the Samuel Powel Elementary School—a
K-4 District neighborhood school in Powelton Village—to strengthen and
expand Powel by creating a partner middle school (grades 5–8) in conjunction with Science Leadership Academy High School, an innovative
magnet STEM high school. By 2014, Drexel had purchased the 14-acre University City High School site in a joint venture with Wexford Science + Technology, with the long-term goal of building a new facility to house both
schools, as Wexford moved to add commercial, residential and retail developments on other parcels on the site.

The late Philip Lindy, pictured here with West Philadelphia middle school students participating in the Lindy Scholarly Program, inspired and supported community outreach at Drexel including the Lindy Center for Civic Engagement. (Office of University Communications.)

The capacity to expand Drexel's neighborhood collaboration efforts, and to fully engage the university in the work, was dramatically bolstered by a $15 million gift from philanthropist Philip B. Lindy in 2011. Lindy's gift helped expand the existing Center for Civic Engagement, housed initially in the Pennoni Honors College, to the Lindy Center for Civic Engagement, in order to provide "community-based experiential learning for students, faculty, and professional staff."[56]

Where Kerman found existing channels of communication between Drexel and Powelton Village, she observed "what Drexel did not have was much of a sense of engagement in Mantua."[57] Mantua received a HUD-funded Choice Neighborhoods Planning Grant in 2011. Here was a welcome opportunity to sit with Mantua leaders and learn what the priorities for redevelopment were. The timing could not have been better for Drexel, especially since Kerman "came in feeling it wasn't our role to ask Mantua to plan because we wanted them to." Kerman was invited to join the leadership committee. "We were at their table, at their request," she recalls. At the center of the initiative was a public housing project called Mount Vernon Manor, founded by Andrew Jenkins in 1978. By the 2000s Mount Vernon Manor was in disrepair, and was eligible to serve as the centerpiece for the Choice Grant. Building on this momentum, organizations in Mantua like Mount Vernon Manor, who led the *We Are Mantua!* planning process and the People's Emergency Center partnered with Drexel, the Mayor's Office of Community Empowerment and Opportunity (CEO), the Philadelphia City Planning Commission, and the Local Initiatives Support Corporation (LISC) to compete for a federal "Promise Zone" designation. The Obama administration designated Mantua one of the first five Promise Zones in the nation in 2013—opening the way towards preference for federal grants in twenty-five different areas from housing to education to public safety.

During this time, Kerman developed a concept around which she believed Drexel's neighborhood engagement work could proceed: "extension"—an idea with deep roots in American higher education, going back to research partnerships between agricultural communities and universities in the nineteenth century. In discussion with deans across the university, Kerman updated the concept, looking at it as a way to imagine Drexel as a "problem solving" institution working collaboratively with neighborhood groups looking for assistance and expertise.[58] David and Dana Dornsife gave $10 million to Drexel to acquire a property in Mantua, and to launch the extension center—the Dornsife Center for Neighborhood Partnerships, which opened its doors in 2014. The university was also able to attract $3.8 million in New Markets and Historic Tax Credits for this project.

In 2012 Drexel released a new campus master plan, emphasizing four major areas of focus: transformation of the campus into a "vibrant urban university district," improving the streetscape of campus, creating shared spaces, and "expanding the innovation community." *Philadelphia Inquirer*

Drexel alumna Dana Dornsife (with scissors) and her husband, David Dornsife (fourth from left), provided unprecedented support for Drexel's academic and civic activities. Here they celebrate the grand opening of the Dornsife Center for Neighborhood Partnerships, which facilitates collaboration between residents of the Powelton Village and Mantua neighborhoods and Drexel faculty, professional staff and students. (Office of University Communications.)

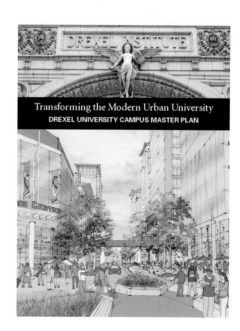

"Transforming the Modern Urban University," Drexel University Campus Master Plan, Office of the President, 2012. (Office of University Communications.)

architecture critic Inga Saffron wrote about the master plan, noting a shift from the old days of acting like an "absolute monarch," to a substantially new approach to planning. Saffron explained: "When Drexel began working on a new master plan in the spring of 2011, it sensed that the time had come for a more benevolent, inclusive approach. Before convening the usual insider group to define its goals, Drexel first set up a Facebook page and a blog . . . to crowd-source ideas from students, faculty, and neighborhood residents. It organized brainstorming workshops and town-hall-style meetings, ultimately getting more than a thousand people to offer their two cents about how the West Philadelphia campus should be reorganized."[59]

And if the mode of planning was to be different, so to was the substance of the effort. Saffron pointed out that Drexel would be *consolidating* its undergraduate footprint into a tighter core, in an effort to end its destructive sprawl into the Powelton Village and University City neighborhoods." New growth would be "mostly upward and eastward, especially around the transit hub of Thirtieth Street Station, where there are large tracts of vacant land."

Building on the fourth element of the 2012 master plan, Drexel came forward in 2014 with a further strategic plan for an "Innovation Neighborhood"—a "dynamic mixed use environment," housing Drexel's education, research, and corporate partners. Seeking to "transform Philadelphia and take a place alongside innovation centers like Cambridge and Silicon Valley," the Innovation Neighborhood looks to expand the university's footprint east of the campus to Thirtieth Street Station, and up the Schuylkill over the old Pennsylvania Railroad yards. The strategic plan for the Innovation Neighborhood explains: "twelve acres of prime undeveloped land adjacent to the third largest rail hub along the Northeast Corridor are owned by Drexel. The land lies within an urban/residential district thriving with world class education, research, health and business leaders, driving Philadelphia's future global brand. An estimated 6.4 million square feet of construction is probable."[60] A key to the success of the Innovation Neighborhood is Drexel forming partnerships with private-sector real estate development companies on key building parcels owned by Drexel, in order to spur the revitalization of the edges of campus.

Harris Steinberg, architect and founder of PennPraxis, joined Drexel in 2015 as the first executive director of the new Lindy Institute for Urban Innovation. An experienced hand at bringing together multiple stakeholders (public and private) in development initiatives, Steinberg added depth to Fry's bench of urban planning experts. Discussing it in 2015, Steinberg outlined perhaps the central challenge of the Innovation

Neighborhood—bringing it to life simultaneously as an economic enterprise and also as an "authentic place . . . not just cut-and-paste urbanism the way you see in other places around the world."[61] As of today, university extension in Powelton Village and Mantua, the physical upgrade of the core campus, and planning and construction in the Innovation Neighborhood all proceed simultaneously.

Conclusions and Projections

And so we conclude where we began this volume, not in the past—but projecting twenty-five years into the future, to the year 2041. Future projections actually tell us more about the people making the projection than they do about any concrete future. If you stop at various moments along the way in Drexel's past you will find administrators, faculty, and students imagining the future of Drexel University, sometimes with high levels of creativity and enthusiasm—in 1891 or in the early 1960s—tempered by concern and outright fear for the survival of the institution at other times (the 1940s and early 1990s).

The material details of a future projection will become dated, the locations of buildings, aspirations for new programs, these will fluctuate. More

View of proposed development of Schuylkill Yards from the east with view of new public square. (© 2016 SHoP Architects PC / West 8.)

interesting, and more central to the health of a university is the underlying set of principles and values upon which a future projection rests. A city is the same.

Looking ahead to 2041, the principles of urban economic dynamism, inclusivity and social equity, and the power of research to transform our lives for the better anchor Drexel's vision. President John Fry can take the last word as we look at that possible future—a future made more meaningful when we know the history that has brought us to this moment in time.

> INTERVIEWER: *Let's use the time machine. In 25 years what is the ideal state of campus and of this part of Philadelphia?*
>
> JOHN FRY: *Drexel is the academic anchor of one of the five great innovation districts in the United States. The Schuylkill, Amtrak, and SEPTA railyard over-build has occurred. There's another couple hundred thousand people living and working in these newly constructed neighborhoods that go all the way up to the Spring Garden bridge. That whole area is completely filled in. You can get to New York in thirty-five minutes, or an hour to Washington via Amtrak. . . . It's a hothouse of invention and entrepreneurship. It's our own version of Kendall Square in Cambridge [MA], except it happened in Philadelphia because our university had the foresight . . . to think about how all that infrastructure could be knit together.*
>
> *And, this may be the most important thing: to do it all while helping the fortunes of distressed neighborhoods nearby to Drexel*

View of Proposed Development Over Rail Yards at 30th Street Station. Looking south from above the Benjamin Franklin Parkway. (Image courtesy Philadelphia 30th Street Station District Plan / Skidmore, Owings & Merrill LLp. 2016.)

*who will take part in that renaissance. So there's no longer this idea
that there are innovation zones over here and federal promise zones
over there, but we've actually been able to knit these places together,
so there is this tidal wave of business and civic innovation, as well
as social and economic equity.*

*By the way, everything I just described is absolutely doable. It
can all happen. It sounds like a big vision now, but it can all happen. It's just a matter of driving towards it, generation after
generation.[62]*

NOTES

1. John A. Fry, Drexel University convocation speech, October 5, 2010.
2. Ibid.
3. Margaret Pugh O'Mara, *Cities of Knowledge: Cold War Science and the Search for the Next Silicon Valley* (Princeton, NJ: Princeton University Press, 2004), 178–79.
4. Ibid.
5. Britt Fremstad et al., "The Quality of Life in Two West Philadelphia Neighbor-hoods: The Case of Belmont and Mantua," December 22, 2006, 29, available at http://www.archives.upenn.edu/histy/features/upwphil/belmont_mantua.pdf.
6. Ibid., 34.
7. "A Lifetime of Service: A Conversation with Rev. Dr. Andrew Jenkins," available at http://funeralforahome.org/story/andys-chest/.
8. "Mantua Community Planners," *The Triangle*, October 31, 1969, 6.
9. Ibid.
10. Scott Gabriel Knowles, ed., *Imagining Philadelphia: Edmund Bacon and the Future of the City* (Philadelphia: University of Pennsylvania Press, 2009).
11. "Congress Reviews CRC; Elects More Chairmen," *The Triangle*, July 19, 1968, 1.
12. "Mini-school Seeking Students as Tutors," *The Triangle*, August 22, 1969, 1.
13. Larry Besnoff, "Community Affairs," *The Triangle*, February 2, 1971, 1; Rob Douse, "Drexel Forms New Consulting Service," *The Triangle*, November 19, 1971, 1.
14. Jim Quinn, "Heart of Darkness," *Philadelphia Magazine*, May 1978, 132–33.
15. W. W. Hagerty letter to Mr. and Mrs. Rubin Berkowitz, August 11, 1977, UR10.1.110/22, University Communications Records, Drexel University Archives.
16. J. K. Lee Smith, "MOVE Statement," c. 1978, UR10.1.110/22, University Com-munications Records, Drexel University Archives.
17. Neil Schmerling, "Security Measures: Powelton Sees the Light," *The Triangle*, Oc-tober 31, 1975, 1.
18. Neil Schmerling, "Security Measures Tightened," *The Triangle*, July 6, 1979, 1.
19. Joe Messina, "Security to Be Revamped," *The Triangle*, November 12, 1993.
20. "PVCA Wants to Control Students," *The Triangle*, February 8, 1991.
21. "PVCA, Drexel Continue Struggle," *The Triangle*, November 19, 1993.
22. PVCA Demands, c. April 1984, UR1.9/4/18, William S. Gaither Administration Records, Drexel University Archives.
23. Ibid.

24. Drexel University PVCA Agreement, February 26, 1985, UR1.9/15/2, 9, William S. Gaither Administration Records, Drexel University Archives.

25. William Gaither and Peter Dodge letter to James Finney, February 26, 1985, UR1.9/15/2, William S. Gaither Administration Records, Drexel University Archives.

26. "Drexel to Install a New President with Undersea Vision," *Philadelphia Inquirer*, April 25, 1985.

27. "Powelton Responds to Inquirer," *The Triangle*, August 21, 1987.

28. "Standing Up to the Scourge in Their Midst," *Philadelphia Inquirer*, August 7, 1988.

29. "Blacks Who Are Taking a New Path," *Philadelphia Inquirer*, July 28, 1991.

30. David A. Paul, *When the Pot Boils: The Decline and Turnaround of Drexel University* (Albany: SUNY Press, 2008), 114.

31. Ibid., 136.

32. Howard Goodman, "Drexel U President Resigning," *Philadelphia Inquirer*, September 22, 1994.

33. C. R. "Chuck" Pennoni, interviewed by Scott Gabriel Knowles, November 2015.

34. Ibid.

35. Ibid.

36. Ibid.

37. Papadakis speech, William Penn Award, Philadelphia, 2008.

38. Chuck Pennoni, interviewed by Scott Gabriel Knowles.

39. Paul, *When the Pot Boils*, 154–55.

40. *The Drexel Interview*, 2003.

41. Paul, *When the Pot Boils*, 159.

42. Ibid., 167.

43. Papadakis speech to Philadelphia Public Relations Association, 2006.

44. Paul, *When the Pot Boils*, 171.

45. Kathy Boccella, "A Coast to Coast Vision: Drexel's Papadakis Has Driven Growth," *Philadelphia Inquirer*, August 19, 2007.

46. *The Drexel Interview*.

47. Powelton Village Civic Association, *Powelton Village Directions: 2011 Neighborhood Plan*, 14.

48. Brian Keech, interviewed by Scott Gabriel Knowles, January 28, 2016.

49. Burt Hill, *Drexel University, 2007 West Philadelphia Campus Master Plan*, May 2007, 9.

50. Richard Greenawalt, interviewed by Scott Gabriel Knowles, December 3, 2015.

51. Susan Snyder, "Fry Selected Drexel's Next President," *Philadelphia Inquirer*, March 11, 2010, B1.

52. John Fry biography, Drexel University Office of the President, available at http://drexel.edu/president/JohnFry/biography/.

53. John Kromer and Lucy Kerman, *West Philadelphia Initiatives: A Case Study in Urban Revitalization* (Philadelphia: Fels Institute of Government, University of Pennsylvania, 2004), 8.

54. John Fry, interviewed by Scott Gabriel Knowles, 26 October 2015.

55. Chuck Pennoni, interviewed by Scott Gabriel Knowles.

56. "Philanthropist Philip Lindy Receives Civic Engagement Award from Drexel," *DrexelNow*, October 25, 2012.

57. Lucy Kerman, interviewed by Scott Gabriel Knowles, 2016.

58. Ibid.

59. Inga Saffron, "Drexel's Big Plans," *Philadelphia Inquirer*, September 8, 2012.

60. Drexel University, "Innovation Neighborhood: A Drexel University Vision," March 31, 2014.

61. Frank Otto, "A Q&A with the Lindy Institute's Harris Steinberg," *DrexelNow*, July 16, 2015.

62. John Fry, interviewed by Scott Gabriel Knowles.

Contributors

Lloyd Ackert is Associate Teaching Professor of History at Drexel University.

Cordelia Frances Biddle is an independent scholar and novelist, and a direct descendant of Francis Martin Drexel, grandfather of Saint Katharine Drexel.

Paula Marantz Cohen is dean of the Pennoni Honors College and Distinguished Professor of English at Drexel University.

Donna Marie De Carolis is founding dean of the Charles D. Close School of Entrepreneurship and the Silverman Family Professor of Entrepreneurial Leadership at Drexel University.

Roger Dennis is founding dean and Professor of Law at the Thomas Kline School of Law at Drexel University.

Richardson Dilworth is director of the Center for Public Policy and Professor of Politics at Drexel University.

Gloria Donnelly is former dean and Professor of the College of Nursing and Health Professions at Drexel University.

Kevin D. Egan is director of the Center for Interdisciplinary Inquiry in the Pennoni Honors College at Drexel University.

Alissa Falcone is a staff writer in the Office of University Communications at Drexel University.

David Fenske is dean emeritus and Professor in the College of Computing and Informatics at Drexel University.

John A. Fry is president of Drexel University.

Stephen F. Gambescia is Clinical Professor of Health Services Administration in the College of Nursing and Health Professions at Drexel University.

Marla Gold is dean emerita and Professor of Health Management and Policy at the Drexel University.

Charles Haas is L.D. Betz Professor of Environmental Engineering and head of the Department of Civil, Architectural, and Environmental Engineering at Drexel University.

Kathy Harvatt is assistant vice president of strategic communications at Drexel University Online.

Daniel Johnson is a history major at Drexel University.

Jeannine Keefer is an architectural historian and the visual resources librarian at the University of Richmond.

Larry Keiser is executive director for Special Projects, Communications and Administration in the School of Education at Drexel University.

Michael Kelley is a budget analyst at the Johns Hopkins University School of Medicine. He received his bachelor's degree in history in 2010 from Drexel University, where he was a brother of the Delta Rho chapter of Alpha Epsilon Pi fraternity.

Scott Gabriel Knowles is Associate Professor and interim head of the Department of History at Drexel University.

Jason Ludwig is a 2016 graduate of Drexel University, where he majored in history.

Jonson Miller is Associate Teaching Professor of History at Drexel University.

Julie Mostov is senior vice provost for Global Initiatives at Drexel University.

Danuta A. Nitecki is Professor in the College of Computing and Informatics and Dean of Libraries at Drexel University.

Anthony M. Noce is chair of the Drexel University Alumni Association Board of Governors, and was cofounder and past president of the Drexel Inter-Fraternity Alumni Association.

Steven J. Peitzman is Professor of Medicine at the Drexel University College of Medicine.

David Raizman is Distinguished University Professor in the Department of Art and Art History, Antoinette Westphal College of Media Arts and Design, Drexel University.

Tiago Saraiva is Assistant Professor of History at Drexel University.

Amy E. Slaton is Professor of History at Drexel University.

Nathaniel Stanton is a 2016 graduate of Drexel University, where he majored in history.

Virginia Theerman is a Drexel University undergraduate dual-majoring in art history and design and merchandising.

Laura Valenti is executive director, College Engagement, Marketing and Communications, College of Nursing and Health Professions at Drexel University.

James Wolfinger is associate dean in the College of Education, and Associate Professor of History and Education, at DePaul University.

Eric A. Zillmer is director of athletics and Carl R. Pacifico Professor of Neuropsychology at Drexel University.

INDEX